ANNALS OF THE NEW YORK ACADEMY OF SCIENCES

Volume 296

CONCEPTUAL AND INVESTIGATIVE APPROACHES TO HYPNOSIS AND HYPNOTIC PHENOMENA

Edited by William E. Edmonston, Jr.

The New York Academy of Sciences
New York, New York
1977

Library of Congress Cataloging in Publication Data

Main entry under title:

Conceptual and investigative approaches to hypnosis
and hypnotic phenomena.

(Annals of the New York Academy of Sciences; v. 296)
Papers from a conference held by the New York Academy
of Sciences, Jan. 11-13, 1977.

Includes index.

1. Hypnotism—Congresses. I. Edmonston, William E.
II. New York Academy of Sciences. III. Series: New
York Academy of Sciences. Annals; v. 296. [DNLM:
1. Hypnosis—Congresses. W1 AN626YL v. 296 / WM415
C744 1977]

Q11.N5 vol. 296 [BF1119] 508'.1s [154.7'7] 77-10880
ISBN 0-89072-042-8

PCP
Printed in the United States of America
ISBN 0-89072-042-8

ANNALS OF THE NEW YORK ACADEMY OF SCIENCES

VOLUME 296

October 7, 1977

CONCEPTUAL AND INVESTIGATIVE APPROACHES
TO HYPNOSIS AND HYPNOTIC PHENOMENA *

Editor and Conference Organizer
William E. Edmonston, Jr.

CONTENTS

Introduction. *By* WILLIAM E. EDMONSTON, JR. 1

Part I. The Nature of Hypnosis

Hypnosis from the Standpoint of a Contextualist. *By* WILLIAM C. COE AND
THEODORE R. SARBIN 2
The Construct of Hypnosis: Implications of the Definition for Research and
Practice. *By* MARTIN T. ORNE 14
Hypnosis, Suggestions, and Altered States of Consciousness: Experimental
Evaluation of the New Cognitive-Behavioral Theory and the Traditional
Trance-State Theory of "Hypnosis." *By* THEODORE X. BARBER AND SHERYL
C. WILSON 34
The Problem of Divided Consciousness: A Neodissociation Interpretation.
By ERNEST R. HILGARD 48

Part II. Research Tactics in Hypnosis

Hypnosis Research and the Limitations of the Experimental Method. *By*
LEWIS R. LIEBERMAN 60
Clinical and Experimental Hypnosis: Implications for Theory and Metho-
dology. *By* JOSEPH REYHER 69
Research Strategies in Evaluating the Coercive Power of Hypnosis. *By* EUGENE
E. LEVITT 86
The Problem of Relevance Versus Ethics in Researching Hypnosis and Antiso-
cial Conduct. *By* WILLIAM C. COE 90

Part III. Capacity for Hypnosis

Body Morphology and the Capacity for Hypnosis. *By* WILLIAM E. EDMON-
STON, JR. 105
Issues and Methods for Modifying Responsivity to Hypnosis. *By* MICHAEL JAY
DIAMOND 119
The Hypnotic Induction Profile (HIP): A Review of Its Development. *By*
HERBERT SPIEGEL 129

* This series of papers is the result of a conference entitled Conceptual and Investigative
Approaches to Hypnosis and Hypnotic Phenomena, held by The New York Academy of
Sciences on January 11, 12, and 13, 1977.

Part IV. Psychological Concomitants of Hypnosis

On Attempts to Modify Hypnotic Susceptibility: Some Psychophysiological
Procedures and Promising Directions. *By* IAN E. WICKRAMASEKERA 143
EEG Alpha Activity and Its Relationship to Altered States of Consciousness.
By DAVID A. PASKEWITZ 154
Hypnosis and Sleep: The Control of Altered States of Awareness. *By* FRED-
ERICK J. EVANS 162
A Comparison of Hypnosis, Acupuncture, Morphine, Valium, Aspirin, and
Placebo in the Management of Experimentally Induced Pain. *By* JOHN A.
STERN, M. BROWN, GEORGE A. ULETT, AND IVAN SLETTEN 175

Part V. Cognitive Aspects of Hypnosis

Incongruity in Trance Behavior: A Defining Property of Hypnosis? *By* PETER
W. SHEEHAN 194
Experienced Involuntariness and Response to Hypnotic Suggestions. *By* NICHO-
LAS P. SPANOS, STEVEN M. RIVERS, AND STEWART ROSS 208
Hypnosis: An Informational Approach. *By* KENNETH S. BOWERS 222

Part VI. Selected Phenomena of Hypnosis

Hypnotherapy: Patient-Therapist Relationship. *By* HAROLD LINDNER 238
The Role of Hypnosis in Behavior Therapy. *By* L. MICHAEL ASCHER 250
Variables Influencing the Posthypnotic Persistence of an Uncanceled Hypnotic
Suggestion. *By* CAMPBELL PERRY 264
Perceptual Processes and Hypnosis: Support for a Cognitive-State Theory
Based on Laterality. *By* KENNETH R. GRAHAM 274
Models of Posthypnotic Amnesia. *By* JOHN F. KIHLSTROM 284

Author Index 302

Subject Index 303

INTRODUCTION

William E. Edmonston, Jr.

Department of Psychology
Colgate University
Hamilton, New York 13346

More than three years ago, when I was first invited to propose a conference for The New York Academy of Sciences, I decided to develop the program around the theme of inquiries into the fundamental nature of hypnosis. Although hypnosis has been investigated and applied, in a variety of formats, for centuries, its precise nature has not been clarified. I felt that the best way to enhance our future efforts to understand hypnosis would be to review our present general fund of knowledge by bringing together the major investigators in the field.

The first two sessions were attempts—quite successful, I believe—to review, first, the major theoretical orientations of hypnotic investigations, and, second, the basic research tactics used by workers in the field. Naturally, no examination of hypnosis would be complete without a review of the traditional areas of interest: capacity for hypnosis, physiological concomitants, pain control, amnesia, hypnotherapy, and the like. But also necessary for a conference that is to be future-directed by the past is a look at the newer areas of investigation into creativity, dreams, imagination, and altered states. All of these areas were covered in the conference.

Did the conference accomplish its purpose of illuminating pathways for hypnotic investigations yet to come? I hope so, although the whims of individual investigators will be another strong influence.

Can I summarize the conference in a sentence or two, or, now that the conference is complete, define hypnosis with any more assurance than before? To the latter, probably no, but to the former I would say that three major investigative directions emerged: (1) I think we are going to see a resurgence of studies into those special characteristics of individuals who are highly capable of hypnosis, particular personality, physique, and physiological variables that are related to hypnotic susceptibility. (2) There will be an expansion of investigations of hypnosis as an analgesic agent. Three different individuals from three different laboratories all reported the positive analgesic effect of hypnosis. Such replication can now form the core for new studies further clarifying the limitations of the analgesia obtained through hypnosis. Finally, (3) our understanding of consciousness will be enhanced through and by future work in hypnosis, and this, in turn, will aid our understanding of hypnosis; for we know a phenomenon by its related phenomena, and understanding comes through contrast.

1

HYPNOSIS FROM THE STANDPOINT
OF A CONTEXTUALIST

William C. Coe

California State University
Fresno, California 93740

Theodore R. Sarbin

University of California, Santa Cruz
Santa Cruz, California 95064

The task of this conference is to make sense of unexpected and unusual actions, the counterexpectational conduct of the hypnotic subject. A person is told that his arm is stiff and that he cannot bend it. It is of little interest to scientists and philosophers if he bends his arm; such actions are expected under usual circumstances. But if he appears to try to but does not bend his arm, our interest is aroused. More dramatic examples of counterexpectational conduct include persons' claims of not experiencing pain when painful stimuli are applied, claims that ordinarily remembered recent events are forgotten, and claims of seeing and hearing happenings contrary to fact. Counterexpectational conduct, including conterfactual statements, make up the fabric of hypnosis.

We address the question: "How to make sense of counterexpectational conduct?" The answer will flow from the placement of the conduct in a framework where such conduct is expected, that is, no longer contrary to expectations. A reference case will illustrate.

We observe a man holding his arm out in front of him, and he says, "I cannot bend my arm." With no more information, the man's behavior is contrary to expectation. Without further infromation we are perplexed.

As, however, we learn more about the context of this counterexpectational conduct, his actions are more likely to be perceived as expected under the special circumstances and are therefore understandable. For example, we might observe that the man is wearing the uniform of an Army private and that his commanding officer has told him to hold out his arm and not to bend it. Or, in another context, we may observe that he is being examined by a neurologist after suffering a severe blow to his head. In yet another context, we may discover that the man is in the presence of a hypnotist who has told him that his arm is stiff and that he cannot bend it.

In each of these cases, identifying the context renders the man's conduct expectational. In the instance of the Army private, we would expect his conduct from our knowledge of the military code of discipline. In the neurologist's office, we would probably attribute his inability to bend his arm to an injury of the brain. And in the presence of a hypnotist, we might suppose that he could not bend his arm because he was "hypnotized."

Each context provides information that makes counterexpectational conduct expectational. However, the explanatory statements are not equally convincing. Many of us are familiar with the military code of discipline and are aware of the severe, negative consequences that may be incurred if it is violated. The man's statement that he "cannot" bend his arm thereby makes sense in that we

2

understand it as his way of avoiding punishment. The neurological context is probably less familiar than is the military context. But even though many lay persons do not understand the workings of the nervous system, the deleterious effects of brain damage on the motor system are well-documented and generally agreed upon by experts. It therefore makes sense that the man cannot bend his arm. The explanation from the hypnotic context is less convincing. "Being hypnotized" is not a univocal term, and even in scientific circles there is lack of agreement on what constitutes "being hypnotized." The observation that some people cannot bend their arms when they are so instructed by a hypnotist makes the conduct expectational only if "hypnosis" is seen as sufficient cause. But, to the critical observer, more information is needed about what we mean by hypnosis before its use is very helpful in making sense of the man's conduct.

The foregoing analysis implies that some models or theories make more sense in accounting for the observations of counterexpectational conduct. Our task is to decide which model or models best perform this function, a task to which we now turn.

MODELS AND UTILITY

Our analysis to this point has shown that when an event is isolated from its context it is likely to be viewed as counterexpectational. Conversely, the more fully the context is identified, the more likely it is that the event becomes expectational; that is to say, the more likely it is that we will be able to make sense of it. Our chances of understanding are therefore increased if we select a model that allows us access to the greatest amount of information about the context, a model which is not constrained to isolated aspects of it.

A Contextualist Model

It is our position that of the models currently available, the dramaturgical model carries the least constraints and therefore the greatest utility. The dramaturgical model flows from the world view of contextualism, a view of the world that postulates that in order to understand the nature of mankind, one must view his actions within the context of their occurrence. Human beings are seen as active, ever-changing participants in the world, and in order to understand their conduct, one must take into account all of the conditions that make up the context of their actions. The metaphors of the drama guide us to those aspects of the context which may be important in making sense of our observations. Persons are metaphorically described as actors, who, like actors on the stage, enact various roles. The actor's personal characteristics are of importance, to be sure, but other aspects of the context are also significant, such as the characteristics of the stage, the other actors, the audience, the director, the plot, and so on.[1-5]

Formist and Mechanist Models

Most modern theories of hypnosis follow from the world views of formism and mechanism, or some mixture of these two. The formist view emphasizes the notion that the world may be organized on the basis of similarities and differences among entities, that there exists an ideal, natural form for things—norms, if you will. Theories that flow from this view postulate forms like the mind, personality, and the psyche. These theories usually elaborate these basic concepts with subordinate concepts such as ego states, traits, and states of consciousness. The mechanist views the world through the metaphor of the machine. Man's actions, like those of machines, may be explained by the transmission of forces along cause-and-effect chains. The clearest examples in psychology are the stimulus-response and the computer analog models.[6] When the formist and mechanistic views are combined, the models postulate the intervention of hypothetical mental structures and causal chains of energy. A good example from psychoanalytic theory is the transmission of psychic energy through levels of consciousness.[6]

Models that arise from formism and mechanism are generally quite constrained in regard to their capacity to study the larger contexts in which human behavior occurs. They are usually limited to the study of the individual abstracted from his context and to the operation of mental structures; context is either ignored or futile attempts are made artificially to hold it constant.

Our position does not deny that formist and mechanistic views are useful. No identified world view has a monopoly on "truth" or the "real" nature of things—all world views are simply metaphorical ways of constructing the world. One or another of these world views may have greater utility as our focus of interest changes. The utility of the mechanistic view increases as our focus becomes more and more limited to tiny aspects of the context. For example, in the neurologist's examining room the mechanistic, cause-effect view of the relationship between the damage to the cortex and the paralysis of an arm has utility. Formist models generally have their greatest utility in moral and ethical enterprises. Their utility is clearly demonstrated in social control movements where forms are endowed with moral judgments of "good" and "evil." Concepts such as "mental illness," "mind," "love," and "soul" make use of the notion of forms. Formist models depend upon the postulate of permanence. They have generally held little utility for making sense of complex human conduct, conduct that flows from change and novelty. A review of the history of hypnosis, especially during the last half century, accents the emergence of attention to context. Although their theories do not necessarily make use of a contextual world view, such writers as Barber, Shor, Orne, Hilgard, and others have reported observations that emphasize how hypnotic conduct depends upon identifiable contexts.

We have expounded the utility of role theory for many years.[1, 2, 7] Our earlier, less-refined concepts and observations led to the conclusion that hypnotic performance could best be regarded as a role enacted as part of a social drama, the role behaviors of the subject being seen as parallel to the role behaviors of stage actors engaged in their professional employment.

Role Enactment and Faking

Although we have explicitly defined role enactment as not coterminous with faking, dissimulation, deception, or fraud, our arguments appear not to have convinced all of our contemporaries. In this paper, we shall do more than assert that "hypnosis" as role enactment is not to be perceived as faking. We shall attempt to dismiss this misunderstanding and at the same time offer fresh dimensions that may assist us in making sense of hypnotic behavior.

To begin with, we should point out that the terms "enacting" and "faking" are taken from different families of concepts. Enacting a role is not the same as faking a role. Enacting is parallel to other action terms like entering, contributing, and so on; all indicate that people are doing something. No value judgments are implied about the goodness or badness of the actions in themselves, although a judgment may be made about the quality of the enactment; for example, X is an inept quarterback. The term *faking*, on the other hand, belongs to a family of concepts concerned with moral judgments and ethical issues, with categories such as sincerity, honesty, truthtelling, and so on. The word itself carries moral connotations and is employed to describe the reasons and purposes behind an enactment. Thus, interchanging the words *enacting* and *faking* represents a category error. *Enacting* and *faking* cannot legitimately be substituted one for the other.

Let us take a common case. A person enacts in turn the roles of father, husband, employee, church member, golfer, and voter. One does not ordinarily ask: "Do role theorists mean that the 'real' person is faking? That he is play-acting each role?" Such questions are not asked, because we have come to accept the use of the role metaphor in everyday social conduct, where persons enact roles to validate the positions they occupy. Concern with dissimulation is appropriate if the observer has reason to question whether the person is legitimately occupying the position that his actions are supposedly validating. For example, in Orne's simulator design, subjects are purposely instructed to fake being good hypnotic subjects.[8]

The ready acceptance of the role metaphor for ordinary social roles has not generalized to all roles. The use of the root metaphor, "life is theater," is probably behind the misconception that role enactment is faking. Only an uncritical, unsophisticated glance at professional actors acting on a stage promotes the ideas that role enactment is equivalent to faking. When Richard Burton portrays the role of Hamlet, the spectator knows that the actor is not the character, whether or not he reads the program. This is not to gainsay the observation that the spectator may become so involved in the actions of the drama that the *character* becomes the object of attention, *not* the actor who recites the lines. That is, if Burton is enacting his role with conviction, the spectator may lose perspective momentarily and become involved with the character "Hamlet" rather than with the actor Richard Burton. Alternately, Burton may set aside his role as self-spectator and temporarily "become" Hamlet. In any case, it is absurd to say that Burton is faking the role Hamlet.

We now turn to describing in more detail the dramaturgical model in understanding episodes that are labeled "hypnosis." As we proceed, it will become clearer that role enactment and faking are concepts drawn from two separable contexts.

Let us take a reference case and describe it in ordinary language. Two persons are involved: one is designated the hypnotist and the other the subject. The hypnotist utters a statement with counterexpectational implications, "You will not remember anything that happened during the time you were hypnotized." The statement is counterexpectational in the sense that we ordinarily expect a person to remember recent events. When the subject is subsequently queried about what happened, he says, "I don't remember." Upon presentation of an agreed-upon cue, the subject remembers.

Among the alternative explanations for this observation are those that follow from the formist metaphysic: for example, amnesia is a characteristic of special mental states; or from the mechanistic metaphysic: for example, the spread of cortical inhibition blocks recall. An alternative metaphysic, contextualism, provides a dramaturgical description. We would begin with the sentence: The subject is enacting a role that calls for not remembering and for saying, "I don't remember."

THE DRAMATURGICAL VIEW

Because of space limitations, we wish to emphasize the roles of the hypnotist and the subject, the actors in our drama. A dramaturgical description of the hypnotist's and subject's conduct is especially relevant to an analysis of the interesting studies of pain control which E. R. Hilgard and his associates have been conducting.[9, 10] We will turn to these studies momentarily.

It is important to make clear that the actors are but a part of the total context. Before turning our focus to them, we shall therefore briefly examine some other strands in the context. As we look at these, we will at the same time be showing how a dramaturgical model is capable of revealing a broader view of the context for counterexpectational conduct. In addition to the actors, the stage, the audience, and the plot are also important in the context of explaining hypnotic behavior.

Stage, Audience, and Plot

The stage includes the physical trappings that surround the actors. The particular characteristics these take may encourage, restrain, or in other ways modify the conduct of the actors. Included, among other things, are the buildings, the furnishings, and the costumes. The nature of the stage will, to a degree, limit the plot of the drama. The stage differences in the scientist's laboratory, the practitioner's office, and the entertainer-hypnotist's scene each suggests a somewhat different plot which in turn modifies the actors' scripts and expected conduct. For example, unlike the therapist-practitioner, the scientist-experimenter rarely expects his subject to reveal highly personal information, nor does he seek it. Also, neither the therapist nor the experimenter, unlike the entertainer-hypnotist, conducts himself in ways meant to entertain.

As we have pointed out elsewhere, the audience affects the ongoing drama by reinforcing the actors' conduct and providing them with feedback.[1] The audience does not have to be physically present; hypnotists and subjects may create imaginary audiences. For example, the scientific researcher might modify his actions because of his impressions about how the scientific community will accept his work. Striking examples are seen in cases where data are purposely altered; less obvious examples are seen where experimenters lead their subjects to behave in ways that support the experimenter's hypothesis.[11, 12] Subjects may also modify their behavior for imaginary audiences like those which represent personal and communal codes of conduct. These effects are sometimes labeled "role demands" or "propriety norms"[1] or, in more specific contexts, "demand characteristics" of the experiment.[8]

Plots are the general themes or purposes of social interactions. They limit within a context the ways in which actors conduct themselves and the goals to which they aspire. The plot in the usual laboratory is to discover information by employing knowable conditions and observing what happens. In stage dramas, the plots are predetermined and previously agreed upon by the cast; in most everyday interaction the plot is not so clear, nor is it so readily agreed upon by the participants. In fact, much of what goes on between people in everyday interactions may be viewed as attempts to discover a common plot that will make their interactions more comfortable. The same may be said about the laboratory scientist's experiment, the practitioner's therapy, or the stage hypnotist's show. In any event, the actors' perception of presumed plots modify ways in which they interact with each other. More will be said about these matters as we focus on the role of the actors in hypnosis.

The Characters: Hypnotist and Hypnotic Subject

It is now time for a more detailed analysis of the characters. The dramaturgical model casts our observations within the general metaphor "life is theater." As scholars and scientists, we examine metaphors deliberately in hopes that they will help make sense of perplexing, counterexpectational conduct, and we try to select one that provides the most satisfying answers. In trying to make sense of the hypnosis scene, the hypnotic subject may also cast about for a suitable metaphor. The context may be supportive of his adopting the dramatistic metaphor, and he may then enact the role as he perceives it, given such conditions as settings, experimenter variables, skills, and others. Merely telling the subject that "this is a hypnosis experiment" may be sufficient to call out the dramatistic metaphor, and he may enact the role as he has acquired it through mass media, personal observation, and so on.

Perhaps the most important single event that sets the stage, so to speak, for the subject to structure the hypnotic experiment as a dramatic episode is the experimenter's utterance of counterfactual propositions. The experimenter says "you are becoming drowsy" or "you hear a mosquito buzzing around your ear" or "your unconscious mind is now active." The subject may be quick to recognize these statements as counterfactual, and he may take them as cues that a miniature drama is about to be performed, a drama in which both the experimenter and the subject engage in counterexpectational, counterfactual conduct. We propose that the counterfactual statement of the experimenter, within the total situation, serves the same function as the stage director's more explicit instruction: "Mr. Burton, you play the role of Hamlet." A parallel may also be drawn from the observation of children at play when one child says to his playmate. "You be the doctor and I'll be the nurse." In short, there are direct and indirect ways of casting actors in specific roles, of communicating that we are about to participate in a dramatic scene. To be sure, the subject may accept or reject the role-casting. If the implied plot interests or excites the subject, then he is likely to accept the role-casting. In this sense, then, he is like the professional actor who becomes excited about participating in a dramatic scene when he reads the script or is told about the script by his agent.* If, however, the subject is more literal in his view of the world, he

---

* Several studies have already supported a strong link between interest in drama and hypnotic responsiveness.[13-17]

is less likely to respond in kind to the hypnotist's invitation to participate in a dramatistic encounter.

Simply accepting the dramatic possibilities of a situation is not enough, however, for a convincing role enactment. The subject is now faced with the task of making credible his enactment as hypnosis subject. Like the actor on the stage, he must use his knowledge and skills in order to enact his part in ways that are credible to other participants, in the present case, the hypnotist and other spectators. He must enhance his credibility through verbal and nonverbal channels of communication. Space does not permit a detailed discourse on the concept of credibility enhancement discussed in previous writings.[1] Suffice it to note that the subject's knowledge of what is expected and the skills that are necessary to fulfill these expectations interact in determining the effectiveness of his performance.

From the dramaturgical standpoint, it is no less important to observe the actions of the hypnotist than the actions of the subject. Both are actors, both are engaged is reciprocal communication. Both must consider ways of enhancing credibility, that is, of making their role enactments convincing. Observe the typical hypnotist in the act of casting the subject in the hypnotic role. How does he communicate that his counterexpectational or counterfactual statement should be taken as a cue for the subject to participate in the miniature drama? His speech patterns vary from those when his communications are expectational and/or factual. He may drop his speech an octave, he may decrease the rate of speech, he may repeat phrases monotonously, he may place accents in unusual places, and so on. All this is done to insure his credibility in the role of hypnotist. If the subject assigns a high degree of credibility in the hypnotist's role enactment, then he may choose to join the action and enact the corresponding counterexpectational role. The conditions for a successful role enactment as subject are canceled if the subject assigns no credibility to the hypnotist.[18, 19]

The Self-Report

To this point, we have deferred discussion of one of the most important issues: the validity of subjects' self-reports. Elsewhere we have elaborated characteristics associated with self-report including the psychology of believing, the psychology of secrets, and the psychology of self-persuasion.[20] Self-reports are the primary data in most studies, including Hilgard's and his coworkers' recent studies on pain control, to which we now turn.[9, 10, 21-24]

HYPNOTIC ANALGESIA AND THE "HIDDEN OBSERVER"

We make use of Hilgard's important reports on hypnotic analgesia to illustrate the heuristic value of a theory that employs dramatistic categories. Hilgard's studies confirm the observation made repeatedly over the past 200 years that for selected subjects, suggestions of analgesia produce convincing self-reports of analgesia. More significant is the finding that the employment of so-called automatic writing and automatic talking procedures (again, in selected subjects) results in the subject's contradiction of his prior or concurrent self-reports of analgesia. The latter findings, at first perplexing and apparently counterexpectational to Hilgard and his associates, called for a metaphor that would help reduce the strain of perplexity. For communicative purposes, the "hidden observer" metaphor was employed—the clearly metaphoric quality of the term being indicated by quotation marks. As data accumulated and theorizing progressed, Hilgard advanced a neodissociation theory to account for the puzzling observations. The theory posits cognitive systems that are relatively autonomous from one another. The theory is elaborated with the aid of a number of opaque terms, among them *cognitions, barriers, consciousness, awareness,* and *communication channels.* In keeping with scientific—that is, the mechanistic—idiom, Hilgard identifies certain correspondences between the neodissociation theory of hypnotic analgesia and the neurological theory of pain perception developed by Melback and Wall.[25]

It is clear from reading Hilgard's reports that the counterexpectational findings are to be rendered expectational (and understandable) only through entering the individual to scrutinize his cognitive processes and/or his neurological pathways. The hoped-for outcome of this strategy is an equation that connects stimuli and responses, that is to say, a formula that relates communications of the hypnotist to both analgesia self-reports and the self-reports which contradict analgesia. Like so many hypothetical constructs, dissociation —at first a figure of speech employed to describe metaphorically the mechanics of counterexpectational behavior—has taken on the semblance of a platonic form. It may suffer the same fate as other forms employed to account for hypnosis, such as trance, odylic force, animal magnetism, and psychic states.

In this connection, a brief glance at one segment of the history of hypnotism might be instructive. It is only in the past half-century that students of hypnosis have been seriously concerned with individual differences in responsiveness. In earlier times, questions about counterexpectational conduct were framed in the formist idiom: "What is hypnosis?" The emphasis was on the posited form, the mental state, the divided consciousness, the dissociated self, and so on. When experimental psychologists approached the subject matter of hypnotism, the formist question was replaced by the current, more scientific, individual-differences questions, such as, "What are the characteristics that differentiate persons who are responsive to hypnotic induction procedures from those who are not?" This question evolved into a more detailed question which has since guided the study of most contemporary workers in hypnosis: "What are the characteristics of persons, settings, instructions, etc., that lead some persons and not others to perform actions that are contrary to expecations, which are apparently discontinuous from ordinary conduct?"

The studies in analgesia under discussion can easily lead us back to the formist question: "What is hypnosis?" By working only with preselected, highly responsive subjects, individual-differences questions are set aside. Strategies are employed to discover empirical justification for the construct employed in the first place as a metaphor, a fiction, to help describe the discontinous conduct. To avoid this return to formism, we are well-advised to keep the individual-differences question prominently before us, to sample widely among subjects, and also to heed Brunswik's counsel and sample widely among situations.

Analgesia

Let us return now to Hilgard's findings and account for them through the application of the dramaturgical model. First, let us consider the observation that some people, but by no means all, report analgesia following hypnotic instructions. It is not counterexpectational, not perplexing to the dramatistically inclined theorist that social conditions can be arranged for selected persons to enact specific roles. In preselecting subjects with high scores on hypnotizability scales, the experimenter automatically selects persons who have demonstrated (1) a readiness to engage in a miniature drama in response to the counter-factual statements of the hypnotist, and (2) a skill in employing actions that lead to credibility enhancement. To the role theorist, preselection of subjects on these dramatistic dimensions makes hypnotic analgesia expectational.

The subject employs whatever skills, techniques, and maneuvers he can to disattend the pain stimulus. In this respect, he is like the youth who engages in the macho game of not expressing pain through grimacing, flinching, weeping, or shouting when ferociously pinched by his antagonist. He may use distraction techniques such as talking, counting, laughing, imagining a contrary state of affairs, or others. Meditation, relaxation, fantasy, prayer, and laying on of hands are some of the distraction procedures that have been successful with some persons in producing analgesia. *Distraction* (or disattending) is a more transparent term than dissociation. It is a term that denotes actions, actions that are observable and even measurable.[26] †

It is important to note that the subject is cast in the role of actor. If he accepts the casting, he becomes the agent, the doer, the performer of intentional acts. He tries as best he can to be pain-free, and he also tries to communicate to the hypnotist that he is without pain. Lest we be accused of oversimplifying, we are quick to point out that there are other strands in the texture of explanation of the social act of communicating analgesia. In addition to motoric and cognitive skills already mentioned, we might point to the relationship between the hypnotist and the subject or patient, prior experiences with analgesia, prior experiences with hypnosis, the specific role demands of the situation and so on.

Contradictory Reports

We now turn to a second observation derived from reports of a so-called hidden observer, those reports which contradict the prior reports of analgesia. The instructions are worth repeating here. The hypnotist says to the subject:

> When I place my hand on your shoulder, I shall be able to talk to a hidden part of you that knows things are going on in your body, things that are unknown to the part of you to which I am now talking. The part to which I am now talking will not know what you are telling me or even

---

† If neurological categories were required to justify the distraction hypothesis, we could cite the important work of Beecher, a long-time leader in the field of anesthesiology. Beecher proposes competing afferent inputs to account for analgesia through distraction. Our perspective, however, is social psychological. We recognize that the human being is grounded in biology; however, his intentional social acts are not explicable as combinations of muscle twitches.

that you are talking. . . . You remember that there is a part of you that knows many things that are going on that may be hidden from either your normal consciousness or the hypnotized part of you. . . .[9]

The receiver of this communication is free to assume that this instruction contains categories that are isomorphic with the structure of a mind or brain, for example, "the hidden part of you." If taken literally, the assumption encourages the use of the metaphor of hidden observer.

Talking and writing about the hidden observer as a metaphor implies the statement, "It is *as if* there is a hidden observer." Following the mechanistic credo of science, Hilgard seems to demand more than an "as if" statement, more than a metaphorical description. A set of propositions in the traditional language of science is more congruent with the aims of the mechanistic enterprise. He employs terms that have the warrant of history, although not always the warrant of clarity, e.g., "divided consciousness," "dissociated cognition," and "neurological pathways." These constructs are employed according to the basic paradigm of mechanistic science: the transmission of energy.

At this point, it would be appropriate to ask: Is the dissociation explanation of the contradiction of analgesia the result of literalizing the metaphor of dissociation, of assigning a high degree of credibility to a fiction? If so, it would not be the first time in the history of science that a useful metaphor has been transformed to a reified entity.

Now let us consider the hidden observer instructions to the subject from the dramatistic perspective. We have said before that the experimenter's utterance of a counterfactual proposition is sufficient to invite the subject to join in a dramatistic enterprise. If the subject accepts the invitation, he, like the hypnotist, will enact his role in ways that enhance credibility. It is likely, given the obvious dramatistic atmosphere of the setting, that the hidden-observer instructions are interpreted as metaphoric stage directions. In effect, the stage directions instruct the subject to shift his orientation from that of agent or actor to that of spectator. To be able to report analgesia, the subject as actor engages in certain actions that for the moment reduce his involvement in the sensory stimulus. To be able to note his actions, he must actively adopt another perspective, that of spectator. Our language is clearly not the opaque language of mental states, nor is it the mechanistic language of physiology. The vocabulary of everyday life is well-suited to talk of actors and of spectators.

Hardly anyone would support the statement that so-called automatic writing and automatic talking are literally automatic. Such acts require effort, decision, choice. The dramatic stage direction to engage in automatic communication is a counterfactual statement, the content of which is to become a spectator. As before, the subject may take this communication as a further invitation to participate in the drama, to participate as a spectator. It requires no elaborate theory or neurological exegesis to account for the commonplace observation that a person may shift his perspective from actor to spectator.

The highly selected subjects in Hilgard's experiments, we hold, are persons who are justifiably characterized as imaginative, as good role-takers, as ready for dramatic encounters. We propose that the implications of the hidden observer instructions direct the subject to participate in particular kind of dramatic enterprise, a monodrama. In addition to the more obvious dramatic encounter between two actors, the subject and the hypnotist, a monodramatic enterprise takes form. We can liken the monodrama to a play within a play.

Although the main action is between players, the hypnotist and the subject, a subsidiary plot unfolds around the subject, who enacts both parts in the monodrama, agent and spectator. Parenthetically, we are reminded of the seminal contribution of George Herbert Mead that the person is both an *I* and a *me*. The subject simultaneously adopts both perspectives, that of the agent or doer and that of the spectator or audience. As a spectator, he can be his own dramatic critic.

From the perspective of the spectator, the subject can now report both the happenings and the doings of the analgesia scene. He can report the immediate sensory experience, a happening over which he has little control; he can report his efforts to minimize the *effects* of the sensory experience, he can report the anguish and suffering; and he can report the actions taken to reduce overt communication about anguish and suffering.

With the aid of these concepts, the self-reports of subjects under hidden-observer directions lose some of their mystery. The direction to take the perspective of the spectator grants license to the subject to serve as his own dramatic critic, the result of which is the contradiction of the self-report of analgesia.

SUMMARY

We set out to formulate a theory that makes counterexpectational conduct expectational. Our contextualist position has led us to the dramaturgical perspective. This perspective guided our examination of the hypnotic performance, and we noted that both the hypnotist and the subject are actors, both enmeshed in a dramatic plot, both striving to enhance their credibility. The dramatistic concepts of actor and spectator helped us make sense of the contradictory self-reports in Hilgard's analgesia studies.

We underscore the proposition (long overlooked) that the counterfactual statements in the hypnotist's induction are cues to the subject that a dramatistic plot is in the making. The subject may respond to the cues as an invitation to join in the miniature drama. If he accepts the invitation, he will employ whatever skills he possesses in order to enhance his credibility in enacting the role of hypnotized person. This proposition emphasizes the need for analyzing the implied social communications contained in any interaction.

REFERENCES

1. SARBIN, T. R. & W. C. COE. 1972. Hypnosis: A Social Psychological Analysis of Influence Communication. Holt, Rinehart and Winston. New York, N.Y.
2. SARBIN, T. R. & M. L. ANDERSEN. 1967. Role-theoretical analysis of hypnotic behavior. *In* Handbook of Clinical and Experimental Hypnosis. J. E. Gordon, Ed.: 319–344. Crowell-Collier and Macmillan. New York, N.Y.
3. SARBIN, T. R. & V. L. ALLEN. 1968. Role theory. *In* Handbook of Social Psychology. G. Lindzey and E. Aronson, Eds.: 488–567. Addison-Wesley. Reading, Mass.
4. BURKE, K. 1945. A Grammar of Motives. Prentice-Hall. New York, N.Y.
5. GOFFMAN, E. 1959. Presentation of Self in Everyday Life. Doubleday Co. New York, N.Y.
6. HALL, C. S. & G. LINDZEY. 1970. Theories of Personality. 2nd edit. John Wiley and Sons. New York, N.Y.

7. SARBIN, T. R. 1950. Contributions to role theory: hypnotic behavior. Psychol. Rev. **57:** 255–270.
8. ORNE, M. T. 1972. On the simulating subject as a quasi-control group in hypnosis research: What, why and how? In Hypnosis: Research Developments and Perspectives. E. Fromm and R. E. Shor, Eds. : 399–443. Aldine-Atherton. Chicago, Ill.
9. KNOX, V. J., A. H. MORGAN & E. R. HILGARD. 1974. Pain and suffering in Ischemia: the paradox of hypnotically suggested analgesia as contradicted by reports from the "Hidden Observer." Arch. Gen. Psychiat. **30:** 840–847.
10. HILGARD, E. R., A. H. MORGAN & H. MacDONALD. 1975. Pain and dissociation in cold pressor test: A study of hypnotic analgesia with "hidden reports" through automatic key pressing and automatic talking. J. of Abnormal Psychol. **84:** 280–289.
11. BARBER, T. X. 1973. Pitfalls in research: Nine investigator and experimenter effects. In Handbook of Research on Teaching. 2nd edit. R. M. Travers, Ed. : 382–404. Rand McNally. Chicago, Ill.
12. ROSENTHAL, R. & R. L. ROSNOW. 1969. Artifact in Behavioral Research. Academic Press. New York, N.Y.
13. COE, W. C. 1964. Further norms on the Harvard Group scale of hypnotic susceptibility, Form A. Int. J. Clin. Exper. Hypnosis **12:** 184–190.
14. COE, W. C. & T. R. SARBIN. 1966. An experimental demonstration of hypnosis as role enactment. J. Abnorm. Psychol. **71:** 400–406.
15. COE, W. C. & T. R. SARBIN. 1971. An alternative interpretation to the multiple composition of hypnotic scales: A single role-relevant skill. J. Abnorm. Psychol. **18:** 1–8.
16. SABRIN, T. R. & D. T. LIM. 1963. Some evidence in support of the role taking hypothesis in hypnosis. Int. J. Clin. Exper. Hypnosis **11:** 98–103.
17. HILGARD, J. R. 1970. Personality and Hypnosis: A Study of Imaginative Involvement. University Chicago Press. Chicago, Ill.
18. BARBER, T. X. & D. C. CALVERLY. 1964. Effect of E's tone of voice on "hypnotic-like" suggestibility. Psychol. Rep. **15:** 139–144.
19. COE, W. C. 1976. Effects of hypnotist susceptibility and sex on the administration of standard hypnotic susceptibility scales. Int. J. Clin. Exper. Hypnosis **24:** 281–286.
20. COE, W. C. 1976. Posthypnotic amnesia and the psychology of secrets. Paper presented at ann. mtg. Soc. Clin. Exp. Hypnosis. Philadelphia, Pa.
21. HILGARD, E. R. 1973. A neo-dissociation interpretation of pain reduction in hypnosis. Psychol. Rev. **80:** 396–411.
22. HILGARD, E. R., J. C. RUCH, A .F. LANGE, J. R. LENOX, A. H. MORGAN & L. B. Sachs. 1974. The psychophysics of cold pressor pain and its modification through hypnotic suggestion. Amer. J. Psychol. **87:** 17–31.
23. HILGARD, E. R. 1974. Toward a neo-dissociation theory: Multiple cognitive controls in human functioning. Perspectives in Biology and Medicine. **17:** 301–316.
24. HILGARD, E. R. & J. R. HILGARD. 1975. Hypnosis in the Relief of Pain. William Kaufmann, Inc. Los Altos, Calif.
25. MELBACK, R. & P. D. WALL. 1965. Pain mechanisms: A new theory. Science **150:** 971–979.
26. KNOX, V. J., L. CRUTCHFIELD & E. R. HILGARD. 1975. The nature of task interference in hypnotic dissociation: An investigation of hypnotic behavior. Int. J. Clin. Exper. Hypnosis **23:** 305–323.

THE CONSTRUCT OF HYPNOSIS:
IMPLICATIONS OF THE DEFINITION FOR RESEARCH
AND PRACTICE *

Martin T. Orne

*The Institute of Pennsylvania Hospital and
University of Pennsylvania
Philadelphia, Pennsylvania 19139*

Although hypnotic phenomena have been well delineated since the Marquis de Puységur's historic description, controversy persists concerning the nature of hypnosis and even its very existence. It is my hope that, in this paper, by asking what it is that makes hypnosis interesting—to some, even implausible—and exploring how the phenomena have been defined, it will be possible to lay to rest some disagreements about hypnosis. In particular, I will seek to address issues about the reality of hypnosis that are in fact controversies about the mechanisms responsible for what is observed. Such an effort is intended to clarify definitional issues and distinguish between those questions which require empirical as opposed to those which demand conceptual clarification.

WHAT MAKES HYPNOSIS A COMPELLING PHENOMENON?

Consider for a moment what occurs with a responsive subject following a simple hypnotic induction procedure administered by a comparative stranger. Following arm levitation, a number of standard hypnotic phenomena are suggested and the specific suggestion that on awakening, "You will forget what has occurred during hypnosis until I start writing down notes," is made. Further, the hypnotist adds, "Each time I remove my spectacles your right hand will lift to smooth your hair." Hypnosis is then terminated, and when asked what has occurred, the subject is able to describe the experience of watching the hand and seeing it begin to float upward, but insists that he is unable to recall more than one or two disjointed events that occurred subsequently. Despite encouragement to remember, the subject continues to assert that he simply cannot recall more of what has occurred. However, during his conversation, I twice remove my eyeglasses and each time he smooths his hair. Finally, I begin to take notes about what is being said, and suddenly, with a somewhat puzzled expression followed by a smile, the subject says, "It suddenly came back to me. . . . Now I remember. . . ." Indeed, the subject does now remember and reports systematically most, though not necessarily all, that has transpired.

Such a series of events holds great fascination for the observer, be he layman or psychologist. What is it that makes this series of events interesting? The subject's actions taken separately are unremarkable. He may have raised

* The substantive research upon which the theoretical outlook presented in this paper is based was supported in part by grant MH 19156–06 from the National Institute of Mental Health and by a grant from the Institute for Experimental Psychiatry.

his hand somewhat more slowly than usual. When told to place his hands together and that he would be unable to take them apart, he did not separate them until told to do so. On awakening, he reported that he did not remember what had happened and then twice smoothed his hair—a trivial action—all of which again merely involved in some sense doing what he had been asked to do.

The Failure of Behavioral Compliance to Index Hypnosis

It is not the trivial items of behavior that cause us to call this set of events hypnosis but rather an inference about the subjective events reflected in these behaviors. The subject was not instructed to raise his hand slowly; rather he had been told that his fingers and arm were getting light and would float upward. The observer may wonder whether the subject actually experienced his hand and arm becoming light—which expressed itself in the hand slowly lifting upward—or whether he simply chose to raise his hand slowly. Similarly, when on awakening the subject says, "I can't remember what happened," the observer may be curious about whether that is true or whether the subject really does remember and chooses to act as though he cannot. Again, with the posthypnotic response the issue is whether the response of smoothing the hair is carried out without the subject's awareness, as it appears to be, or whether it represents a purposive going along with the hypnotist's request.

If the observer learned that he happened to have come upon a rehearsal of a play and the participants were actors, he would quickly lose interest since there would be no reason to assume that the observed behavior had reflected changes in the individual's subjective experience. In other words, it is not the overt behavioral compliance that is elicited by the hypnotist which distinguishes the phenomenon. Thus, the drill sergeant can and does elicit behaviors involving greater efforts, a higher degree of compliance, and extending over a longer period than do most hypnotic suggestions. Although some might focus on the vague resemblance to hypnosis with regard to the automaticity of behavior in both situations, the soldier's actions seem to involve quite different processes.

These differences are important for an appreciation of what makes hypnosis unique. In the case of the drill sergeant, the social context defines his authority over the soldier. Elaborate, formal and informal sanctions exist to compel obedience to the sergeant's orders. Finally, these orders invariably demand behaviors that—though requiring effort—the soldier can carry out if he chooses to do so. Contrast this with the hypnotic situation. Hypnotist and subject may be strangers, but beyond the agreement to participate in hypnosis (and the absence of a hostile relationship), social sanctions which would compel compliance on the part of the subject are not required. Given a minimum of cooperation, the subject's hypnotizability—a reasonably enduring trait—seems to be the single most important determinant of the subject's response.[1]

Even though the hypnotized subject may respond to the suggestions of the hypnotist in an apparently automatic fashion, there is no compelling evidence that hypnotized individuals will do things in hypnosis that they are not prepared to do in the same social context without hypnosis. Thus, hypnosis is never induced in a vacuum and generally occurs in one of three settings: (1) in a therapeutic context, (2) in an experimental context, and (3) in the context of a demonstration with a volunteer subject. In all three settings the range of behavior which an individual will carry out if requested to do so is vastly greater than is generally believed. This willingness to comply is such that it has been difficult to document any increment of control following the induction of hypnosis over and above that already present prior to hypnosis.

Some time ago I summarized the evidence [2] that, contrary to my own early views,[3] the hypnotizable individual is not more motivated than the unhypnotizable individual to comply with the requests of the hypnotist that do not involve hypnotic phenomena. In this I was particularly impressed with the striking and oft-ignored observations originally made by London and Fuhrer [4] that unhypnotizable subjects are more willing to exert themselves in feats of endurance prior to hypnosis or following the induction of hypnosis than hypnotizable individuals. A similar tendency was reflected in a higher pain threshold of unhypnotizable subjects prior to an experiment.[5] Again, using punctuality as the measure of motivation, as is often done in a therapeutic setting, one finds that highly hypnotizable individuals are more likely to arrive late or even miss appointments than those subjects who have more difficulty in entering hypnosis.[6]

It is *only* when hypnotic phenomena are suggested that the apparent increase in compliance of the hypnotized subject becomes evident. Thus, the hypnotizable individual will not hold a kilogram weight longer than his unhypnotizable counterpart,[3] but his arm soon begins to float upward when suggestions of lightness are given, and while he may promptly forget what has transpired when suggestions of amnesia are given, unhypnotizable individuals exposed to the same suggestions fail to respond.

The Alteration of Subjective Experience in Hypnosis

What characterizes the hypnotizable subject is *not* the tendency to comply with any and all requests but rather the *specific tendency or ability to respond to suggestions designed to elicit hypnotic phenomena.* In other words, what strikes the observer is the profound change that can apparently be brought about in the *experience* of the hypnotized subject, which suggests that hypnosis must involve some basic and profound alterations. Paradoxically, however, the induction of hypnosis does not require an intense interpersonal relationship or even an intense wish on the part of the subject to be hypnotized. Furthermore, the induction procedure is hardly impressive, and it strikes an observer as most implausible that such a simple set of operations would lead to such profound consequences.

If hypnosis were the consequence of some drastic procedure, be it a drug, an intensely stressful experience, prolonged isolation, or some other obviously significant intervention, we would find it easy to understand and accept. It strikes me that it is the paradox between the apparently trivial induction procedure and the apparently dramatic consequences that is responsible for many of the difficulties which have surrounded hypnosis since its discovery.

HYPNOSIS: STATE VERSUS HOAX?

The reactions to hypnosis that seem to evolve among both serious lay observers and scientists seeking to understand hypnosis appear to polarize into one of two major categories (see Sutcliffe's distinction between "credulous" and "skeptical" views [7]). One group seems convinced that hypnosis is a uniquely powerful state that results in almost magical abilities. They report that hypnotized individuals can perform feats of strength and have control of both body and mind beyond the ken of the normal individual. Not only can cures of psychological problems be effected but even a wide range of bodily processes can be altered in a unique fashion. Finally, in novels and the lay press, this view leads to the imaginative leap that the hypnotist is able to exert a wide range of control over the subject which, if not restrained by ethical strictures, would make it possible to compel the hypnotized individual to do whatever the hypnotist desires. Scientifically, the extreme state view tends to be associated with the conviction that hypnosis must involve a major neurophysiological alteration. Typically, it is argued that specific bodily symptoms, which the trained hypnotist can readily appreciate and identify, characterize hypnosis. Furthermore, it is generally believed by these workers that unique neurological changes exist during hypnosis that either already have or would soon be demonstrated by rigorous research. This general view of hypnosis has been particularly popular among medically trained and biologically oriented individuals. The tradition is exemplified by Mesmer,[8] Braid,[9] Charcot,[10] to some extent by Erickson,[11] and, most recently, by Spiegel.[12]

An almost opposite response to hypnosis has been to argue that unique characteristics of hypnosis do not exist; the extreme version of this view holds that hypnosis reflects some kind of elaborate hoax. Early examples of this position are the writings of C. R. Hall [13] in the middle of the nineteenth century and those of E. Hart [14] at the turn of the century. Because rigorous investigators have been able to show that many of the claims concerning the effects of hypnosis have simply not stood up to close scrutiny, this position has found considerable support. Historically, Mesmer's animal magnetism, the Marquis de Puységur's lucid somnambulism, and innumerable other more or less plausible claims about the effects of hypnosis have been questioned and discarded following careful studies. The work of investigators such as P. C. Young,[15, 16] Pattie,[17, 18] and Hull [19] gradually delineated hypnotic phenomena, as quantitative methods were applied to the study. More recently, Barber [20] and Sarbin and Coe [21] have forcefully expressed more extreme versions of the skeptical position.

In the context of a conference such as the one on which this volume is based, one often tends to minimize differences between positions and point to the gradual convergence of views taking place in the last few years. Undoubtedly, to some extent there has been a convergence of views; however, the way in which one conceptualizes the phenomenon and, even more importantly, the way one operationally defines it, will have profound consequences for the manner in which it is empirically studied and for the kinds of conclusions that follow from such studies. I hope to show that it is not necessary to assume neurophysiological changes unique to hypnosis (for which no solid evidence as yet exists) in order to appreciate the potential utility and subjective reality of hypnotic phenomena. By the same token, it is very difficult and perhaps impossible to design studies that can document the behavioral consequences of alterations in subjective experience from a position which basically rejects the study of subjective experience as an attainable scientific goal. That which attracts our attention to hypnosis is the apparent change in subjective experience; while it is essential to find ways of demonstrating these changes in behavioral terms, it is necessary to identify those behaviors which reflect these changes. From this point of view, a definition of hypnosis will be discussed to facilitate rigorous, systematic research while taking into account the central characteristics of the phenomenon under investigation.

THE DEFINITION OF HYPNOSIS

If we are to advance beyond the stage of arguing state versus hoax, it is essential for any systematic study of hypnosis to begin with a reasonable operational definition of the phenomenon. The two major ways in which hypnosis has been defined is (1) in terms of what is done to the subject, and (2) in terms of the subject's response.

Traditionally, hypnosis has been defined in much the same way as psychotherapy: An interaction that occurs when a trained individual, the hypnotist (or psychotherapist), carries out what he calls hypnosis (or psychotherapy), respectively. In other words, the qualifications of the hypnotist and the fact that he hypnotizes and asserts that the patient is hypnotized are the criteria. Unfortunately, the consensus within the field is by no means sufficient, and experts do not necessarily agree whether a given patient has in fact been hypnotized. While the inadequacies of such a loose definition seem evident, a variant of this approach has found considerable favor in the neobehaviorist scientific community.

Most notably, Barber [20] and his students have defined hypnosis by its antecedent events; in other words, hypnosis is that which occurs following a standardized induction procedure. Unfortunately, the response of unselected individuals to hypnotic induction procedures varies widely, depending upon their ability to respond. Typically, some 15% will be profoundly affected, some 5%–10% will show hardly any response, and the remaining individuals will show varying levels of responsivity—with the whole group more or less approximating the normal distribution.

Even more troublesome, moreover, is Bernheim's classic observation that all hypnotic phenomena can be elicited in suitable individuals without any formal induction procedure. Clearly, if a hypnotic induction is unnecessary for some individuals and not sufficient to induce hypnosis for others, it cannot be used to define hypnosis.†

The alternate approach recognizes that we are dealing with a phenomenon which cannot be identified by specific antecedent events, and for which no invariant psychological or physiological concomitants have been isolated. Under these circumstances it seems reasonable to approach the identification of hypnosis as a problem analogous to the diagnosis of a state such as depression or sleep (without recourse to EEG).

In its simplest form one would define hypnosis as that state or condition which exists when appropriate suggestions will elicit hypnotic phenomena. Hypnotic phenomena are then defined as positive responses to test suggestions

---

† It is worth noting that an induction procedure defines the hypnotic context for all subjects, regardless of whether they are hypnotized. This change in context can bring about significant alterations in the interpersonal relationship that, in the therapeutic situation at least, may have profound consequences for behavior. Such consequences may be unrelated to the presence of hypnosis but follow solely from the hypnotic context.

which on analysis all turn out to involve suggested alterations of perception or memory.

The construct of hypnosis as a subjective state in which alterations of perception or memory can be elicited by suggestion is operationalized in standardized scales of hypnotic susceptibility of which the Stanford Scales [22, 23] have been the most useful. These scales present a variety of hypnotic items to the subject and measure the individual response in a standardized fashion. Though it is necessary to specify responses in behavioral terms, it should be emphasized that the resulting scores validly reflect the hypnotic process only to the degree that the behavior reflects alterations in the individual's subjective experience.[2] Fortunately, there is a high degree of concordance between what the subject independently describes as his experience and how he behaves in properly administered standardized tests. There are some circumstances, however, such as when a test is repeatedly administered with intervening treatments (as in studies designed to evaluate procedures proposing to increase hypnotizability), when the subject's objective behavior may be affected more than his subjective experience. It therefore seems crucial that investigators keep in mind that objective scales are valid only to the degree that they continue to accurately reflect altered subjective events.

For reasons such as these, and because with relatively small samples it becomes very important not to increase error variance by including subjects who are less responsive than they appear to be, we have always felt the most appropriate criterion measure of hypnosis is a diagnostic session [24] where an experienced clinician tries to induce a broad range of hypnotic phenomena in whatever fashion appears best suited to a particular subject. The response to hypnotic suggestion is evaluated behaviorally as well as by means of an extensive posthypnotic discussion which explores in detail the individual's experience. The diagnostic judgment is based on the congruence between the kind of suggestions given, the behavioral response, and the subject's description of what he experienced. In many ways this procedure is a rigorously operationalized form of the traditional way of defining hypnosis by an experienced clinician's judgment based on extensive work with a particular subject. We have been able to achieve high levels of reliability between observers and routinely use two independent diagnostic sessions with two different investigators. Further, we do not view this type of evaluation as a substitute for at least two standardized tests of hypnotic responsivity. Rather, the diagnostic sessions are intended to supplement standardized procedures by the careful establishment of the concordance between the subject's description of what he experiences and how he behaves.

In summary, I have tried to define hypnosis as that state or condition in which subjects are able to respond to appropriate suggestions with distortions of perception or memory. It should be clear that such a definition is descriptive rather than explanatory. Moreover, it may well be that the hypnotized subject carries out a suggested action also because he is in hypnosis; however, since we have found no actions which subjects would not carry out when requested to do so in the waking state,[25] simple behavioral compliance cannot be used to identify hypnosis. Although it would appear that not all individuals have the capacity to respond to hypnotic suggestions, those individuals who do have this ability vary in their responsiveness to suggestion, depending on the circumstances.

The basic questions that need to be resolved are the differences between those individuals who have the skill of entering hypnosis and those who do not; the circumstances that facilitate and/or respectively inhibit the tendency to respond to hypnotic suggestion in those individuals who have the ability to do so; and the consequences of being in hypnosis for an individual's psychobiological functioning.

One final point: In phrasing the definition, I have sought to be as theoretically neutral as possible. It is appropriate, however, to translate this definition into another conceptual framework. Thus, it is entirely compatible with my view to describe hypnosis, as Sarbin [26] does: a role that is played with such conviction as to become totally compelling to the individual. It would be crucial, however, that the individual experience the role as real, rather than that he is consciously acting a part. The role metaphor, if used in such a fashion, is operationally indistinguishable from my formulation. Equally acceptable, and, in my view, operationally indistinguishable, is to describe hypnosis as a "believed-in imagining." [21] The crucial point in such a formulation is that the individual, for the time being, becomes unable to distinguish between his fantasy and other life experiences.

THE REALITY OF HYPNOSIS

Whether hypnosis is "real" or a hoax is a question that has been raised ever since hypnotic phenomena were first described. The main reason why this issue remains with us today is, in my view, largely related to the tendency to confuse the several different questions that are in fact subsumed under this deceptively simple problem.

There are four distinct major issues around which at one time or another controversy about the reality of hypnosis has revolved. 1) Is the mechanism which a given investigator has postulated to explain the phenomenology of hypnosis valid; e.g., is there such a thing as animal magnetism? 2) Does a formal hypnotic induction procedure bring about unique changes different from those seen without hypnotic induction, e.g., the paradigm followed by Barber and his students? 3) Can hypnotic suggestion lead to the transcendence of normal volitional capacity; e.g., in hypnotic age regression, do the thought processes come to resemble those of a child? Is an individual able to remember accurately what happened during childhood? 4) Does the hypnotized individual experience what he appears to experience? Does his behavior reflect his phenomenal awareness; e.g., when hypnotic analgesia is induced and a pain stimulus administered, does the subject who asserts that he is comfortable nonetheless feel the pain?

While these four sets of issues do not necessarily exhaust what has been implied by the question of whether hypnosis is real, they may be sufficient to illustrate the range of issues that are involved. Hopefully, such an analysis will help explain both how and why investigators have often talked past each other, even though they seem to be addressing the identical question, the reality of hypnosis.

The Mechanisms by which Hypnosis is Explained

Explanatory mechanisms inevitably seem to become an integral part of an investigator's way of thinking about the phenomenon. Particularly because the dramatic effects of hypnosis do not appear justified by equally dramatic causes, investigators have tended to postulate some new kind of psychobiological explanatory mechanism. The controversy about hypnosis would then focus on the validity of the particular explanatory principle that has been postulated.

Already in Mesmer's time, the disputes surrounding his work illustrate this process. Mesmer sought to explain the cures following his treatment as the effects of an invisible fluid or force—animal magnetism. The Royal Commission appointed to investigate the claims of the Mesmerists initially agreed to study the results of treatment, and members of the commission appeared impressed with some of the observed results. However, the inquiry soon shifted its focus to the question of whether the magnetic fluid the Mesmerists had postulated actually existed. Although the commission acknowledged that many patients seemed to be helped by the Mesmerists' procedure, it was felt that such cures could best be explained as the consequences of "mere" imagination. Because the experiments failed to provide evidence for a magnetic fluid, Mesmer's claims were rejected and the phenomenon was dismissed as not real.

A similar controversy was basic to the famous dispute between the schools of Nancy and Salpêtrière. The distinguished neurologist Charcot described what he believed to be invariant stages reflecting basic neurological changes associated with hypnosis. Bernheim rejected this position and insisted that the effects of hypnosis were the product of suggestion. Further, he showed that formal induction of hypnosis was not necessary in order for a responsive subject to manifest all hypnotic effects; suggestion alone could be sufficient. To Charcot's followers, the acceptance of Bernheim's view was tantamount to denying the reality of hypnosis—hypnosis could be explained away as mere suggestion. Again, what appeared to many to be a controversy concerning the reality of hypnosis was quite clearly a dispute about the mechanisms that produce it. Indeed, Bernheim, who was presumably accused of denying the reality of hypnosis, made the practice of hypnotherapy his life's work.

Similar issues persist to the present day. Whenever a new explanatory principle is evoked to account for hypnosis, there is a tendency to argue that hypnosis is not real if experimental work fails to document the postulated mechanism. Ultimately, we will, of course, need to understand how it becomes possible for some individuals to distort their experience so dramatically. Without a meaningful theory the phenomenon continues to elude scientific clarification. By the same token, however, the absence of a satisfactory theory to explain the phenomena of hypnosis does not explain them away. Evidence that a given mechanism postulated to explain hypnotic phenomena fails to do so speaks to the inadequacy of a particular theory but tells us nothing about the reality of those events for which the theory has unsuccessfully tried to account.

Does a Formal Hypnotic Induction Procedure Result in Unique Changes?

Whether with unselected individuals unique effects of hypnotic induction can be demonstrated is by no means established. From the perspective of this discussion, however, even more troublesome is the tendency to confuse that question with questions about the reality of hypnosis. Since the early 1960s, Barber [20] and his students have systematically tried to study hypnosis by comparing individuals exposed to an induction procedure with individuals who are treated in a different fashion. Typically, few if any differences emerge when unselected subjects exposed to hypnotic induction are compared with unselected subjects exposed to a task-motivated condition, fantasy instructions, and the like. As I have pointed out earlier, such a design appears to address the reality of hypnosis only if hypnosis is defined exclusively by its antecedent events. Such a definition fails to take into account the nature of the phenomenon under investigation. Furthermore, the task-motivated instructions are likely to produce effects that mimic the behavior of hypnotized individuals without necessarily bringing about a change in the individual's subjective experience. On the other hand, some types of fantasy instructions are more likely to produce the same phenomenon as other kinds of hypnotic induction procedures.

Though one might argue, as does Barber, that the absence of dramatic differences between hypnotic induction groups and control groups given different types of instructions challenges the utility of the construct of hypnosis, such a position fails to account for the dramatic changes in subjective experience that seem to be brought about *in some individuals* following a variety of different antecedent events. It is the occurrence of a sequence of events such as we described at the beginning of this paper which needs to be understood; the demonstration that it does not depend upon formal induction procedures speaks to that issue, but it does not address the reality of the phenomenon that is observed.

Transcendence of Normal Volitional Capacities and the Correspondence of Subjective Experience and Verbal Report

Whether hypnosis can lead to the transcendence of normal volitional capacity and whether the hypnotized individual actually experiences what his behavior and his verbal reports seem to indicate are the kinds of questions about the reality of hypnosis that concern the nonspecialist when he asks whether hypnosis is real. These two questions are conceptually distinct. It is possible that the answer to one of these is affirmative and to the other, negative. However, an empirical resolution of these questions would seem essential for the development of any definitive theory to account for hypnotic phenomena. It is these issues which the bulk of our research has tried to address. How these problems are formulated and translated into operational definitions will, however, depend in large part on how hypnosis has been defined.

The discussion to follow will strive to clarify some of the problems of research in this area: why we have developed some special methodological tools to deal with them and selected findings which, in my view, document the subjective reality of hypnosis and may, one hopes, lay to rest the concern about this problem which has perhaps inadvertently been encouraged by some of the observations about hypnosis in recent years.

Some Methodological Considerations

In his major monograph on hypnosis and suggestibility, Hull [19] set the standard for modern research in this field. Because it was time-consuming to identify highly responsive hypnotic subjects, he favored an experimental design comparing the response of the same individual while hypnotized with that while in a waking state. He carefully counterbalanced the order of presentation in an effort to control for order effects. However, he himself already recognized some of the serious difficulties potentially inherent in such a design, particularly that it was possible for a subject to depress his waking performance in order to enhance the relative level of the hypnotic performance.

This difficulty, as well as the problem of treating subjects in the same way whether they are hypnotized or awake, and the likelihood of unwittingly biasing the subject's response in the manner in which some instructions are given, and finally, from my point of view particularly important, the extent to which a within-subjects design can communicate what is expected—or wanted —of the subject's performance, convinced me that additional controls were required.[27] I rejected an independent group design,‡ partly because of the extreme cost involved in finding highly responsive subjects and also because an independent group design does not solve the problem of experimenter bias. From the observation of other investigators, I had noticed that hardly anyone gave instructions to hypnotized individuals in the same manner as to waking subjects, a tendency that I found difficult if not impossible to eliminate when I ran subjects myself. To deal with these issues, a special simulator comparison group was developed.

Elsewhere [29] I have described in detail the merits and demerits of using as a comparison group unhypnotizable subjects instructed to simulate hypnosis. The logic of the design is based on that developed by Hull, using highly responsive subjects as their own controls, in hypnosis and in the wake state. The simulating subjects who are run in exactly the same fashion as deeply hypnotized subjects have the purpose of establishing whether motivated un-hypnotized subjects could figure out the responses that are desired from the totality of cues available to them—including prior information, the experimental procedure, and subtle (perhaps unwitting) cues from the experimenter. Simulators are not intended to be true controls to be compared directly with hypnotized individuals. Rather, they indicate whether an unhypnotized subject could successfully mimic the behavior of the hypnotized individual for an investigator-hypnotist who is blind to their true status. The model demands that unhypnotizable subjects be used as simulators, since it is the only way to assure that these subjects will not enter hypnosis. (Obviously, we confound hypnotizability as a trait with the presence of hypnosis as a state.§)

‡ Independently, Sutcliffe [28] adopted in his own work an independent group design to minimize practice effects. Since his studies resulted in essentially negative findings, concerns about experimenter bias are not [2] relevant criticism of his work. The issue of experimenter bias would become relevant only if he had found differences on the particular parameters he was examining. In such a case, one would be required to run additional studies in order to exclude the alternative hypothesis of experimenter bias that might account for differences.

§ If there are no differences between real and simulating subjects, it becomes impossible to determine whether this is due to the selection of inappropriate dependent variables or whether it is because there are no differences between these groups. In any case, a lack of differences indicates that a particular experimental procedure is inadequate to establish a particular effect. The fact that unhypnotizable subjects are used in the comparison group is irrelevant in the case of null findings. If, however, differences are noted, they cannot be explained as a function of differential treatment

It should be emphasized that simulating subjects must not receive any special training in how to simulate, and they must be aware that the hypnotist does not know their true status and be convinced that he will terminate the experiment if he comes to believe they are faking. The hypnotist, by the same token, must in fact be unaware of the subject's true status. As I have reported, it is not possible for experienced hypnotists to distinguish between these two groups of subjects during a simple induction procedure and without special tests or extensive contact. In practice, the hypnotist is also required to guess the status of the subject, which provides further assurance concerning possible differential treatment of these two groups by the hypnotist.

This design provides the opportunity for a rigorous test about the myriad assertions concerning changes that are unique to hypnosis, concerning abilities that are unique to hypnotized individuals, and concerning what the subject might or might not figure out from the experimental procedure concerning the desires of the hypnotist which are not explicitly suggested to him.¶

An Example from Hypnotic Age Regression

A hypnotic phenomenon of both theoretical and practical importance is hypnotic age regression. In an early study,[31] a highly responsive subject was given appropriate suggestions to regress to age six; accordingly, he began acting like a child, talking like a child, and apparently thinking like a child. After he had completed some drawing in regression, I asked him to put his name at the bottom of the drawing, which he did in typical childlike printing. On a hunch, I then asked him to continue to write, and dictated, "I am conducting an experiment which will assess my psychological capacities." He printed slowly and laboriously but with perfect spelling. It struck me that such an obvious discrepancy may be the cause of much controversy about hypnosis. Not only does it say to those who would argue that age regression is a full return to early childhood that this is not the case, but the cynic would seize upon such data to show that age regression is a fraud. If, however, it were a true fraud, if the subject were merely seeking to put one over on the hypnotist, would he be so stupid as to write such a sentence without spelling errors? This subject's behavior can therefore be taken as evidence that we are not dealing with mere conscious role-playing and that, at the very least, the hypnotized individual's judgment is affected. Though I view this argument as plausible and correct, you may not choose to agree with me. It is precisely to evaluate the likelihood of such an event that the simulator design was developed.

The subtlety of the problem is illustrated in a later study of hypnotic age

---

by the hypnotist-experimenter, but they may be related to differences in hypnotizability as a trait, or to the presence of hypnosis in the experimental group, or to the effect of instructions to stimulate in the comparison group. To distinguish definitively between these possible alternatives, additional experimental data are needed.

¶ As I have pointed out in detail elsewhere, our work should not be taken to suggest that the spontaneous simulation of hypnosis is a common occurrence. It rarely occurs in either clinical or experimental contexts, and as will be seen later, it should not be assumed to explain the hypnotic phenomena that are observed. Further, while I devised the real-simulator model to deal with certain kinds of methodological problems, it is by no means either an appropriate or necessary control in much hypnotic research.[23, 30]

regression. Reiff and Scheerer,[32] in a major monograph, had compared the behavior of individuals age-regressed to ages ten, seven, and four, with role players instructed to role-play ages ten, seven, and four, respectively, using a variety of Piaget-type tasks and other behavioral items. One somewhat different test was devised by the investigators. While subjects were regressed to age four, playing in a sandbox, the experimenter asked whether the subject wanted a lollipop. All subjects responded affirmatively; he then removed the wrapper and handed to the regressed subject, whose hands were covered with mud, a lollipop, while holding it by the stick in such a way as to make it awkward for the subject to reach for the stick. Hypnotized subjects were satisfied to take the eating end of the lollipop into their dirty hands and put it into their mouths. Role players, however, awkwardly reached around to the stick and would not put their hands on the part that was to go into their mouths.

On replication, using simulating subjects where the hypnotist was blind to their true nature, both reals and simulators took the lollipop at its eating end with their dirty fingers. This aspect of the study clearly indicates something about the cues the hypnotist puts into the situation. Lest one make an inappropriate inference, we also examined what four-year-olds did under these circumstances. To our surprise, none of the four-year-olds was willing to take the lollipop by its eating end—all sensibly insisting on taking it by the stick! [33]

Other Issues of Transcendence of Normal Volitional Capacities

It appears that when the hypnotized subject's performance in hypnosis is compared with his performance in the waking state he is able to transcend his normal abilities to a considerable degree, but this observation must be qualified by evaluating what highly motivated waking subjects can be induced to do. For example, it was possible to show that by motivating subjects in the waking state they could be induced to exceed their previous hypnotic performance on an endurance task.[3] Simulating subjects can serve as an independent control group to study this kind of question.[3, 5, 34, 35] To answer transcendence questions, task-motivated groups [20] are equally appropriate controls. Summarizing the work on the transcendence of normal volitional capacities, all of the claims concerning significant changes due to hypnosis can be mimicked by highly motivated individuals in well-controlled studies.

We would, however, be loath to conclude that hypnosis would not result in increased performance on some of the many dependent variables that have not yet been rigorously studied. For example, I find it difficult to believe that simulating subjects would calmly tolerate major surgery without benefit of anesthesia, although we have long since learned to be cautious about even such improbable possibilities. At the present time we can only suggest that any claims for abilities unique to hypnosis require careful validation, using the real-simulator model.

HYPNOTIC PHENOMENA THAT CANNOT BE EXPLAINED AS VOLITIONAL ROLE PLAYING

As has been suggested earlier, the question that ultimately bothers the observer of hypnosis is whether the subject's behavior truly reflects what he experiences. Does the hand that rises really feel light? As he struggles to separate his hands in a hand clasp, does he really feel unable to take them apart? When he seems to have forgotten what has happened, is he really unable to recall?

These questions, of such interest to the naïve observer, also seem to me central to the study of hypnosis, though they are unfortunately hardly considered in many of the neobehaviorist studies of hypnosis, probably because of the admittedly difficult problem of operationalizing subjective experience. Similarly, role theory,[26] as it addresses hypnosis, has provided for the possibility of role playing on a nonconscious level, which would make hypnosis real in the limited sense in which it has been discussed here. By the same token, role theory [21] tends also to speak of playing a role in a conscious sense, sliding from one position to the other with little difficulty and without an apparent need to draw a distinction between them. Conscious role playing, however, would be the same as spontaneously simulating hypnosis. It is hardly surprising, therefore, that an investigator who intentionally uses simulating subjects as a comparison group to clarify the behavior of the hypnotized individual would view the distinction between conscious and nonconscious role playing central to his understanding.‖

Perhaps the best clinical evidence for the subjective reality of hypnotic effects derives from the treatment of chronic pain and the use of hypnosis as an anesthetic. Though environmental contingencies certainly affect the expression of pain, the repeated choice of hypnosis as an analgesic when alternatives are readily available is difficult to explain without assuming that the anesthesia suggestions effectively alter the individual's experience.

Systematic studies, however, are perhaps more relevant in this context. Particularly interesting are those which are counterexpectational; that is, where the simulating subject is unable to predict accurately what the deeply hypnotized individual will do—resulting in a difference between these groups which may be ascribed to hypnosis, to the presence of hypnosis, or to being hypnotizable, but not likely to be a function of simulation as an independent treatment. An example of this kind is the spontaneous occurrence of evidence of trance logic, which does not occur with all subjects but often will be seen in deeply hypnotized individuals.

For instance, when a subject who is able to do so is given the suggestion to hallucinate a person sitting in a chair and is asked to describe what he sees, he may say, "I can see him . . . he is there . . . . But it is strange, I can also see the outline of the chair through him." Although this response occurs spontaneously in only 25–30% of deeply hypnotized individuals who are able to hallucinate a person, I know of no instance where a simulator has *spontaneously* ** reported seeing the chair through the hallucinated person.

‖ There is, of course, no doubt that phenomenologically, especially with subjects in the midrange of hypnotizability, one frequently encounters mixtures of conscious and nonconscious role playing. While there is a continuum in the relative amounts of volitional compliance and experiential changes that occur in individuals, it is nonetheless important to determine whether we are dealing with two distinct, qualitatively different processes.

** Obviously, if simulating subjects are asked a direct question such as "Do you, or do you not, see the back of the chair through Joe?" (in a context where "Joe" was the hallucinated person), many will catch on to what is wanted and reply affirmatively,

The mixing of hallucination and percept seems to occur spontaneously only with those subjects who are deeply hypnotized. This finding has been corroborated in two independent experiments that have explored it.[37, 38]

A related kind of phenomenon is source amnesia, studied by Evans [39] and Evans and Thorn.[40] Here a subject in deep hypnosis is asked a number of questions, including some such as "An amethyst is a blue or purple gemstone; what color does it turn when it's heated?" Almost no one is familiar with the answer, and when the subject in deep hypnosis says he doesn't know, the experimenter casually answers yellow, and then goes on to the next item. He then induces amnesia and awakens the subject. When asked what transpired, the subject insists that he cannot remember. The subject is then given a simple test of information which includes the amethyst item; when asked what color it turns when it's heated, he responds "yellow" in an almost automatic fashion. If then asked how he knows this, he may offer some plausible possibility such as learning the information in a geology class. In short, the subject (who is no longer in hypnosis) displays no knowledge of the true *source* of his information. Hence the term "Source Amnesia."

Such a response might possibly be taken as evidence that amnesia is not real, since the subject clearly has the information that he had presumably forgotten. However, the conclusion should be precisely the opposite. No one shamming amnesia would be so naïve as to admit knowledge that he acquired during a time for which he is supposed to have had amnesia. In this instance, however, you need not accept my opinion. We have data! In a study [41] using reals and simulators, approximately a third of the deeply hypnotized subjects showed source amnesia, while not a single simulator ever admitted having known the answers to questions he had learned during hypnosis. On reflection it becomes clear that one needs to have amnesia in order not to recall the source of what has just been learned.

In another study, where we investigated what happened if the hypnotist disappeared, we found that when the study was carefully carried out, simulating subjects typically stopped simulating when they were left alone.[42] They had lost the audience for the role they were required to play. Deeply hypnotized individuals continued in trance for some minutes, only gradually arousing themselves over time—suggesting a state, or, in Sarbin's metaphor, the synonym, a high level of organismic role enactment.[43]

In another study, we tested the effect of a posthypnotic suggestion that the subject run his hand over his hair whenever he heard the word EXPERI-MENT; this test took place outside of the experimental context in a situation where the hypnotist would neither know nor care about the subject's response. Under these circumstances, simulating subjects did not respond, but those who had been deeply hypnotized were as likely to respond in the absence of the hypnotist as in his presence. Simulators, moreover, actually responded more frequently in the hypnotist's presence than deeply hypnotized subjects, who occasionally failed to hear the posthypnotic cue when it was well embedded in a sentence, something that very rarely occurred with simulators.[44]

Building upon his observation that deeply hypnotized subjects ceased to respond to the word EXPERIMENT when they were given the instruction, "When I count to three, you will no longer run your hand over your hair

---

thereby eliminating any possible differences between hypnotized and simulating subjects (see Johnson *et al*.[36]).

every time you hear the word EXPERIMENT"—even though the hypnotist had yet to count to three—Sheehan [45] carried out a series of studies that manipulated preexperimental expectancies. When subjects were given the expectation that a hypnotically induced automatic response persisted until a specific cue was given lifting the suggestion, simulators tended to behave in accordance with these expectations. Deeply hypnotized individuals, however, still tended to discontinue their automatic behavior once it was clear to them that a suggestion was about to be terminated. These observations would seem to support the view that the deeply hypnotized individual is highly attuned to the hypnotist's explicit and implicit wishes, which come to determine his experience, whereas the simulator is more influenced by prior knowledge and expectations.

Perhaps the most exciting finding is the recent work of Evans and Kihlstrom [46] and Kihlstrom and Evans,[47] which investigates the effect of suggesting posthypnotic amnesia on the order of recall. These studies do not involve simulators; rather, they study an unsuggested consequence of suggested hypnotic amnesia where an unobtrusive measure in the sense of Webb *et al.*[48] was used. It was shown that in response to amnesia suggestions, those individuals who were hypnotized but nonetheless had some recall remembered those items they did recall in a random order. On the other hand, less hypnotizable individuals who remembered the same number of items were likely to recall them in the order in which they had occurred. This novel observation appears to reflect a robust phenomenon that is not destroyed either by exhorting subjects to remember, providing them with honesty instructions, or even asking them to put the material in a correct temporal sequence.[49] The disorganization of recall is thus an unsuggested consequence of a suggestion to have amnesia. It is, however, not seen, regardless of the level of the hypnotic response, unless amnesia is specifically suggested. Particularly interesting is the recent study by Spanos and Bodorik,[50] which replicates the finding of disorganized recall in hypnotized subjects but fails to find this effect in individuals given task-motivated instructions.

CONCLUSIONS

As I have tried to point out, controversies about the very existence of hypnosis have persisted since the phenomenon was first described. Over the past 25 years, however, we have witnessed an unprecedented amount of research on hypnosis that has been accompanied by a distinct shift in the way hypnosis is perceived. Prior to that time, there had been a developing consensus that hypnosis was effective in bringing about certain types of therapeutic changes [51] and was a powerful technique in controlling human behavior,[52] that it made possible unusual feats of strength,[19] unusual feats of memory,[53] and unusual types of control over an individual's biological processes.[54] Though acknowledged to be a powerful phenomenon, it was rarely integrated into general textbooks of psychology and received scant systematic attention even in psychiatry. Little systematic effort was made to understand hypnotic phenomena within the broader framework of psychobiological principles.

Ensuing work led to the development of novel and more appropriate methodological approaches that challenged some of the widely believed and apparently well-established evidence [19] that hypnosis led to the transcendence of normal volitional capacities. As this evidence became widely disseminated, it was inappropriately used for the argument that hypnosis was not real. In such a context my demonstration that even highly trained clinicians were unable to identify hypnotized individuals from simulators in a single session contributed to the overall confusion.

It took a surprising amount of work to document what I had been careful to explain in the first publication on the use of simulators in research [3]—that despite the superficial similarity of the hypnotized individual's behavior, the underlying mechanisms are by no means identical. Thus, we have now shown with careful, detailed studies systematic differences that are likely to be a function of the hypnotizable individual's being hypnotized rather than due to the absence of simulation. Some of these differences help clarify the nature of the hypnotic phenomenon. Perhaps equally important, they help to document that the hypnotized individual's behavior cannot be explained as a conscious effort to please the hypnotist or as some form of conscious role playing. Whether the hypnotized individual is characterized as responding to a world created by the hypnotist's words while disregarding much of the circumstances of the real world, or whether the hypnotized subject is characterized as deluded,[28] or as a form of role enactment,[26] or responding to a believed-in imagining,[21] does not matter. Regardless of how we describe hypnosis, it is real in the sense that the subject believes in his experience and is not merely acting as if he did. To say that an individual who has been regressed to age four believes that he is four does not, however, mean that he therefore knows only what he knew when he was four and is really like a child. To some degree we may indeed see an increase in accurate recall of events that once transpired; to some extent hypnosis will also facilitate the creation of pseudomemories. Indeed, perhaps the most striking characteristic we have noted about hypnotized individuals—in contrast to simulators—is their remarkable willingness to mix the experiences in the world suggested by the hypnotist with the percepts of the real world, often in a remarkably uncritical fashion.

Having obtained evidence for the subjective reality of the hypnotic phenomenon and at the same time evidence that hypnosis does not result in physiologically real color blindness, uniocular blindness, uniaural deafness, or what you will, we remain confronted with the puzzle of the ultimate significance of the fact that some individuals can for a time alter their perception or memories. Is it merely a curious quirk of the mind that can be seen under some circumstances or does it reflect important processes that can have profound consequences, both therapeutically and for an understanding of human mental functions? Although I am firmly convinced the latter is true, much work needs to be done to characterize the difference between the effect of just having a fantasy as opposed to the effect of having a fantasy and for a time accepting it as real.

Having documented substantial differences between simulating and real subjects, it is also necessary to recognize, as Bowers [55] has aptly emphasized, that the simulating model is not suited to explore the effects of suggestions which are widely recognized and known within the subject population. For example, the tendency of the hypnotized individual to become relaxed and initially to speak in a low, somewhat colorless voice is sufficiently well known to be inevitably mimicked by all simulators. This should not be taken to mean, however, that these characteristics are therefore not typical of hypnotized individuals. The important systematic studies of pain and its suppression by hypnosis carried out by Hilgard and Hilgard [56] present lawful information about pain, even though simulating subjects can mimic most of these changes. Fortunately, experimental subjects are, on the whole, honest, and it is neither feasible nor necessary to set up byzantine procedures in each instance to test the validity of subjective reports. Obviously such reports have problems, many of which are closely analogous to those of psychophysics. While psychophysics has had to concern itself with questions of response set and other kinds of bias, it has appropriately not worried about purposive simulation.

Although studies using simulators and other related forms of comparison groups will continue to be needed to test some particular questions or striking claims not otherwise easily resolved, it is my hope that the need for such elaborate procedures will diminish as we rethink our search for psychological or physiological correlates that are unique to hypnosis. It seems likely that it will be more productive to focus on identifying basic cognitive, social psychological, and neurophysiological mechanisms that link hypnosis with other psychobiological processes.

An example of this kind follows from the work of Shor,[57, 58] Ås,[59] and Tellegen and Atkinson,[60] which has shown that an individual's tendency to have naturally occurring trancelike experiences or the ability for absorption—which appears to be an underlying mechanism for the occurrence of such events—relates to the ability to enter hypnosis. This process involves an individual's increased ability to become absorbed either in his own thoughts or by some particular feature of the external environment in a manner that causes him to exclude other external stimuli which would normally capture his attention. The ability to focus attention has long been acknowledged as important to the ability to enter hypnosis. However, one would hardly expect the ability to focus attention to be a unique attribute of hypnotizable individuals. Nonetheless, the psychobiological processes reflecting such deployment of attention have been the subject of considerable study in other contexts and may well provide some important empirical links between hypnosis and other related phenomena. For these reasons, we are currently examining such basic mechanisms as habituation, the orienting response, and measures of cognitive effort as means for empirically assessing the deployment of attention.

Our hope is to establish links between hypnosis and other phenomena rather than searching for any unique psychobiological correlate of hypnosis. In such an effort we have little concern about whether a particular process can be mimicked and even less about whether the process is unique to hypnosis. Instead, we are seeking to identify a variety of mechanisms that may be associated with hypnosis that may begin to provide an understanding of how hypnosis relates to other circumstances that involve the focusing of attention and the ability to choose for a time to ignore significant aspects of the real world. It is our hope that as such an understanding evolves we will ultimately be able to understand how in hypnosis it is possible to gain control over the subject's information input, how the mechanism of recall can be affected, and the consequences of such events for the individual's total psychobiological functioning.

ACKNOWLEDGMENTS

The author would like to thank Frederick J. Evans, A. Gordon Hammer, Emily Carota Orne, William M. Waid, and Stuart K. Wilson for their substantive comments during the preparation of this paper. Especial appreciation is due to Mae C. Weglarski for her editorial assistance.

REFERENCES

1. HILGARD, E. R. 1965. Hypnotic Susceptibility. Harcourt, Brace & World. New York, N.Y.
2. ORNE, M. T. 1966. Hypnosis, motivation and compliance. Amer. J. Psychiat. **122:** 721–726.
3. ORNE, M. T. 1959. The nature of hypnosis: Artifact and essence. J. Abnorm. Soc. Psychol. **58:** 277–299.
4. LONDON, P. & M. FUHRER. 1961. Hypnosis, motivation and performance. J. Pers. **29:** 321–333.
5. SHOR, R. E. 1964. A note on the shock tolerance of real and simulating hypnotic subjects. Int. J. Clin. Exp. Hypnosis **12:** 258–262.
6. EVANS, F. J., E. CAROTA-ORNE & P. A. MARKOWSKY. 1977. Punctuality and hypnotizability. Paper presented at East. Psychol. Ass. Boston, Mass. April.
7. SUTCLIFFE, J. P. 1961. "Credulous" and "skeptical" views of hypnotic phenomena: Experiments on esthesia, hallucination, and delusion. J. Abnorm. Soc. Psychol. **62:** 189–200.
8. MESMER, F. A. 1948. Mesmerism by Dr. Mesmer: Dissertation on the Discovery of Animal Magnetism. 1779. Translated by V. R. Myers. Published with Gilbert Frankau. Macdonald. London, England.
9. BRAID, J. 1960. Braid on Hypnotism: Neurypnology. A. E. Waite, Ed. George Redway. London, 1889. Reprinted: Julian Press, Inc. New York, N.Y.
10. CHARCOT, J. M. 1882. Sur les Divers États Nerveux Déterminés par l'Hypnotisation chez les Hystériques. Comptes rendus hebdomadaires des seances de l'Académie des Sciences [D] **94:** (Paris) 403–405.
11. ERICKSON, M. 1939. The induction of color blindness by a technique of hypnotic suggestion. J. Gen. Psychol. **70:** 61–89.
12. SPIEGEL, H. 1972. The eye-roll test for hypnotizability. Amer. J. Clin. Hypnosis. **15:** 25–28.
13. HALL, C. R. 1845. Mesmerism: Its Rise, Progress, and Mysteries. Burgess, Stringer & Co. New York, N.Y.
14. HART, E. 1898. Hypnotism, Mesmerism, and the New Witchraft. D. Appleton & Co. New York, N.Y.
15. YOUNG, P. C. 1927. Is rapport an essential characteristic of hypnosis? J. Abnorm. Soc. Psychol. **22:** 130–139.
16. YOUNG, P. C. 1940. Hypnotic regression—fact or artifact? J. Abnorm. Soc. Psychol. **35:** 273–278.
17. PATTIE, F. A., JR. 1935. A report of attempts to produce uniocular blindness by hypnotic suggestion. Brit. J. Med. Psychol. **15:** 230–241.
18. PATTIE, F. A., JR. 1941. The production of blisters by hypnotic suggestion: A review. J. Abnorm. Soc. Psychol. **36:** 62–72.
19. HULL, C. L. 1933. Hypnosis and Suggestibility: An Experimental Approach. Appleton-Century-Crofts. New York, N.Y.
20. BARBER, T. X. 1969. Hypnosis: A Scientific Approach. Van Nostrand-Reinhold. New York, N.Y.
21. SARBIN, T. R. & W. C. COE. 1972. Hypnosis: A Social Psychological Analysis of Influence Communication. Holt, Rinehart & Winston. New York, N.Y.

32   Annals New York Academy of Sciences

22. WEITZENHOFFER, A. M. & E. R. HILGARD. 1959. Stanford Hypnotic Susceptibility Scale, Forms A and B. Consulting Psychologists Press. Palo Alto, Calif.
23. WEITZENHOFFER, A. M. & E. R. HILGARD. 1962. Stanford Hypnotic Susceptibility Scale, Form C. Consulting Psychologists Press. Palo Alto, Calif.
24. ORNE, M. T. & D. N. O'CONNELL. 1967. Diagnostic ratings of hypnotizability. Int. J. Clin. Exp. Hypnosis 15: 125–133.
25. ORNE, M. T. 1970. Hypnosis, motivation and the ecological validity of the psychological experiment. In Nebraska Symposium on Motivation. W. J. Arnold & M. M. Page, Eds. : 187–265. Univ. Nebraska Press. Lincoln, Neb.
26. SARBIN, T. R. 1950. Contributions to role-taking theory: I. Hypnotic behavior. Psychol. Rev. 57: 255–270.
27. ORNE, M. T. 1973. Communication by the total experimental situation: Why it is important, how it is evaluated, and its significance for the ecological validity of findings. In Communication and Affect. P. Pliner, L. Krames & T. Alloway, Eds. : 157–191. Academic Press. New York, N.Y.
28. SUTCLIFFE, J .P. 1958. Hypnotic behavior: Fantasy or simulation. Unpublished Ph.D. Thesis. University of Sydney. Sydney, Australia.
29. ORNE, M. T. 1971. The simulation of hypnosis: Why, how, and what it means. Int. J. Clin. Exp. Hypnosis 19: 183–210.
30. ORNE, M. T. 1972. On the simulating subject as a quasi-control group in hypnosis research: What, why, and how. In Hypnosis: Research Developments and Perspectives. Erika Fromm & R. E. Shor, Eds. : 399–443. Aldine-Atherton. Chicago, Ill.
31. ORNE, M. T. 1951. The mechanisms of hypnotic age regression: An experimental study. J. Abnorm. Soc. Psychol. 46: 213–225.
32. REIFF, R. & M. SCHEERER. 1959. Memory and Hypnotic Age Regression: Developmental Aspects of Cognitive Function Explored through Hypnosis. International Universities Press. New York, N.Y.
33. O'CONNELL, D. N., R. E. SHOR & M. T. ORNE. 1970. Hypnotic age regression: An empirical and methodological analysis. J. Abnorm. Psychol. 76 (Monogr. Suppl. 3): 1–32.
34. DAMASER, E. C., R. E. SHOR & M. T. ORNE. 1963. Physiological effects during hypnotically requested emotions. Psychosom. Med. 25: 334–343.
35. ORNE, M. T. & F. J. EVANS. 1965. Social control in the psychological experiment: Antisocial behavior and hypnosis. J. Pers. Soc. Psychol. 1: 189–200.
36. JOHNSON, R. F. Q., B. A. MAHER & T. X. BARBER. 1972. Artifact in the "essence of hypnosis": An evaluation of trance logic. J. Abnorm. Psychol. 79: 212–220.
37. McDONALD, R. D. & J. R. SMITH. 1975. Trance logic in tranceable and simulating subjects. Int. J. Clin. Exp. Hypnosis 23: 80–89.
38. PETERS, J. E. 1973. Trance logic: Artifact or essence of hypnosis? Unpublished Doctoral Dissertation. Penn. State Univ. College Park, Pa.
39. EVANS, F. J. 1965. The structure of hypnosis: A factor analytic investigation. Unpubilshed Doctoral Thesis. University of Sydney. Sydney, Australia.
40. EVANS, F. J. & W. A. F. THORN. 1966. Two types of posthypnotic amnesia: Recall amnesia and source amnesia. Int. J. Clin. Exp. Hypnosis 14: 162–179.
41. EVANS, F. J. 1971. Contextual forgetting: A study of source amnesia. Paper presented at East. Psychol. Ass. New York, N.Y. April.
42. EVANS, F. J. & M. T. ORNE. 1971. The disappearing hypnotist: The use of simulating subjects to evaluate how subjects perceive experimental procedures. Int. J. Clin. Exp. Hypnosis 19: 277–296.
43. SARBIN, T. R. 1956. Physiological effects of hypnotic stimulation. In Hypnosis and its Therapeutic Application. R. M. Dorcus. 4/1–4/57. McGraw-Hill. New York, N.Y.
44. ORNE, M. T., P. W. SHEEHAN & F. J. EVANS. 1968. Occurrence of posthypnotic behavior outside the experimental setting. J. Pers. Soc. Psychol. 9: 189–196.

45. SHEEHAN, P. W. 1971. Countering preconceptions about hypnosis: An objective index of involvement with the hypnotist. J. Abnorm. Psychol. **78:** 299–322.
46. EVANS, F. J. & J. F. KIHLSTROM. 1973. Posthypnotic amnesia as disrupted retrieval. J. Abnorm. Psychol. **82:** 317–323.
47. KIHLSTROM, J. F. & F. J. EVANS. 1976. Recovery of memory after posthypnotic amnesia. J. Abnorm. Psychol. **85:** 564–569.
48. WEBB, E. J., D. T. CAMPBELL, R. D. SCHWARTZ & L. SECHREST. 1966. Unobtrusive Measures: Nonreactive Research in the Social Sciences. Rand McNally. Chicago, Ill.
49. KIHLSTROM, J. F. 1975. The effects of organization and motivation on recall during posthypnotic amnesia. Doctoral Dissertation, Univ. Penn. Dissertation Abstracts International **36:** 2473B–2474B. Univer. Microfilms no. 75–24082.
50. SPANOS, N. P. & H. L. BODORIK. Suggested amnesia and disorganized recall in hypnotic and task-motivated subjects. J. Abnorm. Psychol. In press.
51. WOLBERG, L. R. 1948. Medical Hypnosis. Grune & Stratton. New York, N.Y.
52. ESTABROOKS, G. H., Ed. 1943. Hypnotism. Dutton. New York, N.Y.
53. ERICKSON, M. H. 1943. A controlled experimental use of hypnotic regression in the therapy of an acquired food tolerance. Psychosom. Med. **5:** 67–70.
54. DUNBAR, H. G. 1943. Psychosomatic Diagnosis. Paul B. Hoeber. New York, N.Y.
55. BOWERS, K. S. 1976. Hypnosis for the Seriously Curious. Brooks/Cole. Monterey, Calif.
56. HILGARD, E. R. & J. R. HILGARD. 1975. Hypnosis in the Relief of Pain. William Kaufmann, Inc. Los Altos, Calif.
57. SHOR, R. E. 1960. The frequency of naturally occurring 'hypnotic-like' experiences in the normal college population. Int. J. Clin. Exp. Hypnosis **8:** 151–163.
58. SHOR, R. E., M. T. ORNE & D. N. O'CONNELL. 1962. Validation and cross-validation of a scale of self-reported personal experiences which predicts hypnotizability. J. Psychol. **53:** 55–75.
59. Ås, A. 1963. Hypnotizability as a function of non-hypnotic experiences. J. Abnorm. Soc. Psychol. **66:** 142–150.
60. TELLEGEN, A. & G. ATKINSON. 1974. Openness to absorbing and self-altering experiences ("absorption"), a trait related to hypnotic susceptibility. J. Abnorm. Psychol. **83:** 268–277.

HYPNOSIS, SUGGESTIONS, AND ALTERED STATES OF CONSCIOUSNESS: EXPERIMENTAL EVALUATION OF THE NEW COGNITIVE-BEHAVIORAL THEORY AND THE TRADITIONAL TRANCE-STATE THEORY OF "HYPNOSIS" *

Theodore X. Barber

Research Department, Medfield State Hospital
Medfield, Massachusetts 02052

Sheryl C. Wilson

Medfield Foundation
Medfield, Massachusetts 02052

The new Cognitive-Behavioral Theory of "hypnosis" [1-3] postulates that regardless of whether or not a trance-induction procedure is administered, subjects are responsive to test-suggestions for limb heaviness, anesthesia, time distortion, age regression, and so on, to the extent that they think along with and imagine the themes that are suggested. The theory also postulates that subjects do not think along with and imagine with the suggested themes when they have passive attitudes, negative attitudes, or cynical attitudes toward the test situation. Following these postulates of the Cognitive-Behavioral Theory, one could predict that a very proficient method for producing a high level of responsiveness to test-suggestions in unselected subjects would include instructions designed both to remove passive or negativistic attitudes and also to demonstrate to the subjects how to think and imagine with the themes of the suggestions (Think-With Instructions).

The traditional Trance-State Theory postulates that (1) responsiveness to test-suggestions is a function of a "hypnotic trance" state, and (2) a trance-induction procedure is the most effective method we have available for producing a hypnotic trance in the largest number of subjects.

The experiment presented below pitted the new Cognitive-Behavioral Theory [1-3] against the traditional Trance State Theory. Subjects who were randomly assigned to one of three experimental treatments were tested on response to ten standardized test-suggestions after they had been exposed to either a trance-induction, Think-With Instructions, or a control treatment. The Cognitive-Behavioral Theory would be supported if subjects exposed to Think-With Instructions are more responsive to test-suggestions than those exposed to the trance-induction or control treatment. On the other hand, the traditional Trance-State Theory would be supported if subjects exposed to a traditional trance-induction are more responsive to test-suggestions than those exposed to Think-With Instructions or the control treatment.

To measure responses to test-suggestions in this experiment we used a recently constructed instrument that has been named the Creative Imagination Scale.[4, 5] This standardized scale, which takes 18 minutes to administer,

* This research was supported by grant MH28432 from the National Institute of Mental Health, U.S. Public Health Service.

measures responses to the following ten test-suggestions: arm heaviness, hand levitation, finger anesthesia, water "hallucination," olfactory-gustatory "hallucination," music "hallucination," temperature "hallucination," time distortion, age regression, and mind-body relaxation. The Creative Imagination Scale can be administered either to an individual or to a group, and either with or without a prior trance-induction procedure. The test-suggestions are worded nonauthoritatively and phrased to guide subjects in imagining those things which are described. The scale has been shown to possess split-half reliability, test-retest reliability, and factorial validity.[4, 5]

The Creative Imagination Scale was chosen as the measuring instrument for this experiment because most previous scales designed to measure responses to suggestions, such as the Stanford Hypnotic Susceptibility Scales and the Harvard Group Scale, were constructed to be administered after a trance-induction procedure and are thus inappropriate for control subjects.* A second reason why we used the Creative Imagination Scale instead of one of the Stanford Hypnotic Susceptibility Scales or our own Barber Suggestibility Scale is that all of these earlier scales include test-suggestions that (1) are within the subjects' range of expectations when the experimental situation has been defined to them as "hypnosis" but (2) are unexpected, discordant, and incongruous for control or "non-hypnotic" subjects. For instance, the earlier scales include such dictatorial commands or "suggestions" as the following: ". . . your throat and jaw are solid and rigid. . . . They're so solid and so rigid, that you can't speak . . . you can't say your name. . . . You can't talk! Try; you can't . . . try harder; you can't."[7] (p. 245) These kinds of dictatorial commands are unexpected, incongruous, and discordant when the situation is *not* defined as "hypnosis," that is, when subjects are in a Control group or in a group that is shown how to think-with the suggestions. Although these kinds of authoritarian commands do not violate the implicit contract between the hypnotist and the subject in a "hypnosis" situation, they clearly violate the informal contract between the experimenter and the "non-hypnotic" subject, because the contract states that the subject is participating in an experiment in which he is expected to use his own imagination abilities.

METHOD

Subjects

Sixty-six student nurses (65 females and 1 male) who were taking a course in psychiatric nursing at Medfield State Hospital were asked by the first author to participate in an experiment on imagining in which they would be tested in small groups on the Creative Imagination Scale. They

---

* An experimenter could possibly administer these scales without also administering the trance-induction procedure which was designed to precede them. In this case, however, the test-suggestions would have incongruous aspects because they were originally worded to be given after a trance induction. For example, the following statements from one of the test-suggestions (Verbal Inhibition) of the Stanford Hypnotic Susceptibility Scale (Form A) are worded to apply to subjects who have been exposed to relaxation suggestions as part of a trance induction and are incongruous for control subjects: "You are very relaxed now . . . deeply relaxed . . . think how hard it might be to talk while so deeply relaxed . . . perhaps as hard to talk as when asleep."[6]

were also told that they would each receive two dollars at the end of the 45-minute experimental session. All 66 student-nurses who were asked to participate in the experiment agreed to do so. None had participated in our previous experiments.

Procedure

The 66 subjects were randomly assigned to one of three experimental treatments—Think-With Instructions, Control, and Trance Induction—with 22 subjects to each treatment. Under each of the three treatments, one experimenter (S.C.W.) tested the subjects in small groups of four to seven subjects.

Immediately following each treatment, the Creative Imagination Scale was administered to the subjects by a tape recording of the experimenter's voice.†

The experimental treatments were as follows:

Think-With Instructions. The 22 subjects assigned to this treatment were given Think-With Instructions designed to demonstrate how to think along with the imaginatively focus on the suggested themes. These Think-With Instructions, which extended over a period of seven minutes, are presented verbatim in the APPENDIX to this paper. They can be briefly summarized as follows.

1. The subjects were first told: "I'm going to give you a series of tests in which I'll ask you to focus your thinking and to use your imagination creatively. . . ."

2. The experimenter then said: "Let me give you an example of the kind of tests I might give you. I might, for example, ask you . . . to feel as if you're looking at a T.V. program." The experimenter then described and modeled the following three ways in which the subjects could respond to this test: (1) They could say negative things to themselves, such as "This is ridiculous, there is no T.V. there," and nothing at all would happen; (2) they could passively wait for a T.V. screen to appear and, again, nothing at all would happen; and (3) they could let their thinking and imagination move with the suggestion by recalling a T.V. program they liked and letting themselves "see" it again in their mind's eye.

3. The experimenter next gave the subjects a second example of the kind of tests they might be given: they might be asked to hold a pendulum with the tips of two fingers and to think of the pendulum moving back and forth. The experimenter then held such a pendulum and demonstrated how the pendulum clearly moves in an interesting way when one thinks and imagines that it is moving. The experimenter then demonstrated that it does not move when one says negative things to oneself, e.g., "It can't move," or when one waits passively for it to move.

4. Finally, the experimenter told the subjects, "Although you could respond in any of the ways I've described, I'd like you to respond in the way in which you'll benefit most from the tests, and that is to focus your thinking and to imagine to the best of your ability. Just let your thinking and your creative

---

† Experimental studies [8,9] have demonstrated that similar responses to test-suggestions are obtained when the test-suggestions are presented either in spoken form by the experimenter or by a tape-recording of the experimenter's voice.

imagination go along with the instructions so you can fully experience the many interesting and useful things your mind can do."

Immediately following the Think-With Instructions, the Creative Imagination Scale was administered by a tape recording of the experimenter's voice.

Control. The 22 subjects assigned to the control treatment were tested on the Creative Imagination Scale after they were told, "In this study you will be given a series of tests in which you will be asked to focus your thoughts and to imagine certain events. When asked to do so, please focus your thoughts and imagine to the best of your ability."

Immediately following the control treatment, the ten test-suggestions of the Creative Imagination Scale were administered by a tape recording of the experimenter's voice and the subjects' responses were assessed.

Trance Induction. Upon entering the experimental room, subjects assigned to the trance-induction treatment were told by the experimenter that, if they agreed, they would be hypnotized in the experiment and then tested on the Creative Imagination Scale. All 22 of the subjects assigned to this treatment agreed to be hypnotized and to continue in the experiment. A standardized 11-minute trance-induction procedure was then administered by a tape recording of the experimenter's voice.‡ The characteristic features of this trance-induction procedure included: (1) motivational instructions (e.g., ". . . if you pay close attention to what I say and follow what I tell you, you can easily learn to fall into a hypnotic sleep. . . . Your cooperation, your interest is what I ask for" . . .); (2) suggestions of eye-fixation, eye-heaviness, and eye-closure; (3) repeated suggestions of muscular relaxation, regular, deep breathing, drowsiness, and sleep; and (4) suggestions of being in a unique state (a trance state) of deep hypnosis in which it is possible to have interesting and unusual experiences.

In the same way as the subjects assigned to the other two treatments, the trance-induction subjects were then assessed on the ten test-suggestions of the Creative Imagination Scale which are described next.

Creative Imagination Scale

A verbatim account of the ten test-suggestions that comprise the Creative Imagination Scale is presented elsewhere.[4, 5] The ten test-suggestions, in the order they were presented, can be briefly summarized as follows:

1. *Arm Heaviness.* Starting with the subject's left arm extended and horizontal, with the palm facing up, suggestions were given to guide her in imaginging that three heavy dictionaries were being placed in her outstretched hand, causing her arm to feel heavy.

2. *Hand Levitation.* Starting with the subject's right arm extended and horizontal, with the palm facing down, suggestions were given to guide her in imagining that a strong stream of water from a garden hose was pushing against the palm of her hand, pushing her hand up.

3. *Finger Anesthesia.* Starting with the subject's left hand in her lap, with

‡ The trance-induction procedure, which is a group adaptation of the procedure used in earlier experiments by Barber,[7] (pp. 251–259) is presented verbatim by Wilson.[4]

the palm facing up, suggestions were given to guide her in imagining that Novocain had been injected into the side of her hand next to the little finger, causing two fingers to feel numb.

4. *Water "Hallucination."* Suggestions were given to guide the subject in imagining that she was drinking a cup of cool mountain water.

5. *Olfactory-Gustatory "Hallucination."* Suggestions were given to guide the subject in imagining smelling and tasting an orange.

6. *Music "Hallucination."* Suggestions were given to guide the subject in thinking back to a time when she heard some wonderful music and to re-experience "hearing" it.

7. *Temperature "Hallucination."* Starting with the subject's hands resting in her lap, with the palms facing down, suggestions were given to guide her in imagining that the sun was shining on the top of her right hand, causing it to feel hot.

8. *Time Distortion.* Suggestions were given to guide the subject in imagining that time was slowing down.

9. *Age Regression.* Suggestions were given to guide the subject in recreating the feelings that she experienced when she was a child in elementary school.

10. *Mind-Body Relaxation.* Suggestions were given to guide the subject in imagining that she was lying under the sun on a beach and becoming very relaxed.

Immediately following the administration of the Creative Imagination Scale, the subject was given a written questionnaire—the Self-Scoring Form of the Creative Imagination Scale—to score her own subjective experiences.§ On the Self-Scoring Form, which is presented verbatim elsewhere,[4, 5] each subject was asked to score her experience of each of the ten test-suggestions on a scale ranging from "Not at all the same" as the real thing (score of 0) to "Almost exactly the same" as the real thing (score of 4). For example, the scoring of Item 2, Hand Levitation, read as follows:

> In the second test you were asked to think of a strong stream of water from a garden hose pushing up against the palm of your hand. Compared to what you would have experienced if a strong stream of water were actually pushing up against your palm, what you experienced was:

0	1	2	3	4
0%	25%	50%	75%	90+%
Not at all the same	A little the same	Between a little and much the same	Much the same	Almost exactly the same

Since the score on each of the ten test-suggestions can range from 0 to 4, scores on the Creative Imagination Scale can range from 0 to 40.

§ There are at least two reasons why subjective scores (subjects' self-scoring of their own experiences), as used in the present experiment, are no more and also no less reliable than objective scores (observers' ratings of the subjects' observable responses): (1) previous studies[7] indicate that subjective and objective scores on suggestibility scales are highly correlated, and these correlations are as high as test-retest correlations of either subjective scores or objective scores on the same scale; and (2) if subjects exaggerate or inflate their subjective responses they can just as easily exaggerate their objective responses; e.g., when given suggestions of arm heaviness, they can just as easily lower the arm slowly (objective response) as they can say that the arm feels heavy (subjective response).

RESULTS

Total Scores on the Creative Imagination Scale

A one-way analysis of variance showed that there was a significant difference among the three treatments in scores on the Creative Imagination Scale ($F = 6.5$, df $= 2/63$, p $< .005$).¶ To localize the significant-treatment effect, a Duncan Multiple Range test was performed upon the three treatment means. The Duncan test showed that the mean score on the Creative Imagination Scale of subjects receiving the Think-With Instructions (26.3) was significantly higher ($p < .05$) than the mean score of subjects receiving the traditional trance induction (20.8) and those receiving the control treatment (22.1). Also, the Duncan test showed that the mean score under the trance-induction treatment did not differ significantly from the mean score under the control treatment. In brief, the Think-With Instructions were effective in raising responsiveness to test-suggestions above the base level (control treatment) and also above the level obtained with a traditional trance induction.‖

Let us look more closely at the degree of enhancement produced by the Think-With Instructions. The mean score on the Creative Imagination Scale under all three experimental treatments—that is, for all 66 subjects—was 23. As TABLE 1 shows, scores of 23 or higher (at or above the overall average) were obtained by 100% of the subjects given the Think-With Instructions, 45% of those exposed to the trance induction, and 55% of those assigned to the control treatment. In other words, *all* of the subjects receiving the Think-With Instructions obtained relatively high scores on the Creative Imagination Scale, whereas under the other two treatments, some subjects scored relatively high, some medium, and some low.**

¶ A test for homogeneity of variance showed that the standard deviation under the Think-With Instructions treatment (2.5) was significantly smaller than the standard deviations under the Trance Induction and Control treatments (6.5 and 6.0, respectively). Although there is evidence to indicate that the F test from the analysis of variance is robust under such heterogeneity of variance,[10, 11] some statisticians have argued that nonparametric tests are more appropriate when there are significant differences among the variances of the experimental groups. Consequently, we also performed a Kruskal-Wallis nonparametric test on the scores on the Creative Imagination Scale under the three treatments. The results of the Kruskal-Wallis test were consistent with the results of the F test; the scores on the scale differed significantly among the treatments (p < 0.01).

‖ Analyses of variance and Duncan Multiple Range tests were also performed separately on each of the 10 test-suggestions that comprise the Creative Imagination Scale. These analyses showed that (1) subjects under the three treatments did not obtain significantly different scores on the first three test-suggestions, but (2) on the remaining seven test-suggestions, subjects given Think-With Instructions generally obtained higher scores than subjects tested under the trance-induction or control treatments.

** These results are also reflected in the fact (noted previously) that the standard deviation under the Think-With Instructions treatment was relatively small (all scores were bunched up rather close together above the overall mean), whereas the standard deviations under both the trance induction and the control treatment were relatively large (scores under these treatments were spread out below and above the overall mean).

TABLE 1

NUMBER OF SUBJECTS OBTAINING SCORES OF 0–40 ON THE CREATIVE
IMAGINATION SCALE UNDER THINK-WITH INSTRUCTIONS, CONTROL,
AND TRANCE-INDUCTION TREATMENTS

Score	Think-With Instructions		Control		Trance-Induction	
33–40	0		0		0	
32	1		0		0	
31	1		1		1	
30	1		0		0	
29	1		1		0	
28	2	100%	3	55%	2	45%
27	2		0		1	
26	3		3		2	
25	7		2		1	
24	2		1		1	
23	2		1		2	
22	0		0		2	
21	0		2		3	
20	0		1		0	
19	0		1		0	
18	0		2		1	
17	0		1		0	
16	0		0		1	
15	0		1		1	
14	0	0%	0	45%	0	55%
13	0		0		1	
12	0		1		1	
11	0		0		0	
10	0		0		0	
9	0		0		0	
8	0		0		1	
7	0		1		1	
0–6	0		0		0	

DISCUSSION

In this experiment a prediction deduced from the new Cognitive-Behavioral Theory was pitted against one deduced from the traditional Trance State Theory. The Cognitive-Behavioral Theory would predict that Think-With Instructions would be more effective than a traditional trance induction in enhancing responses to suggestions of age regression, anesthesia, and so on. On the other hand, the traditional Trance State Theory would predict that subjects exposed to a traditional trance induction would be more responsive to these types of suggestions than subjects told how to think with and imagine those things that are suggested.

The experimental results indicated that the Think-With Instructions were effective in raising responsiveness to test-suggestions on the Creative Imagination Scale above the base level (control treatment) and also above the level obtained with a traditional trance-induction procedure. More specifically, *all* of the subjects receiving the Think-With Instructions obtained relatively high scores (above the overall mean), whereas in the other two groups, some subjects scored relatively high, some medium, and some low. The important finding thus was that the Think-With Instructions were more effective than the trance induction in producing a high level of response to test-suggestions and, consequently, the data support the Cognitive-Behavioral Theory and do not support the traditional Trance State Theory.

Cross-Validation and Extension

Soon after the above experiment was completed, an attempt was made to cross-validate it and extend it in a doctoral dissertation that was carried out by De Stefano [12] at Temple University, Philadelphia, Pa. De Stefano conducted essentially the same study as the one we described above, with one major extension: the subjects were assessed on the ten test-suggestions of the Creative Imagination Scale and then, without interruption, were also assessed on the eight test-suggestions of the Barber Suggestibility Scale. De Stefano found that (1) the Think-With Instructions produced a significantly higher level of response to the test-suggestions on the Creative Imagination Scale than either the traditional trance induction or the control treatment, and (2) subjects who received the traditional trance-induction procedure did not score significantly higher than those who received the control treatment. In brief, our experimental results were dramatically cross-validated in an experiment conducted at an independent laboratory. Since De Stefano's results were essentially the same as our results, his data also offered further strong support for the Cognitive-Behavioral Theory and contradicted the traditional Trance State Theory.

As stated above, De Stefano also administered the Barber Suggestibility Scale immediately after the Creative Imagination Scale. The results with the Barber Suggestibility Scale were as follows: (1) the average score of the Think-With Instructions group (11.9) tended to be higher ($p < .10$) than the average score of the trance-induction group (9.5),†† (2) the average score of the Think-With group was significantly higher ($p < .05$) than the average score of the control group (8.0), and (3) the average score of the trance-induction group did not differ significantly ($p > .10$) from that of the control group. In brief, De Stefano found that the Think-With Instructions tended to be more effective than the traditional trance induction and the control treatment in producing high scores on the Barber Suggestibility Scale, and this part of his experiment also provided support for the Cognitive-Behavioral Theory and contradicted the traditional Trance State Theory.

Another recent study, carried out independently in a different laboratory, also supports the Cognitive-Behavioral Theory and contradicts the traditional Trance State Theory. In this study by Katz,[11] a group of subjects were first given information to correct misconceptions and to increase favorable attitudes toward hypnosis. Next, these same subjects were given instructions that were derived from one of our earlier experiments [15] and were similar to the Think-With Instructions that we described above. Specifically, the experimenter

---

†† Responses to the Barber Suggestibility Scale were self-scored by the subject in the manner described by Barber and Calverley.[13] Since these subjective scores could vary from 0 to 3 on each of the eight items on the scale, the subjective scores on the Barber Suggestibility Scale could vary from 0 to 24.

described aloud his own thoughts while he was successfully responding to several autosuggestions. For example, the experimenter held his own right arm straight out and verbalized the following: "I imagine my arm is becoming stiffer and stiffer, as though it were a bar of iron, with the elbow welded stiff, and the whole arm heavy and metallic. I imagine the dull silver of the metal, feel the weight of the metal, and I can't bend it. I really can't. Try and bend my arm! As long as I continue to let myself believe my arm is steel, welded, solid and rigid, then I—and you—can't bend it. . . . Oh, this is ridiculous, I can bend my arm. As soon as I decide to stop imagining my arm is stiff, it bends easily." [14] (p. 139)

Subjects exposed to these instructions were significantly more responsive to the test-suggestions of the Stanford Hypnotic Susceptibility Scale (Form C) than other subjects who were randomly assigned to a traditional trance-induction treatment. Although the instructions used in the experiment by Katz and those used in our experiment presented above were composed by investigators working in different laboratories and were thus worded differently, they both aimed to help the subject think with and imagine the themes that are suggested. Since both sets of "Think-With Instructions" were more effective than a traditional trance induction, both experiments support the Cognitive-Behavioral Theory and contradict the traditional Trance State Theory of hypnosis.‡‡

Let us place the experiments described above in a broader historical context. For more than a hundred years it has been commonly assumed that a trance-induction procedure comprised of repeated suggestions emphasizing relaxation, drowsiness, sleep, and hypnosis was the most effective method for eliciting a high level of response to test-suggestions for age regression, anesthesia, time distortion, and so on. During the 1960s and early 1970s this assumption was shown to be invalid. A series of studies, summarized by Barber [1, 3, 7] showed that subjects who were exposed to brief one-minute instructions that exhorted them to try to the best of their ability to imagine those things that are suggested (Task Motivational Instructions) were generally as responsive to test-suggestions as subjects who were exposed to a traditional trance-induction procedure. Although these studies found Task Motivational Instructions generally to be as effective as a traditional trance induction, the Task Motivational Instructions were *not* found to be superior to a trance induction for eliciting a high level of response to test-suggestions. However, the present experiment, and other recent experiments by De Stefano [12] and Katz,[14] have shown that a procedure that was derived from the Cognitive-Behavioral Theory is generally *more* effective than a traditional trance-induction procedure in enhancing response to test-suggestions. These experiments strongly indicate that it is generally more effective simply to tell a subject directly how to respond to—that is, how to think along with—the test-suggestions, rather than using an indirect procedure such as a traditional trance induction. Of course, a traditional trance-

‡‡ In another recent study [16] half of the subjects were exposed to a traditional trance induction emphasizing relaxation, drowsiness, sleep, and entering a hypnotic state. The other half of the subjects were told that they were to participate in an experiment that was the "opposite of hypnosis," and they were exposed to suggestions that they were becoming more awake, aware, alert, and joyous, and more capable of intense, heightened experiences. Subjects exposed to the latter "hyperempiric" (heightened experience) suggestions were significantly more responsive to the test-suggestions of the Harvard Group Scale than those exposed to the traditional trance-induction procedure.

induction procedure comprised of repeated suggestions of relaxation, drowsiness, sleep, and hypnosis is an indirect method for attempting to enhance a subject's responsiveness to test-suggestions because the subject is not given any direct information regarding what he can do in order to respond effectively to the test-suggestions.

The results of the present experiment, and the confirmatory experiments by De Stefano [12] and by Katz,[11] have a number of important implications. For instance, clinicians might find it more efficacious to use the direct Think-With Instructions rather than the indirect trance-induction procedure to enhance their patients' responsiveness to suggestions for pain relief, age regression, slowing down of time, mind-body relaxation, symptom removal, and so on. If the clinical practice of "hypnosis" changes, that is, if Think-With Instructions, rather than a traditional trance induction, are typically administered prior to the test-suggestions, we can expect a change in the attitudes of clinicians toward theories of hypnosis. Since the acceptance of theories often follows a change in practice, we can expect that the Cognitive-Behavioral Theory will be more accepted by clinicians who find that, in their practice, the Think-With Instructions are generally more effective than a traditional trance induction in enhancing their patients' responsiveness.

The results of the present experiment and the confirmatory experiments by De Stefano [12] and Katz [14] suggest a number of areas that require further research. For instance, studies are needed to determine (1) which components of the Think-With Instructions are most effective in enhancing responses to test-suggestions and (2) whether instructions can be constructed that are even more effective than the ones used in these experiments in helping the subject think along with and imagine those things that are suggested.

Further studies are also needed to determine to what extent the effectiveness of Think-With Instructions, trance-induction procedures, and other types of treatments [3, 15] are contingent upon the types of test-suggestions that are administered. For instance, a traditional trance-induction procedure may be more effective than Think-With Instructions when the test-suggestions are consistently worded as authoritarian commands that imply that the subject is supposed to be under the control of a hypnotist, e.g., "You can't open your eyes," "You can't bend your arm," "You can't see," "You can't hear," and so on.

Further studies are also needed to determine whether Think-With Instructions are as effective in heightening responses to test-suggestions when the situation is defined to subjects as "hypnosis" rather than as a "test of imagination" and whether Think-With Instructions are more effective when combined with a trance-induction procedure rather than when they are given alone.

All studies that involve either suggestions or "hypnosis," including the studies discussed in this paper, are open to the criticism that the subjects may exaggerate their experiential reports in order to be "good" subjects, or to please the experimenter or hypnotist, or to comply with the "demand characteristics" of the experimental situation.[17-19] To ascertain to what extent the subjects may be exaggerating (or, possibly, underemphasizing) their experiences, researchers can use a technique adapted from Bowers: [20] the subjects could be interviewed after the experiment by a person other than the experimenter and strongly urged to give unexaggerated or literally truthful reports concerning what they experienced. We can predict from previous studies that used this kind of postexperimental inquiry,[15, 21, 22] that (1) all experimental groups—e.g., trance induction, Think-With Instructions, and control—will to some degree reduce their estimates pertaining to how intensely they experienced the suggested effects, and (2) the degree of reduction in the experiential reports will be more or less equal among all groups.

SUMMARY

Sixty-six subjects were tested on a new scale for evaluating "hypnotic-like" experiences (The Creative Imagination Scale), which includes ten standardized test-suggestions (e.g. suggestions for arm heaviness, finger anesthesia, time distortion, and age regression). The subjects were randomly assigned to one of three treatment groups (Think-With Instructions, trance induction, and Control), with 22 subjects to each group. The new Cognitive-Behavioral Theory predicted that subjects exposed to preliminary instructions designed to demonstrate how to think and imagine along with the suggested themes (Think-With Instructions) would be more responsive to test-suggestions for anesthesia, time distortion, age regression, and so on, than subjects exposed to a trance-induction procedure. On the other hand, the traditional Trance State Theory predicted that a trance induction would be more effective than Think-With Instructions in enhancing responses to such suggestions. Subjects exposed to the Think-With Instructions obtained significantly higher scores on the test-suggestions than those exposed either to the traditional trance-induction procedure or to the control treatment. Scores of subjects who received the trance-induction procedure were not significantly different from those of the subjects who received the control treatment. The results thus supported the new Cognitive-Behavioral Theory and contradicted the traditional Trance State Theory of hypnosis.

Two recent experiments, by De Stefano and by Katz, confirmed the above experimental results and offered further support for the Cognitive-Behavioral Theory. In both recent experiments, subjects randomly assigned to a "Think-With Instructions" treatment were more responsive to test-suggestions than those randomly assigned to a traditional trance-induction treatment.

ACKNOWLEDGMENTS

We are indebted to R. F. Q. Johnson, Donald S. Scott, Judie Kaiser, Peter M. Litchfield, and Kimberly Kiddoo for critically reading a preliminary draft of the manuscript.

REFERENCES

1. BARBER, T. X. 1970. Suggested "hypnotic" behavior: the trance paradigm versus an alternative paradigm. Medfield Foundation. Medfield, Mass. Reprinted in Hypnosis: Research Developments and Perspectives. E. Fromm & R. E. Shor, Eds. Aldine Publishing Company. Chicago, Ill.; 1976. *In* Advances in Altered States of Consciousness and Human Potentialities. Vol. 1. T. X. Barber, Ed. Psychological Dimensions. New York, N.Y.
2. BARBER, T. X. & M. W. HAM. 1974. Hypnotic Phenomena. General Learning Press. Morristown, N.J.

3. BARBER, T. X., N. P. SPANOS & J. F. CHAVES. 1974. Hypnosis, Imagination, and Human Potentialities. Pergamon Press. Elmsford, N.Y.

4. WILSON, S. C. 1976. An experimental investigation evaluating a Creative Imagination Scale and its relationship to "hypnotic-like" experiences. Doctoral dissertation. Heed University. Hollywood, Fla.

5. WILSON, S. C. & T. X. Barber. 1976. The Creative Imagination Scale: Applications to clinical and experimental hypnosis. Medfield Foundation. Medfield, Mass.

6. WEITZENHOFFER, A. M. & E. R. HILGARD. 1959. Stanford Hypnotic Susceptibility Scale: Forms A and B. Consulting Psychologists Press. Palo Alto, Calif.

7. BARBER, T. X. 1969. Hypnosis: A Scientific Approach. Van Nostrand Reinhold. New York, N.Y.; 1976. Psychological Dimensions. New York, N.Y.

8. HOSKOVEC, J., D. SVORAD & O. LANC. 1963. The comparative effectiveness of spoken and tape-recorded suggestions of body sway. Int. J. Clin. Exp. Hypn. 11: 163–164.

9. BARBER, T. X. & D. S. CALVERLEY. 1964. Comparative effects on "hypnotic-like" suggestibility of recorded and spoken suggestions. J. Consult. Psychol. 28: 384.

10. NORTON, D. W. 1952. An empirical investigation of some effects of non-normality and heterogeneity of the F-distribution. Doctoral dissertation. State University of Iowa. Ames, Iowa.

11. LINDQUIST, E. F. 1956. Design and Analysis of Experiments in Psychology and Education. Houghton Mifflin Company. Boston, Mass.

12. DE STEFANO, R. 1976. The "inoculation" effect in Think-With Instructions for "hypnotic-like" experiences. Doctoral dissertation. Temple University. Philadelphia, Pa.

13. BARBER, T. X. & D. S. CALVERLEY. 1966. Toward a theory of "hypnotic" behavior: experimental evaluation of Hull's postulate that hypnotic susceptibility is a habit phenomenon. J. Personality 34: 416–433.

14. KATZ, N. W. 1975. Comparative efficacy of sleep/trance instructions and behavior modification procedures in enhancing hypnotic suggestibility. Doctoral dissertation. Washington University. St. Louis, Mo.

15. COMINS, J. R., F. FULLAM & T. X. BARBER. 1975. Effects of experimenter modeling, demands for honesty, and initial level of suggestibility on response to "hypnotic" suggestions. J. Cons. Clin. Psychol. 43: 668–675.

16. GIBBONS, D. E. 1976. Hypnotic vs. hyperempiric induction procedures: an experimental comparison. Percept. Mot. Skills 42: 834.

17. ORNE, M. T. 1962. On the social psychology of the psychological experiment: with particular reference to demand characteristics and their implications. Amer. Psychol. 17: 776–783.

18. ROSENTHAL, R. 1966. Experimenter Effects in Behavioral Research. Appleton-Century-Crofts. New York, N.Y.

19. BARBER, T. X. 1976. Pitfalls in Human Research: Ten Pivotal Points. Pergamon Press. Elmsford, N.Y.

20. BOWERS, K. S. 1967. The effect of demands for honesty on reports of visual and auditory hallucinations. Int. J. Clin. Exp. Hypn. 15: 31–36.

21. SPANOS, N. P. & T. X. BARBER. 1968. "Hypnotic" experiences as inferred from subjective reports: auditory and visual hallucinations. J. Exp. Res. Pers. 3: 136–150.

22. SPANOS, N. P., T. X. BARBER & G. LANG. 1974. Cognition and self-control: cognitive control of painful sensory input. In Thought and Feeling: Cognitive Alteration of Feeling States. H. London & R. E. Nisbett, Eds. Aldine Publishing Company. Chicago, Ill.

Think-With Instructions

In this study I'm going to give you a series of tests in which I'll ask you to focus your thinking and to use your imagination creatively to produce certain effects and to experience certain events. You'll benefit from these tests if you let yourself think along with the instructions. When you think along with the instructions you'll find that you can use your mind to do many interesting and useful things.

Let me give you an example of the kind of tests I might give you. I might, for example, ask you to close your eyes and feel as if you're looking at a T.V. program. Now, there are a number of possible ways to respond to these tests. For instance, if someone asks me to close my eyes and to imagine I'm watching a T.V. program, one way I could respond is to close my eyes and say to myself, "There's no T.V. screen there. I can't see a T.V. show when there's no T.V. there. This is ridiculous. It's a lot of baloney. I can't do it." Obviously, if I take this kind of negative attitude and say these negative things to myself, nothing's going to happen. I'm not going to visualize a T.V. screen or feel as if I'm looking at a T.V. program, and I won't find this to be an interesting or worthwhile experience.

There is another way of responding to this test in which I also do not benefit from the test. This way is to close my eyes and passively wait for a T.V. screen to appear. Once again nothing will happen, because only my own mind, my own thoughts, can make a T.V. screen appear before my eyes. It won't happen magically by itself.

A third way I could respond, and this is the way in which I benefit most from this test, is when somebody tells me, "Close your eyes and imagine you're watching a T.V. program," I let myself think of a T.V. program that I like or one that I can remember easily, like "All in the Family." Then I close my eyes [experimenter closes her eyes] and tell myself that I'm looking at Archie Bunker and I see him in my mind's eye. I visualize him walking in his front door, in his own way, hanging up his hat and jacket on the hook by the door as he calls to Edith that he's home and then yells at Michael to get up off of his chair. And I feel as if I'm looking at the T.V. program [experimenter opens her eyes], and I find this to be a very interesting experience. In the same way, I could feel as if I'm watching the newscast or a football game or any other program on T.V. By using my creative imagination and thinking of a T.V. program I've seen previously, I create it myself and I see it in my mind's eye. Now, everybody can do this although not everyone does. Some people block themselves by negative attitudes such as telling themselves that it's silly and can't happen, or by passively waiting for something to happen to them.

Now, I'll give you another example of the kind of test I might give you. I might, for example, ask you to hold a pendulum like this and to think of it moving back and forth. Again, there are a number of ways you could respond.

For instance, if someone says to me, "Hold this pendulum [experimenter holds pendulum and models how to think along with the instructions] and think of it moving back and forth. Think that it's moving faster and watch for it to actually begin to move back and forth, back and forth, faster and faster, back and forth." When I think along with these instructions and I focus my thinking and think of it moving back and forth, I find that it actually does move back and forth [experimenter stops holding pendulum]. Now, there's nothing magic or mysterious about it moving. My own thoughts cause the pendulum to move. Focusing on the thought that the pendulum is moving back and forth causes slight little movements in the muscles of my fingers. These movements are unconscious in the sense that I'm not aware that my muscles are moving. Then, this movement is amplified by the pendulum and it seems to me that the pendulum is moving by itself. In psychology, this is called ideomotor action; that is, our muscles or our body and our mind are so intimately related that it would be impossible for us to think vividly of the pendulum moving back and forth without moving our muscles slightly.

Now, this is the kind of thing that I'm referring to when I tell you that by letting your thoughts go along with the instructions you can have some interesting experiences and see how your mind and your body function together in amazing and useful ways.

However, when asked to think of the pendulum moving back and forth, there are a couple of other ways I could respond that would block the whole thing so that I could not benefit from these tests. I could say to myself, "It isn't moving back and forth. This is silly. It just can't move like that. That is ridiculous." And, of course, with this kind of negative attitude nothing will happen.

Another way in which nothing will happen is if I just wait for it to move by itself without thinking of it moving back and forth. Again, nothing will happen because it won't move by magic, only my own mind can make it move.

Now, I'm going to give you a number of interesting tests like these. Although you could respond in any of the ways I've described, I'd like you to respond in the way in which you'll benefit most from the tests, and that is to focus your thinking and to imagine to the best of your ability. Just let your thinking and your creative imagination go along with the instructions so that you can fully experience the many interesting and useful things that your mind can do.

THE PROBLEM OF DIVIDED CONSCIOUSNESS:
A NEODISSOCIATION INTERPRETATION *

Ernest R. Hilgard

Department of Psychology
Stanford University
Stanford, California 94305

The unity of consciousness is an illusion, resulting in part from the filling in of the gaps of memory through recognition and recall. Once the continuity of memories is restored after there has been a disruption, consciousness seems to have been continuous and hence integrated all along. It was Pierre Janet, an early practitioner of hypnosis, who did much to introduce the concept of dissociation, implying that consciousness might not be so unified but could go on in more than one stream, with memories not equally available to both streams. The clinical illustrations came from fugues and multiple personalities, but laboratory analogues can be found in automatic writing, posthypnotic suggestions, and other familiar aspects of hypnosis.

Ordinary life is not free of multiple tasks going on at once, as in carrying on a conversation while driving a car. The operation of the car is quite automatic until the traffic snarls, at which time the conversation gets interrupted. A tune may get started and haunt the person throughout the day, even while he is engaged in doing other things and wishing that he could get rid of the tune running through his head. It is very common these days to point out that hypnosis and everyday experiences are not so very different, as is indeed the case. Nearly all the experiences characteristic of hypnosis can be found present on occasions in which no hypnosis, at least no formal hypnosis, has been involved. I have pointed out elsewhere that one of the defining characteristics of a hypnotic situation is that many different experiences associated with hypnosis can be demonstrated in a single short session, and this variety of hypnotic-like behaviors is never found except in the context of hypnosis.[1] That could be in part a matter of social practice or convenience, however, and the extreme position of those who like to point out the similarity between hypnotic experiences and those of everyday nonhypnotic life is that the concept of hypnosis is useless and expendable.

When so much remains to be found out, controversies over conceptual matters may divert energy from getting on with the task; reformulations are unprofitable unless the new conceptualizations harmonize more data than the old and lead to new discoveries or inventions. My purpose here is to present some recent data that may indeed modify some of the ways we look at hypnosis and that may possibly serve to mediate between controversial viewpoints.

My preference in discussing hypnosis is to refer directly to hypnotic procedures and practices and to use expressions such as *hypnotic responsiveness* to characterize the relatively enduring talent that makes some individuals more

* Assisted by a grant from the National Institute of Mental Health, Department of Health, Education, and Welfare (grant MH–03859).

hypnotizable than others; *hypnotic induction* for the procedures used in inviting a nonhypnotized person to become hypnotized; the established *hypnotic state* for the condition that permits the responsive subject to know that he is hypnotized; and *depth of hypnosis* to refer to the degree of involvement in hypnosis, varying from time to time and readily judged by the subject himself. This language is readily understandable and is appropriate at the descriptive or phenomenal level, for it reflects the findings from measurement and from what the hypnotized person reports to the hypnotist. Fortunately, now that cognitive psychology has overtaken the excesses of behaviorism and the related operationalism, we are freer than we once were to recognize what the subject tells us as a valid source of information. In many instances that is the only useful source, and if cautiously appraised it provides orderly and reproducible data frequently more valid than that read from physiological records.

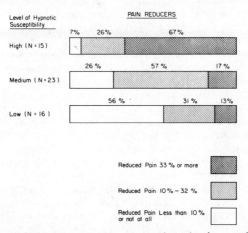

FIGURE 1. Reduction of pain through suggested analgesia as related to susceptibility to hypnosis. The subjects were 54 university students whose prior experience of hypnosis had been limited to standard tests of hypnotic responsiveness following formal induction procedures. By permission of the publishers of Acta Neuro. Biol. Exp. (Warsaw).[3]

A TWO-COMPONENT INTERPRETATION OF HYPNOTIC PAIN CONTROL

The data that I am about to present bear on hypnotic consciousness when a subject, in the laboratory, is given suggestions to reduce pain. For this purpose I shall limit my remarks to pain produced by the placement of one hand and forearm in circulating ice water for a short time, the so-called cold pressor response. This has been studied a great deal in our laboratory,[2] but I shall be presenting some new data along with that already reported, leading to a two-component interpretation of response to analgesia suggestions.

The importance of hypnotic responsiveness, as a talent the subject brings to the experiment, is well indicated by the results on pain reduction. Only a few can eliminate the pain entirely and feel nothing following hypnotic analgesia suggestions, but a reduction of a third or more suffices to keep the pain at a tolerable level. Even that much pain reduction typically requires a high level of hypnotic responsiveness, as illustrated in FIGURE 1. Success depends upon degree of hypnotizability, but even in the highest group, as classified here, only two thirds could reduce their pain by a third or more of the normally felt pain.

When pain reduction is indicated as due to analgesia suggestions within hypnosis, a great deal is unmentioned, particularly the active participation of the subject in bringing about the experience. He may, in fact, work hard at it, and it is as much his active participation as the commands of the hypnotist that is responsible for his success. The talent for the behavior that the subject possesses is central to the experience. Those who favor a role interpretation of hypnosis commonly emphasize the compliant behavior of the subject in trying to come up to the expectations of the hypnotist. Such behavior is clearly present, as the evident efforts of the subjects to reduce their pains indicate. It is, however, an insufficient explanation of the success in pain reduction, for without the necessary talent many compliant subjects are unsuccessful. That what the successful persons do may be to satisfy themselves rather than the hypnotist is shown by the frequent use of the pain-reducing techniques for pain reduction in natural settings when there is no hypnotist to please. Had these subjects not experienced genuine pain reduction there would have been no reason for them to try to comfort themselves in emergencies by the techniques that they had been taught, now in circumstances when there was nobody else around to please. A few illustrations will suffice. One male student had an accident on a ski slope, resulting in a compound fracture of his leg. It took a long time for the rescue sled to be brought up the slopes in order to take him to the emergency hospital at the bottom. He hypnotized himself and remained comfortable throughout, and the attendants at the hospital could not understand how someone with such a severe injury could arrive after the protracted delay in an obviously relaxed and comfortable state. Another young man broke a bone in his foot when he was about to appear in a leading part for several performances in a college play requiring vigorous Mexican-style dancing. After having appropriate x rays he discussed with his physician the possibility of permanent damage if he were to use the foot without a cast for the duration of the play. The physician agreed that the bone was not in a position in which placing stress on the foot would do any permanent damage, although putting weight on it would undoubtedly be very painful. Using what he had learned in the laboratory, he eliminated the pain hypnotically during each performance, and fulfilled all his obligations before having the foot placed in a cast until the bone might heal. He reported only a single episode when he felt pain: one of the others in the play stepped on his foot; fortunately, he was able to recover and make it painless again. A young woman student had cut her knee seriously, the repair requiring 38 stitches. Because of an allergy to novocain, she controlled the pain subjectively by blocking everything from her mind, concentrating on breathing, and picturing her head filled with something like foam rubber that would block sensation. This is complaint behavior, but compliant to her own demands for achieving comfort in the face of normally noxious stimulation.

Although in obtaining the results shown in Figure 1 the subjects had undergone a prior attempted induction of hypnosis, suggestions of analgesia may be given without such an induction in what is commonly called waking suggestion. Differences in experimenter preference regarding the conception of hypnosis introduce subtle differences in the instructions that are given, with consequent differences in data that may appear to be empirical contradictions when, in fact, they are readily interpretable. For example, if the experimenter doubts that there is any special hypnotic condition produced by induction, he proceeds to give the waking suggestions of analgesia without saying anything restrictive. If, however, he believes that there are some changes related to the hypnotic condition, when he tests for responsiveness in the nonhypnotic (waking) condition, he tells the subject not to drift into hypnosis, or to arouse himself if he finds himself drifting into hypnosis. That is, you have an alternative of defining hyposis operationally as what happens to some people following a hypnotic induction, or defining hypnosis as that same condition reached by some people in other ways *whether or not there has been a formal induction.* This makes a great deal of difference, because highly hypnotizable persons readily drift into hypnosis when given any kinds of suggestions, so that a comparison of waking and hypnotic condition is inappropriate if the comparison is made of waking and hypnotic suggestion without correcting for drifting into hypnosis in the so-called waking condition. The question may well be raised whether or not the choice between the two procedures is an arbitrary one, reflecting a difference between two paradigms of hypnosis.

There are some questions about the logic of science that are being considered here. If the purpose is merely reproducibility of data, then the choice between the two procedures is arbitrary; the result of a comparison between waking suggestion and hypnotic suggestion, uncorrected for drifting into hypnosis, repeated by someone else in another laboratory, will find results consistent with the first experiment being replicated. The different results, by those who correct for drifting into hypnosis, can also be replicated. From my point of view, the choice between the two methods of testing the difference between waking suggestion and hypnotic suggestion is not arbitrary, because if one is fair to the phenomena, he is not free to ignore phenomena that present themselves upon inquiry. Because subjects are able to tell when they drift into hypnosis, it is proper to test the independent influence of waking suggestion under conditions in which they are told *not* to drift into hypnosis. Highly hypnotizable subjects become adept at self-hypnosis, and if not advised against it will use their hypnotic abilities when given suggestions in the waking state, especially if confronted with something unpleasant, such as a pain they would like to get rid of and are capable of eliminating through self-hypnosis.

Despite the restriction against drifting into hypnosis, subjects, both hypnotizable and nonhypnotizable, can achieve some measure of pain reduction through analgesia suggestions given in the waking condition. *This reduction, which takes place through diversion of attention, relaxation, and reduced anxiety, is available to all subjects, not only to those with hypnotic talent.* Waking suggestion in our experiment results in an average reduction to about 80% of the normal pain and represents the first component of the two-component interpretation of pain reduction. The fact that this component is available to the nonhypnotizable person who is cooperating with the hypnotist may well account for the belief by some practicing hypnotists that, in principle, everyone is hypnotizable. Therapeutic results may be obtained through hypnotic procedures that do not require any significant degree of hypnotic responsiveness. We often find in our hypnotically unresponsive subjects who have just completed one of our hypnotic susceptibility tests under experimental conditions that they feel very good and marvelously relaxed, and believe that a repetition of the experience would be of benefit to them.

The second component of the hypnotic pain reduction is available only to those who are hypnotizable and involves an amnesic-like process; it accounts for the much greater successes on the part of the highs as compared with the lows, as previously shown.

The two components are represented for low hypnotizable subjects and high hypnotizable subjects in FIGURE 2. These are based on an interrogation after the experiment by someone not the hypnotist, to be sure that the reports correspond to actually felt pain. The low hypnotizable subjects, when in the hypnotic condition, have simulated hypnosis in order to have whatever advantage comes from playing the role of a hypnotized person as skillfully as to fool the hypnotist; only the honest reports are shown in FIGURE 2.

Note that in waking analgesia the highs and the lows scored essentially alike, reducing the pain to about 80% of normal, some, of course, more and some less. When the analgesia suggestions have been preceded by a hypnotic induction, however, the truly hypnotized reduced their pain to an average level of about 20% of the normal pain, whereas the low hypnotizables *remained at the same level as in waking suggestion;* the second component was not available to them.

The interpretation that there are two components to the pain reduction receives further support from another method in use in our laboratory, which seeks a report of *covert* pain in hypnotic analgesia, compared with the *overt* pain that is reported. Several years ago we introduced a "hidden observer" technique similar to automatic writing in which the subjects in our pain experiments reported covert pain at a hidden or subconscious level that was above that reported overtly, orally, when pain had been reduced by hypnotic analgesia suggestions.[5] Another method that by analogy was called automatic talking yielded the same information in a form that could be discussed with the subject.[6, 7]

The pertinent hypothesis that can be tested with the aid of data from the study of overt and covert pain is this: *If there are two components of pain reduction, one associated with the special capacity of the highly hypnotizable*

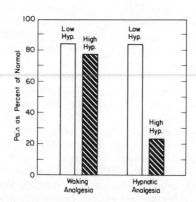

FIGURE 2. Pain reduced through waking suggestion and through hypnotic suggestion in subjects unresponsive to hypnosis and in those highly responsive. Twelve subjects in each group, selected on the basis of prior tests of hypnotic responsiveness. The low hypnotizables in the hypnotic condition were simulating hypnosis, but the data are from their honest reports based on the subsequent inquiry. (By permission of Wiley-Interscience.[4])

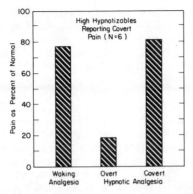

FIGURE 3. Waking analgesia and hypnotic analgesia (overt and covert) as reported by high hypnotizable subjects. The subjects are the 6 from the 12 in FIGURE 2 who reported a difference between overt and covert pain in hypnotic analgesia. Note that the covert hypnotic analgesia equals the waking analgesia. (Unpublished data, Stanford Laboratory.)

for amnesia-related processes, then the covert pain that is reported following hypnotic analgesia should eliminate only the special hypnotic component. Hence, the covert pain should be the normal waking pain as reduced by the first component that is available as well to the hypnotic unsusceptible. In other words, the *covert* pain revealed by the special techniques should equal in magnitude the pain reduced by waking suggestion. For this purpose it is important that the comparisons be made for those who do indeed report covert pain; otherwise, the mean residual pain would be a meaningless mixture of that reduced overtly by those who do not report covert pain and the residual pain of those who have access to a covert report. Such a comparison has been made in FIGURE 3. It can be seen that the results conform to the prediction; the covert pain is indeed equal to that experienced by these subjects in waking analgesia.

The data presented here are new, actually replications of data obtained earlier, from which the two-component interpretation arose, so that the factual situation is well established.

In any experiment on hypnosis the problems of demand characteristics and compliance with the expectations of the hypnotist have to be taken seriously. It is of the essence of hypnosis that the hypnotist communicates his demands to the subject. When the hypnotist tells him to experience a rabbit in his lap, the highly hypnotizable subject is expected to experience a rabbit, not a kitten or a kangaroo. Hence when Orne proposes the use of simulating subjects to determine something about the essence of hypnosis he does not imply that there should be no compliance with the hypnotist's demands.[8] He is particularly interested in what the subject *adds to* the hypnotist's suggestions, and the method that he has designed serves the purpose of showing that what the simulators add may be different from what the reals add to the suggestions they receive. There are many subtle issues here into which I shall not enter, except to point out that when both the simulator and the hypnotic real yield the same behavior it does not mean that hypnosis is discredited. For example, it is obviously easy to simulate seeing a rabbit in your lap; hence if simulator and hypnotic real both see rabbits, the issue is not that they both report rabbits in their laps. The issue is rather one of the quality of the hallucinated experience. When reporting honestly, the simulator will say that he did not actually see a rabbit, the hypnotic real will say that he did actually see a rabbit, although the hallucinatory experience need not have been that of a flesh-and-blood rabbit. In our two-light test, in which one light is real and one light hallucinated, subjects who actually see two lights commonly know which is real, because the hallucinated light may float above the box or have no reflection in its bright surface. This is the kind of report that distinguishes the experiences of the reals from those of the simulators. Unless one relies on careful verbal reports, simulation of cognitive experiences is too easy to be critical. Of course the simulator often overreacts; this limits Orne's method, because it can be used well only with very highly hypnotizable subjects who do so well that the detection of simulation cannot be made easily on the basis of the overreaction of the simulators. Even compared with very high hypnotizables, simulators still commonly overreact, but one can question just how high the reals have to be in order to make the comparison a strict one. Against randomly selected subjects, simulators of high hypnotizables would *always* tend to overreact. For various reasons the behavioral differences in many instances will be less crucial than the subjectively reported ones, when the simulators and reals are both reporting honestly.

We have compared a group of 12 simulators with 12 reals in the pain experiments of overt and covert pain, and the simulation was remarkably good at both the overt and covert levels of reporting, whereas the high hypnotizables, the reals, were reporting honestly and the low hypnotizable simulators were deceiving the hypnotist by acting as they thought they would if they were high hypnotizables. However, the differences showed up readily when the simulators reported honestly. Some comparisons are given in FIGURE 4.

The first thing to note is the success of the simulators in duplicating the results of the reals, in the overt analgesia and in the covert report. The simulators overreacted as expected, in the overt analgesia, although the difference was barely significant by statistical standards, $p = .05$, one-tailed. For example, six of the twelve simulators reported no pain at all, compared with three of the twelve reals. This is one of the difficulties of the method, as already mentioned. Had reals been preselected to yield no pain at all, then the difference might have been reversed. When it came to reporting covert pain, some simulators guessed that reals would have experienced increased pain, others guessed they would not. Those who guessed that covert pain would be reported very sensibly reported the pain that they had actually felt in the experiment while simulating hypnotic analgesia, which turned out to be equivalent to their pain reduced by waking suggestion. Because this was actually what the reals felt, the results for reals and simulators are very much alike. When honest reports were obtained, however, the picture became very different: the reals did not change their reports, for they had been honest all along; the simulators commonly gave an honest report equal to what they had reported as covert pain, but they indicated that this was in fact the pain that they had actually felt while reporting reduced pain in hypnotic analgesia. Hence their honest results conformed to just what would be expected from nonhypnotizable subjects.

As in the case of overreaction to the hypnotic analgesia suggestions, there are many other evidences of differences between the reals and the simulators. For example, half the reals yielded no covert increase in pain, and none of them indicated any change in their honest report; one fourth of the simulators chose to deny a covert increase in pain over their simulated hypnotic analgesia, but all of them reported that they had actually felt pain equivalent to that felt in waking analgesia.

These contrasts were extended in the interviews that followed the experiments. The simulators were very puzzled about the possibility of covert pain experiences, and had simply chosen such reference points as they could, that is, what they had reported in simulated analgesia, or what they actually felt. The reals, who were often surprised or puzzled by their covert reports, had no doubt of the reality of the change between overt and covert reporting.

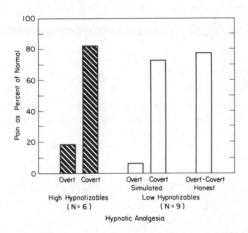

FIGURE 4. Overt and covert pain as reported by "reals" and "simulators" who indicated a difference between overt and covert pain. The results are from 6 of the highly hypnotizable subjects and 9 of the low hypnotizables from FIGURE 2. Because the simulators, when reporting honestly, had experienced only one level of pain, their honest reports are alike for overt and covert pain, as shown in the right-hand column. The reals did not change their reports under honesty instructions. (Unpublished data, Stanford Laboratory.)

The two-component interpretation of pain reduction has implications for hypnotherapy that go beyond problems of pain. As mentioned earlier, the two-component interpretation helps account for some disagreements between experimenters and clinicians. Many practitioners of hypnotherapy believe that everyone is hypnotizable, while experimenters characteristically believe that only a small proportion of the population can be hypnotized sufficiently to yield substantial amnesia, hallucinations, and other evidences of profound hypnotic involvement. The two-component theory points out that therapeutic practices using hypnotic methods can be of benefit to nearly everyone through relaxation, anxiety reduction, diversion of attention, improved self-confidence, even though, in a careful assessment setting, some of those helped would be shown to be barely hypnotizable at all.

If one understands the two-component theory, the less hypnotizable and the more hypnotizable would be treated according to somewhat different therapeutic models. For example, biofeedback, with its emphasis on acquiring voluntary control of the realities of bodily responses—heartrate, blood pressure, muscular relaxation, or hand temperature—differs from hypnosis in that such biofeedback changes are available to those who can use only the first component of hypnotic responsiveness. The setting may be hypnotic, as in autogenic training, which grew out of Schultz's hypnotic experience, but the person treated does not have to be very susceptible to hypnosis. More profound hypnosis commonly involves distortion of the awareness of bodily processes—denying the pains of burns or broken bones—and success here depends on the second component, not available to many who can use feedback successfully. In fact, hypnotizability may make biofeedback contraindicated because of the person's tendency to substitute hallucination for reality when under stress. A lack of correlation between hypnosis and feedback [9] does not, of course, mean that all hypnotizable persons cannot use feedback; all it means is that it is not possible to predict from success in one procedure to success in the other.

Toward a Neodissociation Interpretation

Although the detailed data as presented were all obtained from studies of laboratory pain, there are implications beyond this limited sphere. We have been able to demonstrate covert experiences, available through the hidden-observer technique, in a wide variety of hypnotic behaviors, including hypnotic deafness and positive and negative visual hallucinations. The nature of the hidden observer, representing as it does a fractionated part of consciousness, bears on cognitive activities within hypnosis and has led to the development of a neodissociation theory.[4]

Discontinuity in the Distribution of Hypnotic Talent

If there is a qualitative change that appears when hypnotic responsiveness is present to a high degree, this will bear on the interpretation of the hypnotic consciousness, because something may have to be said that applies to the highly hypnotizable that does not apply to others who respond in some milder form to hypnotic suggestions. Some discontinuity is indicated by the biomodal distributions that are commonly found when large populations are carefully tested for hypnotic susceptibility. The finding is particularly impressive in studies of posthypnotic amnesia,[10] but it is found in more general tests of hypnotizability as well.[11] Studies of suggested hallucination have shown, for example, that many moderately responsive subjects will report some degree of hallucinatory behavior, but only a small fraction of subjects experience hallucinations as genuine, that is, as if they are perceiving external reality, as if something seen is really there or some music is heard as if produced by a real orchestra. A recent experiment has shown again that the reports of hallucinations, both auditory and visual, correlate positively with hypnotizability as measured by the Barber Suggestibility Scale, but the most realistic hallucinatory experience is confined to about two percent of their subject population.[12] Despite the cooperation of the subjects and the strong suggestions to hallucinate, half the subjects *did not imagine at all,* and another 31% imagined only vaguely. The results are entirely coherent with the interpretation that a fully acceptable auditory or visual hallucination requires a very high order of hypnotic talent. The indifferent hallucinations of the majority of subjects described by them as imagined, rather than as seen or heard, represent what I have called the first component of response to suggestion and require little in the way of hypnotic procedures and talent to produce them. The first component will correlate with hypnotizability, but it is limited as a predictor of the abilities of the truly hypnotizable. The second component, dramatized by the socalled somnambule or the hypnotic virtuoso, as I prefer to describe him, yields the more advanced phenomena, such as the better-established hallucinations, which, when genuine, are typical of a profound hypnotic involvement.

The State-Nonstate Issue

If the phenomena that the experimenter keeps in focus are those of the first component as I have described it, the evidence will favor a nonstate theory, because these phenomena of response to suggestion do not require a change in state. If the phenomena that interest the experimenter are those of the second component, he is more likely to entertain a state conception, in view of what the highly hypnotizable tells him about his experiences within hypnosis and how they differ from his experiences when he is not hypnotized.

Whether or not the bimodality of distribution of hypnotic talent represents a sharp discontinuity, all careful observers can detect a variety of changes in the hypnotic consciousness from essentially no change at all to a profound change associated with deep hypnosis.

I have found a neodissociation interpretation useful as a way of resolving the state/nonstate issue, because dissociation may be interpreted as a matter of degree. For example, there are dissociations associated with both components of the two-component interpretation. In the first component, the modifications that are noted are in executive control systems, without any appreciable change in the total state; that is, modification of controls is in evidence when a voluntary movement cannot be inhibited by an attempt, or when an inhibition of movement cannot be overcome by intentional effort. Such ideomotor modifications are readily produced by waking suggestion and require very little alteration in consciousness. Some simple cognitive processes can also be modified in the first component, as in suggesting that the subject has a taste of salt or sugar in his mouth. The dissociations that are produced for those who have available the abilities associated with the second component are more extensive, as when, in age regression, the person feels himself a child again and, as a child, takes initiative and makes demands on those around him appropriate to the child's age, or, when hallucinating a person, carries on a realistic conversation with that person without doubt of his reality.

The interpretation of these dissociations within hypnosis—and in nonhypnotic experiences as well—I refer to as a neodissociation interpretation because I wish to avoid the excesses that came to be associated with the classical dissociation theory.

The essence of the neodissociation viewpoint can be stated rather simply, since it bears upon hypnosis and the state/nonstate issue.

First, a dissociated activity is identified by a shift in cognitive controls rather than by a change in the quality of consciousness. A shift in executive controls is evident when an activity, normally voluntary, becomes involuntary or inaccessible to voluntary management; less frequently, an involuntary activity may be brought under voluntary control. The loss of voluntary control is found not only in motor activity but in the retrieval of memories. A shift in perceptual or observational functions is illustrated by positive and negative hallucinations, departing as they do from the normal realistic, critical observation of events in the external world or in the person's own body.

Second, dissociated activities or controls can vary from minor or limited ones to profound and widespread evidences of altered controls. The twitch of a single finger in response to a posthypnotic signal would represent the persistence of a minor dissociation; a fugue lasting several days or weeks would be a massive dissociation.

Third, dissociations imply a change of the total state only when they are sufficiently widespread. According to this position, it is futile to argue that a change of state is essential in order to produce responses to suggestion characteristic of the first component in hypnotic responsiveness. There are many simple responses to suggestion that no one would attribute to a hypnotic state. Some natural conditioned responses can be interpreted in this way; for example, it is not hard to demonstrate how easy it is to produce salivation by having a person watch a lemon being squeezed, even though he does not taste the juice. Call it conditioning if you wish, but it is also a simple response to suggestion. The same holds for simple arm movements, which are yielded by almost all subjects who are cooperating in a hypnotic induction. When, however, the dissociations are more massive, as evidenced by the variety of responses yielded by the highly hypnotizable person when hypnotized and by his own self-reports, a description of the change according to a hypnotic state or hypnotic trance is entirely appropriate.

Because dissociations can be partial or widespread, a person does not have to continue in the hypnotic state in order to have an analgesia persist for a day after he is no longer hypnotized; he does not have to reenter hypnosis in order to carry out a simple posthypnotic suggestion. Were this position more widely adopted, we would no longer argue that the behavior of a hypnotized person does or does not depend on his being in a hypnotic trance. Instead, we would inquire as to the degree of hypnotic involvement necessary for the performance under study and the basic hypnotic talent required. Theoretically, the degree of involvement required would be stated according to the pervasiveness of the dissociations required.

REFERENCES

1. HILGARD, E. R. 1973. The domain of hypnosis, with some comments on alternative paradigms. Am. Psychol. **28:** 972–982.
2. HILGARD, E. R. & J. R. HILGARD. 1975. Hypnosis in the Relief of Pain. William Kaufmann, Inc. Los Altos, Calif.
3. HILGARD, E. R. & A. H. MORGAN. 1975. Heart rate and blood pressure in the study of laboratory pain in man under normal conditions and as influenced by hypnosis. Acta Neuro. Biol. Exp. (Warsaw). **35:** 741–759.
4. HILGARD, E. R. 1977. Divided Consciousness: Multiple Controls in Human Thought and Action. Wiley-Interscience. New York, N.Y. In press.

5. HILGARD, E. R. 1973. A neodissociation interpretation of pain reduction in hypnosis. Psychol. Rev. **80:** 396–411.
6. KNOX, V. J., A. H. MORGAN & E. R. HILGARD. 1974. Pain and suffering in ischemia: The paradox of hypnotically suggested anesthesia as contradicted by reports from the "hidden observer." Arch. Gen. Psychiat. **30:** 840–847.
7. HILGARD, E. R., A. H. MORGAN & H. MACDONALD. 1975. Pain and dissociation in the cold pressor test: A study of hypnotic analgesia with "hidden reports" through automatic key-pressing and automatic talking. J. Abnorm. Psychol. **84:** 280–289.
8. ORNE, M. T. 1972. On the simulating subject as a quasi-control group in hypnosis research: What, why and how. *In* Hypnosis: Research Developments and Perspectives. E. Fromm and R. E. Shor, Eds. : 399–443. Aldine-Atherton. Chicago, Ill.
9. ROBERTS, A. H., J. SCHULER, J. G. BACON, R. L. ZIMMERMAN & R. PATTERSON. 1975. Individual differences and autonomic control: Absorption, hypnotic susceptibility, and unilateral control of skin temperature. J. Abnorm. Psychol. **84:** 272–279.
10. COOPER, L. M. 1972. Hypnotic amnesia. *In* Hypnosis: Research Developments and Perspectives. E. Fromm and R. E. Shor, Eds. : 217–252. Aldine-Atherton. Chicago, Ill.
11. HILGARD, E. R. 1965. Hypnotic Susceptibility. Harcourt Brace Jovanovich. New York, N.Y.
12. SPANOS, N. P., N. CHURCHILL & J. D. MCPEAKE. 1976. Experiential response to auditory and visual hallucinations in hypnotic subjects. J. Consult. Psychol. **44:** 729–738.

HYPNOSIS RESEARCH AND THE LIMITATIONS OF THE EXPERIMENTAL METHOD

Lewis R. Lieberman

Psychology Department
Columbus College
Columbus, Georgia 31907

Five years ago I was invited to address a symposium on hypnosis organized by Dr. Edmonston. In preparation for my present paper, I reread that last effort.[1] In the parts of that paper that I can still understand, one thing stands out clearly; namely, my belief in the value of the experimental method.

In the past five years, I have been pondering by myself and with my philosopher friend, Dr. J. T. Dunlap, the nature of the experimental method. I have found what appear to be some rather severe limitations in the experimental method. My objective this afternoon is to describe to you these limitations as clearly as I can, and to show how the points apply to hypnosis research.

I don't mind telling you from the start that the findings I shall discuss are rather distressing to me. It has been my belief that psychology was in the business of understanding behavioral events and that such events were to be understood by the relating of other events to them in general causal statements. I believed that when such relations could be *experimentally* verified, one was as close as one could get to truth. I am no evangelist for experimentation; the point is that there are not any good alternatives. To believe in explanations based on tradition, majority opinion, or somebody's gut reaction seems unbearably tenuous.

I trust you know the feeling of comfort that faith in our methodology brings, so that you can sympathize with my own anxiety at having found faults in the very foundation of my discipline. I warn you in advance of my upset in hopes that you can supply some necessary therapy. I envision this therapy to be in either of two forms: either someone can explain to me that these limitations I have described are like Zeno's paradoxes—apparent but not real—or, if they are real, perhaps someone can help me follow them to their proper conclusions, a step which in my upset condition, I seem incapable of taking.

Let us begin by making sure that we understand what is meant by the experimental method. I think of an experiment in the behavioral sciences as a situation devised by some experimenter to test some general causal hypothesis about behavior. The hypothesis is usually of the form that says "such-and-such change in conditions will lead to [is sufficient for] such-and-such change in behavior." It is important for what follows to bear in mind that no one is interested in what particular subjects do. No one is particularly interested in the fact that Jane Doe fooled the experimenter into thinking she was hypnotized; what is important is how the results bear on the hypothesis being tested. Second, it is important to keep in mind the fact that the experimenter is in control of the conditions. This control allows the experimenter to be pretty sure that the changes that occur in the behavior are the result of his manipulation rather than some extraneous factor.

As an example, let us consider an experiment from social psychology. In this study by Aronson and Mettee,[2] the general hypothesis was that lowered self-esteem would cause cheating. (I have simplified the details of this study, for clarity.) Esteem was lowered by the reading of a phony report of a personality test, and cheating was measured by observing behavior in a game in which subjects thought that cheating would not be detected. Half the subjects were given a poor personality report, half were given a good report. Which subject got which treatment was determined randomly, so that results could not be attributed to any characteristic of the subjects. The general hypothesis received support when statistical analysis showed that significantly more persons in the low-esteem group cheated.

It is assumed in experiments that the experimental manipulation and the behavior being observed are fairly unambiguous. The rules for classifying conditions and behavior should be clear and objective, which results in the experiment's being replicable.

I hope at this point we have before us a clear idea of the behavioral experiment. I have tried to present it in a favorable light before analyzing its limitations. There are two limitations that are well-known, and that I shall mention briefly.

The first limitation stems from the fact that the hypothesis being tested is general and is about *all* members of a certain class of events. Since there is no way to gather all the members of a class in an experiment, and since what has happened before is never a guarantee about what will happen in the future, the hypothesis can never be absolutely certain. This kind of uncertainty I am willing to tolerate.

The second limitation to the experimental method is that it is a method of verification, rather than discovery. It is not a method for answering a question such as, what are the powers of hypnosis, or what can hypnosis do? Rather, one must propose an answer (e.g., hypnosis can cure insomnia) before the experimental method can be employed. It seeks to verify answers proposed, in itself it does not tell us where to get the answers.

THE PSYCHOMETRIC DILEMMA

Now I embark on less familiar territory. The first misgivings I had arose in a different context. In a paper I wrote called "The Psychometric Dilemma," [3] I set out to show that questions about whether blacks or whites were more intelligent could not be answered by standardized intelligence tests. I tried to show this by comparing the question to the question, "Which is more intelligent, males or females?" This question cannot be answered by standard IQ tests because any items that favor one sex or another are eliminated from the tests. Test-makers have decided that the sexes are not different in intelligence and regard as erroneous items that do not support this assumption. Similarly, a test-maker who assumes that the blacks and whites are not different in intelligence should rule out any items that suggest such differences, and there is no way to say that his test is any more or less valid than tests that do not conform to his assumption. Even a test-maker who does not find such items cannot be assured that such items do not exist.

Of course, the questions of whether color and sex are correlated with intelligence are not experimental questions, since one cannot manipulate sex or color at will and assign them randomly to subjects, but the psychometric dilemma faces any experiment in which behavior is measured by a test. An excellent recent example is the study of the "risky shift" phenomenon. It was discovered that after a group discussion, subjects tended to become less cautious in their answers to questions presumed to be assessing risk-taking tendencies. Aften ten years of research on this phenomenon, it was discovered that whether the change was toward risk or toward caution depended upon the items in the "test." One could, by a judicious selection of items, show a risky shift, a cautious shift, or no shift at all. (For a discussion of this, cf. Cartwright.[4])

One obvious application of the psychometric dilemma to hypnosis research is to the several tests of hypnotic susceptibility (Stanford, Harvard Group, Barber). Like an intelligence test, these scales have items that are supposed to be progressively more difficult. But why these particular items and not others which could easily be thought of or which have yet to be thought of? Thus, any studies (like those of Hilgard[5]) that compare scores on these scales with other traits are subject to criticism—actually on two counts, since there is probably no good defense for the items on the scale measuring the other variable which is being correlated with hypnotic susceptibility.

I hope this point is clear. Let me amplify one more time. Suppose that it is the pet hypothesis of some energetic researcher that because hypnotic performance requires imagination, there should be a correlation between hypnotic susceptibility and creativity, and that tests of these two variables should correlate positively. If, in fact, his research showed zero or negative correlation between such tests, then he could (based on his conviction) decide that one or the other of the tests is invalid and attempt to devise new tests that would satisfy his belief. This sounds like cheating, but it is the case that we cannot say whether he cou'd succeed, and if he did succeed, we could not say that his tests were worse than the original tests or better. The original tests were older, but that does not make them more valid.

I think that this psychometric viewpoint gives us an insight into Orne's[6] search for the essence of hypnosis. Research with the quasicontrol groups to uncover the essence of hypnosis is research looking for an item that could be on a susceptibility test and that would discriminate simulators from hypnotized subjects. For a while it was thought that the trance-logic-task (i.e., being told that someone who was seated behind you was seated alongside of you) would be such a task. Simulators would respond as if the subject were alongside them, while hypnotized subjects responded as if the person were in fact in both places. The object of having this task was to separate the two kinds of subjects, and I say that this is analongous to having a task on an IQ test which separates males from females.

EXPERIMENT OR DEMONSTRATION?

The next difficulty or set of difficulties that I discovered with the experimental method arose from some discussions I had with my student, Mr. Gary Peters, and culminated in our paper "Can or Does?"[7] As I recall, Peters and I were looking at some study, and I complained that that was no experiment, it was just a demonstration, and Peters wanted to know what the difference was and we tried to figure it out.

I don't recall what study we were even looking at at this time, but Rosenthal's studies on the so-called experimenter bias effect will do for an example. Barber and Silver have written at least two critiques [8, 9] of this work, but no amount of legitimate criticism can refute Rosenthal's position, since all he is saying is that an experimenter's expectations may bias his results. We always knew this. If Rosenthal's first ten experiments had failed to show this, he could have scored on the eleventh. He couldn't fail. But he is obviously not making the claim that these expectations *always* bias results, or then his own studies would be subject to doubt and he would be in a logical morass (like the barber who shaves all those and only those who do not shave themselves). The work on the Experimental Bias Effect has not given us anything that would allow us to predict or explain any results; it demonstrates, I say, what we already knew.

In trying to elucidate the distinction between experiment and demonstration, let us return to the basic definition of "experiment." Recall, we said that an experiment was a situation designed to test a general proposition of the sort "a change in X causes a change in Y." The verb in such a general statement implies an invariant relationship; that is, we mean that a change in X does invariably cause a change in Y. When it turns out that a particular experiment merely supports the proposition that a change in X can—or may—cause a change in Y, then we have a demonstration. Demonstrations are interesting, but of little explanatory power.

Here is the situation: the concepts in the hypothesis must be general to be of value. In the actual experiment the general concept must be realized in a particular way. This is usually called an operational definition, but this is a misnomer, for while it definitely specifies an operation, it is no definition. We are forced to focus on a single instance of the general condition specified in the hypothesis in order to do the experiment, but when we are through, we do not know that the results can be generalized to other instances of the conditions specified in the hypothesis.

To make this clearer, take the example used above of the experiment testing whether a lowering of self-esteem causes cheating. Low self-esteem was operationalized by giving subjects a fake report from a personality test. While I am easily willing to admit that this operation belongs to the class of operations that would lower self-esteem, how can we know that the results would generalize to the multitude of other operations that might reduce self-esteem? The point of the study is that the folks cheated because their self-esteem was lowered, that low self-esteem was the essential feature of the situation *qua* cheating. It is true that the investigators have instituted controls to make sure the result is not due to having had to take the test or simply to getting some kind of feedback, but from the viewpoint of subjects in the experimental condition, the operation of giving unpleasant feedback while having the characteristic of lowering self-esteem has other characteristics, too. It may be one of these that is causing the result. For example, such feedback might be insulting to the subjects who cheat for revenge; or the feedback may make them anxious and it is the anxiety-arousing feature that makes them cheat. Thus, if it is the insulting aspect which makes them cheat, then perhaps some condition that does not lower self-esteem but is insulting would make them cheat. If this were true, the hypothesis of the study would be false, even though the study seemed to support it.

In order for the operational definition to be acceptable, the investigators must assume that this particular situation is representative of all situations that lower self-esteem, an assumption for which there is no independent evidence. Therefore, this study constitutes a demonstration that lowered self-esteem can cause cheating, but surely not that it does so invariably; it does not even much increase the probability of the latter statement.

The same criticism is true in spades for the concept of cheating. Does the cheating in the experimental situation represent all cheating? It could represent merely cheating-when-you-know-you-are-not-going-to-get-caught, or cheating-when-getting-caught-has-no-ill-consequences, or cheating-when-the-issue-is-trivial. Perhaps if something important were in the balance, the subjects would not cheat no matter how terrible the personality report. In fact, the famous studies of Hartshorne and May,[10] that honesty is not a unitary trait (i.e., subjects who are honest in some situations will be dishonest in others and vice versa) seem good evidence for my contention. The burden of proof, however, is on the experimenters to show that their situation is representative of the general concept. I am not sure it can be shown.

In a sense the "Can or Does" issue and the "Psychometric Dilemma" are the same. In the latter case, I questioned how we could know that a given set of items was representative of the general variable that was supposed to be being measured, and in the former case we are asking how the single situation chosen to represent the experimental condition is representative and also how the behavior being observed is representative of that general concept for which *it* is supposed to stand. Cheating on that single game in the Aronson and Mettee study is a single-item test of cheating; how do we know another item with the same face validity would be responded to by subjects in the same way?

The most obvious application of the can-or-does criticism to hypnosis experiments has to do with the hypnotic-induction instructions. Many hypnosis experiments use a standard induction instruction, usually tape-recorded. Such a procedure is clearly an operational definition of hypnosis. There seems to me a very large question of whether we have any right to generalize conclusions from laboratory experiments with a recorded standard induction on college students to all hypnotic inductions in all situations. There is some evidence I know of, a study by Gur and Reyher,[11] in which they varied what they called the style of induction, in which differences attributable to induction instructions were found. In fact, it is surprising that there are not studies on the effects of different kinds of induction instructions, live vs. recorded, with-audience vs. without, in-office vs. in-laboratory, experienced vs. inexperienced operators, and so on.

An even more obvious example of this criticism comes from considering the generality of Barber's task-motivating instructions. Assuming that with respect to something like analgesia, in a laboratory setting task-motivation is as effective as hypnotic induction, would anyone be willing to expect that in a consulting-room situation the 60-second task-motivation would be equally effective?

THE ROLE OF CONTROL

I come to the final limitation I want to discuss. The point I want to make is developed in a paper by Dunlap and myself [12] entitled "The Role of Control in Psychological Experiments." The starting point for this paper, as I recall, was my posing for Dunlap the problem of the underlying logic of an experiment— a problem that didn't make any sense at all to Dunlap. I was able to clarify the question only after I discovered a paper by Boring [13] in which he talks about the experiment as following this logical model: From the experimental group results we can conclude "if X, then Y," and from the control group, we can conclude "if not X, then not Y," and the experiment as a whole allows us to conclude "X if and only if Y." In this model X is the independent variable and Y the dependent.

It is clear that even in the best experiment, where there are no exceptions, one cannot conclude that the independent variable is the necessary and sufficient condition for the dependent variable. If, for example, in some experiment all the hypnosis subjects showed some phenomenon and none of the controls showed it, we certainly could not conclude that this phenomenon can be produced *only* by hypnosis.

After much discussion and debate, we decided that in behavioral experiments, the independent variable is added on to an ongoing system, and the role of the control group is to assess the effects in this ongoing system—i.e., what would have happened without the introduction of the experimental factor? For example, in the low-esteem-cheating study, if we had only the data from the experimental group, we would know that subjects who had had their esteem lowered did in fact cheat a bit, but we wouldn't know that without the esteem-lowering operation they might not have cheated just as much. Therefore, the control group gives us an estimate of the forces already in the ongoing situation that might produce cheating.

Given this as the role of control, how might we express this in logical symbols? I suggested that we symbolize the ongoing situation as C (for control). Now the control group can be symbolized (1) "If C, then not-Y," and the experimental situation can be symbolized (2) "If C & X, then Y." And what we wish to conclude is (3) "If X, then Y"; that is, we wish to conclude that X is sufficient for Y, in our example, that lowering self-esteem is sufficient for cheating, but there might be other ways to induce cheating.

When we say we can conclude statement (3) above, we are asserting that with (1) and (2) as premises, (3) can be logically deduced. But, in fact, it cannot! This is a fundamental belief about experiments, that what the experimental subjects do that the controls do not is caused by the difference in treatment. This, in fact, is the kind of statement the experiment is designed to test. To discover that the experiment does not lead to this conclusion is startling. Perhaps the suggested symbolization is wrong. Maybe it is, but some reflection shows that this symbolization has provided an important insight.

The fact is that the experimental factor may indeed not be the cause of the result, but that the experimental factor interacting with something in the situation, a part of the ongoing system, may be causing the effect. For example, 60-second task-motivating instructions may be effective with college students in a laboratory, but may be considered absurd if used in the consulting office with paying, adult neurotics. I am suggesting that the task-motivating instructions interact with some characteristic of the laboratory situation to produce compliance; this factor is absent in the consulting office.

If my analysis is correct here, then I must conclude that all the Orne-type simulation studies and all the Barber-type task motivation studies are inadequate. In the simulator studies, the fact that the behavior of simulators is indistinguishable from the hypnotized subjects proves nothing. It shows, simply, as my landlady Mrs. Johns used to say, that there are more ways to choke a dog than on butter. Introducing a concept like "demand characteristics" is of no help to the logic of the situation. The simulators are presumably responding to these demand characteristics, but just because subjects exposed to an induction behave the same way does not logically prove that they, too, are responding to these "demands." They may be, but they may also not be. Let me reinforce this by an analogy. Two groups are responding to a paired associates list: when the experimenter presents the stimulus item, the subject gives the appropriate response item. One group has learned to do this by memorizing the list; the other group has the list written out in front of them. The performance is indistinguishable, but the manner of producing the behavior is much different.

The case with the Barber-type task-motivation study reduces to two subclasses. In some of these experiments, it is simply assumed that the "standard" induction instructions are task-motivating, and so the control group gets special task-motivating instructions, whereas the experimental group gets entirely different (hypnotic) instructions. This case is like the simulator case; similar outcome in no way proves similar causes. However, in some of the task-motivation studies, the experimental subjects are exposed to the identical task-motivating instructions as the controls after the hypnotic-induction instructions. Similar outcome here, however, does *not* prove similar cause, either, but the reason in this case is the possibility of interaction. Let me elaborate a little.

Barber has repeatedly criticized the trance concept on the grounds that there are no independent reliable signs of trance other than the hypnotic phenomena it is supposed to bring about, and that this presents a circular logic. The fact remains, however, that just because there is at present no independent criterion for trance, this does not rule out the possibility of such being found. Stated this way, my argument sounds petulant, but there is subjective evidence for postulating a trance state.

If, for the sake of argument, we assume that there is a state called "trance" and that this may be induced by a set of recorded hypnotic-induction instructions, then once the subject enters this state, he is no longer like the nonhypnotized person in the control group, and the effect of the task-motivating instructions on him may no longer be the same. In other words, the experimental factor may interact with some factors in the control situation.

IMPLICATIONS

I have now finished my catalogue of complaints against the experimental method. As I said before, I honestly wish someone would show me where I am wrong. In the meantime I have been trying to assess the impact of my indictment, and again I am most uncertain of what it all means.

One implication that I have toyed with is that in the behavioral sciences, experiments are used mostly for political purposes to gain followers and disciples for the experimenter. The experimenter is tolerated so long as he doesn't step on anybody's toes, so long as he doesn't challenge any vested interests. When this happens, there is a flurry of criticism of his experiments and attempts to carry out experiments that refute him. Since the experiments were never compelling to begin with, this is not difficult. Such is the situation in hypnosis when theorists who wish to uphold that hypnosis is nothing but [14] "role-taking" or "task motivation" buck the traditional view that it is a trance. We may have failed to reach a conclusion in this matter because the competing theories are too vague or because it is too soon, but it could also be that the experimental method is too weak ever to do the job.

In this view, the experimental method is seen as a conservative force, one used by the Establishment to fend off attack and also to keep behavioral scientists busy. I believe that this position is consonant with that of Kuhn [15] and clearly places psychology today in a preparadigmatic state.

An alternate kind of implication is that if the experimental method is weak, then what needs to be done is to strengthen it. An obvious example of the method being successful is the physical sciences. How come it works here? There are, of course, three answers to this question: one is that it really doesn't work there. This is Kuhn's answer: our experiments in the physical world are the result of our outlook on this world, and this outlook is subject to change called by Kuhn a "scientific revolution."

The second answer is that indeed there is something about the nature of the physical world that lends itself to experimental investigation: one gas is very much like another, as it turns out, and it is a feature of the physical world to be regular, hence our knowledge of it stated as regularities is satisfactory and adequate for our purposes. The human world, on the other hand, does not lend itself to such treatment because the nature of the human world is that it is infinitely variable and contains only those regularities which men impose.

The third answer is that the method can be fruitful in the behavioral sciences as soon as we work the kinks out of it. I, of course, do not see how the method can be repaired. My feeling about it is that if progress is to be made, it needs to happen in the conceptual sphere. We need concepts that will work out so that several demonstrations that X causes Y will allow us to believe it in general. We need it to be the case that when a set of items is supposed to measure some variable, we have some guarantee through some conceptual scheme that those items are representative of the domain covered by that variable.

As you can see, I am not on strong ground in discussing these implications.

As a final point, I think I should mention to you how this has effected me personally. I find that I have been going on conducting experiments even though I can see how noncompelling they are. Why am I doing this? In part, it is a kind of functional autonomy. In part, it is a suspicion that my reasoning is fallacious somewhere and will be shown up sooner or later. And finally, it is because I don't know what else to do.

REFERENCES

1. LIEBERMAN, L. R. 1972. Appropriate controls in hypnosis research. Am. J. Clin. Hypn. 13(4): 229–235.
2. ARONSON, E. & D. METTEE. 1968. Dishonest behavior as a function of different levels of self-esteem. J. Pers. Soc. Psychol. 9: 121–127.
3. LIEBERMAN, L. R. 1970. The psychometric dilemma: Psychological difference or item bias. Paper read at Southeastern Psychological Association Annual Convention.
4. CARTWRIGHT, D. 1973. Determinants of scientific progress: The case of research on the risky shift. Am. Psychol. 28(3): 222–231.
5. HILGARD, E. R. 1965. Hypnotic Susceptibility. Harcourt, Brace & World. New York, N.Y.
6. ORNE, M. T. 1959. The nature of hypnosis: Artifact and essence. J. Abnorm. Soc. Psychol. 58: 277–299.
7. LIEBERMAN, L. R. & R. G. PETERS. 1973. Can or does? An inquiry into the experimental method in psychology. Paper read at Southern Society for Philoso-

phy and Psychology Annual Convention. (A contribution to the Memorial Symposium for Richard M. Griffith.)

8. BARBER, T. X. & M. J. SILVER. 1968. Fact, fiction, and the experimenter bias effect. Psychol. Bull. Monogr. **70**(6) (part 2): 1–29.

9. BARBER, T. X. & M. J. SILVER. 1968. Pitfalls in data analysis and interpretation: A reply to Rosenthal. Psychol. Bull. Monogr. **70**(6) (part 2): 48–62.

10. HARTSHORNE, H. & M. A. MAY. 1928. Studies in Deceit. Macmillan. New York, N.Y.

11. GUR, R. E. & J. REYHER. 1973. Relationship between style of hypnotic induction and direction of lateral eye movement. J. Abnorm. Psychol. **82**: 499–505.

12. LIEBERMAN, L. R. & J. T. DUNLAP. 1976. The role of control in psychological experiments. Paper read at Southern Society for Philosophy and Psychology Annual Convention.

13. BORING, E. G. 1969. Perspective: Artifact and control. *In* Artifact in Behavioral Research. R. Rosenthal & R. L. Rosnow, Eds. Academic Press. New York, N.Y.

14. GORDON, J. E. 1967. Conclusions. *In* Handbook of Clinical and Experimental Hypnosis. J. E. Gordon, Ed. Macmillan. New York, N.Y.

15. KUHN, T. 1962. The Structure of Scientific Revolutions. University of Chicago Press. Chicago, Ill.

CLINICAL AND EXPERIMENTAL HYPNOSIS: IMPLICATIONS FOR THEORY AND METHODOLOGY

Joseph Reyher

Psychology Department
Michigan State University
East Lansing, Michigan 48823

The seemingly inexhaustible techniques of inducing hypnosis implies that the induction of hypnosis has nothing to do with the induction procedure *per se*, and that the gradual development of an alleged state of hypnosis is an illusion, an artifact of the induction procedure. This illusion is reinforced by the progression of item difficulty on standard susceptibility scales, and by the impression of increasing relaxation in the physical and facial appearance of subjects undergoing an induction. I will present evidence supporting the notion that the obtained enhancement of suggestibility is immediate. If this is indeed the case, then its enhancement must be obscured by the administration of the standard susceptibility scales. Another implication is that the trait theory underlying these scales is inappropriate; to wit, giving heterogeneous items equal weight when they do not all represent the same underlying system or function. Quite aside from this conceptual issue, these scales suffer from severe shortcomings with respect to item difficulty, which can lead to erroneous inferences regarding the nature of suggestibility or hypnosis. An alternative approach to the problem of measurement will be considered after I present some of the conceptual issues surrounding suggestibility and hypnosis.

My main argument, buttressed by hard data, is that suggestibility is increased simply upon the subject's adoption of a passive-receptive, open-minded attitude wherein she/he waits silently for instructions. Operationally, this assertion reduces to that of persons silently following instructions, whether this be systematic desensitization, biofeedback, acupuncture, implosive therapy, alpha feedback, TM, exorcism, faith healing, a physical examination by a physician, LeMaze and natural methods of training for childbirth, being born again, or a formal induction of hypnosis. The obvious methodological implication is that there is the same enhancement of suggestibility for waking-resting, simulating, and imagination-control groups. The assessment of suggestibility involves its enhancement, and the shared goals of the participants function as suggestions.

To explain this alleged enhancement of suggestibility, I have been exploring the explanatory value of the two disparate modes of information processing believed to characterize the two cerebral hemispheres. With respect to perception, the right cerebral hemisphere subjects different sources of sensory input to synthesizing Gestalt principles while under the modulating influence of the neural records of past perceptions. This influence is mediated by analogical functions * (seeing sameness in differences) along gradients of similarity (physical, functional, and qualitative). Fresh perceptions are effortlessly and

---

* Although the right cerebral hemisphere is incapable of expressive speech, it has retained receptive functions at least at the level of competence of childhood, before the lateralization of these functions was completed.

unconsciously synthesized and are characterized by such analogically based cognitions as recognition, familiarity, and novelty. Therefore, I find it advantageous to designate the joint effect of synthesizing principles and analogical functions as the analogic-synthetic mode of information processing. These synthesizing and analogical functions are otherwise known as condensation and displacement, respectively, and constitute the two main components of so-called primary process thinking in psychoanalytic theory.[27]

With respect to speech, the left cerebral hemisphere mediates a volitional and effortful selection of discrete bits (words) of information and arranges them in a particular order according to certain rules (syntax) for the purpose of communication. This represents an analog (potentials) to digital (words) conversion.† Unlike a perception or a visual image, a word is a vehicle of representation; it stands for something other than itself. A word is a symbol, which means that there is a semantic relationship obtaining between its graphic or phonetic structure and its referent (a natural or conceptual object). Differentiated meaning is determined by the syntactic ordering of words to form sentences. Gradients of similarity and Gestalt principles of organization are not involved; therefore, I find it advantageous to designate the joint operation of word meaning and sentence structure as the expressive semantic-syntactic mode of information processing. It can be either overt or covert. This is secondary process in psychoanalytic theory.

Listening, or the receptive semantic-syntactic mode of information processing, involves a digital to analogue conversion ‡ that must be mediated by

---

† The neuropsychological theorizing of Pribram,[1] which I have adopted, is complementary to these constructs. They represent another domain of theory which need not be tied to the psycholinguistic theory developed in the text. Although highly speculative, these constructs appear to possess redeeming heuristic value, as have earlier conceptual excursions of my own.[23] ". . . the view taken here is that the slow potential pattern 'computes' both the spatial neighborhood interactions among neural elements and, to some extent, the temporal interactions over a range of sites by a continuous (analogue) rather than a discrete, all-or-none (digital) mechanism." (p. 18)

"In short, nerve impulses arriving at junctions generate a slow potential microstructure. The design of this microstructure interacts with that already present by virtue of the spontaneous activity of the nervous system and its previous 'experience.' The interaction is enhanced by inhibitory processes and the whole procedure produces effects akin to the interference patterns resulting from the interaction of simultaneously occurring wave fronts. The slow potential microstructures act thus as analogue cross-correlation devices to produce new figures from which the patterns of departure of nerve impulses are initiated. The rapidly paced changes in awareness could well reflect the duration of the correlation process." (p. 105).

‡ The receptive, semantic-syntactic mode accomplishes a conversion of digital syntaxically distributed symbols into enduring configurations of slow potentials which immediately becomes integrated into the overall synthesis forged by the analogic-synthetic mode. One facet of this analogic-synthetic processing is the spontaneous visual imagery and affective experiencing that accompanies listening, particularly in response to story telling. Another facet is the spontaneous recall of past experiences as the records of past perception are reactivated by virtue of gradients of similarity and are incorporated into the ongoing synthesis. Listening is practically effortless if the words are concrete and the sentences are short. Under these conditions, the configuration of slow potentials generated by the receptive semantic-syntactic mode produces a flow of impulses to other cortical areas. In contrast, abstract words and complex sentences require the listener to retain denotative meanings of words, phrases, and clauses

a distinctive cortical area, as in expressive and receptive aphasia. Because listening and covert speech (analytical or critical thinking) represent disparate modes of semantic-syntactic information processing, they cannot proceed concurrently without some degree of interference (i.e., losing the thread of conversation; forgetting what one wanted to say). This interference is maximized, perhaps to the point of mutual exclusivity, during listening and overt speech. Fortunately, the two semantic-syntactic modes are not always reciprocally cueing and interfering: The receptive semantic-syntactic mode is not bound by reciprocal cueing for the individual who listens uncritically and silently. Consequently, a digital to analogue conversion (words to potentials) is mediated by the receptive semantic-syntactic mode and is incorporated into the ongoing synthesizing function of the analogic-synthetic mode which enables suggestions to influence perceptual, cognitive, and neurophysiological processes. Therefore, suggestibility is

---

until the sentence is complete and syntax provides the meaning of the sentence. Paying attention is effortful and analytic, thereby sustaining the expressive semantic-syntactic mode. When listening and speaking are articulated, as in conversation, they serve as the matrix or substrate for each other. In a sense, their energies are bound, which means that the slow potential microstructure generated by the input of the receptive semantic-syntactic mode is not incorporated into the ongoing, overall synthesizing function of the analogic-synthetic mode. This binding of energy is also true while a person is engaged in critical, covert thinking and analytic listening. Thus, the increase in suggestibility produced by prolonged sensory deprivation [24] may result from the breakdown of the reciprocal innervation between the receptive and expressive semantic-syntactic modes. I owe these refinements in theory to Maria Della Corte at Michigan State University. The expressive semantic-syntactic mode has the opposite task. It must accomplish an analogue (meaning) to digital (language) conversion. Meaning is considered to be a configuration of slow potential microstructure that can become a macrostructure (CNV) under certain circumstances involving motility. A microstructure is created by specific intentions and drives. Like the dynamic schematizing activity of Werner and Kaplan,[25] meaning is a cortical sensory-motor and affective anlage, which includes Broca's area. However, because of the digital nature of words, only one facet of an anlage can be represented at a time by the expressive semantic-syntactic mode, although a sentence may include several facets. For example, words are seldom sufficient vehicles of meaning, particularly the affective component, between lovers, during bereavement, and other affective states. Since the affective quale associated with the anlage is particularly difficult to represent linguistically,[2] the universal appeal of poetry and ballads can be better understood. Their appeal lies in the abrogation (poetic license) of precise criteria for denotative reference, the suspension of grammatical rules, and, with the addition of rhyme, rhythm, melody, and dance, the individual experiences the contours of the sensory-motor-affective anlage, rather than cognitively understanding and communicating discrete facets of the anlage. The repetition involved in these more discursive vehicles recruits limbic system long circuiting and intensifies sensory-motor and affective input into the psychic experience. Expressive behavior (facial expression, gesture, carriage, tone of voice) are shaped by this anlage, and it may even be responsible for dreams and other constitutive marks of Freud's dynamic unconscious. The expressive mode is an active, intentional, effortful, encoding process which involves sensory-motor servomechanisms, particularly proprioceptive feedback from the articulators. Drives and intentions activate an anlage of meaning, and incipient muscle movements constitute the digital, linear substrate for the conversion from an analogue to linguistic (digital) vehicles. If this is the case, then a paralysis of the neuromuscular apparatus for speech should eliminate all expressive, semantic-syntactic functions, including implicit thinking, writing, and typing.

increased whenever there is a cessation in either the covert or overt expression of the expressive semantic-syntactic mode of information processing.

Clinical observation [16, 26] indicates that there may be even a further increase in suggestibility beyond that realized by the cessation of the expressive semantic-syntactic mode. This happens under circumstances when people face a threat to their physical well-being or life, and they lack the skills to diagnose and to treat their affliction. This insufficiency of the requisite skills produces acute anxiety, which, in turn, pressures the helpless individual into a passive-dependent relationship with the attending physician.[3] I contend that this dependency striving [4] is the critical psychodynamic factor that is instrumental in producing the impressive results of suggestion in the clinical, particularly medical, setting. I also will present both hard and soft data in support of my argument, but before I do, I want to identify the putative dimensions on the basis of which patients in medical hypnosis differ from subjects undergoing hypnosis for research purposes.

Purpose of Hypnosis. The manifest purpose of the hypnosis is determined by either one of the two participants. In the medical situation, patients seek out the physician for professional consultation and intervention. In a crisis situation, their need for help is immediate, and a physician is summoned on their behalf. Since the patient is objectively dependent, dependency strivings are likely to be activated. In contrast, the scientific investigator is the one seeking out subjects to help him/her gather data.

Setting of the Induction. The medical and laboratory settings are obviously different in a variety of ways. The medical situation usually is distinguished by being housed in a professional building. In addition, there are other waiting patients, there are intermediaries between the patient and the physician, and there are all the impressive accoutrements of the medical profession. These facets of the medical situation tend to stimulate two major reactions in patients: 1) anxiety concerning the actual or potential significance of one's physical condition, and 2) the hope that one's condition will be cured or at least ameliorated. Both these facets foster the development of dependency strivings. By contrast, the psychological setting is more likely to create awe, if it is well equipped, and apprehension stemming from the personal threat posed by hypnosis *per se* and by the experimental procedures. Dependency strivings are not fostered.

The Hypnotist. The credentials of physicians and laboratory investigators most often differ; one is a healer and the other is a scientist. The physician tends to be paternalistic and authoritative, and readily assumes responsibility for the welfare of individuals. All of this encourages the development of dependency strivings in the patient. In contrast, the laboratory investigator presents the individual with a circumscribed task and does not assume responsibility for the treatment of anything. Dependency strivings are not encouraged.

Anxiety. The source of anxiety is different for laboratory and medical hypnosis. In the laboratory situation with volunteer subjects, the personal implications of hypnosis are anxiety-producing for some individuals and may be intense enough to interfere with suggestibility.[4, 5] Anxiety has the opposite effect in the medical situation because it pressures the afflicted individual into entering a passive-dependent relationship with the attending physician.[3]

Dependency Strivings.

As I previously mentioned, dependency strivings may play a critical role in the further enhancement of suggestibility, and the foregoing factors contribute to its development. Whether or not the individual develops dependency strivings in his/her relationship with the hypnotist can be operationally defined as behavior furthering caretaking behavior on the part of the hypnotist, such as unquestioning compliance, approval seeking questions, placating comments, ego-boosting comments, lack of initiative, and so on.

Summary and Integration

To summarize integratively, medical patients are anxious about their physical plight and cannot help themselves. They are objectively dependent. For some of them, their objective dependency will develop into dependent strivings that are encouraged by the demeanor of the physician and his/her significance as a helping authority. These strivings are reinforced by the treatment connotations of the medical building itself and in a variety of other ways, including difficulty in getting an appointment, sitting in the waiting room with other patients, relating to the physician through intermediaries (nurses), being given prescriptive advice, and the patient's own ideas' being dismissed or discounted.

The volunteer subject for experimental investigations is likely to be motivated by curiosity, money, or credit points, and is not objectively dependent. Anxiety, if present at all, is associated with the personal threat posed by the hypnotic induction procedure. Should dependency strivings be present, they are not encouraged by the demeanor of the hypnotist who generally uses a standardized scale of hypnotic susceptibility. Neither are dependency strivings reinforced by the connotative significance of the hypnotist (who often is a graduate student), nor the setting (often an unimpressive laboratory room).

RELEVANT RESEARCH

In order to test whether the induction procedure is necessary to enhance suggestibility, any induction *whatsoever* must be eliminated, and all preliminary remarks should be kept to an absolute minimum. Josephine Pottinger and I did just this with the Harvard Group Scale of Hypnotic Susceptibility, Form A (HGSHS:A) and found no decrement in the pass percentages of the items (n = 31) as compared to the standard administration of the scale (n = 59). In the light of a growing body of research,[4] this should surprise no one.

In order to answer the question whether the progressive development of suggestibility (or hypnosis) is an illusion due to the increasing difficulty of the items on susceptibility scales, the order of their presentation must be reversed or randomly determined. In an unpublished investigation,[6] I attempted to answer this question and a variety of others. Data on changed orders of item administration was obtained while using our own scale of suggestibility. I developed this scale in order to eliminate the shortcomings of the Stanford and Harvard Scales. The new instrument, of which there are two forms, included the same items as these scales but substituted a uniform format to eliminate

sources of confounding with respect to item difficulty caused by variations in
the phrasing of the items. For convenience I refer to them as Michigan State
Suggestibility Profiles (MSSP). One form is entirely semantic (MSSP:S),
since it does not include any imaginal props. The other form (MSSP:I) includes
visual props on all the items.§ There was no formal induction whatever, and
only brief preliminary remarks were made to the groups of subjects before the
administration of the scale. When the order of item presentation was changed
in a variety of ways, including a reversal, order of presentation did not influence
the pass percentages of the items, and there were no contingencies between
items. The pass percentages for the items were the same at the beginning as at
the end of the scale. This outcome supports the hypothesis that the enhancement of suggestibility is immediate, not progressive. Furthermore, the psychological impact of passing or failing does not influence the subject's performance
on subsequent items.

Item Difficulty

The illusion of a progressive development of suggestibility also is furthered
by spurious indices of item difficulty. I was first alerted to this by obtaining a
pass percentage of 87 for Arm Immobilization on a modified version [7] of the
HGSHS:A. This finding was highly discrepant from the pass percentages of
14 and 48 for this item on the SHSS:A and HGSHS:A, respectively. A comparison of the wording of this item on the modified version with its wording
on the two standard scales revealed the reason for this discrepancy. Both the
Stanford and Harvard scales include an explicit countersuggestion to an implied
catalepsy, "But perhaps in spite of being so heavy, you could lift it a little."
Some good subjects are likely to comply and therefore fail the item.

Uncontrolled sources of variance confounding item difficulty (pass percentages) on the Stanford and Harvard scales are as follows: (1) inconsistency in
phrasing the desired effect; (2) extraneous contingencies, that is, a suggestion
extraneous to the desired effect upon which it is dependent, such as posthypnotic
suggestion being dependent on the development of an amnesia; (3) variation
in whether the desired effect is presented as weak suggestions, strong sugges-

---

§ An illustration of the same item from each form of the MSSP is given below:
Hand Lowering (form S). "Now I want you to lift your left arm straight out in
front of you with the palm of your hand down. You will notice that your arm is
becoming heavy." After five seconds say, "Your arm is becoming heavier and heavier
and soon it will be too heavy to keep up even though you will try. I'm going to
count from one to ten and by the count of ten your arm will be very heavy, so very
heavy you will not be able to keep it up." After each count say, "Heavy, getting
heavier." After the count of ten say, "That's fine, you can stop trying now, just relax."
Hand Lowering (form I). "Now I want you to lift your left arm straight out in
front of you with the palm of your hand down. You will notice that your arm is becoming heavy." After five seconds have elapsed say, *"Imagine in your mind's eye a
weight's pulling your arm down.* Your arm is becoming heavier and heavier and
soon it will be too heavy to keep up. I am going to count from one to ten and by the
count of ten your arm will be very heavy, so very heavy that you will not be able to
keep it up even though you will try." After each count say, *"Imagine in your mind's
eye that a weight is pulling your arm down,* arm heavy; getting heavier." After the
count of ten, say, "That's fine, you can stop trying now, just relax."

tions, or indirect suggestions; (4) the fact that challenges to break motor suggestions are not always given, directly or indirectly; (5) in one case (Arm Immobilization) immobilization implied in the challenge rather than directly suggested; (6) in one case (hallucination of a fly HGSHS:A), inclusion of an affective reaction (annoyance); (7) variation in the use of imaginal props, such as "eyes tightly glued shut," in an attempt to potentiate the desired effect.¶ These spurious indices of item difficulty also permit erroneous conclusions to be drawn from factor analysis as well as give the illusion of a progressive increase of suggestion, or, in terms less susceptible to operational definition, a progressive deepening of hypnosis. To eliminate the seven sources of confounding, all the items of the MSSP follow the same format. The only difference among them is the wording of the target behavior for the suggestion.

TABLE 1

ITEM-BY-ITEM COMPARISON OF MSGSHS:V AND HGSHS:A

Item	MSSP:S N=110	HGSHS:A N=59	χ^2	p
Head Fall	75	73		
Eye Closure	38	71	16.80	.001
Hand Lowering	75	85		
Arm Immobilization	71	34	21.54	.001
Finger Lock	75	54	6.45	.02
Arm Rigidity	73	57	4.01	.05
Moving Hands	76	64	3.74	.10 *
Comm. Inhibition	77	44	18.93	.001
Hallucination (fly)	25	27		
Eye Catalepsy	74	51	8.94	.001
Posthypnotic Sug.	25	22		
Amnesia †	50	32	4.89	.05

* χ^2 for p < .05 is 3.84.
† Pass percentages of 51 (n=299) and 35 (n=278) were obtained for males and females, respectively. This difference was significant, $\chi^2(1)=16.29$, p < .001. This was the only sex difference on the twelve items.

MSSP:S vs. HGSHS:A

When the items of the MSSP:S (n = 110) and HGSHS:A (n = 59) were compared (TABLE 1), the pass percentages were generally larger on the MSSP:S. Eight of these differences were significant at the .05 level. As expected, Arm Immobilization had a high pass percentage (71).

¶ The imaginal props included in MSSP:I failed to increase the pass percentages (MSSP:I vs. MSSP:S). Thus, supplemental, goal-directed fantasies [8] do not increase suggestibility beyond that level attained by purely linguistically phrased suggestions.

Kinetic and Static Items: Eyes Open vs. Eyes Closed

The wide variation in pass percentages (TABLE 2) with the subjects' eyes open was striking. The pass percentages of some items were grossly reduced, whereas others were not affected at all. Those items that involve kinetic ideomotor effects (Head Fall, Hand Lowering, Moving Hands) were dramatically reduced in pass percentage in comparison with those items involving static or inhibitory ideomotor effects (Arm Immobilization, Finger Lock, Arm Rigidity, Catalepsy). This disparity in pass percentages between kinetic and static items can be resolved on the basis of differences in the saliency of cues available to the subject in retrospectively scoring pass or fail in the self-scoring booklet. At the time that subjects with eyes closed are experiencing some suggested ideomotor effect on a kinetic item, they have no way of knowing whether they passed or failed, and they have only the faded memory of

TABLE 2

PERCENTAGES OF SUBJECTS PASSING THE EYES OPEN AND
CLOSED MANIPULATIONS ON MSSP:S

	Eyes Closed		Eyes Open				
	N	%	N	%	diff.	χ^2	p
Head F.	276	75.0	301	56.5	20.4	21.87	.001
Eye C.			577	50.0			
Hand L.	276	69.2	301	43.2	26.0	39.57	.001
Arm I.	276	63.4	301	58.4	4.6	1.48	n.s.
Finger L.	286	77.9	291	73.9	4.0	1.34	n.s.
Arm R.	376	72.6	201	73.6	−1.0	.06	n.s.
Moving H.	276	73.9	301	79.5	24.4	36.02	.001
Comm. I.	276	75.0	301	69.8	10.2	1.94	n.s.
Hal.	376	22.9	201	12.4	10.5	9.18	.01
Eye C.	577	65.9					
Post. S.	376	31.4	201	27.9	3.5	.77	n.s.
Amnesia	376	43.8	201	41.8	2.0	.21	n.s.

proprioceptive cues which most probably are an unreliable basis for making estimates of distance. In contrast, the static items provide immediate highly salient proprioceptive feedback. Even a little movement signals failure of the suggested inhibition. In these instances, many subjects undoubtedly must be surprised afterwards when they read the scoring criteria and discover that they might have passed the item after all. Although they once again must match a faded memory of proprioceptive cues with distance, the distance of movement is comparatively small and more easily estimated.

As a result of the inherent ambiguity in retrospectively scoring kinetic items on the basis of proprioceptive cues, more subjects than not probably will give themselves the benefit of the doubt and score a pass. In the eyes-open condition, however, the degree of ambiguity for kinetic items is materially reduced by the subject's utilization of visual cues. The incorporation of the more objective visual cues into available scoring criteria drastically reduces the pass percentages.

Since static items are not as dependent upon visual cues, they are not as affected by the eyes-open condition as are the kinetic items. In fact, a small movement may be proprioceptively salient but visually imperceptive. Social facilitation in a group induction could not produce this differential effect.

Manipulating Suggestibility: Disengaging the Semantic-Syntactic Mode

The term "suggestibility" is abused whenever anyone uses it as an explanatory term. For example, in two reviews [9, 10] of systematic desensitization, the effects of the procedures are attributed to suggestion or expectancy. These terms do not have scientific status unless their antecedent conditions are known and they are susceptible to manipulation. Wilson [11] accomplished this when he examined the relationship between a passive-receptive attitude and enhanced suggestibility. He constituted three different groups, each characterized by an alleged passive-receptive attitude. Operationally, this simply means that the subjects were silent and carried out instructions. The three groups were: (1) sitting silently while waiting for instructions; (2) directed visual imagery; and (3) silently observing spontaneous visual imagery (free imagery). All the subjects were told that the research involved attention and vigilance. The group means were not expected to differ from each other and from a fourth baseline group which received a formal induction of hypnosis because of the putative disengagement of the semantic-syntactic mode. These groups all were compared to a fifth group wherein the semantic-syntactic mode was engaged. This was accomplished by instructing the subjects to verbalize their free imagery. Suggestibility for the five groups was assessed by presenting virtual (nonexistent) stimuli. The subjects signaled by raising their right hand when they experienced increased brightness through their eyelids, when they heard the song "White Christmas," felt the room get warmer, smelled ammonia, felt their chair tilt, felt their chair vibrate, felt a feather drawn across the back of their hand, and felt their left arm and hand become numb as a result of the experimenter's pressing a "special" nerve in their left shoulder. They also were given an amnesia for these "events" and a posthypnotic suggestion that the room lights would dim.

As expected, the means of the three passive-receptive groups did not differ from one to another nor from the baseline hypnotic induction (4.06). Their means ranged from 3.81 (free imagery) to 5.06 (passive waiting). However, the base line group was significantly greater than the mean (2.13) of the linguistically engaged group. These results were replicated by Robin Hughes using a counterbalanced, within-subjects design involving a comparison between just the silent free imagery and verbalized free imagery conditions. The possibility of anxiety upon verbalizing free imagery having been a confounding variable was discounted by the fact that the state anxiety scores between the two conditions were equivalent.

Not only are these results consistent with the argument that a passive-receptive attitude is associated with an enhancement of suggestibility, but it is the first time, to my knowledge, that conditions for manipulating suggestibility have been identified. Only now is it legitimate to explain phenomena in terms of suggestion or expectancy as did Kadzin and Wilcoxon [9] with respect to the effects of systematic desensitization. If the procedures of a given laboratory investigation or treatment mode require the subject or patient to follow instructions silently, suggestibility should increase. I prefer to conceptualize this enhancement of suggestibility as resulting from a disengagement of the expressive semantic-syntactic mode of information processing. This is what is involved in laboratory investigations of hypnosis.

The results of a recent investigation by Smyth [5] at Michigan State University can be interpreted in this way. He showed that attention (accuracy of signal detection) to two types of stimuli gradually decreased for highly suggestible subjects as the administration of the SHSS:A progressed, but that attention could rebound to baseline level without influencing suggestibility. These results were obtained by a modified attention-controlling method of induction developed by Ruben Gur.[12, 13] The subjects listened to a taped induction of the SHSS:A over one earphone of a headset and sequences of digits over the other earphone. A painless electric shock was administered to the subjects whenever they failed to press a button upon hearing the word "relax." They were also instructed to press the button whenever they heard double digit numbers pronounced by the experimenter who was physically present. Only the highly suggestible subjects experienced progressively increasing errors to both the pronunciation of "relax" and double-digit numbers as the induction proceeded. They showed diffuse attention. Relatively nonsuggestible subjects showed increasing errors to digits only. They showed a concentration of attention on the hypnotist's words. For both low- and high-suggestibility groups, attention rebounded to the initial base line level with the administration of the first item and at least one subsequent item. If a gradual diffusion of attention were a parameter of gradual increase in suggestibility, then the subjects certainly lost it upon being given the first item. Thus, the diffusion of attention for highly suggestible subjects may simply indicate whether the expressive semantic-syntactic mode is disengaged and rebounds reflect an orienting response.

The discrepancy in attention between "relax" and double digits for the nonsuggestible subjects might reflect the continual engagement of the expressive semantic-syntactic mode of the left cerebral hemisphere due to covert, critical or analytical thinking. (See Footnote †.) This inference also is consistent with the relatively greater amplitude of the alpha rhythm associated with the right cerebral hemisphere of highly suggestible subjects [14] and the tendency for suggestibility to be correlated with increasing lateralization of cerebral functions.[15] The putative disengagement of the expressive semantic-syntactic mode of highly suggestible subjects is consistent with the frequently cited observation that hypnotized subjects speak slowly and laboriously, are very literal in their understanding of instructions, lack a sense of humor, and are seemingly uncritical of illogicalities.

Anxiety and Reduced Suggestibility

Two investigations are relevant to the anxiety-producing properties of a hypnotic induction and its effect on suggestibility.

Reyher and Wilson [4] reported that a progressive relaxation procedure significantly increased the GSR frequency and the variance of susceptibility scores when it was designated as a hypnotic induction procedure. The inference drawn from this was that some subjects were made anxious by the personal implications of the term "hypnosis" whereas others were excited by the implication of adventure. Smyth [5] also reported that state anxiety scores were significantly and negatively correlated with suggestibility during the attention-controlled procedure. In both investigations, the induction of hypnosis appears to be the primary source of anxiety.

Manipulating Suggestibility: Anxiety-Driven Dependency Strivings

Field reports [16, 17] show that persons rendered helpless through injury or wounds experience an increase in suggestibility. Quite unwittingly, it appears that one laboratory paradigm for increasing suggestibility approximates the field or medical paradigm. As noted previously in discussing Smyth's investigation, Ruben Gur [12, 13] was the first to develop the attention-controlling method of induction, and he succeeded in enhancing the suggestibility of nonsuggestible subjects. Unlike Smyth, however, he used a very painful electric shock upon the hypnotist's utterance of the word "relax." In these investigations, anxiety was apparent in the behavior of many of the subjects, yet this attention-controlling procedure increased suggestibility instead of decreasing it as would be expected if the source of anxiety were the personal threat posed by hypnosis itself. However, he also found that this increase in suggestibility occurred *only* when the experimenter was physically present in the room. The physical presence of the experimenter is a necessary condition. On the level of empirical constructs, there appears to be a relationship between the threat of painful shock and the physical presence of the hypnotist. This finding is complemented by Smyth's finding that painless shock and the physical presence of the hypnotist resulted in a *decrease* in suggestibility relative to a control group which did not receive painless shock. Unlike Ruben Gur,[12] he did not observe behavioral manifestations of anxiety in his subjects. Smyth's observations are buttressed by two other sources of data: (1) the intensity of shock was judged by his subjects to be painless; (2) the mean state anxiety scores for these subjects were the same as control subjects who did not receive shock. If Gur's threat of painful shock does, in fact, intensify dependency strivings, these could be actualized only when the experimenter was physically present. In the experimenter-absent condition, subjects must rely on their own coping mechanisms. Clearer support for this conclusion must await a replication of Smyth's and Gur's results with the inclusion of operational definitions of dependency strivings.

One interpretation of these findings is that the source of anxiety stems from the prospect of pain, not the induction of hypnosis *per se*. It is also important that all of Gur's subjects received some shock, probably due to fluctuations in attention, thereby producing an element of inevitability and helplessness. If this inference is true, then this laboratory procedure is congruent with the medical situation wherein the client's physical condition is the source of anxiety and the instigator of helplessness and dependency strivings. Consequently, there should be added pressure for subjects to enter a passive-dependent relationship with the experimenter and therefore manifest another increase in suggestibility.

In an investigation including both laboratory and clinical features, Allison Stern [28] found that female volunteers for research involving the enhancement of sexual arousal had group mean susceptibility scores on the Stanford scales substantially higher than the standardization groups. I attribute this presumed heightened suggestibility to a blend of anxiety, hope, and confidence in the therapist-experimenters. An enhancement of sexual arousal was achieved.

Implications for Theory

The foregoing laboratory investigations and clinical observations suggest that a viable theory of suggestibility must include: (1) constructs characterizing interpersonal relationships that foster the adoption of a passive-receptive attitude; (2) constructs identifying the sources of anxiety and dependency strivings; (3) constructs specifying the defenses, and security operations || generated by the anxiety and dependency strivings, and determining the effect of these on suggestibility (e.g., intellectualization and obsessions should reduce suggestibility because they are mediated by the expressive semantic-syntactic mode, whereas hysterical defenses should increase suggestibility because they are mediated by the analogic-synthetic mode.[2] For the same reason, the security operations of "Being a Know-it-All" and "Disparagement" should be associated with low suggestibility, whereas "Instant Compliance" should be associated with high suggestibility); (4) constructs relating modes of information processing to cortical structures and functions; (5) constructs relating modes of information processing to type of defense and security operation; (6) constructs specifying how suggestion influences cognitive, perceptual, and neurophysiological processes, and which specify the limits of suggestibility.

My own integration at the moment is as follows. In terms of empirical constructs, there is a two-step increase in suggestibility. The first occurs as a function of silently carrying out instructions. This one-sided or asymmetrical relationship exists only by agreement in socially or personally sanctioned circumstances. Ordinarily, interpersonal relationships are two-way or complementary, and any attempt by one participant to convert it to an asymmetrical relationship is opposed by the other because of his/her defenses and security operations. Commonplace, sanctioning circumstances include the physical examination by a physician, biofeedback, instruction by a guru (TM), acupuncture, the formal induction of hypnosis, and so on. In terms of theoretical constructs, the moment a passive-receptive attitude is adopted, the expressive semantic-syntactic modes of the left cerebral hemisphere are suspended, their reciprocal cueing ceases, and the analogic-synthetic mode incorporates the instructions—via the receptive semantic-syntactic mode—of the attending person into its own synthesizing functions. This separation of modes of information processing may occur to the extent that the individual's brain is lateralized. Since lower levels of neural integration are analogic-synthetic, there is increased control over perception and some local neurophysiological processes.**

|| Sullivan[2, 18] originated the term "security operation" to designate tactics employed by an individual in order to maintain self-esteem in an interpersonal encounter, e.g. disparagement, boasting, name dropping, and so on.

** Of course, any attempt to explain the clinical documentation of specific or local effects of a suggestion (warts) is patently speculative. Nevertheless, I shall proceed because of the possible heuristic value of such speculations. Spoken words of the hypnotist produce a slow potential microstructure (having both spatial and temporal dimensions) which constitutes their meaning (the receptive, semantic-syntactic mode). This slow potential microstructure is just one contribution to an overall, ongoing synthesis involving the concurrent input of all the sensory modalities and the matching of these against records of past perceptions, all of which serve the adaptive purpose of forging new perceptions to represent veridically the immediate situation. Aspects of this overall synthesis of microstructures are reproduced at lower levels of integration. Thus, if a word denoting a body part is embedded in this synthesis, that body part is

When the induction of hypnosis is the source of anxiety, analytical and critical functions of the expressive semantic-syntactic mode are engaged (this is an active, analytical attitude) and suggestibility is low. If, however, the source of anxiety is one's physical plight or the state of one's soul, which would require a clergyman or faith healer, dependency strivings develop in anyone who does not have the requisite skills for self-help and whose personality does not oppose relating to another person in terms of these dependency strivings. The anxiety, helplessness, and dependency strivings are encouraged by a paternal, caretaking attitude on the part of physicians [4] or their spiritual counterparts, and are reinforced by the connotative significance of their credentials and the setting. This complex of interpersonal and intrapsychic stimuli reactivate early childhood perceptions or reminiscences of omniscient parents who pick them up, change diapers, kiss away hurts, put food in their mouths, and do other marvelous things such as talk, sing, and play music. (Freud [20] called this a regressive transference, which, for him, was a complete definition of hypnosis.) I assume further that the innervation of the cortical and subcortical structures, and their associated brain mechanisms, underlying the reactivation of early childhood reminiscences, have a powerful influence over perception and bodily functions. This influence accounts for the augmentation of suggestibility seen in patients in medical situations and some subjects in laboratory hypnosis who readily enter into a passive-dependent relationship, if they feel safe under the circumstances.

Hilgard [21] has presented frequency distributions consistent with the two-step

---

affected by changes in whatever neurophysiological processes are regulated by that level. Each level controls different processes or is involved in a different aspect of regulation. In fact, a microstructure may not be reproduced unless it can be utilized. Perhaps a lock-and-key paradigm is appropriate. An obvious objection to this explanation is that lower levels of neural integration are patently unable to interpret the meaning of the slow potential microstructure that is reproduced. However, the body schema (image) may enable this type of mediation to take place because it may have linguistic as well as perceptual and somesthetic components. This would not be surprising because limited receptive and expressive, semantic-syntactic functions already are present early in infancy, and the body of the infant becomes a source of great interest and exploration. Since body parts are named while the infant looks at them, moves them, and touches them under varying conditions, it is reasonable to suppose that naming contributes to the development of a body image. Since the body image [18] is a widespread collection of structures that includes the occipital lobe, the thalamus, and spinal projections, a reproduction of a linguistic slow potential microstructure at lower levels of neural integration becomes a possibility. If the particular vehicles are concrete words, then changes in local neurophysiological processes may be affected. There are several immediate implications of this speculative neurophysiological explanation of the centrifugal, cortical mechanisms mediating local suggested effects: (1) those body parts most observable and in the focus of an infant's attention should be most responsive to local suggested effects in the adult (this includes the hands, feet and male genitals, but not the back of the neck); (2) suggestions phrased in the first learned language of bilingual adults should be more effective; (3) local effects in an adult should be increased by repeating the name of a body part of area while touching it, moving it, and looking at it. The alleged enhancement of suggestion under circumstances of anxiety-driven dependency strivings is "explained" by the additional corticofugal neural pathways provided by limbic system involvement and/or by the potentiation of all the pathways participating in the body image. One correlate of limbic system involvement is the reactivation of reminiscences of omnipotent parents.

theory of suggestibility. When the SHSS, forms A and B, are combined and the scores plotted against frequency, a bimodal curve emerges which suggest that two separate populations or phenomena are being measured. Could it be that the first distribution ($\overline{X} = 8.07$; n = 96.5) is generated by the cessation of the expressive semantic-syntaxic mode, and that the second distribution ($\overline{X} = 20.00$; n = 27.5) reveals the substantial increase in suggestibility due to the development of dependency strivings and the reactivation of reminiscences of omnipotent parents (a regressive transference)?

The early literature of hypnosis was generated by practitioners of medicine who treated medically naïve, poorly educated patients and who should have readily entered into a passive-dependent relationship with the physician. Many early practitioners [22] simply used hand passes or discrete stimuli to produce immediately the alleged trance. In modern warfare, even the sophisticated, highly trained soldier requires no induction for the immediate enhancement of suggestibility. Perhaps we should reserve the term "hypnosis" only for inductions that engage dependency strivings. Suitable operational definitions based on the subjects' behavior can be easily formulated. Recall that I gave a few examples earlier. The battlefield physician needs only to say, "I'm a doctor. I will help you. I will count from one to twenty and you will feel secure and sleepy." [26]

Anxiety-driven defenses and self-protective mechanisms deriving from the personal implications of hypnosis are the critical factors delaying or preventing the adoption of a passive-receptive attitude or passive-dependent strivings. A delay reinforces the illusion of a progressive increase in suggestibility (or deepening of hypnosis), and the variety of ways of reducing anxiety gives the impression that there are multiple pathways to hypnosis. The reduction of anxiety takes time and must be of sufficient degree before defenses and security operations mediated by the semantic-syntactic mode can be relinquished. All of this means that we must devise methods and procedures for making systematic observations in clinical settings to further a scientific understanding of the effects produced by hypnotic induction procedures or outright suggestions.

An Alternative to the Trait Model of Hypnotic Susceptibility

The standard scales of hypnotic susceptibility are tied to the trait model. Hypnotic susceptibility is a trait or an ability, and each item is an equal measure of this ability. However, some of the items reflect the involvement of different neuropsychological or psychophysiological systems, with some more easily influenced than others. Some of these items reflect discontinuous psychodynamic and biological mechanisms. A given defense mechanism may be in evidence only when anxiety reaches a given threshold point of intensity, or a given security operation is needed only under certain interpersonal circumstances, or anxiety-producing affects and impulses are aroused only under certain conditions and not others, or a given symptom is manifested only in relation to specific affects and particular defenses under circumscribed conditions. The relevant phenomena are discontinuous or they operate in an all-or-none, on-or-off fashion for a given individual. Although each phenomenon, such as the defense of projection, varies in degree from person to person, a trait model neither takes note of the conditions when it is turned on and off nor assesses its effectiveness. The same is true in biology, particularly with respect to the maintenance of steady states by homeostatic mechanisms. Therefore, to advance our knowledge of suggestibility, we might focus on the particularities of behavior that an ability or trait model ignores or distorts because it dimensionalizes phenomena on abstract continua that do not exist in nature. A profile representation of scores is satisfactory from this point of view, provided that each item reflects only one process, system, or function. We might learn more about neuropsychological processes or systems involved in an item if we conceptualized the differences in percentages of subjects passing as being indicators of the relative ease of influencing these systems. We certainly would want to include in the development of such an instrument items that involve the digestive, eliminative, reproductive, cardiovascular, musculoskeletal, somesthetic, autonomic, and central nervous systems as well as perception and cognitive functions. By focusing on the effects of suggestion on particular processes and systems, rather than on the abstraction of hypnotic ability or susceptibility data can be obtained regarding the limits of direct suggestion, and subsequent research could determine if the degree and extent of influence over any of these systems could be increased by special procedures. As previously discussed, the items in a satisfactory scale of suggestibility should not reflect other sources of variance than the ease of influencing a particular system, function, or process.

I have avoided using the terms "hypnosis" and "susceptibility" because they carry too much vague, surplus meaning; however, it should be evident that I am not adverse to employing theoretical constructs. Theoretical constructs are useful if their surplus meaning is identified. To simplify communication, I designate the first increase in suggestibility as Hypersuggestibility, level I, and the second level as Hypersuggestibility, level II. Only level II is what the early practitioners described as hypnosis.

Implications of Methodology

The most immediate implication of this two-step theory of suggestibility is the constitution of control groups; it disqualifies any control group wherein the instructions to the subjects allow them to adopt a passive-receptive attitude with respect to the procedures. This includes relaxation, waiting, resting, free imagery, and directed imagery. Even the administration of the items with no instructions produces the same enhancement of suggestibility. If there is any validity to my theoretical frame of reference, there is no conceptual basis for a control group. There are only treatment groups. The manipulatable variables are modes of information processing—which includes cerebral, hemispheric relations—anxiety, dependency strivings, defenses, and security operations, all of which are susceptible to operational definitions. Wilson's investigation and its replication by Robin Hughes are good examples of the sole use of treatment groups. The same is true for an investigation [7] by Raquel Gur and myself in which left- and right-lookers were compared on scales tailor-made to suit their preferred mode of information processing. Finally, Ruben and Raquel Gur [15] constituted comparison groups solely on the basis of degree of cerebral lateralization of function; a conventional control group would have been irrelevant.

Implications for Practice

In order to induce hypersuggestibility, level II, the practitioner is advised to adopt a paternalistic or maternalistic demeanor and to reinforce his/her image as an authoritative, helpful professional by displaying impressive credentials in a setting reinforcing these connotative meanings. On the other hand, if the physician were to use a nonauthoritarian or equalitarian induction procedure, such as hand levitation, patients would be forced to cooperate when their dependency strivings dispose them to seek out direction and caretaking behavior. This striving is frustrated, which produces anger. At the same time, their feelings of helplessness are exacerbated, causing anxiety about their ability to become hypnotized. Each of these affective reactions may interfere with the disengagement of the semantic-syntactic mode; consequently, the induction may fail.

Not all medical patients with grave or exquisitely painful conditions can experience hypersuggestibility, level II. The psychodynamic picture is different for medical patients with chronic, terminal, or hysterical conditions who realize that the field of medicine and their particular physicians cannot help them; consequently, medical hypnosis does not foster dependency strivings. Some of these patients become resigned to their fate, whereas others turn elsewhere, such as to religion, chiropracty, occultism, faith healing, acupuncture, biofeedback, and quackery. Buoyed up by fresh hope, dependency strivings are undoubtedly fostered in some of these patients along with the development of hypersuggestibility level II, and presto, "miraculous" remissions occur. Knowing she/he has lost his/her magic, perhaps the physician should encourage selected, chronic patients to seek a "cure" in some charismatic alternative to the medical profession while maintaining a watchful, unobtrusive eye on the course of events.

REFERENCES

1. PRIBRAM, K. H. 1971. Languages of the Brain: Experimental Paradoxes and Principles in Experimental Neuropsychology. Prentice Hall, Inc. Englewood Cliffs, N.J.
2. REYHER, J. Emergent uncovering psychotherapy: the use of imagoic and linguistic vehicles in objectifying psychodynamic processes. *In* The Power of Human Imagination. J. L. Singer & K. S. Pope, Eds. Plenum Publishing Corp. New York, N.Y. In press.
3. JANIS, I. L. 1958. Psychological Stress. John Wiley & Sons, Inc. New York, N.Y.
4. REYHER, J. & J. G. WILSON. 1973. The induction of hypnosis: indirect vs. direct methods and the role of anxiety. Amer. J. Clin. Hypn. 15: 229–233.
5. SMYTH, L. S. 1977. Th influence of attention, anxiety, and brain asymmetry on hypnotic suggestibility. Unpublished Doctoral Dissertation. Michigan State University. East Lansing, Mich.
6. REYHER, J., J. PAPESCH, L. LAWRENCE, K. PICCONE, C. GRAYSON & R. GATES. 1977. Variables influencing the items on the HGSHS:A: suggestion vs. hypnotic susceptibility. Unpublished ms. Michigan State University. East Lansing, Mich.
7. GUR, R. E. & J. REYHER. 1973. Relationship between style of hypnotic induction and direction of lateral eye movements. J. Abnorm. Psychol. 82: 499–505.
8. SPANOS, N. P., J. SPILLANE & J. D. MCPEAKE. 1976. Cognitive strategies and

response to suggestion in hypnotic and task-motivated subjects. Amer. J. Clin. Hypn. **18:** 254–262.

9. KAZDIN, A. E. & L. A. WILCOXON. 1976. Systematic desensitization and nonspecific treatment effects: a methodological evaluation. Psychol. Bull. **83:** 729–758.

10. WILKINS, W. 1971. Desenitization: social and cognitive factors underlying the effectiveness of Wolpe's procedure. Psychol. Bull. **76:** 311–317.

11. WILSON, J. G. 1974. The hypnotic relationship: facilitation and inhibition through indirect procedures. Unpublished Doctoral Dissertation. Michigan State University. East Lansing, Mich.

12. GUR, R. 1973. An experimental investigation of a new procedure for enhancing hypnotic susceptibility. Unpublished Dissertation. Michigan State University. East Lansing, Mich.

13. GUR, R. 1974. An attention-controlled operant procedure for enhancing hypnotic susceptibility. J. Abnorm. Psychol. **83:** 644–650.

14. MORGAN, A. H., H. MACDONALD & E. HILGARD. 1974. EEG alpha: lateral asymmetry related to task, and hypnotizability. Psychophysiol. **11:** 275–282.

15. GUR, R. L. & R. E. GUR. 1974. Handedness, sex, and eyedness as moderating variables in the relation between hypnotic susceptibility and functional brain asymmetry. J. Abnorm. Psychol. **83:** 635–643.

16. HADFIELD, J. A. 1920. Functional nerve disease: an epitome of war experience for the practitioner. In Hypnotism. H. C. Miller, Ed. Hodder & Stoughton, Ltd. London, England.

17. GUR, R. E. & J. REYHER. 1973. Relationship between style of hypnotic induction and direction of lateral eye movements. J. Abnorm. Psychol. **82:** 499–505.

18. SULLIVAN, H. S. 1953. The Interpersonal Theory of Psychiatry. W. W. Norton & Co., Inc. New York, N.Y.

19. PEELE, T. L. 1961. The Neuroanatomic Basis for Clinical Neurology. McGraw-Hill Book Co. New York, N.Y.

20. KLINE, M. V. 1958. Freud and Hypnosis. Julian Press. New York, N.Y.

21. HILGARD, E. R. 1965. Hypnotic Susceptibility. Harcourt, Brace, and World. New York, N.Y.

22. MOLL, A. 1958. The Study of Hypnosis. Julian Press. New York, N.Y.

23. REYHER, J. 1964. Brain mechanisms, intrapsychic processes and behavior: a theory of hypnosis and psychopathology. Amer. J. Clin. Hypn. **VII(2):** 107–119.

24. SANDERS, R. & J. REYHER. 1969. Sensory deprivation and the enhancement of hypnotic susceptibility. J. Abnorm. Psych. **74:** 375–381.

25. WERNER, H. & B. KAPLAN. 1963. Symbol Formation: An Organismic-Developmental Approach to Language and the Expression of Thought. John Wiley & Sons. New York, N.Y.

26. KLIENHAUZ, M. 1976. Hypnotherapy of acute psychiatric casualties in war. Paper presented at mtg. 7th Int. Congress of Hypnosis and Psychosomatic Medicine. Philadelphia, Pa.

27. REYHER, J. Spontaneous visual imagery: implications for psychoanalysis, psychopathology and psychotherapy. J. Mental Imagery. In press.

28. STERN, A. B. 1975. Enhancement of female sexual arousal through hypnosis. Unpublished Doctoral Dissertation. Michigan State Univ. East Lansing, Mich.

RESEARCH STRATEGIES IN EVALUATING THE
COERCIVE POWER OF HYPNOSIS

Eugene E. Levitt

Department of Psychiatry
Indiana University School of Medicine
Indianapolis, Indiana 46202

The magnitude of the strength of hypnosis—the extent to which the hypnotic state can compel an individual to behave—is one of the perennially intriguing issues in the field. Nonetheless, the editors of a recent hypnosis compendium [1] did not see fit to devote a chapter to this topic. Surely this is not because there are no findings; on the contrary, there are a number of empirical studies and clinical reports, most of which have been collected and summarized (e.g., Barber [2] and Orne [3, 4]). Certainly this information was available to the authors of the compendium. The reason for the neglect can only be that the data, while fascinating, may not cast any true light on the coercive power of hypnosis. The methodological problems of behavioral research with human subjects are the most intricate and troublesome in the world of science. Within behavioral science, hypnosis research is particularly plagued with these problems, and within the field of hypnosis, the issue of coercive power seems to be a maximally difficult one in which to arrive at a data-based conclusion.

A widely accepted view, which is effectively presented by Orne,[4] contends that the issue of the coercive power of hypnosis cannot be evaluated by empirical means, that it is an area in which it is not possible to develop testable hypotheses. The logic of this view is as follows. One cannot evaluate the power of hypnosis by requiring the hypnotized subject to perform an actual, antisocial or criminal act outside of the laboratory. Such exigencies are contraindicated by obvious legal and moral considerations. The experimenter is therefore restricted to the laboratory situation, in which the subject responds not only to specific suggestions by the hypnotist but also in keeping with his perception of the total situation. The subject assumes quite correctly that the experimenter will not place him in any real jeopardy. If he is requested to perform an antisocial or criminal act, either he is being deceived and the act is not antisocial or criminal, or the experiment has been arranged so that the subject will be protected in some way from the consequences of his behavior. Thus, he feels free to perform all sorts of outrageous acts, either hypnotized or unhypnotized. Orne points out that this position is supported by a high compliance rate both by hypnotized and unhypnotized subjects in experiments designed to evaluate the coercive force of hypnosis.

Despite his argument that the coercive power of hypnosis is experimentally unamenable to examination, Orne [4] adopts a definite position on this issue. Hypnosis, he proposes, may indeed "play a role in bringing about a certain course of events," but it is not a unique force. It is similar in strength to "minimal amounts of alcohol or group pressure," thus simply a facilitating, and not a coercive, agent. Hypnotist and subject play a sort of game of mutual self-deception, a pleasurable *folie à deux*. The subject happily deeds over his ego functions for the nonce to the hypnotist, so that he can be provided with a rationale for acting-out. If necessary, the subject will invoke his hypnotically induced helplessness to escape blame and responsibility. The hypnotist agreeably shares the illusion that he wields true coercive control over his subject, thereby embarking on a gratifying ego trip of his own. Neither chooses to recognize that the control of the hypnotist and the compliance of the subject are, to turn again to Orne's [4] metaphor, "in the manner of a constitutional monarch" who rules "by the sufferance of his subjects."

Orne's logic, while persuasive, is by no means conclusive. One might, for example, begin with the many demonstrations of the use of hypnosis to control pain, to nullify undesirable behavior, and to remove pathological symptoms. The logical immediate inference is that hypnosis must have a powerful motive force. True, these considerations might be argued away on the grounds that symptoms are ego-alien phenomena that the patient would willingly forego, and thus he cooperates fully with the hypnotist. The circumstance is different from one in which the subject is made to perform an act that is allegedly dangerous or in violation of his/her personal moral code. Nevertheless, it is still true that the individual is unable to achieve a desired end without resorting to hypnosis, so that one must assume that it has some power. It is certainly not unreasonable to suppose that this power, if it can function in support of the individual's welfare, can also be turned against his best interests.

Recent experiments by Coe and his associates at California State University [5, 6] and Levitt and coworkers [7-9] at Indiana University seem to suggest that the issue of the coercive power of hypnosis may indeed be testable, if appropriate research strategy is employed. The crux of this strategy lies in convincing the subject that the experimental situation is natural and unprotected, that the danger, whether it be legal or moral, is real, and that the subject will have to bear full responsibility for the consequences of his actions. A comparison of the procedures and findings of the work at California State and Indiana Universities with the classical experiments (e.g., Rowland,[10] Wells,[11] Young,[12] and Orne & Evans [13]) suggests that there are three situational variables that are likely to influence the subject's perception of the experimental milieu and thereby determine the extent to which the experimental situation can be employed to evaluate the coercive power of hypnosis.

These variables are:

1. The physical location of the experiment;
2. individuals other than the subjects who are involved in the experiment;
3. the specific behavior that is requested of the subject.

With a few exceptions, the classical experiments were undertaken by university faculty and were carried out entirely within the university campus, usually confined to a laboratory that must have been unmistakable to the subjects. By contrast, the Coe experiments required the subject to leave either the laboratory or the campus itself. A logical essence seems obvious. The subject must surely feel a greater sense of security within the laboratory and campus, a feeling that seems likely to contribute to his perception of the experimental situation as unthreatening. The subject who is required to leave the campus, on the other hand, might well develop some doubt about the benignity of the experimenter. This would seem to be all the more likely if the experimental task were allegedly a criminal act.

There is no reason to doubt that the experimenters in hypnotic coercion research were either known to the subjects or easily identified as university faculty members. Accomplices, when they were employed, have probably been junior faculty or graduate student assistants, again individuals easily identifiable as university-associated. Attempts to persuade the subject that persons outside the campus setting were involved in the experiment are scarce. Yet, it seems logical that the exclusive presence of academic types in the experimental milieu reassures the subject. Participation of individuals who resemble the stereotype of sociopathy—e.g., unshaven, roughly dressed, lower-class speech pattern— would contribute to an atmosphere of reality, especially when the subject is asked to commit an antisocial or criminal act. The ultimate situation might be one in which the university person, having hypnotized the subject, now pointedly turns him over to the (alleged) outsider and appears to withdraw from the experiment at that juncture.

Traditionally, the self-injurious or antisocial acts that have been required of subjects in coercion experiments have been extreme. Otherwise, how would the experimenter be certain that a coercive agent was needed?

An analysis of the classical experiments suggests that apart from other considerations, the more outrageous the act required of the subject, the more likely he will be to perform it. Again, there seems to be an element of logic. The very outrageousness of the request renders it unreal. The subject's refusal to believe that the snake is dangerous or that there is a blinding acid in the beaker that is to be thrown in someone's face is buttressed by the flagrancy of these acts. The benign experimenter would surely never permit the subject to commit an atrocity. Thus, protection and/or relief from consequences is certain.

The experimenter is thus faced by a dilemma. If he requests an atrocious act of his subjects, they will surely comply, with or without hypnotic force. If he asks for less extreme behavior, the trance may be extraneous. One possible solution is the use of disagreeable but not dangerous or seriously antisocial behaviors, as in the Indiana experiments. The subject who is asked to clean up an actual puddle of vomitus, or to undress, or to mutilate a Bible, obviously faces a situation in which the customary experimenter protection is absent. A fair number of individuals might not perform such objectionable acts in the ordinary experimental situation.

In summary, the aforegoing analysis suggests that the following three experimental circumstances should maximize the possibility that the subject will perceive the experimental situation as natural and unprotected, as realistically threatening, and therefore suitable for examining the coercive power of hypnosis:

1) The experiment, or at least its crucial portion, should take place away from the normal environs of the experimenter, e.g. the campus or hospital.

2) Individuals who are, or appear to be, other than professors, doctors, graduate students, and so on, should be directly involved with the subject in the experimental situation.

3) The experimental task should be objectionable, but not seriously dangerous or antisocial, especially if the first two conditions cannot be met. The allegedly self-injurious act should be avoided; it is most likely to be perceived by the subject as unthreatening.

Combinations of these conditions must depend upon the actual nature of the experimental task that is employed. For example, the first two conditions are less important if an objectionable act is used in the experiment. When the first two conditions are clearly met, a major felony might well be the requested behavior. Obviously, some systematic experimentation is needed to test the efficacy of these conditions and the effects of various interactions among them on subject behavior.

REFERENCES

1. FROMM, E. & R. E. SHOR. 1972. Hypnosis: Research Developments and Perspectives. Aldine-Atherton. Chicago, Ill.
2. BARBER, T. X. 1961. Antisocial and criminal acts induced by "hypnosis": A review of experimental and clinical findings. Arch. Gen. Psychiat. **5:** 301–312.
3. ORNE, M. T. 1961. The potential uses of hypnosis in interrogation. *In* A. D. Biderman and H. Zimmer, Eds. The Manipulation of Human Behavior. John Wiley & Sons. New York, N.Y.
4. ORNE, M. T. 1972. Can a hypnotized subject be compelled to carry out otherwise unacceptable behavior? Int. J. Clin. Exp. Hypn. **20:** 101–117.
5. COE, W. C., K. KOBAYASHI & M. L. HOWARD. 1972. An approach toward isolating factors that influence antisocial conduct in hypnosis. Int. J. Clin. Exp. Hypn. **20:** 118–130.
6. COE, W. C., K. KOBAYASHI & M. L. HOWARD. 1973. Experimental and ethical problems of evaluating the influence of hypnosis in antisocial conduct. J. Abnorm. Psychol. **82:** 476–482.
7. LEVITT, E. E., M. J. MISCHLEY & L. A. MISCHLEY. 1973. Testing the coercive power of hypnosis: A survey of volunteering behavior. Psychol. Rec. **23:** 547–552.
8. LEVITT, E. E., G. ARONOFF, C. D. MORGAN, T. M. OVERLEY & M. J. PARRISH. 1975. Testing the coercive power of hypnosis: committing objectionable acts. Int. J. Clin. Exp. Hypn. **23:** 59–67.
9. LEVITT, E. E., T. M. OVERLEY & D. RUBINSTEIN. 1975. The objectionable act as a mechanism for testing the coercive power of the hypnotic state. Amer. J. Clin. Hypn. **17:** 263–266.
10. ROWLAND, L. W. 1939. Will hypnotized persons try to harm themselves or others? J. Abnorm. Soc. Psychol. **34:** 114–117.
11. WELLS, W. R. 1941. Experiments in the hypnotic production of crime. J. Psychol. **11:** 63–102.
12. YOUNG, P. C. 1952. Antisocial uses of hypnosis. *In* Experimental Hypnosis. L. M. LeCron, Ed. Macmillan. New York, N.Y.
13. ORNE, M. T. & F. J. EVANS. 1965. Social control in the psychological experiment: antisocial behavior and hypnosis. J. Pers. Soc. Psychol. **1:** 189–200.

THE PROBLEM OF RELEVANCE VERSUS ETHICS IN RESEARCHING HYPNOSIS AND ANTISOCIAL CONDUCT

William C. Coe

Psychology Department
California State University
Fresno, California 93740

The purpose of this paper is to examine an approach that will at the same time reduce ethical problems with human subjects and provide meaningful answers to the question "Can hypnotized persons be coerced into committing antisocial acts?" To this end, I plan to bring together a meaningful research design with procedures meant to minimize ethical issues. I will begin with the design, review ethical questions next, and, finally, offer recommendations.

THE DESIGN

The conclusions of other investigators interested in the coercive powers of hypnosis agree with my own in many respects, especially the fact that certain variables must be accounted for before we are able to interpret our results unambiguously.[1-3] To review, four variables appear to be crucial:

1. Subjects must be highly responsive to hypnosis and hypnotized at the time they are requested to perform the antisocial act.
2. The "antisocial" act must be contrary to the subject's system of values and also must be considered serious by cultural standards.
3. The coercive effects of the interpersonal relationship between the subject and the hypnotist must be separated from the coercive effects of hypnosis.
4. Subjects must be unaware that they are participating in an experiment at the time the hypnotist requests them to engage in antisocial conduct.

The results from two of our previous experiments [4, 5] have led me to formulate an experimental approach that I believe takes these four issues adequately into account. That is, I believe the design I am about to propose can produce definitive answers to the basic question "Can persons be coerced to commit antisocial acts through hypnosis?"

FIGURE 1 is a diagrammatic representation of the experimental procedures. Each step will be discussed briefly.

Subject Pool, Measure of Morality, and Screening

A rather large subject pool is initially required, probably in the neighborhood of 400 subjects. They are obtained by soliciting volunteers for a "study on the relationship of hypnotic susceptibility to personal characteristics." Subjects may be seen in rather large groups (20–40) for the first session.

A questionnaire that samples personal traits, vocational interests, and values (five-point scale) regarding a wide variety of moral and criminal acts is first administered. The Harvard Group Scale of Hypnotic Susceptibility (HGSHS) [6] is administered next, after which subjects are requested to note if they would volunteer for further experiments in hypnosis. The critical information at this step is 1) to obtain a premeasure of the subject's values toward specific antisocial acts, including the one they will be requested to perform, and 2) to screen for hypnotic susceptibility.

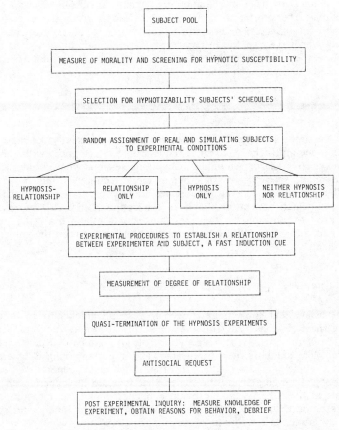

FIGURE 1. A model design to investigate the influence of hypnosis on antisocial behavior.

Selecting for Hypnotizability

The next step, selecting further for hypnotizability, entails individual meetings with subjects who scored high and low on the HGSHS and who also indicated that they would volunteer for further hypnosis experiments. The Stanford Hypnotic Susceptibility Scale, Form C [7] (SHSS,C), a more difficult scale, is administered to confirm high or low responsiveness to hypnosis. Highly susceptible subjects will be requested to continue and will serve as the critical subjects in the final analysis. Low susceptible subjects will be retained as simulating subjects who serve as quasicontrols to help in evaluating the effects of demand characteristics at the time of the antisocial request.[8]

Information is also acquired in this session about the subjects' usual whereabouts each day of the week, with the explanation that it is needed to schedule later sessions. In the case of college student subjects, class schedules may be gathered; work schedules may be obtained for other kinds of subjects. The important thing is to have information that makes it possible for an experimenter to meet the subject in a natural place, apart from the experimental setting, where an antisocial request can be made later in the experiment.

Subjects who have met the criteria thus far are randomly assigned to one of the four experimental conditions, "real" subjects and simulating subjects being assigned equally to each condition.

Hypnosis Experiment

In the remaining sessions all four samples are treated exactly the same up to the time that the antisocial conduct is requested. Subjects meet with the same hypnotist-experimenter for a number of hypnotic sessions where other standard scales of hypnotic susceptibility or other hypnotic techniques may be administered. Other measures, like attitude scales, family background, information, and so forth, which appear justifiable in the context, may also be included.

There are two purposes for these sessions: 1) to establish a rapid, reliable induction cue, and 2) to build a personal relationship between the subject and the experimenter.

Induction Cue

It is necessary that subjects be trained to respond quickly to an induction cue during these sessions. Any number of verbal cues may be employed, for example, the commands, "Go to sleep!" or "Sleep!" Nonverbal cues could be used as well, like touching their foreheads. The important thing is to create a cue that is convincing in its effects. Incorporating "state" reports, self-reports from the subject ranging from one to ten that indicate his experienced depth of hypnosis at the time,[9] would provide a phenomenological measure of the subject's response to the cue. The state report would compliment and supplement the experimenter's estimate of the subject's response, which is made by observing eye closure, relaxation, and perhaps responsiveness to selected suggestions. The subject's state report and the experimenter's observations are used later as measures of the subject's depth of hypnosis at the time of the antisocial request. Training to the cue continues until the subject responds very quickly and reliably during the experimental sessions.

The Relationship

The other important part of these sessions is establishing a relationship between subject and experimenter. The relationship may be enhanced by having the experimenter take a personal interest in the subject's life, empathically exploring any personal difficulties the subject may bring up. Even further, subjects might be told that determining the effects of hypnosis on the resolution of personal problems is part of the experiment, thereby encouraging a strong relationship similar to that which develops between a therapist and client.

Regardless of the particulars during this phase, an objective measure of the subject-experimenter relationship will be obtained before the quasi-end of the experiment is announced. This measure can be embedded in a questionnaire or interview presented as a device for learning more about the subjects' experiences with hypnosis. Some other experimenter, probably a senior investigator, would interview subjects or administer a questionnaire to them after their last hypnotic session. Included among other items would be a statement to the effect that hypnotic subjects tend to develop personal feelings for the hypnotist and that the study is interested in their judging the degree of this phenomenon as it relates to their own experience. The important thing is to obtain the subjects' self-rating of the strength of the relationship with their hypnotists. The experimental attempts to create a relationship may in this way be supported by an independent measure of its degree.

Quasitermination

A formal termination and debriefing is carried out during the last session. After the final information forms are completed the experimenter reviews all that has been done in the previous sessions, explaining in some detail the hypotheses of the "study" and promising to mail a copy of the results to the subject when they have been compiled. Subjects are thanked and/or paid for their participation.

Antisocial Request

At a time after the quasitermination, probably one week or more, subjects are met "inadvertently" at one of the places they usually frequent, for example, after a class meeting. The experimenter approaches the subject as if he/she had just been spotted, or, depending on the nature of the antisocial act, they may be approached as if the experimenter was purposely hunting for them. In either event, it is important to meet subjects away from the experimental setting and to request the commission of the act in a natural setting. Subjects are much less likely to believe that the request is part of an experiment under such conditions. In our earlier study, for example, subjects were met after a class and were requested to help the experimenter sell heroin off campus. Only 23% (6/26) of the "real" and 22% (2/9) of the simulating subjects reported that they suspected the request might be part of an experiment.[5]

Experimental Conditions

The four experimental conditions are designed to differentiate the effects of the relationship from those of hypnosis. The procedure for each is as follows.
1. *Relationship and Hypnosis.* In this condition both the relationship and

hypnosis are employed; that is, a familiar hypnotist hypnotizes the subject and requests antisocial conduct.

Subjects are met by the experimenter who worked with them previously. The experimenter then takes them aside and administers the quick-induction cue, observing their responses and obtaining their state reports. The antisocial request is not made until both the experimenter's and subject's measure of hypnosis indicate that the subject is deeply hypnotized. Subjects are then requested to commit the act. Of course, more conditions may be added to test different methods of requesting the act. For example, one condition might entail directly asking to comply, while another might incorporate "delusional" and/or "hallucinated" material in the request.

2. *Relationship Only.* In this condition, the request for antisocial conduct is made only on the strength of the relationship. Subjects are met by the experimenter who worked with them previously, but they are not hypnotized. The experimenter takes his subjects aside and simply requests their help in committing the act. He offers a reason for needing their help, such as that he is in financial trouble. To equalize the persuasiveness of all conditions, the same reason is included in the other samples as well.

3. *Hypnosis Only.* In this condition hypnosis by itself is used to influence the subjects.

An experimenter whom subjects have never met before (the "strange" experimenter) makes the antisocial request. As in the previous two conditions, he meets subjects inadvertently but with the excuse that he recognizes them from having seen them and knows about them from the hypnosis experiments, admitting he is a friend of the experimenter with whom they worked. He then takes them aside and administers the induction cue, using the same criteria of state reports and his own observations to ensure that subjects are hypnotized before he makes the antisocial request.

4. *Neither Hypnosis Nor Relationship.* This condition may be viewed as a control condition, that is, one in which neither a relationship nor hypnosis is employed to influence the subject's response.

The "strange" experimenter again makes the antisocial request. He meets his subjects as before, but after he takes them aside he simply requests them to help him, offering the same reason(s) as did the experimenter in the "relationship only" condition.

Antisocial Act

The particular antisocial act that is requested may be the same for all subjects as it was in our two previous studies [4, 5] or it may be individualized for subjects depending upon their response to the value questionnaire administered earlier.

There are at least two advantages of using one act for all subjects. One is that the practical arrangements necessary for actually carrying out the study are simplified. It requires a considerable amount of time and effort to set up the natural environment for a contrived antisocial act that may be carried out in a convincing way. The more acts, the more time involved. A second advantage is that the degree to which the act is against a person's values is quite likely to vary across subjects for any one act, making it possible to relate the degree to which an act is opposed to its commission. The secondary hypothesis, that "subjects will only carry out acts which are not against their values," may therefore be tested as well.

On the other hand, tailoring antisocial acts for each subject on the basis of his reported values offers more assurance that the act may be called antisocial from the subject's point of view. Requesting subjects to commit acts which their prereports indicate they are strongly against offers some assurance that the act is actually antisocial.

The degree to which an antisocial act is carried out may also be measured. Most acts are not all-or-none occurrences, although they may be. Subjects may only go so far with the request before deciding they have gone far enough. The distance they move toward completing the act may be recorded and employed as a continuous, dependent variable. In our past experience, however, subjects nearly always completed the act in total or refused to do it at all.

Obviously, the particular nature of the act that is chosen carries its own strength in relationship to ethical values. I would, however, like to discuss these implications in more detail later.

Postexperimental Inquiry and Debriefing

The postexperimental inquiry is conducted by the senior investigator as soon as possible after the commission of the act. It serves three purposes: 1) obtaining an estimate of subjects' knowledge that the antisocial request was part of an experiment; 2) obtaining an estimate of the reasons which led subjects to commit or not commit the act, and 3) debriefing subjects about the experiment.

As far as evaluating whether the subject suspected that the antisocial act was part of an experiment is concerned, we have used a structural interview with freedom to question any interesting leads. Questions were asked like, "What did you think when Mr. X [the experimenter] approached you?", or, "Were you convinced you were selling heroin?" The subjects' responses were recorded and judged by three independent raters on the degree to which they believed the subject suspected that it was an experiment. The same raters also used the interview material to categorize the reasons they believed the subject did or did not commit the act, for example, "against subject's morals," "hypnotized," "fear of legal consequences," "not against morals," and others.

Both of the foregoing judgments may be checked for reliability, and the data can be used to supplement the premeasure of the subjects' moral beliefs.

Debriefing accomplishes three things: 1) it reduces the negative responses that subjects might have to the experiment; 2) it provides them with information as a learning experience; and 3) it enlists their cooperation in not discussing the experiment until it is completed.

Recap

In summary, the foregoing design attempts to meet the four criteria stated earlier in the following ways:

1. Highly responsive subjects who are hypnotized at the time of the antisocial request: a) preselection of high scorers on a difficult, standard hypnotic susceptibility scale, b) training to enter hypnosis on cue, and

c) verification of hypnotic depth following the induction cue with state-reports and experimenter observations.

2. An antisocial act that is contrary to subjects' values and cultural standards: a) preselection of subjects, or selection of acts, based on subjects responses to a value questionnaire, and b) postexperimental inquiry to evaluate subjects' reasons for committing or not committing the act.

3. Separating the effects of the interpersonal relationship from those of hypnosis: the four experimental conditions.

4. Knowledge of participating in an experiment: a) quasitermination of the experiment, b) antisocial request in the natural environment, c) employing simulating subjects as quasicontrols, and d) postexperimental inquiry.

ETHICAL CONSIDERATIONS

A brief review of the ethical questions that arise with human subjects is now in order. I will attempt to summarize a number of articles that have been published on this topic in recent years.[10–17]

Herbert Kelman has pointed out two basic issues that have created concerns about the ethical implications of social research. The first, and most relevant to our analysis, has to do with the process of research; that is, the actual doing of research with human subjects and the issues it raises, like invasion of privacy and the possibility of harm to the subject. The second, which is less relevant to us and will only be touched upon lightly, is the use to which research findings are put, especially the fear that they may be used to control or manipulate one segment of society to the advantage of others.

Kelman's [12] analysis emphasizes as a basic problem the power deficiency of research subjects in their relationship to researchers. One source of subjects' power deficiency is in their relatively disadvantaged positions within the social system; that is, their statuses within a social system are often lower than that of the researcher's, or they are in some way dependent on the system in which the research holds status. Examples are mental hospital patients and college students.

Another source of power deficiency flows from the subjects' position within the research situation itself. In laboratory settings especially, subjects have limited opportunities to question the procedures. The investigator's specialized knowledge and expertise give him a perceived legitimacy and as a consequence increase his power over the subject. Subjects are therefore reluctant to claim their right to question the research procedures.

Deception, a primary issue for our topic, increases subjects' deficit in power because it is even less likely that they will exercise their right to chose not to participate, or to withdraw from a study, if they do not know what is really going to happen. Ethical problems are even further increased when deception is used in an experiment that may be potentially stressful or in some way harmful to the subject—another relevant point to our discussion.

M. Brewster Smith [11] makes us aware of two quite different frames of reference around which our deliberation of ethics in human research revolves. One is what he calls the "libertarian, voluntaristic, 'humanistic' frame captured in the tag phrase 'informed consent'." This frame draws from the philosophy that it is good for people to make their own decisions about what they wish to do as long as they know what it is that they are going to do. Clearly, this framework, even disregarding the many problems of achieving fully informed consent, does not apply to the design I have presented earlier because the subjects are purposely not fully informed until after their participation.

The second framework, "that of the participants welfare or harm," which may be expressed in a "cost/benefit analysis," is clearly the relevant framework for our discussion. Here, individual and/or committee judgments must be made regarding the balance between the potential benefit of the research, both to society and possibly the subject, and the potential harm to the subject as a result of his participation. In the medical sciences this may not be quite so difficult an issue, since it may be possible to weigh the risks to the patient of an experimental "treatment" against the possible gains the patient may derive. But in the social sciences we are mainly referring to the potential benefits to science and society at large, not to the subject, while on the other hand, the costs we consider are to the individual alone. A question also arises about who is to determine which research findings will be good for society and which will not, and who will judge what is really harmful to the subject when the obvious loss of life and limb are rarely involved.

With regard to these questions, I agree with Smith when he says, "There is just no way at all to conceive of a workable cost/benefit formula that could resolve actual issues of research ethics in the social sciences, even though an accounting of potential harms and benefits does provide a useful framework for considering the issues." [11]

THE DESIGN AND THE ETHICS

With this brief background I will now focus more directly on the experimental design I outlined earlier and on the ethical considerations it creates.

Probably the most crucial problem is the use of deception and the potential of harm to the subjects from their participation in the antisocial act.

Deception

First, I will attempt to justify the use of deception. Kelman suggests that serious consideration should be given to three dimensions before deciding to use deception. I should like to examine each of these and the possible ramifications they hold for the design under question.

First, the importance of the study should be considered. Importance refers to its scientific significance, which Kelman admits is a subjective judgment, and to the stage of research that it represents, for example, exploratory versus final. The scientific significance of this study for this audience probably requires little justification; the question to be answered is an age-old one for investigators of hypnosis. Finding the answer to the antisocial question will carry ramifications for the law and criminology as well as the psychology of influence communication and coercion. Further arguments could be made in favor of the study's importance, such as the implications the findings might have for restricting the use of hypnosis. However, in the final analysis, the institutional research committee that actually becomes involved in evaluating the study will have to judge its scientific merits on their own criteria.

As regards the stage of research the study represents, Eugene Levitt's paper [1] and our own research [4,5] documents the refinements that have led to the present design. It would appear to represent the final stages in our search.

Kelman's second dimension to be considered asks about the possibility of using an alternative, deception-free method, or methods, which are capable of producing at least comparable information.

One of the most frequent criticisms of antisocial studies involving hypnosis has been the confounding of the effects of hypnosis with the subjects' knowledge that they are participating in an experiment. It seems highly unlikely at this stage of investigation that any experiment that did not deceive the subjects into believing that they were not participating in an experiment could resolve the issue. Role-playing techniques have been suggested as alternatives to deception, as have models emphasizing participating research where the subject is more actively involved as a participant in a joint effort with the experimenter (Ref. 12, pp. 1003, 1004). Neither, however, would appear to correct the contamination of the knowledge of an experiment and the effects of hypnosis.

The third dimension to be considered is the noxiousness of the deception that refers to both its degree and the probability of harmful effects.

I believe I would have to agree that the deception is quite high; subjects who would eventually complete the experiment are deceived from the beginning. Further, it is planned that they develop a positive, trusting relationship with their hypnotist as part of the deception and the design.

The probability of harmful effects is not so easy to determine. From our study, in which selling heroin was the antisocial act, we found that the possibility of physical harm could not be entirely eliminated, although it was a threat to the hypnotists rather than the subjects. For example, one female subject, after being approached by the "strange" experimenter, enlisted the help of two male friends who restrained the experimenter while she made her escape. In another case, a male subject reported in the postexperimental interview that he went along with the request for the purpose of "beating up" the experimenter and taking the money from the heroin sale. He did not do it, he said, because he began to fear retaliation.

Emotional upset and psychological distress are also difficult to evaluate, but it does not seem to be severe from our observations during the heroin-selling experiment. None of the 35 subjects in that study seemed to require counseling, nor have they requested it, in the three years since. Their usual response was one of two types: a brief show of anger at having been deceived and made anxious, or a show of relief that it was only an experiment after all. Nevertheless, the recommendations I am now going to present are by and large aimed at reducing the impact of psychological stress and preventing the occurrence of inadvertent physical harm.

Prestudy Procedures

Procedures may be employed before the study begins. They may be helpful in isolating especially stressful parts of the experiment so that they may be modified, or they may give an indication of the degree to which one can expect negative responses.

Wilson and Donnerstein [13] suggest that investigators obtain the opinion of members of the subject pool about the noxiousness of the procedures before an experiment is conducted. In our case, subjects would be told the sequential procedures in detail and asked to evaluate the ways in which they believe they would respond to them. Subjects are asked to judge various criteria, such as "would they feel harassed," "had their privacy been invaded," "would they mind being a subject," "would they see a lawyer," and others. Admittedly, their responses might not be the same as they would if they had actually participated in the experiment, but the information gives the investigator an estimate of the noxiousness of his procedures and emphasizes those parts of the procedure which are potentially most stressful. Wilson and Donnerstein also offer norms on these criteria for eight experimental procedures that they evaluated. Thus, it is possible to compare one's own results with other studies in order to judge the severity of its effects. If especially noxious procedures are isolated in this way, the investigator, possibly with the help of the subjects, can explore alternatives that are as effective but less noxious.

Along the same line, Farr and Seaver [17] collected data on subjects' judgment of physical discomfort, psychological discomfort, and invasion of privacy on 30 experimental procedures. One could gather similar data on the antisocial procedures and compare them to these other procedures as an estimate of their potential for discomfort.

Another prestudy procedure is to inform the subjects beforehand that some aspects of the experiment cannot be explained until later because the subjects' knowledge of them would probably affect the way they respond and thereby negate the findings. An "informed" consent form of this type at least lets the subjects know that they are not fully informed and gives them the opportunity to withdraw on these grounds if they wish.

Analysis of Each Procedural Step

I would now like to turn to TABLE 1 and discuss specific modifications that will *minimize risks*.

Step 1: Subject Pool. The selection of the subject pool will make some difference in ethical considerations. As TABLE 1 shows, the subjects with the least power deficit in relation to the investigator are volunteer subjects from the community. Fortunately, such a subject pool will also increase the generalizability of the results to the population at large. The changes that these subjects will exercise their right to leave the experiment are greater than that of institutional subjects and/or paid subjects. The major drawback in choosing community volunteers is the practical matter of arranging appointments and meeting them inadvertently for the antisocial request. Selecting this pool is a choice in the direction of ethics at the expense of experimental time and effort.

Step 2: Screening. During the screening phase, it is possible to insure confidentiality by coding data and other record-keeping procedures. (Campbell and his associates [18] are an excellent source for information on techniques that insure privacy.)

It is probably also desirable at this early stage to administer a screening instrument, like the Minnesota Multiphasic Personality Inventory (MMPI), in order to screen out subjects who appear severely disturbed or very low as

TABLE 1

STEPS IN AN IDEAL, EXPERIMENTAL DESIGN TO INVESTIGATE THE INFLUENCE
OF HYPNOSIS ON ANTISOCIAL BEHAVIOR AND THE ETHICAL CONSIDERATIONS
INVOLVED IN EACH

Steps	Purpose	Ethical Issue(s)

1. Subject pool
  College students
  Community volunteers
  Paid subjects
	Pool definition determines the generalizability of the results, e.g., sex, age, socioeconomic status	Power of experimenter over subject
		  Most power over Subjects who come from an institution where they are dependent upon the experimenters, e.g., college, mental hospital, prison.
		  Least power over volunteers from outside an institution.
		  Increases power over subject regardless of institutional affiliation

2. Screening Subject pool for hypnotic, susceptibility, moral stance and resistance to stress	Select subjects for Level of susceptibility Particular antisocial act Degree of likelihood of negative response to experiment	Deception, confidentiality, safeguarding against excessive emotional upset
3. Experimental procedures: Establishing a relationship, training for "automatic" cue to induce hypnosis	Create a trusting relationship between subject and experimenter and a cue to use at the critical meeting "after" the experiment for a fast induction	Deception
4. Measure degree of relationship	Examine effects of varying degree of relationship between subject and experimenter and/or establish that a positive relationship exists	Deception
5. Quasitermination of the hypnosis experiment	To mislead the subject into believing that the experiment is concluded	Deception

TABLE 1 (*Continued*)

Steps	Purpose	Ethical Issue(s)
6. Random assignment of real and simulating subjects to one of four experimental conditions	Manipulating hypnosis and personal relationship Conditions Hypnosis-relationship Relationship only Hypnosis only Neither	Deception, risk of emotional upset and/or physical harm Lower risk Lower risk Higher risk Highest risk
7. The request for antisocial conduct	Test of the major hypothesis	Deception, confidentiality, emotional and/or physical harm potential to both experimenter and subject
8. Postexperimental inquiry and debriefing	Acquire a measure of knowledge of the experiment and reasons for behavior after antisocial request. Also to remove misconceptions and inform subject of the purpose of the experiment	Emotional upset, confidentiality

far as being able to tolerate stress is concerned. Personal screening should continue in the individual sessions. Any subjects whom the hypnotist considers a high risk to stress could be eliminated before the antisocial request is made. We may sacrifice generalizability of the results by this procedure, but the chances of serious emotional stress are decreased.

Steps 3, 4 and 5. The next three phases are only ethically questionable in that deception is employed. Nothing specific seems called for except that screening for emotional stress should continue as recommended above.

Steps 6 and 7: Four Conditions and Antisocial Request. The greatest potential for physical and/or psychological harm is encountered in Steps 6 and 7.

As we have learned from our previous experiences, the four experimental conditions do not carry equal risk. In the "hypnosis-relationship" and the "relationship only" conditions the risk of something going wrong is comparatively small. The subjects already know the experimenter and have some trust in him. (At least they trusted him to this point.) The subjects in our heroin study were not likely to become upset when the familiar experimenter approached them. They were usually sympathetic and often cooperative, and some even chastised him for wanting to do such a "bad" thing. Subjects may have been anxious and apprehensive while committing the act, but being with a "friend" seemed to reduce their concerns. At the postexperimental inquiry, however, these subjects were likely to show hurt and/or anger at having been manipulated by their friend.

The two conditions involving the "strange experimenter" were much less predictable. Several subjects escaped before they could be told what was really going on, and many of them seemed rather upset and frightened at the time of the request.

After our first negative experiences, we instituted two safeguards which, I believe, helped considerably in reducing unexpected occurrences. I would recommend them here:

First, we made up letters on official stationery which the experimenters carried with them. The letter explained the purpose for their behavior and provided names and phone numbers of responsible persons who could verify the letter. The reason for the letter was to reduce the effects from outside persons who might inadvertently interfere, like the police or bystanders, and/or to reduce unusual upset in a subject should it occur.

The second thing we did seemed especially helpful when the "strange experimenter" approached subjects. We had the experimenters work in pairs, one of the pair always being the experimenter who had a relationship with the subject. One of them would remain out of sight from the subject but available to help should something unexpected occur.

As I stated earlier, the nature of the antisocial act makes a significant difference as far as risk to the experimenter and subject is concerned.

To begin with, I would recommend without hesitation that crimes of violence and crimes against other persons be eliminated as possibilities. Play-guns, blank bullets, and so on are not safeguards in a natural setting against retaliatory actions or interference from citizens. No matter how well-planned and coordinated with authorities such setup crimes may be, the potential for harm seems too great to risk.

The most feasible antisocial acts are nonviolent crimes or immoral (not illegal) acts. They should be carried out in a setting where there are no other persons (or as few as possible) except those who are participants in the experiment.

If illegal acts are chosen, the experimenter must work in cooperation with the local law-enforcement authorities. Even though a real crime is not being committed, the proper authorities should be informed of where and when it is to take place. They can also be quite helpful as consultants on how crimes are committed, making the "pseudocrime" even more convincing. For example, in our heroin-selling experiment the local narcotics agents were most helpful, showing us how heroin is packaged in balloons for passing, and informing us that milk sugar is an excellent mimic for powdered heroin.

In the final analysis, although it increases the time and effort in carrying out the study, antisocial acts should probably be tailored to the individual subjects. To minimize risk, but at the same time retain the true antisocial character of the act, an act can be selected that matches one for which the subject has expressed strong opposition. Individualizing acts allows the experimenter to select one that carries the least risk in its accomplishment from among those acts which the subject opposed.

Step 8: Postexperimental Inquiry. We initially did not tell our subjects that selling heroin was part of our experiment until a day or so later, when they arrived for the postexperimental interview. We found, however, that some of them had spent a rather disturbing time during that period. Some had also felt compelled to discuss their experience with a friend, even though they had been asked not to. We therefore decided it best to tell them it was an experiment right after they had committed the act, or right after they had definitely refused to do so. They were asked not to discuss it with anyone, however, until they had talked with the senior investigator.

I would recommend this procedure because it reduces the potential for emotional upset. It may reduce the validity of the information gathered in the postexperimental inquiry, but it seems a reasonable compromise. Besides, there are other independent sources of data which supplement those that are obtained in the postexperimental inquiry.

Debriefing is very important and should be carried out carefully. Time does not allow an extended discussion of debriefing; rather, I will refer you to an article by Judson Mills [19] that provides a thorough account of the procedure.

I also recommend that subjects be given the choice of whether or not they wish their responses to be used in reporting the research. Being fully informed after debriefing, they are given the opportunity to enter into the experiment in its final analysis if they wish. A signature form should be provided for their consent.

Finally, all subjects should be offered the opportunity for personal counseling if they feel the need.

CONCLUSION

I would like to return to the three considerations that are to be taken into account before the use of experimental deception is justifiable.

1. I believe that the importance of the study and the stage of research it represents warrants the use of deception.

2. I do not believe an alternative, deception-free method is available that will produce comparable information.

3. I believe the degree of deception is high by necessity, but I believe that the safeguards I have recommended considerably reduce the risk to the subjects and to the experimenters.

In short, I believe that on a cost/benefit analysis, the balance falls on the side of benefit.

REFERENCES

1. LEVITT, E. E. 1977. This volume.
2. BARBER, T. X. 1961. Antisocial and criminal acts induced by hypnosis: A review of the experimental and clinical findings. Arch. Gen. Psychiatry **5:** 301–312.
3. ORNE, M. T. 1962. Antisocial behavior and hypnosis: Problems of control and validation in empirical studies. *In* Hypnosis: Current Problems. G. E. Estabrook, Ed. Harper and Row. New York, N.Y.
4. COE, W. C., K. KOBAYASHI & M. D. HOWARD. 1972. An approach toward isolating factors that influence antisocial conduct in hypnosis. Int. J. Clin. Exp. Hypn. **20:** 118–131.
5. COE, W. C., K. KOBAYASHI & M. D. HOWARD. 1973. Experimental and ethical problems of evaluating the influence of hypnosis in antisocial conduct. J. Abnorm. Psychol. **82:** 472–482.

6. SHOR, R. E. & C. ORNE. 1962. The Harvard Group Scale of Hypnotic Susceptibility, Form A. Consulting Psychologists Press. Palo Alto, Calif.
7. WEITZENHOFFER, A. M. & E. R. HILGARD. 1962. Stanford Hypnotic Susceptibility Scale, Form C. Consulting Psychologists Press. Palo Alto, Calif.
8. ORNE, M. T. 1969. Demand characteristics and the concept of quasi-controls. *In* Artifact in Behavioral Research. R. Rosenthal and R. Rosnow, Eds. Academic Press, N.Y.
9. TART, C. T. & E. R. HILGARD. 1966. Responsiveness to suggestions under "hypnosis" and "waking imagination" conditions. A methodological observation. Int. J. Clin. Exp. Hypn. **14:** 247–356.
10. AD HOC COMMITTEE ON ETHICAL STANDARDS. 1973. Ethical Principals in the Conduct of Research with Human Participants. American Psychol. Ass. Washington, D.C.
11. SMITH, M. B. 1976. Some perspectives on ethical/political issues in social science research. Personality Soc. Psychol. Bull. **2:** 445–453.
12. KELMAN, H. C. 1972. The rights of the subject in social research: an analysis in terms of relative power and legitimacy. Amer. Psychol. **27:** 989–1016.
13. WILSON, D. W. & E. DONNERSTEIN. 1976. Legal and ethical aspects of nonreactive social psychological research: an excursion into the public mind. Amer. Psychol. **31:** 765–773.
14. ROMANO, J. 1974. Reflections on informed consent. Arch. Gen. Psychiatry **30:** 129–135.
15. GERGEN, K. J., R. K. SCHWITZGEBEL & D. A. KOLB. 1974. Toward an ethic for research on human behavior. *In* Changing Human Behavior: Principles of Planned Intervention. R. K. Schwitzgebel & D. A. Kolb, Eds. McGraw-Hill. New York, N.Y.
16. RESNICK, J. H. & T. SCHWARTZ. 1973. Ethical standards as an independent variable in psychological research. Amer. Psychol. **28:** 134–139.
17. FARR, J. L. & W. B. SEAVER. 1975. Stress and discomfort in psychological research: Subjects' perceptions of experimental procedures. Amer. Psychol. **30:** 770–773.
18. CAMPBELL, D. T., R. F. BORUCH, R. D. SCHWARTZ & J. STEINBERG. 1975. Confidentiality-preserving modes of access to files to interfile exchange for useful statistical analysis. Protecting Individual Privacy in Evaluation Research. Final report of the Nat'l. Research Council Committee on Federal Agency Evaluation Research. A. Rivlin *et al.*, Eds. Nat. Res. Council, Nat. Acad. Sci. (USA) Washington, D.C.
19. MILLS, J. A procedure for explaining experiments involving deception. University of Maryland. College Park, Md. (mimeo)

BODY MORPHOLOGY AND THE CAPACITY FOR HYPNOSIS

William E. Edmonston, Jr.

*Psychology Department
Colgate University
Hamilton, New York 13346*

More than a decade ago Deckert and West,[1] upon surveying the literature on hypnotizability, confirmed Weitzenhoffer's finding [2] of a decade before, that, despite massive numbers of studies, efforts to relate capacity for hypnosis to age, sex, psychological disturbance, and a host of personality traits had been generally unsuccessful. These authors did point out that one of the major experimental defects was the lack of a uniform methodology for assessing the hypnosis side of these correlational studies. The development of the Stanford Scales [3-5] and their group-administered counterpart—the Harvard Scale [6]—have filled the methodological void and, through similar results from a variety of laboratories, indicated the relative stability of the capacity for hypnosis.

In 1965, Hilgard [7] pointed out that two assumptions appear to underlie what he termed "hypnotic susceptibility": first, that it was a basic, enduring ability, and second, that there was involved a ". . . readily modifiable attitudinal component [p. 69]." Barber [8] has been a particular proponent of the latter, emphasizing the subject's attitudes and motivation in the understanding of both intra- and interindividual differences in the capacity for hypnosis. Since attitudes and motivations are subject to change through various experimental manipulations, the stability of hypnotizability was investigated in a number of studies attempting either to manipulate attitudes or to introduce related training.

Sachs and Anderson [9] found that subjective and objective susceptibility could be significantly increased by utilizing up to six training sessions during which: (1) each subject was provided with a clear conception of the sensory experiences associated with successful performance of each task on the Stanford Hypnotic Susceptibility Scale, Forms A and C; [3, 4] (2) each subject was allowed to make self-paced approximations toward the completion of the performance of each task; and (3) verbal reinforcement and the opportunity for the subject's self-reinforcement were given. Those who had initially scored in the lower range showed the greatest improvement, but this was due to the fact that the upper range of SHSS scores is limited, thus producing a ceiling effect. More recently, Kinny and Sachs [10] have reported successfully using operant conditioning of attention to sensations to increase the capacity for hypnosis. Diamond [11] found that providing disinhibitory and facilitative verbal information, designed to correct misconceptions concerning hypnosis and to maximize the possibility of experiencing hypnosis, led to a statistically significant increase in hypnotizability. Relative improvement could not be judged, because of the ceiling effect imposed by the SHSS.

In 1974, Diamond [12] reviewed the literature regarding the modification of hypnotizability, finding generally that responsiveness to hypnosis can be manipulated experimentally. However, Cooper and coworkers [13] attempted to modify susceptibility in six subjects by using individualized training sessions, using any technique they thought might work for the particular subject. Improvement in susceptibility was minimal, and *relative* susceptibility remained quite stable. The general conclusion was that hypnotic susceptibility is an unusually stable trait. Tart [14] also found that although absolute hypnotic susceptibility scores could be significantly improved, relative susceptibility remained extremely stable. It would appear from such data that whereas all persons can improve their susceptibility scores, there may be inherent capacity for hypnosis which determines the actual percentage of improvement for a subject.

Such a notion is in keeping with the idea of an enduring ability or capacity for hypnosis, which, without deliberate manipulation, remains fairly stable throughout life. Studies both with children and with adults have demonstrated a stability for periods of up to 12 years. Cooper and London,[15] studying 134 5–16-year-olds over a three-year period, concluded that ". . . the magnitude of the relationship even after two years [.57] suggests that some kind of core susceptibility phenomenon exists . . . [p. 495]." Morgan *et al.*[16] were able to locate 85 former Stanford students and reassess their capacity for hypnosis eight to twelve years after their original testing. The test-retest-correlation was .60, with cognitive type items (amnesia) showing the most deterioration over time. Even the longitudinal studies of interindividual differences in the capacity for hypnosis show that the decline of this capacity is gradual from ages nine to twelve onward.[17, 18]

When one thinks of a "core susceptibility phenomenon" or a core capacity, which is modifiable in relative rather than absolute terms, one tends to think of a structurally based function, a biological given, a heritable trait. Surprisingly, investigators in hypnosis have all but ignored this more fundamental of approaches—the heritable structure which makes possible the behavioral functions. It has long been noted that some persons are, at the outset, more responsive to hypnotic suggestions than others, yet only three investigators have even attempted to explore this datum from the hereditary standpoint.

Rawlings [19] and Morgan [20] both have presented evidence for the heritability of a core capacity for hypnosis. Thorkelson [21] found an appreciable hereditary influence on the Field Scale of Hypnotic Depth (a correlation of .51 for 38 pairs of monozygotic twins and .24 for 24 pairs of dizygotic), but little influence on a specially devised susceptibility scale, which combined elements of the Harvard Scale and the Stanford Scale, Form C. While her explanation of the discrepancy involved a two-step combination of correlations between twin pairs and the MMPI Sc scale and correlations between the Field scale and a Paranoid Fantasy scale made up of MMPI Sc and Pa items, it is more direct to suspect that *ad hoc* scales, without normative data, may not measure the same thing as the parent scales. Thus, it is difficult to classify Thorkelson's data with respect to the heritability of hypnotic capacity.

Although Rawlings [19] was not able to establish the heritability of the capacity for hypnotic amnesia in 121 twin pairs, at the very end of his presentation to the Australian and New Zealand Society for the Advancement of Science, he presented a correlation of .67 for identical twins on a hypnotizability score, contrasted with .18 for nonidentical twins. Unfortunately, neither detail nor discussion accompanied these data.

Morgan,[20] in a far more extensive and intensive study, also found evidence for a genetic factor in hypnotizability. Measuring 140 twin pairs on the Stanford Hypnotic Susceptibility Scale, Form A,[3] she found a significant correlation (.52) for monozygotic twin pairs, in contrast to .18 for dizygotic pairs, and a heritability index of .64. This latter figure is quite comparable to those reported for heritability indices for intelligence (.70–.90). In addition, Morgan's data also showed a relationship between personality resemblance and SHSS:A scores for either sexed child and the like-sexed parent, indicating environmental influence through modeling of the like-sexed parent's behavior. Although Morgan [20] concludes that "hypnotizability . . . appears to be the product of both a genetic predisposition and subsequent environmental influences . . . [p. 61]," she has established a hereditary component in this core capacity for hypnosis, through the twin study method.

Although Morgan [20] used behavioral (personality) measures—a Similarity of Child to Parents questionnaire—to relate parents and children, neither she nor anyone else has attempted to relate physical appearance (somatotype) to the capacity for hypnosis. One of the most obvious, observable data in our environment is the fact that offspring look like their parents. This holds true throughout nature. Under usual circumstances, two Dachshunds do not produce a Great Dane. If, then, children genetically resemble their parents in physique (not necessarily stature) and the core capacity for hypnosis has a hereditary component, some relationships should appear between somatotyped physiques and this capacity.

Unfortunately, American psychology has long shunned physical typology, perhaps because of its apparent similarities to phrenology, perhaps because of the imprecise measurement techniques. Even Sheldon and co-workers' constitutional psychology,[22] certainly the major attempt to bring more rigorous order to measurement of physique and temperament relationships of this century, brought little applause from his colleagues. They identified three primary components of body structure: Endomorphy, the predominence of soft roundness in various body regions; Mesomorphy, the predominance of muscle and bone, and Ectomorphy, the predominance of linearity and fragility. Sheldon considered these components, derived from measuring the phenotype or the body as viewed, as approximating the underlying morphogenotype, each being derived from the indicated embryonic layer.

This latter point, however, was contested by Hunt,[23] who pointed out that Sheldon's system was actually based on growth stages rather than embryonic germ layer differences, in that Endomorphy is the product of the growth phase of nine months, Ectomorphy that of nine years, and Mesomorphy that of the adolescent growth phase. He also suggested that the temperaments outlined by Sheldon were also related to growth-phase periods. Hunt [23] did not contest the system, but rather its theoretical underpinnings. Humphreys,[24] on the other hand, took issue with typology per se, correcting Sheldon's intra-type correlations for curvilinearity and unreliability and proposing the trait rather than type approach. Through his corrections, Humphreys concluded that there are actually no more than two physique types, and that Sheldon merely found what he a priori wanted to find.

As one reads Sheldon et al.'s Varieties of Human Physique,[22] the impression is certainly clear that although their photography technique added a dimension of reliability and objectivity to typologies, their method for arriving at the final somatotype suffered from their own subjective impressions. In an attempt to reduce subjectivity and dispense with the embryological theorizing, Parnell [25] developed a system of body typology that minimizes the photography and claims only to produce a phenotype. In his original construction, Parnell [26] found that approximately 90% of his three body components (Fat, Muscularity and Linearity) were within one-half point of Sheldon's comparable somatotypic ratings. A later evaluation of the two systems,[27] however, found that although the shared variances are respectible (35% for Fat and Endomorphy, 44% for Muscularity and Mesomorphy, and 74% for Linearity and Ectomorphy), the two systems are not measuring the same thing. In particular, Parnell's Muscularity scores averaged one point less than Sheldon's Mesomorphy, and is affected by variations in skinfold measures. The authors also found that neither system was reducible to two scores, as Humphreys [24] claimed.

Sheldon regarded the three components of physique as static, but he assigned to temperament the dynamics of the system (Sheldon and Stevens [28]). According to their system, there are three primary components of temperament: Viscerotonia (calm, relaxed, friendly); Somatotonia (assertive, energetic, outgoing, confident); and Cerebrotonia (hypersensitivity to environmental stimuli, gets pleasure from thinking, desires privacy and solitude); each of these correlate highly with Endomorphy, Mesomorphy and Ectomorphy, respectively. It is the possible relationships between physique and temperament that have concerned the few psychologists who have explored this area, but aside from Sheldon's initially high correlations, few stable relationships have been found. Cortes and Gatti,[29] using Parnell's system, reconfirmed the relationships noted by Sheldon. Selecting only individuals in the extremes of the Fat, Muscularity, and Linearity components, self-descriptive adjective selection by the subjects indicated that those individuals high on the Fat component described themselves as "kind, relaxed, warm and soft-hearted"; those with extreme Muscularity, "confident, energetic, adventurous, enterprizing"; and those extreme in Linearity, "detached, tense, shy, and reserved."

Other studies have produced findings consistent with the above. Cortes and Gatti,[30] again using Parnell's system, found a positive and significant relationship between nAch and Muscularity and a significant negative relationship between that same need and Linearity in both delinquents and nondelinquents. Sometime earlier, Smith [31] had shown that individuals with Ectomorphic physiques score high on the Sc and Si scales of the MMPI, whereas Mesomorphic individuals score high on Hy and low on Si. More recently, however, Deabler and associates [32] somatotyped 300 males and compared the somatotypes with 16PF scores. They found no significant correlations between the 16PF and Endomorphy and Ectomorphy, and very few significant correlations with Mesomorphy. The latter did correlate with suspiciousness, anxiety, high Ergic tension, and neuroticism.

In summary, then, it would appear that no matter which system (Sheldon or Parnell) is used, some consistent relationships appear between physique and temperament. By and large, the fat (Endomorphic) individuals tend to be relaxed, warm, and dependent; the muscular (Mesomorphic) individuals tend to be energetic, adventuresome, outgoing and high need achievers; and the linear (Ectomorphic) individuals tend to be withdrawn, shy, socially introverted, and reserved.

Our thinking thus far has been that if the capacity for hypnosis is, in part, genetically determined and an individual's basic physique is genetically determined, then some relationship should exist between anthropometric measures and measures of hypnotic capacity. To strengthen further our hypothesis development, the relationship between physique (somatotype) and behavioral (temperament) measures was explored and related to behavioral concomitants of hypnotic capacity. As noted above and explicated in literature reviews by Deckert and West [1] and Barber,[8] personality (behavioral) traits, as measured with standardized inventories and tests, do not appear to relate in any systematic way to hypnotizability. The one relationship that does seem to be consistent, as reported by several investigators,[33–35] is that stable extroverts and neurotic introverts are more "susceptible to hypnosis" than their reverse counterparts. In addition, Gibson and Curran [35] found that susceptibility—what we are calling capacity for hypnosis—was positively related to introversion and negatively related to extroversion.

The lack of positive relationships between hypnotizability and standardized measures has led investigators to utilize more specifically developed questionnaires [36, 37] and interview techniques [38] in order to tease out what relationships might be present. What has developed from this approach has been the recognition of the role by imagination and imaginative functions in those individuals who have a high capacity for hypnosis.[37–41] Hilgard,[38, 42, 43] for example, has found that individuals who deeply involve themselves in reading, the dramatic arts, and religion, and savor sensory experiences for their own sake are highly capable of hypnosis. These attributes would appear to be closely related to what Tellegan and Atkinson [44] have called "absorption," others [45] earlier called "attention capabilities," and still others [46] have named "concentration capacity." That is, those individuals who are capable of deep involvement in a task, to the relative exclusion of the surround, are also highly capable of hypnosis. Going one step further, such descriptions sound strikingly similar to those applied to the introvert, and more specifically to the Cerebrotonic temperament type of Sheldon. Similar self-descriptive adjectives were selected by Cortes and Gatti's [29] subjects who possessed an extremely Linear physique, as measured by Parnell's phenotype system. Recall, also, that Smith [31] found a significant, positive relationship between social introversion and Sheldon's Ectomorphic component. It would appear reasonable to predict that individuals whose body build tended toward Linearity (Ectomorphy) would be highly capable of hypnosis.

J. Hilgard [38, 42, 43] made one other observation that relates to our thesis of a relationship between physique and hypnosis capacity. She pointed out that individuals who were adventuresome were more hypnotizable than those who were not. Although Cortes and Gatti's [29] Muscularity subjects use "adventurous" to describe themselves, a difference noted by Hilgard in the form this adventuresomeness takes is crucial for our predictive purposes. The highly hypnotizable, adventuresome person is adventurous in a solitary (introverted?), noncompetitive way. He or she revels, not in awards or admiration or defeating a human opponent, but in self-development, in the skills achieved in the motoric activity. Thus, we would not necessarily predict that the muscular Mesomorph would have an outstanding capacity for hypnosis. In fact, we predicted either no relationship between the capacity for hypnosis and the Muscularity component or a negative one.

Finally, the dependency and willingness to please seen in the Viscerotonic temperament type, coupled with its relationship to the Endomorphic physique,[28] leads directly to the prediction of a greater capacity for hypnosis in those scoring higher in the Fat physique component. Murray [47] has already shown a relationship between dependency and the capacity for hypnosis, and the more recent studies noted above [33-35] have demonstrated a positive relationship with stable extroversion—a cluster of behavior depicting the Viscerotonic individual.

METHOD

Subjects

One hundred and thirty-five coerced volunteer Colgate University students (87 males and 48 females) served as subjects as part of a course requirement in General Psychology. The subjects ranged in age from 18 to 20 years.

Procedure

The Harvard Group Scale of Hypnotic Susceptibility (HGSHS) was administered to groups of subjects ranging in size from six to forty individuals.

TABLE 1

MEANS AND STANDARD DEVIATIONS OF HGSHS AND THE FAT, MUSCULARITY, AND LINEARITY COMPONENTS OF PHYSIQUE

	Females (N=48)		Males (N=87)		Total Sample (N=135)	
	$\overline{X}$	s.d.	$\overline{X}$	s.d.	$\overline{X}$	s.d.
HGSHS	6.42	2.27	5.54	2.57	5.85	2.50
Fat	4.20	.76	4.36	.89	4.30	.85
Muscularity	2.69	.94	3.55	1.08	3.24	1.11
Linearity	2.94	1.13	3.05	1.26	3.01	1.21

Subjects were seen individually for the anthropometric measures by like-sexed experimenters. The measures were: height (in inches), weight (in pounds), circumference of the calf and bicep (in millimeters, measured with a tape measure), epicondyle widths of the humerus and femur (in millimeters, measured with an anthropometer), and skin-folds from over the triceps, subscapular, and superiliac areas (in millimeters, measured with a Lange skinfold caliper). These measures were recorded on Parnell's M.4 Standard Deviation Chart and converted to somatotype ratings (one to seven) for the Fat, Muscularity, and Linearity components of physique.

RESULTS

HGSHS scores and the Parnell System components of Fat, Muscularity, and Linearity were tabulated for each subject; means and standard deviations appear in TABLE 1. The latter data compare to those reported by Sheldon,[48] Cortes and Gatti,[29] and Deabler and associates,[32] but show a slight overload

TABLE 2

INTERCORRELATIONS AMONG THE HGSHS AND THE FAT, MUSCULARITY, AND LINEARITY COMPONENTS OF PHYSIQUE (SOMATOTYPES) FOR THE TOTAL SAMPLE (N=135)

	HGSHS	Fat	Muscularity
Fat	.13		
Muscularity	−.19 *	.05	
Linearity	.17 *	−.39 †	−.33 †

* p < .05.
† p < .001.

in the Fat component and underemphasis in Linearity. However, the average height (69.3 in), bicep girth (31.22 cm) and calf girth (36.64 cm) for subjects do not differ appreciably from those reported by Garrett and Kennedy [49] for individuals of Western cultures. Our sample of subjects appears to be reasonably representative of more extensive populations with respect to both the capacity for hypnosis and general physique configuration.

Intercorrelations among the four variables were calculated for the total sample of subjects and for the subsamples of males and females. These data appear in TABLES 2, 3, and 4. All of these tables illustrate the same basic relationships among the three physique components noted by Sheldon,[48] Parnell,[25] and others.[24]

More pertinent to the present investigation are the significant positive correlation between Linearity and the HGSHS scores and the significant negative correlation between Muscularity and the HGSHS scores for the total sample. The correlation between HGSHS scores and Linearity in TABLE 2 appears more attributable to a similar relationship in the male subsample than in the female. The relationship between HGSHS scores and Muscularity appears only in TABLE 2 and may be the result of some combination of factors not evident in either the female (TABLE 3) or male (TABLE 4) subsamples alone. In fact, TABLE 3 and the partial correlation coefficients (see below) make it clear that no relationship exists between HGSHS scores and the components of physique for the female subsample, while for the males, it appears

TABLE 3

INTERCORRELATIONS AMONG THE HGSHS AND THE FAT, MUSCULARITY, AND LINEARITY COMPONENTS OF PHYSIQUE (SOMATOTYPES) FOR THE FEMALE SUBJECTS (N=48)

	HGSHS	Fat	Muscularity
Fat	−.01		
Muscularity	−.18	−.18	
Linearity	.09	−.53 †	−.33 *

* p < .05.
† p < .001.

TABLE 4

INTERCORRELATIONS AMONG THE HGSHS AND THE FAT, MUSCULARITY, AND
LINEARITY COMPONENTS OF PHYSIQUE (SOMATOTYPES) FOR THE MALE SUBJECTS
(N=87)

	HGSHS	Fat	Muscularity
Fat	.21 *		
Muscularity	−.11	.10	
Linearity	.22 *	−.34 †	−.40 †

* p < .05.
† p < .01.

that both the Fat and Linearity components are positively related to the capacity for hypnosis.

Because of the intercorrelations among the physique components themselves, partial correlations between the HGSHS and each of the physique components were derived. The first order partial correlations for the total sample and the male subsample appear in TABLES 5 and 6, respectively. No partial correlations were significant for the female subsample.

In order to clarify further the influence of physique component intercorrelations, second-order partial correlation coefficients were calculated for the total sample and the male subsample. These coefficients appear in TABLE 7. It is clear that both the Fat and Linearity components are positively related to the capacity for hypnosis in males. The similar significant figures for the total sample are attributable to the male rather than the female subsample.

These differential findings with respect to the male and female subsamples —based, we suspect, in part on differences between the male and female physiques [48]—and previous findings suggesting higher capacities for hypnosis in females than in males,[18, 20, 37, 39, 50-53] led us to make a t-test comparison between the HGSHS scores of the males and female subsamples. The females of this sample demonstrated a significantly higher capacity for hypnosis than the males (t = 1.84, p < 05).

Finally, in order to assess more specifically the predictability of hypnosis capacity through physique, regression equations were developed. For the total sample: $Y_{HGSHS} = .65X_F − .28X_M + .44X_L + .27$ (F = 4.16, p < .01); for the

TABLE 5

FIRST-ORDER PARTIAL CORRELATION COEFFICIENTS FOR THE TOTAL SAMPLE (N=135)

Variable Held Constant	Fat	HGSHS with Muscularity	Linearity
Fat	—	−.19 *	.24 †
Muscularity	.14	—	.12 ‡
Linearity	.22 †	−.014	—

‡ p < .10.
* p < .05.
† p <.01.

First-Order Partial Correlation Coefficients for the Male Subjects (N=87)

Variable Held Constant	Fat	HGSHS with Muscularity	Linearity
Fat	—	−.14	.32 *
Muscularity	.23 *	—	.19 ‡
Linearity	.31 †	−.03	—

‡ p < .10.
* p < .05.
† p < .01.

males: $Y_{HGSHS} = .93X_F - .04X_M + .66X_L - .38$ (F = 4.48, p < .005). The regression equation for the female subsample was not significant, and it is suspected that that for the total sample derives its significance from the large male subsample.

DISCUSSION

The findings of this study offer a more detailed understanding of body morphology and the capacity for hypnosis. The significant relationships to emerge appear in both the correlations among variables and the regression equations. The more Fat (Endomorphic) a male physique has, the more likely is that individual to have a high capacity for hypnosis; the same is true of the Linear (Ectomorphic) male physique. The Muscular (Mesomorphic) physique, however, is unrelated to hypnotic capacity in both the male and female subsamples.

The finding of a relationship between Fat and Linearity and hypnosis capacity peculiar to the males and absent in the females is noteworthy. Since Haronian and Sugarman [27] showed reasonable shared variances between the Parnell and Sheldon systems, it is possible that the lack of relationship between physique variables and hypnotic capacity in the females is due to the general nature of the differences between male and female physiques, rather than being attributable to the particular measuring system used. As

TABLE 7

Second-Order Partial Correlation Coefficients for the Total Sample (N=135) and the Male Subsample (N=87)

	Fat	HGSHS with Muscularity	Linearity
Males	.32 †	−.01	.29 †
Total Sample	.21 *	−.12	.20 *

N.B. In each case two components of physique are held constant.
* p < .05.
† p < .01.

Sheldon [48] has shown, female somatotypes tend to cluster to the Endo-Meso-morphic poles, rather than to the Ectomorphic. However, this general cluster-ing and the lack of a relationship between the female Fat component and hypnotic capacity suggest that it is within the hypnotic capacity factor that the basic male-female difference lies.

There is a growing body of literature [18, 20, 37, 39, 50–53] indicating that fe-males do have a slightly higher capacity for hypnosis than do males. The data within our sample suggests the same difference, in that the female sub-sample's HGSHS scores were significantly higher than the male. If these differences have some structural reference, it is certainly not reflected in such gross measures as those obtained through somatotyping. The structural dif-ferences are, as are the hypnotic capacity differences, more subtle than that. Perhaps they are reflected at the cortical level, in that femlaes tend to rely more on their right hemisphere in meeting their environment, and it has been suggested that the capacity for hypnosis may be higher in right-hemisphere individuals than in left, as noted in the laterality of eye movements.[54] Per-haps, on the other hand, such differences are reflected at the subcortical level, notably the preoptic area of the hypothalamus. Male and female brains do differ from one another in hypothalamic structure and function,[56, 57] but the intertwining of hypothalamic and endocrine functions makes it difficult to say which, if either, is regnant with respect to the capacity for hypnosis.

Regarding the Fat (Endomorphic) component, our data demonstrate a stable relationship for males. This was not unexpected, because as early as 1938 Murray had demonstrated a relationship between dependency traits and hypnotic capacity. A number of more recent studies have shown a relation-ship between hypnotic capacity and extroverts,[33, 34] particularly the stable extrovert, although Gibson and Curran [35] report a negative, rather than posi-tive, relationship between extroversion and hypnotic susceptibility. Despite the fact that the relationship has been somewhat elusive, our data suggest that the dependence of the Viscerotonic is systematically related to the capacity for hypnosis.

Furthermore, this finding may relate to Murray [47] and White's [58, 59] early distinction between two kinds of trance, active and passive, the former being attributed to the very dependent, deferent, low-autonomy individual. It may well be that those individuals scoring high on the Fat component (Vicero-tronics in Sheldon's temperament classification) enter a different (alert) type of trance from those who score high on Linearity (Cerebrotonia), the latter possibly utilizing the passive trance. Unfortunately, our data do not allow such a trance distinction, but the relationship is worth further exploration.

In addition, in his critique of Sheldon's somatotypology, Hunt [23] pointed out that Endomorphy is the product, not of the overdevelopment of the endo-dermal embryonic layers, but of the growth phase at nine months of age, It would appear, then, that if the growth phase is maximal during this period, it is not only reflected in a very fat physique, but in certain behavioral pro-pensities as well; i.e., a heightened capacity for hypnosis.

The same sort of growth-phase interpretation can be applied to the Linear physique-capacity for hypnosis relationship, but with an even broader base. Although, the prediction that Linearity would be related to the capacity for hypnosis was derived from many sources dealing with such seemingly disparate areas as the relationships between creativity, imaginative potential, deep involvement, attention capacity, extroversion and social introversion, and hypnosis capacity, as well as relationships between physique and temperament types and self-descriptive adjectives, Hunt's views [23] on physique development are applicable. As with Endomorphy, Hunt [23] pointed out that Ectomorphy is the product not of the overdevelopment of an embryonic layer, but of a growth phase. In this case, the phase indicated was that of nine *years* rather than nine months as in the case of Endomorphy. Nine years—actually 9–12 years—of age is also that period that the maximum hypnosis capacity becomes manifest. [17, 18]

We suspect that it is not fortuitous that the growth phases of the two physiques found to be related to the capacity for hypnosis coincide with: (1) a period of physically imposed dependence (nine months) and (2) a period previously noted to be that of the maximum emergence of hypnotic capacity. This would be additionally revealing if trance types were to coincide with somatotypes, and would suggest the presence of two critical periods for the development of capacities for performing hypnotic behaviors.

The lack of a relationship between the Muscularity component and the capacity for hypnosis is apparent in both males and females, and can be understood through J. Hilgard's findings [38, 42, 43] of personality correlates of hypnosis. Since the highly Muscular physique is related to the "strong man (or woman)" characterature in our society, and included primarily those individuals whose physiques and temperaments led them into competitive situations, Hilgard's notation [38, 43, 44] that it is the adventuresome, but not team-competitive, award-seeking individuals who show a capacity for hypnosis, derives morphological substance in our data. Following Hunt's reasoning [23] again, those individuals who have their greatest growth phase during the adolescent years may be expected to have a stunted development of the capacity for hypnosis.

That heritable physique characteristics are related to the capacity for hypnosis is strongly supported by our data. Looking at the growth phases assumed to underlie physique development and at the peak ages of hypnosis capacity (9–12 years), there is even a hint, a suggestion of critical periods for the development of capacities for performing the types of behaviors generally associated with the terms active and passive trance. From our data, it is suggested that individuals whose major development occurs either at nine months and therefore develop Fat physiques, or in the ninth to twelfth years and therefore develop Linear physiques, will be those individuals with the highest capacity for hypnosis, while those whose peak development is in the adolescent years and therefore project a more Muscular body shape will be least responsive to hypnosis. Although the notion of critical periods for developing hypnotic capacity is admittedly based on the speculative integration of a number of disparate findings, our data do appear, not only to support Morgan's [20] findings of a heritable component to hypnosis, but to show that physique, as a heritable manifestation, is related to the capacity for hypnosis.

Acknowledgment

The author wishes to express his appreciation to the following individuals who assisted in various phases of the study: Steven S. Baumgarten, Carol Capelli, Constance A. Crabtree, Judith M. Isaacson, Cynthia S. Jackson, Joseph L. Kelley, Keith M. Lewis, Dan J. Margolis, Nancy E. Meiman, Gwen Racine, Susan Siegel, and Robert D. Yetvin.

REFERENCES

1. DECKERT, G. H. & L. J. WEST. 1963. The problem of hypnotizability: A review. Int. J. Clin. Exp. Hypn. **11:** 205–235.
2. WEITZENHOFFER, A. M. 1953. Hypnotism, an Objective Study in Suggestibility. John Wiley & Sons, Inc. New York, N.Y.
3. WEITZENHOFFER, A. M. & E. R. HILGARD. 1959. Stanford Hypnotic Susceptibility Scale, Forms A and B. Consulting Psychologists Press. Palo Alto, Calif.
4. WEITZENHOFFER, A. M. & E. R. HILGARD. 1962. Stanford Hypnotic Susceptibility Scale, Form C. Consulting Psychologists Press. Palo Alto, Calif.
5. WEITZENHOFFER, A. M. & E. R. HILGARD. 1963. Stanford Profile Scales of Hypnotic Susceptibility, Forms I and II. Consulting Psychologists Press. Palo Alto, Calif.
6. SHOR, R. E. & E. C. ORNE. 1962. Harvard Group Scale of Hypnotic Susceptibility. Consutling Psychologists Press. Palo Alto, Calif.
7. HILGARD, E. R. 1965. Hypnotic Susceptibility. Harcourt, Brace and World. New York, N.Y.
8. BARBER, T. X. 1964. Hypnotizability, suggestibility and personality: V. a critical review of research findings. Psychol. Rep. **14:** 299–320.
9. SACHS, L. B. & W. L. ANDERSON. 1967. Modification of hypnotic susceptibility. Int. J. Clin. Exp. Hypn. **15:** 172–180.
10. KINNEY, J. M. & L. B. SACHS. 1974. Increasing hypnotic suceptibility. J. Abnorm. Psychol. **83:** 145–150.
11. DIAMOND, M. J. 1972. The use of observationally presented information to modify hypnotic susceptibility. J. Abnorm. Psychol. **79:** 174–180.
12. DIAMOND, M. J. 1974. Modification of hypnotizability: A review. Psychol. Bull. **81:** 180–198.
13. COOPER, L. M., S. A. BANFORD, E. SCHUBOT & C. T. TART. 1967. A further attempt to modify hypnotic susceptibility through repeated individualized experience. Int. J. Clin. Exp. Hypn. **15:** 118–124.
14. TART, C. T. 1970. Increases in hypnotizability resulting from a prolonged program for enhancing personal growth. J. Abnorm. Psychol. **75:** 260–266.
15. COOPER, L. M. & P. LONDON. 1971. The development of hypnotic susceptibility: A longitudinal (convergence) study. Child Dev. **42:** 487–503.
16. MORGAN, A. H., D. L. JOHNSON & E. R. HILGARD. 1974. The stability of hypnotic susceptibility: A longitudinal study. Int. J. Clin. Exp. Hypn. **22:** 249–257.
17. LONDON, P. & L. M. COPPER. 1969. Norms of hypnotic susceptibility in children. Dev. Psychol. **1:** 113–124.
18. MORGAN, A. H. & E. R. HILGARD. 1973. Age differences in susceptibility. Int. J. Clin. Exp. Hypn. **21:** 78–85.
19. RAWLINGS, R. M. 1972. The inheritance of hypnotic amnesia. Presented at Australian and New Zealand Society for the Advancement of Science. University of New South Wales. Sydney, Australia.
20. MORGAN, A. H. 1973. The heritability of hypnotic susceptibility in twins. J. Abnorm. Psychol. **82:** 55–61.
21. THORKELSON, K. E. 1973. The relationship between hypnotic susceptibility and certain personality, physiological, and electroencephalographic variables in monozygotic and dizygotic twin pairs. University Microfilms. Ann Arbor, Mich.
22. SHELDON, W. H., S. S. STEVENS & W. B. TUCKER. 1940. The Varieties of Human Physique. Harper and Row. New York, N.Y.
23. HUNT, E. E. 1949. A note on growth, somatotype and temperament. Am. J. Phys. Anthropol. **7:** 79–89.
24. HUMPHREYS, L. G. 1957. Characteristics of type concepts with special reference to Sheldon's typology. Psychol. Bull. **54:** 218–228.
25. PARNELL, R. W. 1958. Behavior and Physique. Edward Arnold. London, England.

26. PARNELL, R. W. 1954. Somatotyping by physical anthropometry. Am. J. Phys. Anthropol. **21:** 209–239.
27. HARONIAN, F. & A. A. SUGARMAN. 1965. A comparison of Sheldon's and Parnell's method for quantifying morphological differences. Am. J. Phys. Anthropol. **23:** 135–142.
28. SHELDON, W. H. & S. S. STEVENS. 1942. The Varieties of Temperament. Harper and Brothers. New York, N.Y.
29. CORTES, J. B. & F. M. GATTI. 1965. Physique and self-description of temperament. J. Consul. Psychol. **29:** 432–439.
30. CORTES, J. B. & F. M. GATTI. 1966. Physique and motivation. J. Consult. Psychol. **30:** 408–414.
31. SMITH, D. W. 1957. The relation between ratio indices of physique and selected scales of the MMPI. J. Psychol. **43:** 325–331.
32. DEABLER, H. L., E. M. HARTL & C. A. WILLIS. 1973. Physique and personality: Somatotype and the 16PF. Percept. Mot. Skills. **36:** 927–933.
33. FURNEAUX, W. D. & H. B. GIBSON. 1961. The Maudsley Personality Inventory as a predictor of susceptibility to hypnosis. Int. J. Clin. Exp. Hypn. **9:** 167–177.
34. LANG, P. J. & A. D. LAZOVIK. 1962. Personality and hypnotic susceptibility. J. Consul. Psychol. **26:** 317–322.
35. GIBSON, H. B. & J. D. CURRAN. 1974. Hypnotic susceptibility and personality: A replication study. Br. J. Psychol. **65:** 283–291.
36. DIAMOND, M. J., J. GREGORY, E. LENNY, C. STEADMAN & J. M. TALONE. 1974. An alternative approach to personality correlates of hypnotizability: Hypnosis specific mediational attitudes. Int. J. Clin. Exp. Hypn. **22:** 346–353.
37. SHOR, R. E., M. T. ORNE & D. N. O'CONNELL. 1966. Psychological correlates of plateau hypnotizability in a special volunteer sample. J. Pers. Soc. Psychol. **3:** 80–95.
38. HILGARD, J. R. 1970. Personality and Hypnosis: A Study of Imaginative Involvement. University of Chicago Press. Chicago, Ill.
39. BOWERS, K. S. 1971. Sex and susceptibility as moderator variables in the relationship of creativity and hypnotic susceptibility. J. Abnorm. Psychol. **78:** 93–100.
40. PERRY, C. 1973. Imagery, fantasy and hypnotic susceptibility: A multidimensional approach. J. Pers. Soc. Psychol. **26:** 217–221.
41. SUTCLIFFE, J. P., C. W. PERRY & P. W. SHEEHAN. 1970. Relation of some aspects of imagery and fantasy to hypnotic susceptibility. J. Abnorm. Psychol. **76:** 270–287.
42. HILGARD, J. R. 1965. Personality and hypnotizability: Inferences from case studies. *In* Hypnotic Susceptibility. E. R. Hilgard. Harcourt, Brace and World. New York, N.Y.
43. HILGARD, J. R. 1974. Imaginative involvement: Some characteristics of the highly hypnotizable and the non-hypnotizable. Int. J. Clin. Exp. Hypn. **22**(2): 138–156.
44. TELLEGAN, A. & G. ATKINSON. 1974. Openness to absorbing and self altering ("absorption") a trait related to hypnotic susceptibility. J. Abnorm. Psychol. **83:** 268–277.
45. STERN, J. A., W. E. EDMONSTON, G. A. ULETT & A. LEVITSKY. 1963. Electrodermal measures in experimental amnesia. J. Abnorm. Soc. Psychol. **67:** 397–401.
46. SPIEGEL, H. 1974. The grade 5 syndrome: The highly hypnotizable person. Int. J. Clin. Exp. Hypn. **22:** 303–319.
47. MURRAY, H. A. 1938. Explorations in Personality. Oxford. New York, N.Y.
48. SHELDON, W. H. 1954. Atlas of Man. Harper and Brothers. New York, N.Y.
49. GARRETT, J. W. & K. W. KENNEDY. 1971. A Collection of Anthropometry. Aerospace Medical Research Laboratory. Patterson Air Force Base, Ohio.

50. DAVIS, L. W. & R. W. HUSBAND. 1931. A study of hypnotic susceptibility in relation to personality tests. J. Abnorm. Soc. Psychol. **26:** 175–182.
51. FRIEDLANDER, J. W. & T. R. SARBIN. 1938. The depth of hypnosis. J. Abnorm. Soc. Psychol. **33:** 453–475.
52. HILGARD, E. R., A. M. WEITZENHOFFER & P. GOUGH. 1958. Individual differences in susceptibility to hypnosis. Proc. Nat. Acad. Sci. (USA) **44:** 1255–1259.
53. LONDON, P., L. M. COOPER & H. J. JOHNSON. 1962. Subject characteristics in hypnotic research: II. Attitudes toward hypnosis, volunteer status, and personality measures. III. Some correlates of hypnotic susceptibility. Int. J. Clin. Exp. Hypn. **10:** 13–22.
54. BAKAN, J. 1969. Hypnotizability, laterality of eye-movements and functional brain asymmetry. Percept. Mot. Skills **28:** 927–932.
55. GUR, R. C. & R. E. GUR. 1974. Handedness, sex and eyedness as moderating variables in the relation between hypnotic susceptibility and functional brain asymmetry. J. Abnorm. Psychol. **83**(6): 635–643.
56. DORNER, G. 1973. Sex hormone-dependent differentiation of the hypothalamus and sexuality. *In* Horomnes and Brain Function. K. Lissak, Ed. : 47–51. Plenum Press. New York, N.Y.
57. FIELD, P. M. & G. RAISMAN. 1974. Structural and functional investigations of a sexually dimorphic part of the rat preoptic area. *In* Recent Studies of Hypothalamic Function. K. Lederis & K. E. Cooper, Eds. : 17–25. S. Karger. Basel, Switzerland.
58. WHITE, R. W. 1941. An analysis of motivation in hypnosis. J. Gen. Psychol. **24:** 145–162.
59. WHITE, R. W. 1937. Two types of hypnotic trance and their personality correlates. J. Psychol. **3:** 279–289.

ISSUES AND METHODS FOR MODIFYING RESPONSIVITY TO HYPNOSIS

Michael Jay Diamond *

Los Angeles, California 90026

A number of diversified methods have been used to significantly increase hypnotic susceptibility when measured on standardized hypnotic test scales and self-ratings following attempted hypnotic inductions.[8] Included among these methods are *sensory-produced alterations* (e.g. sleep and dream suggestions, music, silence and white noise, psychedelic drugs, and sensory restriction); *hypnotic set and situational variations* (e.g. subject's (*S*'s) attitudes and expectations as well as the hypnotist's behavior); *experiential learning* (e.g. encounter groups and personal growth programs); *psychophysiological training* (e.g. EEG- and EMG-biofeedback; nb: see Wickramasekera [36] for an extensive review of these methods); and *training in hypnotic behavior* (e.g. classical and operant conditioning, observational learning, and informational control). The most methodologically sophisticated modification studies were performed using the latter, more systematic attempts at training hypnotic behavior. I should like to examine the most successful of these methods briefly before raising several pertinent issues with respect to modifying hypnotizability.

The most persistent and generalizable modification effects occur with operant and informational control-based systematic training. Neither classical conditioning nor observational learning procedures produce such effects. The efficacy of operant and informational control procedures is well-established.[7, 10, 12, 18, 25, 33] Moreover, the effects of these two procedures have been demonstrated both for *S*s initially low and more moderate in susceptibility [7, 25] and, on a relatively lasting and generalizable basis.[7, 18, 25, 33] Operant-based training typically involves self-paced successive approximation, provision of a clear conception of the desired sensory behavior, and positive reinforcement. Information control training employs verbal information (direct instructions), presented either observationally or in written form, designed to reduce misconceptions and negative attitudes about hypnosis (disinhibitory information) while providing concrete internal (covert) methods for experiencing hypnosis (facilitative information).

A number of issues and questions require clarification in this area. Too often the motivational differences between clinical and experimental hypnosis (e.g. alleviating distress versus receiving experimental credit) are overlooked, and thus what often seems obvious to a researcher is "Greek" to a clinician (and viceversa). My work both as an hypnosis researcher and practicing clinician has undoubtedly afforded me a unique and advantageous perspective with respect to the phenomenon. I suspect that several points I am about to make will appear "radical" to various experimentalists but "trite" to many clinicians. Certainly, modification data are subject to numerous alternative

* Address correspondence to 974 West Kensington Road #8, Los Angeles, Calif. 90026.

119

interpretations. We hypnosis investigators are limited by our experience much like the blind men in the Sufi parable who, while standing beside an elephant, formed their perceptions of the creature according to the most adjacent bodily part capable of being touched.[28] Campbell Perry [22] has helped me to remember that there is more to modification than meets the eye. Nonetheless, while we agree on the issues in need of addressing, we differ considerably as to how the issues are best dealt with. A more extensive discussion of these differences will shortly be appearing in the *International Journal of Clinical and Experimental Hypnosis*.[9, 22]

Four major issues will be considered here. The issues pertain to *conceptualization, individual differences, methodology,* and *specification.* The *conceptual* issue revolves around the question "How might we best construe hypnotizability?". The issue of *individual differences* stems from the question "Who responds to modification training and how deeply?" The *methodological* issue asks the question "How can we improve upon the methodologies in modification research?" Finally, the *specification* issue derives from the question "What are the core or 'active' components in successful modification training procedures?" I intend to present data-based arguments designed to bridge the clinical-experimental gap while leading toward the resolution of these questions.

THE CONCEPTUAL ISSUE: HOW MIGHT WE BEST CONSTRUE HYPNOTIZABILITY?

My argument is that hypnotizability is most efficaciously construed as a modifiable skill comprised of both aptitudinal and situational factors in need of differentiation.

There are two major ways of conceptualizing hypnotizability. The "trait" viewpoint stems from the psychometric approach to personality and essentially regards hypnotizability as a highly stable, basic underlying personality trait that is not likely to be modified to any large extent unless somehow there are major changes in the personality of the *S.* Any modifications that do occur are considered to result from more transient situational variations rather than from alterations in the enduring underlying components. In contrast, the "skill" viewpoint derives from social learning tradition and construes hypnotizability largely as a skill learned by virtue of one's experiences. Accordingly, this skill can be modified, at least to some extent, by virtue of subsequent learning experiences.

Unfortunately, there is a tendency to confuse these approaches while at the same time failing to see the relationship between one's own trait-skill constructs and subsequent interpretations of the findings. Unlike the more empirically oriented skill theorists, trait theorists like Gur [13] and Perry [22] regard skill-specific training as little more than another situational manipulation.

There are, of course, clear-cut individual differences in hypnotizability that must be accounted for.[14, 15] Trait-theory, which historically is more likely to employ state-based explanatory interpretations,[11, 14, 30] has done a better job in attempting to account for these differences. Skill theoretists, when they have employed explanatory constructs, use terms like "goal directed imagining" [1] and "role enactment" [27] without really examining why some subjects "have it" and others seem not to. Diamond [8] suggested that an empirically oriented skill approach can include state-based explanatory mechanisms. At any rate, there is no reason why skill theoreticians cannot study these differences in the fashion of such developmentally oriented scholars as Josephine Hilgard.[17] Certainly, some basic ability is needed for any kind of skill training to be effective; we can't teach monkeys to speak fluent Chinese. The trait-skill issue, however, revolves around the importance, fluidity, and potential for subsequent learning which is attached to this initial ability level.

A skill-based construction of hypnosis is best assumed in order to generate further research on the more systematic hypnotic training procedures which too often are relegated to a minor position by many experimentalists who implicitly adhere to a trait viewpoint.[9] Additionally, much data further argue against the trait view.[22] Correlational studies typcially indicate small relationships between hypnotizability and various personality traits. Moreover, trait claims relying on test-retest reliability (over varied scales, hypnotists, induction procedures, and time periods) must be seriously questioned. How do these performance consistencies prove the existence of an underlying and enduring personality trait? Behavioral consistencies and stability can just as fruitfully be construed as reflecting test-situational consistency as personality stability.[20] Why should we expect anything but high test-retest reliability following such variations, inasmuch as the tests were designed and validated in order to insure such results? The more pertinent question being asked by more empirically oriented modification researchers is "What happens to test-retest responsivity following systematic training in hypnosis-relevant skills? We shall soon see that even these correlations often fail to hold up following particular kinds of training interventions.

Findings from studies employing hypnosis-specific training indicate that hypnotizability is best conceived as truly modifiable.[8] Perry,[22] however, relied primarily on studies utilizing situational manipulations to suggest that modification changes are typically not very meaningful. He cited the paucity of reports indicating that initially refractory Ss can be brought to experience somnambulism to conclude there are "limitations to the degree of modification possible" and thereby support his contention that alterations do not appear very meaningful. Perry thus implicitly evolved a new criteria for meaningfulness; namely, "profound," "extreme," or "dramatic" change.

These criteria appear rather elitist and somehow more likely to turn up in experimental circles. It is certainly difficult to imagine a clinician disregarding a training procedure simply because his client somehow was not brought to the "expert" level of the somnambulist or "hypnotic virtuoso." Carrying this criterion to other settings, we would be hard pressed to justify virtually any behavior modification or inner-city training program as being "meaningful" simply because few, if any, participants can reach the "virtuoso" status of the initially more skilled or affluent. Apparently, a more limited criterion of "meaningfulness" is needed. We need not assume that modification entails some sort of *tabula rasa* position. Initial differences in ability may indeed limit the effectiveness of any particular change endeavor. Nevertheless, while monkeys cannot learn to speak Chinese, they can be "meaningfully" trained to communicate; similarly, one need not write like William Shakespeare in order to have benefitted from training in creative writing.

The question, then, is what criterion of meaningfulness is best utilized? It appears neither a matter of simple statistical significance nor dramatic or extreme change. Perhaps the most appropriate criteria involve three dimensions: (1) *relativity,* or how much of a change occurs relative to each *S*'s baseline; (2) *clinical utility,* or is the change clinically meaningful in terms of alleviating pain, symptoms, and so on?; and (3) *heuristic value,* or by considering that the change exists, can we better understand and regulate the phenomenon?

The issue of *relativity* dictates an idiographic approach examining changes for each *S* with respect to his own base line performance level. Thus, a training program enabling the experience of hypnotic dreams, regressions, hallucinations, and anosmias can be said to produce relatively meaningful changes for *S*s initially refractory to hypnosis.

Clinical utility requires changes enabling particular qualitative experiences rather than any particular frequencies or depths of experience Most clinicians view hypnotic ability as modifiable and a large number have reported successes in modifying it.[8, 24] In my work as a practicing psychotherapist, I frequently employ hypnosis as an adjunct to assessment and treatment, and I have yet to find a client who is not somewhat capable of learning to experience a degree of hypnosis useful to his/her treatment. Indeed, research does indicate that clinically useful hypnosis does not require particularly good hypnotic *S*s, let alone those capable of deep hypnosis.[16, 19, 23, 26] A successful hypnotic training procedure can apparently aid clients in reducing pain,[26] while lessening symptoms, prompting greater insight, abreaction, and achieving greater cognitive control. I am afraid that the danger of creating self-fulfilling prophecies exists, and some clients might be denied otherwise useful clinical hypnosis when it is assumed that modification procedures do not produce meaningful changes. In this vein, I am reminded of the famous anecdote often told by the eminent hypnotherapist, Milton H. Erickson. Erickson, it seems, once required 300 hours of training before getting a particularly resistant *S* into a trance state. Such perseverance by the hypnotist-clinician is frequently necessary in ameliorating clinical distress.

Heuristically speaking, investigators may more probably develop and improve various modification procedures if they perceive the techniques as capable of producing meaningful changes much in the same way as special educators go about developing behavior modification procedures once they stop seeing certain retarded children as "uneducable." The need for empirical research largely requires that researchers adopt an open-minded attitude with respect to modifying hypnotizability.

A long-standing assumption is that hypnotic performance involves two major underlying components: (1) an enduring aptitude or ability component; and, (2) a modifiable attitudinal component.[11, 14, 21] The attitudinal component is regarded as modifiable by means of interpersonal or situational factors. Unfortunately, however, there has often been an uncritical acceptance of this two-factor assumption that relies on unvalidated hypothetical constructs. The difficulties involved in operationalizing constructs like aptitude and attitude are well known, particularly in the intelligence (IQ) testing field. As in intelligence testing, problems arise for hypnosis investigators when we are too glib in concluding that either of these factors primarily accounts for hypnotizability.

There is indeed evidence that situational "set and setting" alterations have more transitory effects on the initially less susceptible *S*s;[8] nevertheless, this data does not support the assumption that these less susceptible *S*s (low and moderates) are lacking in the aptitudinal factor. Other evidence suggests that initially refractory *S*s have enough ability to increase their hypnotic skills following training,[1, 7, 25] and moreover, some can even become somnambulists.[2, 6]

These findings can as parsimoniously be interpreted as indicating that initially less susceptible *S*s suffer from more hypnosis-hindering situational, attitudinal, and/or interpersonal inhibitions than do highly susceptible *S*s and that, in addition, by virtue of such inhibitions, the initially less susceptble *S* has had far fewer opportunities to practice and develop his/her hypnosis skills. Thus, such *S*s are in need of more potent and frequent skill-enhancing training experiences. This argument runs parallel to the logic of environmentally oriented IQ theoreticians who regard low IQ scores among many urban ghetto residents as reflecting situational inhibitions and developmental deficiencies rather than ability deficits. Could it be that our less susceptible *S*s too are simply in need of more skill-enriching learning and practice experiences?

THE INDIVIDUAL DIFFERENCE ISSUE: WHO RESPONDS TO MODIFICATION TRAINING AND HOW DEEPLY?

It is argued that systematic skill-enhancing training experiences are as effective for initially less susceptible *S*s as for the initially more moderate; meanwhile, the possibility that *S*s can be trained to experience deep hypnosis is left open.

Few modification studies actually report correlations between initial pretraining and posttraining scores. Nonetheless, the reported correlations at least suggest that potent training procedures can meaningfully alter the relationship between initial and posttreatment susceptibility.[9] Hypnotizability thus seems less than "highly stable" and indeed capable of being directly affected by certain forms of training. The effectiveness and value of training would, of course, not be compromised even were the relationship between initial and posttraining skill completely stable. Correlational and relative order relationships are important to the logic of "trait" theorists. An empirical approach to modification does not, however, carry the burden of demonstrating a relationship (or lack of it) to some starting point (i.e., initial level) but rather, only of demonstrating that hypnotic performance is changeable.

Additionally, several studies demonstrated that systematic, hypnotic training procedures were as effective for the initially less susceptible as for the initially more moderate.[1, 7, 10, 25] These findings held up on generalization tests[7] and following correction tests for possible regression effects.[7, 10] Thus, the evidence indicates that even initially refractory *S*s are as capable as more moderate *S*s of learning to experience hypnosis. It does seem, however, that initial differences reflect something more than simple performance tests.[9] Varied training is undoubtedly needed for different entry-hypnotic skills, and presumably, there are multiple training tracks to explore. Empirical research is necessary to discern the limits of this latter pathway.

There is evidence, moreover, that some *S*s may even be trained to experience deep hypnosis or somnambulism.[2, 4, 6, 7] Indeed, there simply is not enough data to warrant any upper limit conclusions. No systematic, hypnosis training procedure ran over seven to ten hours, and training is more typically in the one-hour range. Therefore, it is imperative that we empirically study the effects of more extensive training programs on initially refractory Ss. While we are likely to discover that not everyone can be deeply hypnotized, for a variety of reasons, we are just as likely to find that many otherwise refractory Ss can be brought to deep hypnosis under the right individual, motivation, situation, and training circumstances. The who, what, and why of this possibility remain to be determined.

THE METHODOLOGICAL ISSUE: HOW CAN WE IMPROVE UPON THE METHODOLOGIES IN MODIFICATION RESEARCH?

Several writers have discussed methodological inadequacies and possible artifactual effects in modification research.[8, 9, 13, 22] The points most in need of incorporation include: the determination of base line levels of hypnotizability and criteria for operationalizing "plateau susceptibility"; the role played by compliance; the need for better control groups; the need for studying more "remote effects"; and the need for multimodal, multimethod studies.

Investigations attempting to determine the effects of a change procedure require that base line levels of performance be established in order to insure that effects result from the experimental intervention rather than response variability. Inasmuch as test-retest reliability is extremely high in hypnotic susceptibility studies, modification investigators often settle for two testings to establish a base line. An alternative, albeit more elaborate, criteria termed plateau susceptibility is often operationalized as two consecutive *Stanford Hypnotic Susceptibility Scale: Form C* testings with no S improvement.[31] This plateau is regarded as one's "optimal" hypnotizability established by practice in hypnosis wherein S fears and inhibitions concerning hypnosis no longer operate.[22]

There is a real question as to how this construct is best operationalized. The standard criteria is based on stability and by no means ensures that fears and inhibitions are overcome. We need a parametric study of the phenomenon and a more critical analysis of the utility and validity of the plateau construct. A legitimate question is whether it is worth the time and trouble to establish such a stable base line in comparison with simply establishing one based on a set number of trials (e.g. two or three). It is imperative, however, that a meaningful base line be established, although what constitutes "meaningful" is subject to debate. In most areas of research (biofeedback, operant conditioning, and so on) some variability is an inherent aspect of base line performance, and, although minimizing this variability is the object of the base line notion, establishing session-session consistency, is not regarded as particularly important. At any rate, the data indicate that more than traditionally defined plateau susceptibility is necessary to account for the modification effects.[9, 22]

Additional evidence has also demonstrated that more than compliance is involved in the better modification studies.[8, 22] Nonetheless, more stringent procedures could be developed to insure that Ss are being honest in reporting what they believe to be true. Bowers[3] postexperimental method to minimize "compliance" to pressurizing test instructions has been one useful method.[7, 10, 18] Similarly, these investigators typically employed blind Es to reduce further the potential demand characteristic effects. Finally, Orne's[21] postexperimental clinical interview method using an independent E with no prior experimental involvement appears to have value.[22] Future studies might attempt to employ this latter method along with less explicit statements concerning the experiment's purposes.

There is also a need to employ more adequate control groups in order to determine the potency of specific training procedures. Attention-placebo control groups, which have been recently used in three studies,[7, 10, 33] provide incremental validity over the more frequently used no-treatment control groups. Moreover, corrections for possible regression effects,[13] correlational, as well as (co-) variance analyses are necessary in order to examine modification effects on differential S groupings.[9] As a result of such analyses, the differential effects of training on lows versus moderates can be extended to include such meaningful S groupings as experienced versus inexperienced, highly motivated versus less motivated, and active versus passive learners.

There is a need to carry out both long-term applications of training to determine the upper limits of various training methods and longitudinal studies that provide data about the permanence of the increases in hypnotizability.[8] Similarly, both follow-up and generalization posttesting require continual study to better discern persistence of training effects, the limits of generalization to novel hypnotic suggestions, and the more remote effects of particular training methods on Ss differing in initial susceptibility. The longest term follow-up study ran one month from the post-test;[18] other studies used shorter follow-ups of approximately two to seven days.[7, 13] Apparently, different training methods yield quite different generalization effects; in particular, it appears that the more cognitive, item-specific operant training used by the Sachs researchers[18, 25, 33] produces smaller generalization effects than the more general hypnotic training of Diamond's[7, 10, 12] informational control method. Further research is necessary, however, before any firm conclusions are warranted.

Finally, further research is warranted that tests the value of specific training procedures across such varying modalities as individual versus group training, written versus observation-discussion settings, live versus taped presentations, single versus combination modes (e.g. written and taped) and the like. In addition, we might explore the effects of variously combined modification methods (e.g. direct instructions; music plus operant procedures; relaxation training plus direct instructions; music plus operant training) across subject samples in order to better determine *what* works for *whom* under *which* circumstances.

THE SPECIFICATION ISSUE: WHAT ARE THE CORE COMPONENTS IN SUCCESSFUL MODIFICATION PROCEDURES?

The precise mechanisms accounting for increases in hypnotizability are unknown. Nonetheless, investigators have isolated several dimensions that appear largely responsible for the modification changes they report. These dimensions include both attitudes and specific skills. I will briefly discuss three such dimensions or "core components" that appear particularly important in effective training.

The first dimension, termed *optimal learning factors,* includes *motivation* to experience hypnosis,[1, 4, 7] *attention* (both to the hypnotist's words and to the training procedure itself),[10, 13, 35] *shaping* or successive approximation,[2, 18, 25, 33] *practice* or rehearsal of newly learned internal responses,[4, 25, 33] *reinforcement* in the form of successful hypnotic experience,[2, 7, 25] and *feedback*.[2, 18, 25, 33]

The second component, the *attitudinal and set factor,* includes several dimensions coming into play just prior to the hypnotic experience itself. Regarded as important are *bodily relaxation,*[34, 35] *receptive perception* or more passive, "present-centered" perceptual sets,[34] *interpersonal trust,*[29] and *disinhibiting fears, attitudes and expectations* that otherwise interfere with the hypnotic experience.[4, 5, 7, 10, 12]

The final component, which undoubtedly provides the most important learning augmentation, is termed the *cognitive strategy* factor. It involves teaching Ss correct ways of responding internally in order to experience hypnosis and has been substantiated in research from Barber's,[1, 32] Diamond's,[7, 10, 12] and Sachs'[18, 25, 33] laboratories. Moreover, the use of post-experimental inquiries and subjective questionnaires has been fruitful in further establishing the importance of such strategy learning in modifying hypnotizability. The strategies involved include learning to *suspend reality concerns* by letting go of one's analytic focus and becoming more present-centered;[7, 10, 12] *controlling imagination and imagery* along particular channels congruent with the aims of the suggestion;[1, 4, 7, 32] *focusing thought and attention* along with suggestions;[1, 7, 10, 12, 18, 25, 33] and *learning specific covert contingencies* that typically combine the forementioned strategies, in order to experience such particular hypnotic suggestions as anosmia, amnesia, and hallucinations.[1, 7, 18]

The utility of any modification procedure ultimately rests on discerning these core components and subsequently combining them in the most efficacious manner. The components have been suggested post-hoc by the data; it is time to begin more systematically investigating the role played by the various dimensions of learning, mediation, and covert hypnotic strategy. Such a direction will not only continue to contribute to our understanding of hypnosis and hypnotic phenomena, but, more important, will further enable us to use hypnosis as a tool which improves the quality of people's lives.

REFERENCES

1. BARBER, T. X., N. P. SPANOS & J. F. CHAVES. 1974. Hypnosis Imagination, and Human Potentialities. Pergamon Press. New York, N.Y.
2. BLUM, G. A. 1963. Programming people to simulate machines. *In* Computer Simulation of Personality. S. Tomkins & S. Messick, Eds. John Wiley & Sons. New York.
3. BOWERS, K. S. 1967. The Effects of Demands for Honesty on Reports of Visual and Auditory Hallucinations. Int. J. Clin. Exp. Hypn. **15:** 31–36.
4. BURNS, A. 1976. Changes in hypnotizability following experience. Int. J. Clin. Exp. Hypn. **24:** 269–280.
5. CRONIN, D. M., N. P. SPANOS & T. X. BARBER. 1971. Augmenting hypnotic suggestibility by providing favorable information about hypnosis. Amer. J. Clin. Hypn. **13:** 259–264.
6. DIAMOND, M. J. 1971. The use of observationally presented information to modify hypnotic susceptibility. Doctoral dissertation. Stanford Univ. Stanford, Calif. Ann Arbor, Mich.: Univ. Microfilms. No. 71–19, 672.
7. DIAMOND, M. J. 1972. The use of observationally-presented information to modify hypnotic susceptibility. J. Abnorm. Psychol. **79:** 174–180.
8. DIAMOND, M. J. 1974. Modification of hypnotizability: a review. Psych. Bull. **81:** 180–193.

9. DIAMOND, M. J. 1977. Hypnotizability is modifiable: an alternative approach. Int. J. Clin. Exp. Hyn. In press.
10. DIAMOND, M. J., C. STEADMAN, D. HARADA & J. ROSENTHAL. 1975. The use of direct instructions to modify hypnotic performance: the effects of programmed learning procedures. J. Abnorm. Psychol. **84:** 109–113.
11. GILL, M. M. & M. BRENMAN. 1959. Hypnosis and Related States. International Universities Press. New York, N.Y.
12. GREGORY, J. & M. J. DIAMOND. 1973. Increasing hypnotic susceptibility by means of positive expectancies and written instructions. J. Abnorm. Psychol. **82:** 363–367.
13. GUR, R. C. 1974. An attention-controlled operant procedure for enhancing hynotic susceptibility. J. Abnorm. Psychol. **83:** 644–650.
14. HILGARD, E. R. 1965. Hypnotic Susceptibility. Harcourt, Brace & World. New York, N.Y.
15. HILGARD, E. R. 1973. The domain of hypnosis: with some comments on alternative paradigms. Amer. Psychol. **82:** 972–982.
16. HILGARD, E. R. & J. R. HILGARD. 1975. Hypnosis in the Relief of Pain. Kaufman. Los Altos, Calif.
17. HILGARD, J. R. 1970. Personality and Hypnosis: A Study of Imaginative Involvement. University of Chicago Press. Chicago, Ill.
18. KINNEY, J. M. & L. B. SACHS. 1974. Increasing hypnotic susceptibility. J. Abnorm. Psychol. **83:** 145–150.
19. MELZACK, R. & C. PERRY. 1975. Self-regulation of pain: the use of alpha feedback and hypnotic training for the control of chronic pain. Exp. Neural. **46:** 452–469.
20. MISCHEL, W. 1968. Personality and Assessment. John Wiley & Sons. New York, N.Y.
21. ORNE, M. T. 1959. The nature of hypnosis: artifact and essence. J. Abnorm. Psychol. **58:** 277–299.
22. PERRY, C. 1977. Is hypnotizability modifiable? Int. J. Clin. Exp. Hyn. In press.
23. PERRY, C. & G. MULLEN. 1975. The effects of hypnotic susceptibility on reducing smoking behavior treated by an hypnotic technique. J. Clin. Psychol. **31:** 498–505.
24. SACHS, L. B. 1971. Construing hypnosis as modifiable behavior. *In* Psychology of Private Events. A. Jacobs and L. Sachs, Eds. Academic Press. New York, N.Y.
25. SACHS, L. B. & W. ANDERSON. 1967. Modification of hypnotic susceptibility. Int. J. Clin. Exp. Hypn. **15:** 172–180.
26. SACHS, L. B., M. FEUERSTEIN & J. H. VITALE. 1976. Hypnotic self-regulation of chronic pain. Paper presented at ann. mtg. Amer. Psychol. Ass. Washington, D.C.
27. SARBIN, T. R. & W. C. COE. 1972. Hypnosis: A Social Psychological Analysis of Influence Communication. Holt, Rinehart and Winston. New York, N.Y.
28. SHAH, I. 1970. Tales of the Dervishes. E. P. Dutton. New York, N.Y.
29. SHAPIRO, J. L. & M. J. DIAMOND. 1972. Increases in hypnotizabilty as a function of encounter group training: some confirming evidence. J. Abnorm. Psychol. **79:** 112–115.
30. SHOR, R. E. 1959. Hypnosis and the concept of the generalized reality-orientation. Amer. J. Psychother. **13:** 582–602.
31. SHOR, R. E. & J. C. COBB. 1968. An exploratory study of hypnotic training using the concept of plateau responsivity as a referent. Amer. J. Clin. Hypn. **10:** 178–197.
32. SPANOS, N. P. & T. X. BARBER. 1974. Toward a convergence in hypnosis research. Amer. Psychol. **29:** 500–511.
33. SPRINGER, C. J., L. B. SACHS & J. B. MORROW. 1977. Group methods of increasing hypnotic susceptibility. Int. J. Clin. Exp. Hypn. In press.

34. TALONE, J. M., M. J. DIAMOND & C. STEADMAN. 1975. Modifying hypnotic performance by means of brief sensory experiences. Int. J. Clin. Exp. Hypn. 23: 190–199.
35. WICKRAMASEKERA, I. 1973. The effects of electromyographic feedback on hypnotic susceptibility: more preliminary data. J. Abnorm. Psychol. 82: 74–77.
36. WICKRAMASEKERA, I. This volume.

THE HYPNOTIC INDUCTION PROFILE (HIP):
A REVIEW OF ITS DEVELOPMENT *

Herbert Spiegel †

Department of Psychiatry
College of Physicians and Surgeons
Columbia University
New York, New York 10032

WHY COME UP WITH ANOTHER TEST FOR HYPNOTIZABILITY?

There has been a long-standing need for standardized measurements of hypnotizability appropriate for clinical use. Without measurements, the resulting clinical appraisals are ambiguous. Questions such as "Was the patient hypnotized or not?", "What kind of trance was it?", and "What difference does it make for therapy?" cannot be answered. Ignoring these questions, clinicians who use hypnosis plunge ahead, using some technique (or ceremony) that "works." In fact, many clinicians not concerned with the assessment issue make the assumption that all patients are hypnotizable and that inducing hypnosis depends solely upon the effort and skill of the therapist. Such ceremonies tend to be tailored for the therapist instead of the individual capacity of the patient. Also, consensual validation among therapists is not possible without a standard clinical monitor of trance experience, and further, trance capacity is not differentiated from treatment strategy.

Clinicians have been left in this predicament because laboratory tests for hypnotizability are not feasible for clinical use for many reasons. Practically, these measurements take too much time (an hour or more) out of a therapy session and also may fatigue the patient. Some instructions are aesthetically inappropriate and perhaps embarrassing. There is also the insulting insinuation in the term "susceptibility" that because of a particular weakness, a patient is hypnotizable. Laboratory tests have been standardized on nonpatients (college students), and questions of the impediments caused by psychopathology or neurological deficits have not been considered. Additionally, laboratory tests are based on the assumption that hypnosis is sleeplike, despite the fact that there is no evidence to support this. It is the opposite: attentive, receptive concentration. Asking a subject to "wake up" from a trance or referring to the trance as the opposite of the "awake" state represents sloppy thinking without data-based facts. Furthermore, it is the alertness of the patient in trance that is critical for the treatment interaction.

The Hypnotic Induction Profile (HIP) answers the need for a clinically appropriate test of trance capacity, and it can be used in the laboratory. A brief and quickly paced test,[1] it takes five to ten minutes to administer and works as an alerting operation. Instead of testing a broad range of often embarrassing "hypnotic behaviors" in order to then predict the degree of

* Studies presented in this paper were supported by a grant from the Charles E. Merrill Trust.
† Reprint requests to Dr. Herbert Spiegel, 19 East 88th Street, New York, N.Y. 10028.

hypnotizability present in a patient, it is structured to actually induce trance and use it in the context of therapy while measuring the experience of entry and exit from trance in a standardized way. In addition to the sensory reportage and motor responses that other tests measure, the HIP has a biological measure that theoretically represents an individual's potential capacity to experience trance. The HIP also sets a matrix in which discovery of sensory alteration can occur. It was standardized on a patient population in a clinical setting.[2]

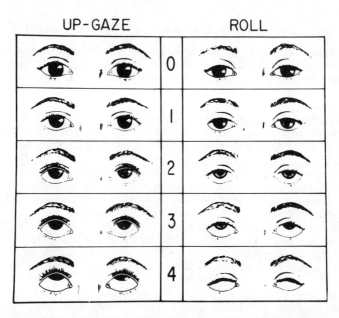

FIGURE 1. The Eye Roll Sign for hypnotizability. The Roll (ER) is a measure of the distance or amount of sclera between the lower border of the cornea and the lower eyelid exhibited while the subject simultaneously gazes upward and slowly closes the eyelid. The Up-Gaze is preparatory, and not an important measure by itself.

HOW IS HYPNOSIS EVALUATED BY THE HIP?

The HIP postulates that hypnosis is a subtle perceptual alteration involving a capacity for attentive, responsive concentration that is inherent in a person, can be tapped by the therapist, and used by the patient for his or her own goals. The biological or structural trait responsible for a person's potential to experience trance is measured by the Eye-Roll sign (ER) while the patient is not in the trance state.[3] Pictured here (FIGURE 1) is the range of five levels of the ER found in our population, represented from no potential (zero) through the highest potential for experiencing trance (four).

The association of the Eye-Roll sign with hypnotizability was discovered after several viewings of a film of a patient with hysterical seizures. Outstanding features were hyperextension of the antigravity muscles, and markedly mobile eye-movements. When tested outside of the trance or seizure, the eye-movements of this patient were also extreme. Later, eye-movement tests were done on other patients. Eyes varied in movement capacity. A clinically nonhypnotizable person with an obsessive character type showed almost no capacity for ER. This led to a tentative hypothesis that ER was related in some way to hypnotizability.

Systematic research has supported the association of the Eye-Roll sign and hypnotizability. In a selected nonpsychotic patient population,[2] it was found that the correlation between the ER and the experiential HIP items was .52 (N = 55). Other investigators using an unselected population have reported a lack of association between the ER and scores on the Harvard Group Scale of Hypnotic Susceptibility (HGSHS)[4, 5] and the Stanford Susceptibility Scale (SHSS).[5, 6] It is, however, important to note that in an unselected patient population (N = 1023), the ER also showed only a weak association to the remainder of the HIP.[2] This suggests that the lack of association between the ER and the HGSHS and the SHSS may have been due to the presence of persons with psychopathology in these samples.

It was observed in clinical use of hypnosis that a high ER was associated with immediate arm levitation, whereas a low ER required reinforcement signals to elicit levitation response. Accordingly, another data point which measured responsivity to structured guidance was developed—the arm levitation. Further, when the patient was asked to compare the sensation of lifting the other arm, he "discovered" that he had more control in the nonhypnotized arm, adding a third data point.

There are two methods for scoring the HIP, one of which is based on these three data points. The Profile scoring postulates that the relationship between potential for trance concentration as indicated by the ER compared with the actual level of trance experience as indicated by arm levitation and the discovery experience is significant. Each of the Profile grades describes a different kind of relationship between a person's trance potential and his or her trance experience. The sensory reportage, motor response, and discovery experience are all experiential measures in contrast to the ER, the fixed biological indicator. The HIP Profile score has been reported to show correlations with HGSHS of .34[4] and .55.[2]

The Induction scoring measures the degree of trance experienced and maintained and is composed of five experiential indicators. It is a standard linear method of scoring; scores range from 0 through 10. This second method of scoring is comparable to other laboratory methods. Studies comparing Induction scoring of the HIP to the HGSHS and the SHSS are currently under way.

A consistent, continuous performance indicates an "Intact" Profile score, representing an intact capacity to sustain the ribbon of attentive concentration. The motor (arm levitation) and discovery (control differential) experiences measure up to the indicated biological potential (ER) (FIGURES 2 & 3). Intact Profile scores range on a normal curve from 0 through 5 where about 50% are hypnotizable with midrange Intact scores, about 10% are above and about 10% are below (FIGURE 4).[2]

Borderline experience of trance is measured where there is indicated potential of trance (ER), the spontaneous discovery experience (control differential), and some sensory reportage, but no crucial motor response (arm levitation)

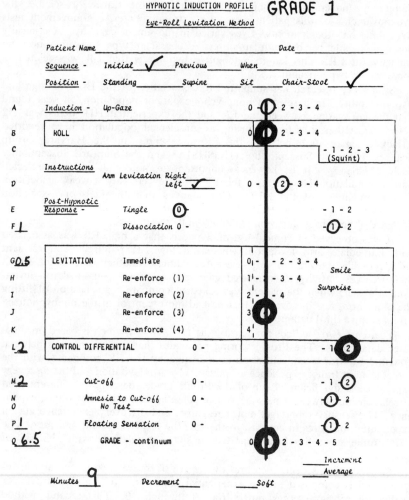

FIGURE 2. Low Intact Profile. (By permission of Soni Medica, Inc., New York, N.Y.)

(FIGURE 5—the Soft Profile). Induction scores that correspond to the Intact and borderline profiles range from approximately 3.5 through 10.[2]

Inconsistent and discontinuous performance indicates a clear break in the ribbon of concentration, a "Nonintact" capacity for trance (FIGURE 6—the Decrement Profile). Here there is indicated potential for trance (ER), but the subtle perceptual alteration has not been sustained long enough for the person to be able to discover a difference in control between the hypnotized and non-hypnotized arm. The Induction score corresponding to the discontinuous Decrement Profile range from 0 through 3.5,[2] also indicating minimal experience of trance, if any.

Two separate series totaling 4,300 clinical cases reveal a bimodal distribution curve where the Decrement (discontinuous) and Soft (borderline) Profiles are discontinuous to the normal distribution of the Intact range (FIGURE 4). The distribution of Induction scores also is represented by the bimodal curve (FIGURE 7). The correlation between the two scoring methods is .84 (N = 1023); the intertester reliability for the Profile scoring is .62 (N = 53) and for the Induction scoring .75 (N = 53); the test-retest reliability for Profile score is .66 and for Induction score .76.[2] A reliable and valid standardized test

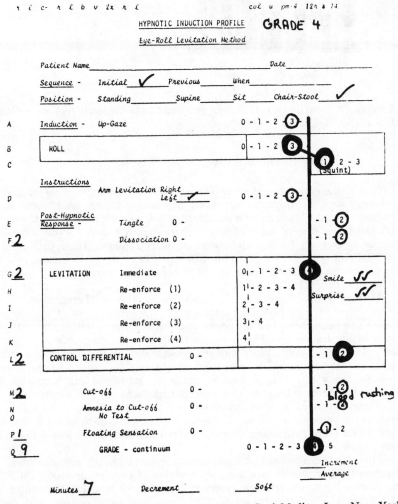

FIGURE 3. High Intact Profile. (By permission of Soni Medica, Inc., New York, N.Y.)

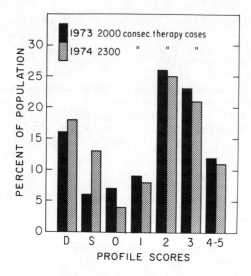

FIGURE 4. Distribution of Profile Scores. D=Decrement; S=Soft.

of hypnotic capacity, the HIP is appropriate as a research tool as well as a clinical one.

THE NONINTACT PROFILE AND PSYCHOPATHOLOGY

One of the early clinical observations was that patients with severe psychopathology such as schizophrenia, severe depression, mental retardation, severe character disorder, patients with neurological deficits such as early Parkinsonism, and patients who were heavily sedated or tranquilized tended to obtain discontinuous Decrement Profiles and sometimes Soft Profiles. These patients were essentially nonhypnotizable or minimally so. They showed biological potential for trance concentration (positive ER), but severe pathology impaired their ability to experience it.

In other words, the essential capacity for hypnosis is characterized by sustained attentive, receptive concentration during which external and internal stimuli can be received and integrated into the experience without breaking the major concentration set. This is similar to Shakow's [7, 8] description of "general set." The collapse or discontinuity characteristic of the Decrement Profile indicates that new stimuli are not incorporated into the experience and distract from the major set. This, in turn, is similar to "segmental set," a concept that Shakow has developed to describe schizophrenic behavior and experience.

These clinical observations eventually led to several studies that confirm the association between a Nonintact Profile and psychopathology, and the HIP grew to do more than assess degree of hypnotizability; it became a diagnostic tool.

First it was predicted that a population selected for the presence of severe psychopathology would show a high proportion of Decrement Profiles. Of 100 psychiatric inpatients tested at Bellevue Hospital, 92 revealed Decrement and Soft Profiles. Furthermore, three of the remaining eight patients with Intact Profiles were considered by the hospital staff to be the most psychologically intact patients on their wards.[9] By contrast, the incidence of Decrement and Soft Profiles in private psychiatric practice is 27%.[2]

In a second investigation, the relation of Profile patterns (Intact, Soft, and Decrement) to psychological health was studied. Data on which health-illness judgments were based were obtained by independent psychological assessment. Decrement and Soft Profiles were found to cluster around the illness end of a five-point Health-Illness continuum and Intact Profiles clustered at the healthy end (FIGURE 8).[9]

The third study in this series compared the severity of psychopathology of those patients with Decrement Profiles (apparent biological capacity, no utilizable capacity) to those patients with Intact but zero-grade Profiles (zero potential in a scale of 0 through 5, and consistent lack of experience). Although both

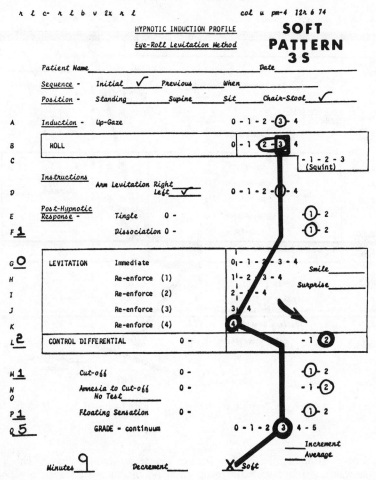

FIGURE 5. Soft Nonintact Profile. (By permission of Soni Medica, Inc., New York, N.Y.)

groups show little or no hypnotizability, we hypothesized that only the collapsed Decrement Profile should be associated with severe psychopathology. It is not nonhypnotizability but rather higher biological than utilizable capacity which should have the strong association. These hypotheses were confirmed: only

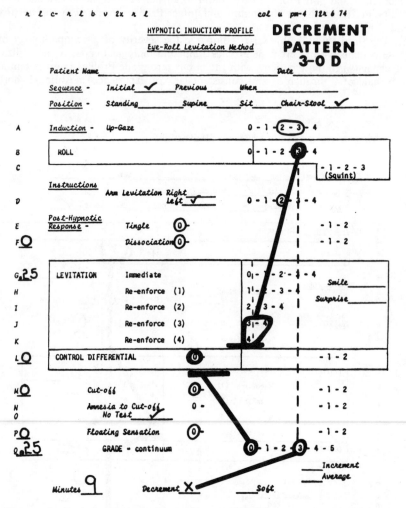

FIGURE 6. Decrement Nonintact Profile. (By permission of Soni Medica, New York, N.Y.)

one in seven straight zero Profiles showed severe psychopathology.[9] This proportion was consistent with the proportion of Intacts with severe psychopathology, and it was significantly lower than the corresponding proportion of Decrements.

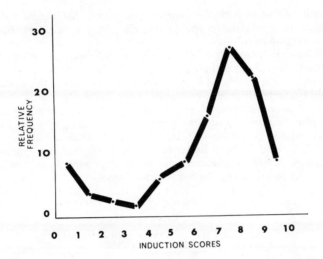

FIGURE 7. Distribution of Hypnotic Induction Scores for a sample of 1,339 patients.

WHAT INFORMATION DO WE GET FROM THE HIP CONCERNING THE KIND OF DISORDER PRESENT?

In the course of clinical work, the characteristic ER's of Decrement and Soft Profiles have lately been noted to be associated with the kind of disorder present. The patients with obsessive-compulsive character disorders and schizoid personality types tend to have Decrement or Soft Profiles with low ER's. The patients with hysteria and depression tend to have Decrement and Soft Profiles with high ER's. Suggested here is a trend from the cognitive disorders through the affective disorders on a continuum from low to high ER. Empiri-

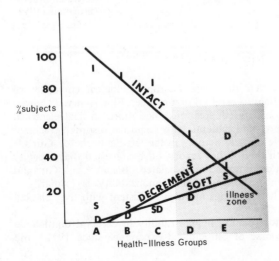

FIGURE 8. Trends for three HIP configurations on the Health-Illness continuum.

cally, this is consistent with the general observation that people with hysteria are prone to be hypnotizable and people diagnosed as schizophrenic are not "good hypnotic subjects."

The following "clinical fall-out" hypothesis has been set up to clarify this trend further: that those pathologic patients with low Profiles or discontinuous Profiles with low ER signs tend to be diagnosed in the area of the schizophrenias, or schizoid character disorders, or obsessive personality disorders. Patients with midrange ER signs (between 2 and 3 on the 0–4 scale) under stress tend to show impulse disorders, borderline personality disorders, and reactive depressions; and stressed patients with high Profiles or discontinuous Profiles with high Eye Rolls tend to have hysterical dissociations with or without somatic manifestations, severe depressions, and manic-depressive syndromes. We are now intensively investigating this hypothesis (TABLE 1).

TABLE 1

HIP SCORE AND TYPE OF PSYCHOPATHOLOGY: HYPOTHESIS

Low Capacity 1	2	Medium Capacity 3	4	High Capacity 5
obsessive-competitive disorders		impulse disorders		hysterical reactions dissociations conversions
schizoid character disorders		sociopathies		manias
paranoid character disorders		passive-agressive disorders		depressions
schizophrenias		depressions (reactive)		hysterical psychoses
Cognitive Disorders (predominantly)				Affective Disorders (predominantly)

BACK TO BIOLOGY

Recent literature suggests that there are neurophysiological correlates to these diagnoses which relate them to cerebral dominance. Flor-Henry[10] showed that patients with affective disorders (depressions) had more cortical electrical activity in the right hemisphere, and patients with cognitive disorders (schizophrenia) had more measurable cortical activity in the left hemisphere. Gur's[11] recent report is consistent with this. Other reports have suggested that capacity to be hypnotized and cerebral dominance are associated. Bakan[12] and Gur and Gur[13] have presented evidence showing that hypnotizability is primarily a right-hemisphere function. These findings are also consistent with the "clinical fall-out" hypothesis presented above.

Another biological indicator relating hypnotizability to cerebral dominance has been uncovered in the course of our clinical experience since 1972: the

Hand Clasp sign. As part of the initial evaluation session, each patient is asked to clasp his or her hands, interlocking fingers. If the patient is right-handed (which is determined by a handedness inventory) and puts the left thumb on top of the right thumb as the hands are clasped, this is identified as a "non-dominant" Hand Clasp. If the patient is right-handed and the right fingers are on top, this is a "dominant" Hand Clasp. The reverse is true for the left-handed person. It was hypothesized that a nondominant Hand Clasp sign, an indicator of right-hemisphere dominance, would be associated with higher hypnotizability, and that a dominant Hand Clasp sign, indicating left-hemisphere dominance, would be associated with lower hypnotizability.

When tested, this hypothesis was statistically confirmed.[11] A dominant Hand Clasp sign was strongly associated with HIP scores indicating lower and non-hypnotizability, and HIP scores indicating higher hypnotizability tended to have nondominant Hand Clasp signs. There were, however, a large number of patients who had nondominant clasps and low HIP scores. It is also interesting to note that when higher and lower hypnotizability was measured by the ER sign alone, there was no association with hemispheric dominance. However, when the HIP Profile score which compares biological potential and experience was used, the significant relationship was found. This brings up many provocative questions: for example, "What light could the Hand Clasp sign shed in questions of psychopathology?" Finally, we are now testing this hypothesis, using the Induction score as a measure of hypnotizability.

Overall, these findings suggest that hypnotizability as measured by the HIP can give us some bearing on hemispheric dominance as well as on a person's style of adaption in the course of mental illness. Perhaps it is hemispheric dominance that is setting a person's personality style altogether? This has led to our next issue.

PERSONALITY AND THE HIP

Although there has been much speculation concerning the relationship between personality and hypnosis, the findings have been conflicting. Hypotheses that relate hypnotizability to sociability, extroversion, or neuroticism have not been confirmed. In summarizing the research on hypnosis and personality, Perry London said:

> There may indeed be personality traits which distinguish persons or relatively different degrees of hypnotic susceptibility, and these traits may be well worth discovering; but it seems quite clear that they are not going to be discovered by any of our existing gross personality inventories. . . . Neither our old Kraepelinian nor current construct categories seem relevant to this trait. It is time to stop doing studies [of this nature] and to seek a fresh approach.[15]

In the course of clinical experience with the HIP, discoveries are being made relating hypnotizability and personality style or structure. These investigations began with a study of the outstanding characteristics of the most highly hypnotizable patients.[16] Eventually, outstanding features of three hypnotizability groups (lows, midranges, and highs) have been identified clinically in terms of spatial awareness, perception of time, and the set of myth-beliefs that each group holds—all of which determine styles of processing and adaptation (TABLE 2).

Typically, the highly hypnotizable person will get so absorbed in an activity that he tends to lose awareness of where he is. He tends to perceive time as predominantly in the present tense, ignoring past and future. The series of myth-beliefs by which he lives his life tend to be characterized by a "heart" rather than a "head" orientation, by a preference to let others set the pace in interpersonal activity, a tendency to be extremely trusting to the point of being vulnerable and gullible, a tendency to affiliate with new ideas without critically appraising them, a preference to acquire new information with close receptors such as touch. In processing new ideas, he tends to get the greater sense of fulfillment from dreaming up an idea rather than implementing it and tends not

TABLE 2

STRUCTURAL THEMES AND HYPNOTIZABILITY

STRUCTURES	GRADE: Hypnotic Induction Profile	0	1	2	3	4	5
	CHARACTER TYPES		APOLLONIAN		ODYSSEAN		DIONYSIAN
	A) Space Awareness (Absorption)		Focal ⁄PERIPHERAL		FOCAL-PERIPHERAL		FOCAL╲ Peripheral
	B) Time Perception		PAST-FUTURE		PAST-PRESENT-FUTURE		PRESENT
	C) Myth-Belief Constellation (Premises)		Affective ⁄COGNITIVE		AFFECTIVE-COGNITIVE		AFFECTIVE╲ Cognitive
	1) Locus of Interpersonal Control		INTERNAL		INTERNAL-EXTERNAL		EXTERNAL
	2) Trust Proneness		LOW		VARIED		HIGH
	3) Critical Appraisal		IMMEDIATE		VARIED		SUSPENDED
	4) Learning Style		ASSIMILATION		ACCOMMODATION		AFFILIATION
	5) Responsibility		HIGH		VARIED		LOW
	6) Preferred Contact Mode		VISUAL		VISUAL-TACTILE		TACTILE
	D) Processing		Premise ⁄IMPLEMENT		MIXED		PREMISE╲Implement
	1) Writing Value		HIGH		VARIED		LOW

to need to process these ideas through language; he processes by "feeling things through." These features are characteristic of the classical Dionysian mode.

By contrast, the persons with a low grade on the Intact hypnotizability scale show characteristics of the Apollonian mode. They usually do not lose space awareness no matter how absorbed they may be in a life experience. Their time perception is focused on the past and/or future with a tendency to miss the present. Their myth-belief premises are characterized by "head" rather than "heart" orientation, a desire to control interpersonal interactions, a tendency to be less trusting than average, a need to critically appraise all new information through distance receptors (vision rather than touch). In processing new ideas, there tends to be a greater sense of fulfillment in the implementation of an idea than in dreaming it up, and implementation is usually accompanied by a strong need to process it verbally.

The midrange style represents an admixture of the two extremes with many combinations. They characteristically negotiate a middle way between Scylla and Charybdis on their odyssey of living. We have identified this mode as Odyssean. For example, during attentive concentration, although there is a capacity for being absorbed, it is not to the point of losing space awareness totally. Time perception is usually divided equally between past, present, and future. The myth-belief constellation is characterized by a balance between head and heart; controlling interaction varies with circumstances. There may be a general tendency to be trusting, but not to the point of gullibility. Or there may be a tendency to be less trusting than average, but not to the extreme of being suspicious. There is a general tendency to critically appraise new information, but not with the extreme rigidity of the low. On some occasions the midrange person can accept new information and delay his judgment about it for some later time as characteristic of a high. In processing new information, there is an equal use of near and remote sensory input. On processing new ideas, there is a tendency to be equally adept at both imagining ideas and implementing them.

This is the latest phase of our study of hypnotic capacity, in which we are now examining the associations between these structural features of the personality, their clusters and associations with the HIP scores. Also, we are comparing HIP grades to a score on a scale of spatial awareness or absorption by Tellegen.[17] Further, we are starting to study whether the theme of the lows is set by the left hemisphere and the theme of the highs is set by the right hemisphere, and whether the midgroup has an equal balance between right and left hemisphere with a tendency to experience the oscillation from frontal to temporal-limbic areas. Or are we, in addition to the lateralization phenomena, in some way measuring a vertical hierarchy from the limbic system through the reticular activating system in relation to the cortex?

SUMMARY AND CONCLUSIONS

1. The HIP is a quick, reliable, and valid test of hypnotizability that measures biological as well as psychological reactive features of trance.

2. It helps in diagnosing clinical psychopathological syndromes that impair integrated concentration.

3. It differentiates the low or nonhypnotizable healthy person from the low or nonhypnotizable due to pathology.

4. It promises to shed light on predictable personality clusters that can influence treatment decisions and can contribute to personality research.

5. The use of the HIP promises to bring a useful measurement into the clinical realm of hypnosis, psychopathology, psychotherapy, and personality as it establishes a new bridge between the laboratory and clinic.

ACKNOWLEDGMENT

I should like to thank Laurie S. Lipman for her assistance in preparing this manuscript.

References

1. Spiegel, H. 1974. Manual for the Hypnotic Induction Profile. Soni Medica. New York, N.Y.
2. Spiegel, H., M. Aronson, J. L. Fleiss & J. Haber. 1976. A psychometric analysis of the Hypnotic Induction Profile. Int. J. Clin. Exp. Hypn. 24: 300–315.
3. Spiegel, H. 1972. An eye roll test for hypnotizability. Am. J. Clin. Hypn. 15: 25–28.
4. Eliseo, T. S. 1974. The Hypnotic Induction Profile and hypnotic susceptibility. Int. J. Clin. Exp. Hyn. 22: 320–326.
5. Wheeler, W., H. T. Reis, E. Wolff, E. Grupsmith & A. M. Mordkoff. 1974. Eye roll and hypnotic susceptibility. Int. J. Clin. Exp. Hypn. 22: 327–334.
6. Switras, J. E. 1974. A comparison of the eye roll test for hypnotizability and the Stanford Hypnotic Susceptibility Scale: Form A. J. Clin. Hypn. 17: 54–55.
7. Shakow, D. 1974. Sequential set: A theory of the formal psychological deficit in schizophrenia. Arch. Gen. Psychiat. 6: 1–7.
8. Shakow, D. 1977. Segmental Set: The adaptive process in schizophrenia. Arch. Gen. Psychiat. 6: 1–7.
8. Shakow, D. 1977. Segmental Set: The adaptive process in schizopherenia. Psychol. 32(2): 129–139.
9. Spiegel, H., J. L. Fleiss, M. D. Aronson, L. S. Lipman & J. T. Janics. 1977. Psychopathology and the Hypnotic Induction Profile. In preparation.
10. Flor-Henry, P. 1976. Lateralized temporal limbic dysfunction and psychopathology. Ann. N.Y. Acad. Sci. 280: 777–795.
11. Gur, R. E. 1977. Motoric laterality imbalance in schizophrenia. Arch. Gen. Psychiat. 34(1): 33–37.
12. Bakan, P. 1969. Hypnotizability, laterality of eye-movements and functional brain asymmetry. Percept. Mot. Skills 28: 927–932.
13. Gur, R. C. & R. E. Gur. 1974. Handedness, sex and eyedness as moderating variables in the relation between hypnotic susceptibility and functional brain asymmetry. J. Abnorm. Pschol. 83: 635–643.
14. Spiegel, H., D. Spiegel & L. S. Lipman. 1977. Hypnotizability and the hand clasp sign. In preparation.
15. London, P. & D. Derman. 1965. Correlations of hypnotic susceptibility. J. Consult. Psychol. 29(6): 537–545.
16. Spiegel, H. 1974. The grade 5 syndrome: the highly hypnotizable person. Int. J. Clin. Exp. Hypn. 22(4): 303–319.
17. Tellegen, A. & G. Atkinson. 1974. Openness to absorbing and self-alteringg experiences ("absorption"), a trait related to hypnotic susceptibility. J. Abnorm. Psychol. 83(3): 268–277.

ON ATTEMPTS TO MODIFY HYPNOTIC SUSCEPTIBILITY: SOME PSYCHOPHYSIOLOGICAL PROCEDURES AND PROMISING DIRECTIONS

Ian E. Wickramasekera *

*Peoria School of Medicine
University of Illinois College of Medicine
Peoria, Illinois 61614*

A technology for the modification of hypnotizability is concerned with the arrangement of conditions to potentiate and stabilize the verbal control of behavior. More specifically, such a technology is concerned with the effectiveness and reliability with which behavioral, physiological, and subjective responses can be brought under the control of antecedent verbal stimuli in an interpersonal or intrapersonal context. These verbal stimuli may originate from within the individual (explicit or implicit self-instructions) or from his social environment. The three response systems (subjective, physiological, behavioral) may vary in their degree of concordance at any given point in time and in their individual responsivity to verbal stimuli. The above phenomena were intensively investigated under the label "hypnotic susceptibility," and have more recently been studied under the label *"in vitro"* systematic desensitization and related procedures.[1]

There is impressive evidence in the hypnotic literature that these three response systems can be effectively and reliably controlled in a minority of the population, within a laboratory situation, and within the context of a set of procedures labeled hypnosis.[2-6] But investigators disagree over the mechanisms of control, and there is yet no compelling evidence that this impressive reliability of hypnotic response is sustained cross situationally (e.g. from laboratory to clinic or consulting room to natural habitat). There is evidence that *low* hypnotic susceptibility may be related to greater responsivity of the behavioral-motor response system (they "try harder") to hypnotic instructions.[7] But low-susceptible subjects lack the concurrent verbal-subjective and autonomic nervous system concomitants that appear to define and give credibility to a hypnotic experience. Specifically, low-susceptible subjects may not report a sense of motor compulsion and profound verbal-subjective involvement or demonstrate rapid instructional control of autonomic functions.

In the clinical situation we observe a measure of ossicilation of hypnotic responsivity that is probably greater than that observed in the laboratory. This instability of response systems may be due to the greater number and variability of intra- and interpersonal factors in the clinical situation as compared to the more limited and standardized laboratory situation. Ideally, the clinical utility of hypnosis would be greatest if more people were reliably responsive to verbal-hypnotic procedures, cross situationally, and if their responsivity were reliably restricted to the high range of hypnotic response.

It appears that this hypnotic responsivity to verbal events has two components: 1) A stable skill or ability component,[2] which may or may not be

---

* Requests for reprints to: 300 E. War Memorial Drive, Peoria, Ill. 61614.

manifest in performance; 2) a less stable situational-motivational component,[4] which strongly influences performance. Shor and associates [8] have stated that it is important to distinguish between variations in hypnotic performance and the modification of hypnotizability. It is also important to note that all statements about changes in hypnotizability are necessarily still inferences from hypnotic performance, since hypnotizability *per se* is an unobservable construct. Hypnotizability sets an upper limit to hypnotic performance.

The psychoanalytic model of Gill and Brenman [9] predicts an enhancement of hypnotic susceptibility by sensory restriction procedures. From the psychoanalytic viewpoint, the mechanism of enhancement is assumed to be a greater probability of "regression" under conditions of sensory restriction. Curiously enough, social-learning motivational models would seem to lead to identical predictions, but for different reasons. Three interpretations of this behavioral enhancement phenomena have been suggested from the social-learning position. 1) An interpretation consistent with the Gewirtz and Baer [10] hypothesis regards the restriction of *social* stimuli as the critical procedure. It assumes that the reinforcer value of social stimuli are subject, like physical reinforcers (e.g. food, water), to alteration by deprivation and satiation procedures; 2) Walters *et al.*[11] have hypothesized that sensory restriction procedures activate *anxiety,* and anxiety arousal is responsible for the facilitation effect; 3) Cairns [12] has suggested an interpretation consistent with the enhancement of *attention.*

A pilot study [13] using 16 females between the ages of 18 and 22 supported the hypothesis that one-half hour of sensory restriction enhanced hypnotizability as measured by Forms A & B of the Stanford Hypnotic Susceptibility Scale (SHSS). Subjects were randomly assigned to either a control ($N = 8$) or experimental ($N = 8$) group. Experimental subjects were subjected to auditory and visual restriction. They also wore heavy cotton gloves and were instructed to remain motionless for one-half hour. Control subjects were simply told to come back after one-half hour for posttesting. No information on the expected effects of the procedure were provided. TABLE 1 presents the pre- and posttest scores, means, and standard deviations of the experimental and control groups.

Encouraged by the results of the previous study, we proceeded to a more careful and extensive study [14] of this apparent facilitation phenomenon. The subjects in the second study were 45 white male prisoners. Subjects who had previous histories of homicide or psychiatric therapy, or who were mentally or physically handicapped were eliminated from the initial pool. Forty-five subjects were randomly assigned to one of three groups of 15 subjects each. There was no significant difference between the groups in regard to age, education or Beta IQ. The subjects in group I were pretested on Form A of the SHSS and simply spent one hour sitting on a chair, listening to music, and looking at magazines prior to retesting on Form B of the SHSS.

Subjects in group II were exposed to a one-hour sensory restriction period identical to the one in the first study, prior to posttesting on Form B of the SHSS.

Subjects in group III were read a set of "anxiety arousing" instructions

TABLE 1

PRE- AND POSTTEST SCORES AND MEANS ON THE STANFORD HYPNOTIC
SUSCEPTIBILITY SCALE

	Experimental				Control		
S	Pre	Post	Diff.	S	Pre	Post	Diff.
1	5	3	−2	9	9	9	0
2	10	12	2	10	10	10	0
3	3	11	8	11	6	6	0
4	4	6	2	12	3	2	−1
5	6	11	5	13	4	4	0
6	5	11	6	14	4	4	0
7	7	11	4	15	5	5	0
8	6	11	5	16	6	4	−2
x	5.75	9.50	3.75		5.88	5.50	−.38
S.D.	1.98	3.00	2.86		2.32	2.58	.70

about the dangers of sensory restriction prior to the imposition of the sensory restriction procedure used with group II (TABLE 2).

The results of this study confirmed the observations of the first study. Subjects in the two experimental groups increased significantly in hypnotizability, but controls did not. Analysis revealed that the three groups were equated on initial susceptibility. The addition of "scare" instructions did not appear to significantly ($p < .10$) increase hypnotizability over sensory re-

TABLE 2

HYPNOTIC SUSCEPTIBILITY SCORES

Subjects	Control Group			Experimental Group I			Experimental Group II		
	A	B	(B-A)	A	B	(B-A)	A	B	(B-A)
1	12	12	0	12	12	0	11	12	1
2	10	10	0	10	11	1	10	12	2
3	9	9	0	10	11	1	9	12	3
4	8	7	−1	9	11	2	8	11	3
5	8	9	+1	8	10	2	8	11	3
6	7	7	0	8	10	2	7	10	3
7	7	8	+1	7	12	5	7	12	5
8	7	7	0	7	9	2	7	9	2
9	6	6	0	6	5	−1	7	8	1
10	5	5	0	5	9	4	6	12	6
11	5	5	0	5	8	3	5	7	2
12	4	5	+1	4	7	3	4	9	5
13	2	2	0	3	5	2	3	10	7
14	2	2	0	2	3	1	2	7	5
15	2	2	0	2	5	3	1	3	2
Total	94	96		98	128		96	145	
x	6.266	6.40		6.53	8.53		6.40	9.6	

striction alone. When this second study was being prepared for publication, Professor Hilgard [15] brought to my attention an unpublished study by Pena,[16] which also used male prisoners. Pena used a control group plus two experimental groups receiving, respectively, one and one-half and three hours of sensory restriction. He found that the enhancement scores of the three groups were ordered in a direction that was consistent with the enhancement hypothesis. Group III obtained the greatest enhancement, and the control group the least. A study by Sanders and Rehyer,[17] which used previously "resistant" subjects, also found that four to six hours of sensory restriction significantly increased hypnotizability. I know of no studies involving hypnotizability that failed to replicate the above observations. It appears that sensory restriction in a laboratory situation reliably enhances hypnotizability.

EMG Feedback and Hypnotizability

Relaxation instructions are one of the independent variables that increase suggestibility.[4] It would seem that increasing the precision of relaxation training with EMG feedback may increase suggestibility even more significantly. In a preliminary study [18] with white male volunteers between the ages of 18 and 22, we found that EMG feedback training significantly increased hypnotic susceptibility (TABLE 3).

The twelve subjects were assigned randomly and equally to either an experimental or control group for a study of "relaxation training and hypnosis." After pretesting individually on the Stanford Hypnotic Susceptibility Scale, Form A, subjects were assigned to either a response contingent (true) or false feedback group for six 45-minute sessions. Subjects were trained on a large padded recliner, and electrodes were first placed on forearm and later on frontalis. The control procedure was an auditory tape of the first six sessions of a psychiatric patient in feedback training. The feedback tone declined over time but noncontingently.

Encouraged by these preliminary observations, we attempted to replicate the above observations, using again twelve white volunteer subjects and an experimental design identical to the previous study. The only differences were that in the present study,[19] 1) There were ten 30-minute feedback training sessions; 2) the posttesting for hypnotic susceptibility was done by a research assistant who was blind to the nature (true or false) of the feedback training the subjects received. We again found that response contingent (true) feedback training increased hypnotic susceptibility quite significantly ($p = .001$) (TABLE 4)

In both of the above studies, verbal instructions to the subjects were limited to taped verbal instructions that told them that they were to be

TABLE 3

PRE- AND POSTTEST SCORES ON THE STANFORD HYPNOTIC SUSCEPTIBILITY SCALE

Group	Pretest	Posttest	Difference
Experimental	4.83	10.16	5.33
Control	5.00	5.16	.16

TABLE 4

PRE- AND POSTTEST SCORES ON THE STANFORD HYPNOTIC SUSCEPTIBILITY SCALE

	Experimental				Control		
Subject	Pretest	Posttest	Difference	Subject	Pretest	Posttest	Difference
1	5	9	4	7	4	6	2
2	8	10	2	8	6	3	−3
3	2	8	6	9	6	6	0
4	2	11	9	10	2	3	1
5	6	11	5	11	6	7	1
6	6	12	6	12	6	6	0

trained to relax and that feedback training could increase their ability to relax. The above observations need independent replication. But within the constraints of both our experimental and clinical procedures with tension-headache patients, we have reliably observed that those who succeed in learning to reliably drop (approximately 3 uV.P-P) EMG levels become more responsive to hypnosis. It is tempting to "explain" these changes by invoking a concept like greater tolerance for "fading generalized reality orientation." [20]

EMG FEEDBACK AND DISINHIBITORY VERBAL INSTRUCTIONS ABOUT HYPNOSIS

We have previously [18, 19, 21–24] hypothesized that relaxation training (a low-arousal state produced by EMG, heart rate, or temperature feedback) will potentiate the expectancy-instructional control of behavior. Five white males, ages 25 to 35, volunteered for a study of "relaxation and hypnosis." They were pretested with the SHSS, Form A, and next received ten 40-minute sessions of contingent EMG feedback training from frontalis. At the termination of the third session of feedback training and while the subjects were still in a relaxed state (approximately 3 uV.P-P) their earphones were disconnected from the EMG unit and plugged into a tape player. While the subjects continued to relax, the tape provided the first of eight two-minute messages on the nature of hypnosis and how to resonate with it most effectively. These segments were prepared from the "positive" information texts used by previous investigators [25, 26] and from the inductory section of the Stanford Scale, Form A. After the final EMG feedback training session and the eighth informational input, the subjects were immediately retested on Form B of the Stanford Scale. Hypnotizability was the dependent variable here. TABLE 5 shows the mean Stanford pre (Form A) and post (Form B) scores and the mean pre and post EMG feedback training scores.

Inspection of the posttest scores appears to indicate some increase in hypnotic susceptibility in this sample. One cannot determine from this data if the disinhibitory information was potentiated by delivery in a relaxed state and/or the EMG feedback training. But the enhancement effects appear to be larger than those observed by Havens,[25] who used a similar procedure minus low-arousal training.

In one sense this may be regarded as a study in attitude modification, specifically, in an attitude (hypnotizability) that is a dependent variable, that has the advantage of being potentially quantifiable along verbal- subjective behavioral and physiological dimensions.

THE MODIFICATION OF HYPNOTIZABILITY AND THETA FEEDBACK TRAINING

The only criteria used in selecting subjects for this study was that they had to have low base line frontalis EMG levels. The pioneering systematic work [27] done in the laboratory of Budzynski *et al.* suggested the need for the above condition.

The subjects in this preliminary study were four adult, white males, ages 27, 32, 52, and 44, who had volunteered for a study of hypnosis and "twilight learning." [28] Twilight learning refers to learning assumed to be occurring in the transitional zone just prior to sleep. The twilight learning system (model TL-1) † is described in the manual as representing "some of the most recent functional characteristics deemed necessary to carry on research on the effects of inputting tape recorded information to a subject only when

TABLE 5

Subjects	Pretest (Form A–SHSS)		Posttest (Form B–SHSS)
1	3		7
2	7		11
3	2	Positive Information	6
4	4	and EMG Feedback	6
5	5		10
	x=4.2		x=8

he is in certain brainwave states." The functional logic of the Theta part of the system is described in the manual as follows:

In the THETA MODE, two tape recorders are used. The ALPHA recorder is turned on and its output fed to phones in response to threshold crossings. . . . The filter used in this mode, the ALPHA/BETA INHIBIT filter, passes frequencies from the low alpha range, around 8 Hz, and gradually boosts increasing frequencies up into the Beta range around 20 Hz and finally adds a very steep dip in response at 60 Hz.

Whenever frequencies from the A/B INHIBIT filter cross the preset ALPHA THRESHOLD, the THETA TAPE recorder is turned off and its output is cut off from the headphones. The THETA TAPE recorder is turned on and its output fed to the headphones whenever EEG frequencies are present in the THETA LEARN filter frequency band. This band extends from a low frequency of about 2 Hz to an upper frequency of 7 or 8 Hz selected by the THETA LOPASS switch. Unlike the ALPHA recorder, the volume of the THETA recorder output fed to the headphones is varied in accordance with the amplitude of the signal passing through the THETA LEARN filter.

The volume of the THETA information heard by the subject is varied in response to the amplitude of the THETA EEG he is producing. If the EEG

† Biofeedback Systems, Inc., Boulder, Colo. 80301.

frequencies begin to drift lower than 4 or 3 Hz, a low frequency boost in the THETA LEARN filter raises the volume of the THETA information above the levels which were being heard for the mid-THETA EEG frequencies and acts to keep the subject from proceeding into Stage 2 sleep.

The purpose of this study was to determine the effects of delivering disinhibitory and inhibitory information about hypnosis while the subject is in a twilight state, or to determine how reliably a belief system (a group of related expectancies about hypnosis) could be turned on and off by careful arrangement of antecedent contingencies.

PROCEDURE

The four white adult males (ages 28, 26, 54, and 41) were first pretested on the SHSS, Form A. Next they were each given ten sessions (1 hour each session) of training on the twilight learning system (TL-1). Finally, all subjects were posttested on Form B of the Stanford Scale.

The subjects were not told in advance what material the theta tape would contain nor if the material on it would be inhibitory or disinhibitory. They were simply told that this was a study of "hypnosis and alpha-theta feedback for relaxation."

The alpha tape delivered the abbreviated autogenic phrases of Schultz and Luthe [29] against a background of "pink" noise. EEG cup electrodes were placed over the left hemisphere (left mastoid, left occipital, and left central parietal) of all these right-handed subjects. It was assumed that reduced cortical arousal over the left hemisphere would immobilize critical, skeptical analytic chatter from the major hemisphere, thus improving the reception of the signal or message.

Two theta tapes were prepared. The first one delivered a message to disinhibit hypnotizability or to inculcate positive attitudes toward hypnosis. The second tape delivered a message to inhibit hypnotizability or to inculcate negative attitudes toward hypnotizability. In addition, a simple naturalistic suggestion was added to the inhibitory theta tape of the fourth subject. He was told that soon after he entered my waiting room he would feel a strong impulse to go outside to check the tires on his car for possible deflation by fragments of glass. It was stressed that he would have this feeling only in my waiting room. The door to my waiting room contains a buzzer that is activated each time the door is opened. Hence I was able to count from my consulting room the number of times the subject complied with this suggestion, and my research assistant was able to verify his compliance by observing him through her window.

RESULTS

The results of these instructional and procedural arrangements are shown in TABLE 6 and should be considered as tentative in view of the small size of the sample and the lack of control for expectancy effects. It appears that instructional material delivered in a twilight state reliably altered suggestibility in these subjects within the constraints of this study. From this study it cannot be determined if inputting information in a twilight state is more effective in modifying hypnotizability and producing complaint motor behavior than inputting the same information in a waking, alert state. If, however, we were to compare it to the alterations in hypnotizability reported by Havens,[25] using an instructional approach in the waking alert state, there appears to be some potentiation of the instructional signal. The subject in whom the experimental compulsion was arranged was apparently unaware of the source of this compulsion and emitted it between one and three times on three subsequent visits to my office.

DISCUSSION

It appears that a variety of disparate procedures (sensory restriction, EMG, and theta feedback training) can potentiate the instructional manipulation of complex human behaviors within the constraints of the laboratory situation. In the real world, such instructionally arranged (antecedents) changes are more likely to be sustained if they are supported by expected consequences (operant conditioning). Verbal manipulation procedures have several advantages when used with subjects who present with well developed and

TABLE 6

Pretest (SHSS–A)			Post (SHSS–B)	Pretest (SHSS–A)			Post (SHSS–B)
1	5	Positive	12	1	5	Negative	1
2	4	Information and Theta Feedback	10	2	7	Information and Theta Feedback	2

differentiated cultural-verbal repertoires. Generally these advantages have to do with the potential specificity of intervention goals, the economy of time and energy of intervention, and the transferability of behavior change across situations. It appears that both at the low [18, 19] and at the high arousal [31, 32] ends of the continuum, the installation of internalized central cognitive changes may be the most efficient way to develop *new* behavior rapidly.

During the last seven years I have clinically used the relaxed state to potentiate and stabilize ego-strengthening or more specific suggestions. It does not appear to be particularly important whether the relaxation was produced by EMG feedback,[18, 19] heart-rate feedback,[23] temperature feedback,[22] or taped tension-relaxation muscle exercises.[21, 33] As our clinical procedures become more sophisticated, greater attention ᴖo the individual patient's psychophysiological profile may require a revision of the above preliminary hypothesis. But because of confounding of variables, no conclusions can be drawn from these clinical observations in the last seven years. I am generally encouraged, however, by the measure of behavioral compliance and subjective changes associated with *talking* to patients in profoundly relaxed physical states. Profound physiological relaxation produces a mental attitude functionally similar to that produced by effective delivery of the "core conditions",[34] which also inhibits critical analytic thought.

I am also impressed by the measure of behavioral compliance associated with talking to patients under carefully arranged stressful conditions.[31, 32] A large clinical series (N = 22) with a highly treatment-resistant group of chronic (as defined by police records) sexual exhibitionists reliably demonstrates that instructional interventions are potentiated under conditions of internally generated high arousal. The outcome measures include verbal reports and physiological and behavioral (police records) measures. These data will not be presented here, but it is worth noting that these subjects also spontaneously become "dissociated" during the ABR procedure.[31, 32]

We have in the last seven years collected from our phobic, anxious, and chronic pain patients verbal reports of spontaneous phantasies, images, and other unexpected "messages" received during systematic *in vitro* desensitization and during feedback training in the relaxed state. Some apparent consistencies in these messages from the "preconscious" suggest the need for a uniform and reliable system to decipher the hieroglyphics of this apparently independent third signaling system. Recently encouraged by the pioneering work of Dr. Elmer and Alice Green, I have become more interested in listening diagnostically to these messages from the preconscious or third signaling system, and even in incorporating their apparent meaning into the therapeutic suggestions I give my patients. I realize that this shift from *talking* to *listening* to the preconscious, appears in some respects to parallel the early development of psychoanalysis and that nothing new may come of this effort. But perhaps the investigations are proceeding with tools more widely applicable, more reliable, and with more known properties. There is a sense of rediscovering a territory that has a few more known landmarks because of Freud's pioneering voyages. Additionally, there is a lingering sense of wonder when confronted by observations and patient reports that simply do not fit ones typical categories of understanding.

CONCLUSION

I have presented some preliminary data that indicate that a variety of psychophysiological procedures, including sensory restriction and low-arousal training, can, under laboratory conditions, potentiate the verbal control of human behavior. I have also referred to two clinical studies of mine that suggest that under conditions of high arousal the verbal control of behavior is potentiated. The modification of hypnotic susceptibility can be regarded as a subzone within the larger zone of behavior modification. The power of a technology like behavior modification that leans heavily on programming the external *consequences* of behavior can be considerable. But its effectiveness appears limited to such programmed environments. A recent review [30] of controlled Skinnerian studies found no compelling available evidence that behavior changes associated with such procedures transfer to unprogrammed environments. A technology that focuses on *antecedent* events and their internalization may not be limited to the original programming environment. A technology that carefully arranges both the antecedents and consequences of behavior with a view to potentiating cognitive variables may increase our ability to predict and control complex human behavior.

In conclusion, are we any closer to developing a technology that can use both the low- and high-arousal ends of the activation continuum to potentiate and stabilize the instructional control of complex human behavior? Will we be able eventually to refine this technology to enable us to precisely, powerfully, and reliably modify belief systems? If such a technology can be developed so that belief systems can be *made* and *unmade* at will, where would such a *technology* leave the ultimate questions of human life—questions like the existence of God, the nature of truth, beauty, and justice, and so on? What would be the implications of such a technology for the fundamental problems of epistemology?

REFERENCES

1. KAZDIN, A. E. & L. A. WILCOXON. 1976. *Psychol. Bull.* **83:** 5, 729–758.
2. HILGARD, E. R. 1965. Hypnotic Susceptibility. Harcourt, Brace and World. New York, N.Y.
3. HILGARD, E. R. & J. R. HILGARD. 1975. Hypnosis in the relief of pain. William Kaufmann. Los Altos, Calif.
4. BARBER. T. X. 1969. Hypnosis: a Scientific Approach. Van Nostrand. New York, N.Y.
5. SARBIN, T. R. & R. W. SLAGLE. 1972. Hypnosis and psychophysiological outcomes. *In* Hypnosis Research Developments and Perspectives. E. Fromm and R. E. Short, Eds. Aldine. Chicago, Ill.
6. MORGAN, A. H., D. L. JOHNSON & E. R. HILGARD. 1974. The stability of hypnotic susceptibility: A longitudinal study. J. Clin. Exp. Hypn. **22:** 249–257.
7. ROSENHAN, D. & P. LONDON. 1963. Hypnosis expectation, susceptibility and performance. J. Abnorm. Soc. Psycho. **66:** 77–81.
8. SHOR, R. E., M. T. ORNE & D. H. O'CONNEL. 1966. Psychological correlates of plateau hypnotizability in special volunteer sample. J. Personality Soc. Psychol. **3:** 80–95.
9. GILL, M. M. & M. BRENMAN. 1959. Hypnosis and Related States. Int. Universities Press. New York, N.Y.
10. GEWIRTZ, J. L. & D. W. BAER. 1958. Deprivation and saturation of social reinforcers as drive conditions. J. Abnorm. Soc. Psychol. **57:** 165–172.
11. WALTERS, R. H., W. E. MARSHALL & J. R. SHOOTER. 1960. Anxiety, isolation and susceptibility to social influence. J. Personality. **28:** 518–529.
12. CAIRNS, R. B. 1969. Towards an Alternative to the concepts of dependency and attachment. Paper presented Soc. Res. on Child Development. Santa Monica, Calif.
13. WICKRAMASEKERA, I. 1969. The effects of sensory restriction on hypnotic susceptibility. Int. J. Clin. Exp. Hypn. **17:** 217–224.
14. WICKRAMASEKERA, I. 1970. Effects of sensory restriction of susceptibility to hypnosis: a hypothesis and more preliminary data. J. Abnorm. Psych. **76:** 69–75.
15. HILGARD, E. R. 1969. Personal communication.
16. PENA, F. 1963. Perceptual Isolation and Hypnotic Susceptibility. Unpublished Ph.D. Thesis. Washington State University. Pullman, Wash.
17. SANDERS, R. S. & J. REHYER. 1969. Sensory deprivation and the enhancement of hypnotic susceptibility. J. Abnorm. Psychol. **74:** 375–31%.
18. WICKRAMASEKERA, I. 1971. Effects of EMG feedback training on susceptibility to hypnosis. Preliminary observations. Proc. 79. Ann. Convention Amer. Psychol. Ass. **6:** 785–784 (summary).
19. WICKRAMASEKERA, I. 1973. The effects of EMG feedback on hypnotic susceptibility: more preliminary data. J. Abnorm. Psychol. **82:** 74–77.
20. SHOR, R. E. 1959. Hypnosis and the concept of the generalized reality—orientation. Amer. J. Psychother. **13:** 582–602.

21. WICKRAMSEKERA, I. 1972. Instructions and EMG feedback in systematic de-
     sensitization: a case report. Behav. Ther. **3:** 460–465.
22. WICKRAMASEKERA, I. 1973. Temperature feedback for the control of migraine.
     J. Behav. Ther. Exp. Psychiat. **4:** 343–345.
23. WICKRAMASEKERA, I. 1974. Heart rate feedback and the management of cardiac
     neurosis. J. Abnorm. Psychol. **83:** 578–580.
24. WICKRAMASEKERA, I. 1976 Biofeedback, Behavior Therapy and Hypnosis. Po-
     tentiating the Verbal Control of Behavior for Clinicians. Nelson Hall. New
     York, N.Y.
25. HAVENS, R. 1973. Using Modeling and Information to Modify Hypnotizability.
     Unpublished Ph.D. Thesis. West Virginia University, Morgantown, W. Va.
26. DIAMOND, M. J. & D. HARADA. 1973. The Use of Direct Instructions to Modify
     Hypnotic Susceptibility. Upublished manuscript. University of Hawaii. Hono-
     lulu, Hawaii.
27. SITTENFIELD, P., T. BUDZYNSKI & J. STOYVA. 1976. Differential shaping of EEG
     theta rhythms. Biofeedback and Self Regulation **1:** 31–46.
28. BUDZYNSKI, T. 1972. Some applications of biofeedback produced twilight states.
     Fields Within Fields **5:** 105–114.
29. SCHULTZ, J. H. & W. LUTHE. 1959. Autogenic Training. Grune and Stratton,
     Inc. New York, N.Y.
30. KELLEY, S. M., K. M. SHEMBERG & J. CARBONELL. 1976. Operant clinical inter-
     vention: behavior management or beyond. Where are the data? Behav.
     Ther. **7:** 292–305.
31. WICKRAMASEKERA, I. 1972. A technique for controlling a certain type of sexual
     exhibitionism. Psychother: Theory, Res. Prac. **9:** 207–210.
32. WICKRAMASEKERA, I. 1976. Aversive behavior rehearsal for sexual exhibitionism.
     Behav. Ther. **7:** 167–176.
33. WICKRAMASEKERA, I. 1970. Desensitization, Resensitization and Desentization
     Again. J. Behav. Ther. Exper. Psychiat. **1:** 257–262.
34. TRAUX, C. R. & R. R. CARKHUFF. 1967. Experimental manipulation of thera-
     peutic conditions. J. Clin. Consult. Psychol. **29:** 119–124.

EEG ALPHA ACTIVITY AND ITS RELATIONSHIP
TO ALTERED STATES OF CONSCIOUSNESS *

David A. Paskewitz

Psychosomatic Laboratories
Department of Psychiatry
University of Maryland School of Medicine
Baltimore, Maryland 21201

Ever since the discovery of the human electroencephalogram in the late 1920s by Berger,[1] the alpha rhythm has stood out as the most prominent feature of the waking EEG. Alpha rhythm is characteristically defined as ranging in frequency from 8 to 13 cycles per second (Hz), with the usual frequency centered around 10 Hz.[2] The amplitude of this rhythm is typically between 30 and 80 microvolts, although sometimes more or less. The appearance of the alpha rhythm in the EEG is subject to many influences. From its discovery it was observed to wax and wane, apparently at random.[1] In addition, it is highly responsive to disruption by external stimuli, particularly visual stimulation.[2, 3] The rhythm is most likely to appear when an individual is resting with his/her eyes closed.

Alpha activity disappears whenever the subject becomes drowsy and starts to fall asleep. In sleep research, the presence of alpha activity is a sign of wakefulness, and its absence signals the start of the process of falling asleep.[4] Alpha activity has also been shown to block numerous kinds of stimuli, including almost all environmental sources of stimulation.[5] Cognitive or mental operations such as mental arithmetic, visualizations, or imagery may lead to alpha blocking as well.[6–8] These two situations, drowsiness and stimulation, at either end of an arousal continuum, both lead to decreased alpha activity. This observation has led some authors to postulate an "inverted U-shaped function" to describe the relationship of alpha activity to arousal.[9, 10]

Following several earlier attempts,[11, 12] there has been a recent renewal of interest in efforts to characterize subjects according to their typical alpha densities. Many of these efforts are attempts seeking to relate alpha activity to subject characteristics like personality traits or hypnotizability.[13, 14] We certainly are aware that when we look at alpha activity under relatively constant, standardized conditions there is marked variation between individuals with respect to the amount of alpha activity they display within a given period of time. There are, in fact, at least two sources of variation in alpha activity, one within a given subject across differing levels of arousal, stimulus situations, task sets, and so on, and the other between individuals, and reflecting, presumably, a more stable trait of the individual.

To the extent that we are interested in determining a level of alpha activity characteristic of an individual, it is important to obtain some form of optimal level of activity, rather than to obtain a level which is situationally

* The data reported here were collected at the Unit for Experimental Psychiatry, Institute of the Pennsylvania Hospital, Philadelphia, Pa. Their collection was supported, in part, by grant MH 19156–06 from the National Institute of Mental Health.

depressed by one or another factor. To the extent that a given measurement is depressed because of excessively high or low arousal levels or other stimulus condition, it will reflect transient situational factors rather than a stable attribute typical of the individual. Only by attempting to establish an optimal situation and an optimal level can we be assured that we have a point from which to measure the effects of various manipulations on alpha activity. This argument does not minimize the importance of changes in alpha activity with varying manipulations. Note, however, that very low levels of alpha activity during a mental task may mean quite a different thing in a subject who has previously shown high base line levels when compared to those same low levels in a subject who has never exhibited any but low levels. Furthermore, optimal levels are not necessarily the most reliable. The most reliable assessment, in fact, would be obtained during a complex visual tracking task, where almost every subject would consistently show near-zero levels of alpha activity. How, then, does one conceptualize such an optimal level? It is certainly neither the active processing of stimulation nor drowsiness.

Literally scores of investigators have studied the blocking of alpha activity with stimulation. As a component of the orienting reflex, it has been subjected to attempts at conditioning and studies of its habituation.[15] This blocking has been linked by some to scanning mechanisms,[16] or to the concept of visual attention.[17, 18] In an attempt to clarify the relationship of alpha activity to the concept of attention, Mulholland and his associates have carried out an interesting series of studies indicating that it is the "looking," not the "seeing," which attenuates alpha activity.[17, 19–21] They have described the blocking of alpha activity in subjects engaged in pursuit tracking, accomodation, and fixation activities. The lack of these occulomotor commands resulted in the production of alpha activity, even when subjects were required to pay attention to their visual sensations. No consistent relationship was found with saccadic movements.

This "oculomotor hypothesis" regarding alpha variations, as it has come to be known, has suggested to some authors that since fixation, accomodation, and eye movement in the direction of a stimulus are likely to be part of an overall orienting reaction, such occulomotor processes would account for the alpha blocking seen under novel stimulus conditions.[21, 22] Additionally, various cognitive and imagery conditions that block alpha activity may be conceptualized as involving the production of occulomotor commands, even when subjects are in a dark room or have their eyes closed. Certainly the work on right- and left-lookers comes to mind in this regard.[23] There is evidence that certain individuals may actually increase alpha activity with mental effort,[24] although such effort may be associated with a cessation of occulomotor control in such subjects while others may use visualization as an aid to mentation.

Many of these issues have emerged in light of the current interest in the feedback control of the alpha rhythm, or alpha biofeedback. Early reports of subjects enhancing alpha activity with feedback claimed that the process was accompanied by feelings of calm and well-being, and that marked increases in alpha activity over previously measured base lines could be obtained.[25–29] Such claims have been attacked by a number of authors, both in terms of the subjective reports and the suprathreshold enhancement of alpha activity.[30–35] We have held the evidence to indicate that the essence of the alpha-enhancement phenomenon lies in the process of habituation of those factors in the training situation that serve to block alpha activity.[30, 31, 35] Some support has accumulated in the literature for this position,[35, 36] and some studies have explicitly linked this disinhibition to occulomotor control strategies.[22] In contrast, Hardt and Kamiya have recently argued that significant enhancement of alpha activity occurs beyond the process of habituation, although they do not rule out the possibility that such enhancement may involve the occulomotor system.[37]

The issue of the learned enhancement of alpha activity beyond that resulting from habituation is most crucial to a discussion of individual differences in alpha activity, and an issue that must be addressed before issues of the relationship between alpha activity and its increase, on the one hand, and states of consciousness on the other, can be resolved. We have maintained that the amount of alpha activity for a given individual is a stable characteristic, given its assessment under conditions optimal for its appearance in that individual. This notion of an optimal situation includes issues of drowsiness, of expectancies, sets, and surroundings, and of the immediate stimulus situation.

There are several implications of such a position. First of all, it is biased against an easy plasticity of the optimal alpha rhythm. We are not aware of convincing evidence that optimally or near-optimally obtained alpha densities can be significantly increased. Note that I am not discussing here demonstrations of the *control* of the alpha rhythm. Such demonstrations are quite easy, given the already present ability of subjects to exercise occulomotor control mechanisms to block alpha activity. Indeed, it is rare to find a subject who requires more than a minute of feedback and the instructions to turn off the tone to achieve almost complete success. Even bidirectional control is not terribly difficult to show, given the hazards of establishing an optimal base line, as we shall see. A second implication of this position is that learned increases in alpha activity involve learning to produce near-optimal alpha activity in situations that are less than optimal. Third, it prompts a close look at all elements in any experimental situation to determine those which render that situation less than optimal for a given subject.

What is the evidence for a characteristic alpha density in individuals? We have, on several occasions, had groups of subjects who participated in multiple sessions under relatively constant conditions. When such a group of subjects is measured for a relatively short period of time, two or three minutes, we find that subjects will order themselves in a remarkably similar manner from occasion to occasion with respect to alpha densities. When 30 subjects were run in a conditioning study, for instance, rank order correlations between the two sessions were $r_s = .85$ for the base lines with eyes opened, $r_s = .69$ for eyes-closed base lines, and $r_s = .82$ when the highest contiguous minute was chosen from among the two base lines for each session.[38] In another group of 13 subjects run for three sessions, rank order correlations ranged from $r_s = .74$ to $r_s = .90$ with eyes opened. With eyes closed, far lower correlations were observed, falling as low as $r_s = .31$. In another paper we have commented on the probable reason for such low coefficients during the eyes closed condition.[39] In that study, 24 subjects were measured over the course of six different base line periods with eyes closed. The correlations ranged from $r = .67$ to $r = .95$, with an average intercorrelation of $r = .76$. We felt, however, that a three-minute eyes-closed period is sufficient time for a subject to become drowsy, and it was likely that drowsiness played a large part in reducing the orderliness of the data. On examination, some base lines for a given individual were clearly atypical. Based on the concept of an optimal value, we chose to focus on those base line minutes which fell below 50% of the highest contiguous minute of alpha activity observed in that subject during any of the base lines. Of the 144 base line periods so examined, 67 were found to contain one or more minutes of atypical density by the above criterion. Further analysis of the records indicated a significant relationship between an atypical minute and the presence of slow eye movements indicating the beginning of sleep.

We also sought to identify some characteristic of alpha activity itself that would separate drowsy base lines from those more nearly optimal. The relative range of variation in alpha density, derived by taking the difference between the largest and smallest fifteen-second epoch densities and dividing by the average density for each minute, proved to be such a characteristic, correctly identifying more than 85% of the base lines as containing or not containing an atypically low minute when separated by means of a median split in relative range. The effects of this sort of drowsiness are not trivial, since it occurred in roughly 46% of the base lines studied, nor are such effects restricted to later base lines, but occurred in about one-fourth of the first session base lines as well. It is difficult to become aware of such drowsiness without access to data from short epochs during the base lines or access to slow eye-movement records.

Mulholland and his associates have commented on the stabilizing effects of feedback on the alpha rhythm.[40] In a study of nine subjects that explored a variety of tasks and situations over six sessions, we looked at the session-to-session intercorrelation matrices for several of the standard situations. For the initial eyes-closed base lines on each day, correlations ranged from $r = .28$ to $r = .93$. Interestingly, the correlations between the first day and succeeding days were all less than $r = .40$, although all other correlations, save one, exceeded $r = .66$ and were statistically significant. Very similar patterns were observed in the eyes-open base line data, although here the first and second days were also significantly related, probably indicating that the blocking effects encountered on the first day have not completely vanished by the second. In contrast, the correlations during the feedback portion of the sessions, with instructions to increase the amount of alpha activity as signaled by a change in feedback tone pitch, were high from day to day, even with the first day. They were all significant, and ranged from $r = .85$ to $r = .98$, with an average of roughly $r = .91$.

What relevance do these issues have for the assessment of the relationship between alpha activity and state of consciousness such as hypnosis? The literature on alpha and hypnosis has been equivocal, to say the least. Engstrom [41] has reviewed a large number of studies, and feels that the evidence supports a "moderate relationship" between alpha activity and hypnotic susceptibility. Many of the studies cited suffer from problems. Subjects in most of the studies were aware that alpha activity and hypnosis were being related, or could guess from the design of the study. Evans [42] has pointed out that in the few studies where the connection was not obvious, no relationship was found. The dangers of interpretation surrounding situations where subjects are free to help or hinder experiments have been previously discussed in detail.[43] Second, Evans again points out that the relationships that have been noted seem to involve subjects with low to medium hypnotizability scores. Apart from the situational effects on alpha base line measures just discussed, it may well be that these subjects are more prone than those with higher scores to the same kinds of situational effects on hypnosis-scale scores that are seen with alpha activity.[42] I am tempted to say that relating alpha and hypnosis is a little like standing in a quicksand bog to measure the height of a pile of Jello. It's a wonder any regularity emerges at all. Nonetheless, let me hazard to talk about data from 15 subjects who were run in a two-session study.† The first day consisted of standard base lines, eyes open and closed, followed by a series of trials of an aversive classical conditioning paradigm. Those subjects returning for the second session again received standard base lines, and then were given alpha biofeedback under conditions in which a light stimulus changed from red to green with the presence of alpha activity. There were ten trials, each lasting two minutes, and separated by one-minute rest periods in total darkness. Subjects were asked to keep their eyes open, in order to see the feedback stimuli. Some time after these data were collected, standardized Form A and Form C Stanford scores were obtained from the subjects. I have calculated rank order correlations between the Stanford scores and a number of base line and dynamic characteristics of the alpha rhythm. None of the correlations are over $r_s = .50$, although many are significant in the statistical sense. It is the patterns of the relationships, however, that is of primary interest. First of all, in every case the correlation between Form A and the alpha variable was lower in absolute magnitude than the corresponding Form C correlation. The values ranged from $r_s = .05$ to $r_s = .44$. Second, the correlation between eyes-closed base lines on the first day of the study and Form A was $r_s = .14$; with Form C it was $r_s = .44$. Similar correlations on the second day were $r_s = .04$ for Form A and $r_s = .17$ for Form C. Correlations between the Stanford scales and mean alpha densities during feedback on the second day, however, were $r_s = .15$ and $r_s = .41$ for Forms A and C, respectively. Measures of relative increases, recovery from blocking, and percent of base line reached all correlated between $r_s = .29$ and $r_s = .35$ with the Form C, less with Form A.

In light of the previous discussion of alpha measurements, which of the levels measured in this experiment reflects subjects' characteristic alpha densities? For a number of reasons, I believe that the day-two eyes-closed base line data for several subjects are contaminated by drowsiness, and consequently this measure is less stable than we would like. Although the addition of visual feedback in this study did not lead to increases in subjects' optimal alpha densities, it did stabilize densities, reflecting the dynamic reaction of alpha densities to the stimulus and task demands in the particular situation. Such a dynamic alteration is apparently also present in the first day base line; indeed, the correlation between the average feedback trial density and the day-one base line is slightly higher than with the day-two base line, though issues of drowsiness also enter here.

These data are relatively encouraging. Particularly comforting is the fact that higher correlations were obtained between the more stable measures of both alpha activity and of hypnotic susceptibility. This finding suggests that a real relationship may exist between characteristics of hypnotic susceptibility and alpha density, provided we can obtain stable measures of each, and examine each in detail. It further suggests that quick, one-shot studies of the relationship are not likely to provide us with definitive answers. A single Form A score did not relate well to any of the alpha measures. Although the data are encouraging, it is likely that alpha level *per se* is not the important variable to study, but

† These subjects were run by Doctor James J. Lynch.

rather that a study of alpha dynamics, the changes that occur in response to differing situations, will lead to a better understanding of the alpha-hypnosis relationship. The data I have described here were gathered from subjects who were trained with visual stimuli, in light, and who learned to increase their alpha activity almost in spite of the feedback stimulus, although never to exceed their eyes closed base line levels. Their task was to learn not to look, but to be aware.

In the past, studies have sought to relate various aspects of personality in general and hypnotizability as a specific trait to alpha density under resting conditions. With the upsurge of interest in feedback techniques, the ease with which subjects learn to increase alpha density has seemed to several investigators an appropriate correlate of the ease with which subjects might enter hypnosis.[41, 44] Current work is seeking to explore the now more likely view that changes in alpha density which reflect the volitional control over attentional processes will prove to have a significant relationship with hypnotizability, a characteristic that appears, at least in part, to reflect similar mechanisms.

ACKNOWLEDGMENTS

I wish to thank Martin T. Orne, Emily Carota Orne, and Frederick J. Evans for their collaboration, assistance and comments, and the staff of the Unit for Experimental Psychiatry, past and present, for their assistance in gathering these data.

REFERENCES

1. BERGER, H. 1929. Uber das Elektrencephalogram des Menschen. J. Psychol. Neurol. **40:** 160–179.
2. STORM VAN LEEUWEN, W., R. BICKFORD, et al. 1966. Proposal for an EEG terminology by the terminology committee of the IFSECN. Electroenceph. Clin. Neurophysiol. **20:** 293–320.
3. MULHOLLAND, T. 1968. Feedback electroencephalography. Activitas Nervosa Superior (Prague) **10:** 410–438.
4. RECHTSCHAFFEN, A. & A. KALES. 1968. A manual of standardized terminology, techniques and scoring system for sleep stages of human subjects. Public Health Service. U. S. Government Printing Office. Washington, D.C.
5. ADRIAN, E. D. & B. A. C. MATHEWS. 1934. The Berger rhythm: Potential changes from the occipital lobes in man. Brain **57:** 355–385.
6. GLASS, A. 1964. Mental arithmetic and blocking of the occipital alpha rhythm. Electroenceph. Clin. Neurophysiol. **16:** 595–603.
7. EBERLIN, P. & D. YEAGER. 1968. Alpha blocking during visual after-images. Electroenceph. Clin. Neurophysiol. **25:** 23–28.
8. KLINGER, E., K. C. GREGOIRE & S. G. BARTA. 1973. Physiological correlates of mental activity: Eye movements, alpha, and heart rate during imaging, suppression, concentration, search, and choice. Psychophysiology **10:** 471–477.
9. MALMO, R. B. 1959. Activation: A neuropsychological dimension. Psychol. Rev. **66:** 367–386.
10. LINDSLEY, D. B. 1960. Attention, consciousness, sleep and wakefulness. In Handbook of Physiology. Section 1. Neurophysiology. J. Field, Ed. Vol. **1:** 1553–1593. American Physiology Society. Washington, D.C.
11. SAUL, L. J., H. DAVIS & P. A. DAVIS. 1937. Correlations between electroencephalograms and psychological organization of the individual. Trans. Am. Neurol. Assoc. **63:** 167.

160   Annals New York Academy of Sciences

12. WALTER, W. G. 1959. Intrinsic rhythms of the brain. *In* Handbook of Physiology. Section 1. Neurophysiology. J. Field, Ed. Vol. 1: 279–313. American Physiology Society, Washington, D.C.
13. TRAVIS, T. A., C. Y. KONDO & J. R. KNOTT. 1974. Personality variables and alpha enhancement: A correlative sutdy. Br. J. Psychiat. 124: 542–544.
14. LONDON, P., J. T. HART & M. P. LEIBOVITZ. 1968. EEG alpha rhythms and susceptibility to hypnosis. Nature 219: 71–72.
15. JASPER, H. H. & C. SHAGASS. 1941. Conditioning the occipital alpha rhythm in man. J. Exper. Psychol. 28: 373–388.
16. GIANNITRAPANI, D. 1971. Scanning mechanisms and the EEG. Electroenceph. Clin. Neurophysiol. 30: 139–146.
17. MULHOLLAND, T. B. 1969. The concept of attention and the electroencephalographic alpha rhythm. *In* Attention in Neurophysiology. C. R. Evans and T. B. Mulholland, Eds. : 100–127. Butterworths. London, England.
18. MULHOLLAND, T. B. 1973. Objective EEG methods for studying covert shifts of visual attention. *In* The Psychophysiology of Thinking. F. J. McGuigan and R. A. Schoonover, Eds. : 109–151. Academic Press. New York, N.Y.
19. PEPER, E. 1970. Feedback regulation of the alpha electroencephalogram through control of the internal and external parameters. Kybernetik 7: 107–112.
20. PEPER, E. 1971. Reduction of efferent motor commands during alpha feedback as a facilitator of EEG alpha and a precondition for changes in consciousness. Kybernetik 9: 226–231.
21. MULHOLLAND, T. B. & E. PEPER. 1971. Occipital alpha and accomodative vergence, pursuit tracking, and fast eye movements. Psychophysiology 8: 556–575.
22. PLOTKIN, W. B. 1976. On the self-regulation of the occipital alpha rhythm: Control strategies, states of consciousness, and the role of physiological feedback. J. Exp. Psychol. General. 105: 66–99.
23. BAKAN, P. & D. SVORAD. 1969. Resting EEG alpha and asymmetry of reflective lateral eye movements. Nature 223: 975–976.
24. ORNE, M. T. & S. WILSON. 1976. Alpha, biofeedback and arousal/activation. Paper presented at First NATO Symposium on Biofeedback and Behavior. Munich, Fed. Rep. Germany. July 29–30.
25. KAMIYA, J. 1968. Conscious control of brain waves. Psychology Today 1: 57–60.
26. KAMIYA, J. 1969. Operant control of the EEG alpha rhythm and some of its reported effects on consciousness. *In* Altered States of Consciousness. C. T. Tart, Ed. : 507–517. John Wiley & Sons. New York, N.Y.
27. NOWLIS, D. P. & J. KAMIYA. 1970. The control of electroencephalographic alpha rhythms through auditory feedback and the associated mental activity. Psychophysiology 6: 476–484.
28. BROWN, B. B. 1970. Recognition of aspects of consciousness through association with EEG alpha activity represented by a light signal. Psychophysiology 6: 442–452.
29. BROWN, B. B. 1971. Awareness of EEG-subjective activity relationships detected within a closed feedback system. Psychophysiology 7: 451–464.
30. LYNCH, J. J. & D. A. PASKEWITZ. 1971. On the mechanisms of the feedback control of human brain wave activity. J. Nerv. Ment. Dis. 153: 205–217.
31. PASKEWITZ, D. A. & M. T. ORNE. 1973. Visual effects on alpha feedback training. Science 181: 360–363.
32. BEATTY, J. 1972. Similar effects of feedback signals and instructional information on EEG activity. Physiol. Behav. 9: 151–154.
33. WALSH, D. H. 1974. Interactive effects of alpha feedback and instructional set on subjective state. Psychophysiology 11: 428–435.
34. TRAVIS, T. A., C. Y. KONDO & J. R. KNOTT. 1974. Alpha conditioning: A controlled study. J. Nerv. Ment. Dis. 158: 163–173.

35. LYNCH, J. J., D. A. PASKEWITZ & M. T. ORNE. 1974. Some factors in the feed-back control of human alpha rhythm. Psychosom. Med. **36:** 399–410.
36. ORNSTEIN, H. B. & B. MCWILLIAMS. 1976. Variations in electroencephalo-graphic alpha activity under conditions of differential lighting and auditory feedback. Biofeedback Self-Regulation. **1:** 423–432.
37. HARDT, J. V. & J. KAMIYA. 1976. Some comments on Plotkin's self-regulation of electroencephalographic alpha. J. Exp. Psychol. General. **105:** 100–108.
38. LYNCH, J. J., D. A. PASKEWITZ & M. T. ORNE. 1974. Inter-session stability of human alpha rhythm densities. Electroenceph. Clin. Neurophysiol. **36:** 538–540.
39. PASKEWITZ, D. A. & M. T. ORNE. 1972. On the reliability of baseline EEG alpha activity. Paper presented at Ann. Mtg. Soc. Psychophysiol. Res. Boston, Mass.
40. MULHOLLAND, T. B., T. MCLAUGHLIN & F. BENSON. 1976. Feedback control and quantification of the response of EEG alpha to visual stimulation. Biofeedback Self-Regulation. **1:** 411–422.
41. ENGSTROM, D. R. 1976. Hypnotic susceptibility, EEG-alpha, and self-regulation. *In* Consciousness and Self-Regulation: Advances in Research. G. E. Schwartz and D. Shapiro, Eds. : 173–221. Plenum. New York, N.Y.
42. EVANS, F. J. 1972. Hypnosis and sleep: Techniques for exploring cognitive ac-tivity during sleep. *In* Hypnosis: Research Developments and Prespectives. E. Fromm and R. E. Shor, Eds. : 43–83. Aldine-Atherton. Chicago, Ill.
43. ORNE, M. T. 1962. On the social psychology of the psychological experiment: With particular reference to demand characteristics and their implications. Am. Psychol. **17:** 776–783.
44. ENGSTROM, D. R., P. LONDON & J. T. HART. 1970. Hypnotic susceptibility in-creased by EEG alpha training. Nature **227:** 1261–1262.

HYPNOSIS AND SLEEP: THE CONTROL OF ALTERED STATES OF AWARENESS *

Frederick J. Evans

Unit for Experimental Psychiatry
The Institute of Pennsylvania Hospital and
University of Pennsylvania
Philadelphia, Pennsylvania 19139

In spite of some obvious phenomenological similarities between hypnosis and sleep, they appear to be unrelated physiologically. It will, however, be hypothesized in this report that hypnosis and sleep may share some control mechanism that may partly account for individual differences in the ability to experience hypnosis and in the ease of falling asleep and maintaining voluntary control of sleep processes.

HYPNOSIS AND SLEEP: SIMILARITIES AND DIFFERENCES

Phenomenological Similarities

If he had not witnessed the induction procedure, the casual observer might well believe a typical hypnotized subject was asleep. It was this sleeplike appearance that led Braid to coin the term "hypnosis" from the Greek *hypnos* (to sleep) and "somnambulist" from the Latin *somnus* (sleep) and *ambulare* (to walk), to describe the deeply hypnotized person. There are indeed many phenomenological parallels between sleep and hypnosis. Not only does the deeply hypnotized individual often appear to be asleep, he may subsequently describe the experience as sleeplike. When awaking from either condition, the person often remembers little of what has transpired. Like the sleep-walking somnambulist, the hypnotized person may move about and talk, and he maintains contact with selected aspects of the external world. Vivid dreams may occur in both sleep and hypnosis. The long historical association between hypnosis and sleep is still reflected in many of the standard induction suggestions that subjects should enter into a deep, relaxed, restful sleep.

The Relationship between Hypnosis and Sleep

In a previous review,[1] some aspects of the possible relationship between hypnosis and sleep were examined. The existing research literature indicates that there are no basic similarities between hypnosis and sleep in terms of the

---

* This research was supported in part by grant no. MH 19156–07 from the National Institute of Mental Health, United States Public Health Service; in part by contract no. DADA17–71–C–1120, U.S. Army Medical Research & Development Command; and in part by the Institute for Experimental Psychiatry.

well-documented EEG characteristics that typically define sleep.[2] Hypnosis is characterized by waking EEG patterns; not those of sleep.†

The review [1] also summarized earlier studies showing that hypnotizability may be related to the ability possessed by some individuals to respond, even while remaining asleep, to meaningful environmental stimuli that are presented exclusively during sleep. Thus, some hypnotizable individuals can respond while sleeping (particularly in stage REM sleep) to behavioral suggestions administered during sleep without having any awareness of their response in the subsequent waking state. Nevertheless, these individuals are able to maintain the response during sleep the next night, or even six months later.[13, 14]

Other hypnotizable subjects have been able to recognize some simple, paired-associate material presented during REM sleep, provided that an appropriate suggested set is established prior to sleep.[1, 15] In general, those subjects who are able to experience dissociative hypnotic phenomena appear to be able to maintain contact with their external environment and are even able to respond to it without their responses necessarily disturbing their sleep (monitored by conservative EEG criteria).

The sleep-responsive subjects (who were highly hypnotizable) reported that they normally fall asleep easily and quickly, sleep without being disturbed by noise or light, and awaken easily in the morning to a significantly greater extent than the unresponsive subjects. This was supported by the EEG sleep data, since these same sleep-responsive subjects also seemed to sleep more soundly whenever they were stimulated during the night, and they fell asleep more rapidly in the laboratory than did nonresponsive, unhypnotizable subjects. Thus, it appears that there may have been an underlying ability whereby these subjects could maintain some kind of cognitive control over their own sleep processes.

Do Hypnotizable Subjects Fall Asleep Easily?

The observation that hypnotizable subjects fall asleep in a sleep laboratory by EEG criteria significantly more quickly than insusceptible subjects ($N = 19$, $p < .05$)[1, 14] provides some empirical support for the historical association between sleep and hypnosis, particularly the frequent juxtaposition of hypnosis with the proximal occurrence of sleep. The somnambulistic sleeplike state studied by Braid [16] was already quite different in appearance from animal magnetism as practiced by Mesmer.[17] Nevertheless, for Mesmer sleep was an important aftereffect of the crises, or hysterical seizures, that were associated with his patients' recovery from their illnesses.

† Following the observation of the apparent correlation by London et al.,[3] several studies reported that hypnotizable subjects manifest higher levels of EEG alpha activity, a common rhythm traditionally associated with relaxed wakefulness rather than sleep. However, these earlier observations, reviewed elsewhere,[1] of a correlation between alpha and hypnosis stemmed from pilot studies that had serious methodological limitations. In general, it was concluded that the relationship between hypnotic susceptibility and alpha density seemed to be either nonexistent or weak, and more recent studies [4-9] (reviewed in this volume by Paskewitz [10]) have continued to yield equivocal results. In addition, recent research has questioned the traditionally accepted relationship between alpha and arousal.[10, 11] These findings suggest that any relationship between EEG activity and hypnosis will indeed be complex.

Other incidental observations also suggest that there is an easy and flexible interchangeability of the two states. If the hypnotized subject is left alone, or if specific suggestions are given, the subject may pass into a natural sleep. Similarly, given appropriate suggestions, the sleeping subject may sometimes awaken directly into a hypnotic state rather than a normal waking state.[18] Whether the individual is in a sleep, hypnotic, or normal state at a given time may depend upon how he perceives what he is expected to do.[19] In a study [20, 21] in which tape-recorded hypnosis sessions were "inadvertently" terminated by a power failure, deeply hypnotized subjects seemed to slowly terminate hypnosis after a period of about 20 minutes. Surprisingly, after a few minutes of activity several of these subjects appeared to fall asleep in a defensive reaction to the inexplicable disappearance of the hypnotist—a behavior not observed in insusceptible, simulating subjects.

These anecdotal and empirical observations seem to point to the conclusion that hypnotizable subjects may be able to fall asleep easily and, in general, may possess an ability to maintain control over sleep processes and cognitive activity associated with sleep. The main aim of this report is to document and test this hypothesis and its implications. However, in order to study the relationship between hypnotizability and the ability to fall asleep easily and maintain control of sleep processes, more data were required to explore individual differences in sleep patterns to determine if indeed such control of sleep is a reliable characteristic. Unfortunately, data addressing questions concerning the voluntary control of falling asleep (or staying awake) do not exist.

The Control of Sleep: A Dimension of Subjective Sleep Patterns

In order to investigate meaningful patterns among subjective reports of sleep habits, a factor analytic investigation was conducted of responses to a sleep questionnaire that has routinely been used in our laboratory to explore some of the parameters of subjects' typical sleep habits.[22] In that study, five independent clusters of items were isolated and replicated in two samples (92 and 180 subjects). The largest contribution to reliable variance was made by a dimension involving *dream recall,* including questions about dreams every night, dreams about daytime happenings, and dreams in color. Two separate dimensions seemed to involve different kinds of sleep problems. The first, *sleep-onset difficulty,* included difficulty in falling asleep, takes sleep medication, nights of dreamless sleep, and trouble sleeping before an exam. The second, *inability to maintain sleep,* involved awakens at sounds, often wakes up during the night, has to get up at night, and light sleeper. The intriguing possibility that these two dimensions represent normal manifestations of the more extreme sleep-onset and sleep-maintenance insomnias often noted in the differential diagnosis of depression and anxiety still need to be explored. Another factor apparently involved the *cognitive control of sleep mentation,* including changes of dream content at will, deciding beforehand what to dream about, and awakens to find sound in dream was real. It may be most relevant to our earlier work on information processing during sleep.[13]

The most relevant of the five factors for this report was tentatively labeled *voluntary control of sleep.* Related questions included items involving falling asleep easily, taking daytime naps, going to sleep at will, and falling asleep during a movie or a concert, or on a plane or train trip.

Subjects who score higher on the Control of Sleep factor report that they fall asleep more quickly at night than those with low scores. This finding has been confirmed by EEG criteria of sleep onset in two studies, one involving nighttime sleep $(N = 19)$,[13] and one involving habitual nappers and non-nappers $(N = 33)$ who were asked to take a laboratory nap. In addition, nappers (who score high on the Control of Sleep dimension) report that they are more likely to delay going to bed at night, particularly if their schedule permits a nap either before or after their late night, and generally go to bed at more variable times than nonnappers (who score lower on the control dimension).

CONTROL OF SLEEP AND HYPNOTIC RESPONSIVITY

In our previous research, there were relatively few significant correlations between the 33 items on the sleep questionnaire discussed above and responsive-

TABLE 1

MEAN HGSHS:A SCORES FOR SUBJECTS WITH HIGH AND LOW SCORES ON THE VOLUNTARY CONTROL OF SLEEP (CS)

	Sample 1			Sample 2		
	N	$\overline{X}$	S.D.	N	$\overline{X}$	S.D.
High CS	17	7.88	2.2	124	6.73	2.6
Low CS	13	4.62	3.2	89	6.00	2.6
t	3.16 (p <.005)			2.03 (p <.05)		

ness to hypnosis. However, the conceptual framework provided by the factor analytic study, and particularly the notion of individual differences in the degree of control over the sleep process, suggested a more direct analysis. In TABLE 1, mean scores on the Harvard Group Scale of Hypnotic Susceptibility, Form A (HGSHS:A)[23] are presented for volunteer college student subjects who scored in approximately the upper and lower quartile of the estimated Control of Sleep factor scores. Data are reported for a sample of subjects $(N = 60)$ who volunteered for a hypnosis experiment, and also for a larger group $(N = 372)$ drawn from three separate hypnosis studies in which subjects volunteered initially for psychological and psychophysiological studies.

Subjects who score high on the Control of Sleep cluster also have significantly higher scores on HGSHS:A than subjects with poor control of sleep. This result can also be shown when subjects are categorized in terms of high (9–12) and low (0–4) hypnotizability on HGSHS:A. The mean scores on the Control of Sleep dimension are 14.8 and 12.6, respectively $(df = 39, t = 2.29, p < .02)$ and 14.3 and 13.8 respectively $(df = 191, t = 1.80, p < .10)$ for the smaller and combined samples. These results support the predicted relationship between hypnotizability and the voluntary control of sleep.‡

Control of Sleep and Hypnotizability Among Nappers

One of the main variables defining the Control of Sleep dimension is the occurrence of napping. It seemed likely that the nature of the relationship between hypnotizability and the ability to control sleep processes would be clarified during our ongoing research on napping. The items concerned with falling asleep easily and quickly at night and the capacity to sleep in circumstances such as a movie theater or a concert represent phenomena that were explored in more detail in another questionnaire that was designed to look at the parameters of napping.[24] This questionnaire included items exploring in more depth an individual's ability to sleep under unusual circumstances. A significant relationship between the items that appeared to be related to the control of sleep, the occurrence of napping, and hypnotizability was predicted. The obtained results, however, were more complex, but perhaps more meaningful, than such a simple relationship would imply.

The napping questionnaire was administered to 469 students who had volunteered to participate in a hypnosis experiment. These subjects were divided into 259 nappers (those who reported they napped "sometimes," "usually," or "always") and 210 nonnappers (those who reported napping "rarely" or "never"). A number of items that seemed similar to those involving the voluntary control of sleep in a variety of circumstances had been shown in a prior sample of 430 students to discriminate significantly between nappers and nonnappers, differences which were replicated in the present sample of 469.

Contrary to our predictions, the mean HGSHS:A score of nappers (7.19) did not differ significantly from the mean HGSHS:A score of nonnappers (7.11). The correlation between HGSHS:A and the response to the question concerning napping frequency (from "always" to "never" on a five-point scale) was .07.

To the extent that it was clear that there were both hypnotizable and unhypnotizable nappers, it seemed relevant to seek possible differences in other aspects of the Control of Sleep dimension that might differentiate between nappers who differ in hypnotizability. However, of the 76 comparisons made on sleep and napping patterns between nappers of high and low responsivity to hypnosis, only six borderline significant differences occurred. This is probably a chance distribution of differences. It seems clear from these results that nappers who differ in hypnotizability do not report different patterns of sleep or napping, or different attitudes toward napping.

Voluntary versus Involuntary Napping

Although napping is one of the main variables defining the Control of Sleep dimension, an alternative hypothesis is that the apparent speed and ease

‡ Although not directly relevant to this report, it should be noted that there were also significant differences in the two samples indicating that hypnotizable subjects scored higher on the dream-recall dimension (p <.02 in both cases).

of falling asleep may reflect a complete *lack of control* over sleep onset, rather than a volitional decision as to when, where, and whether to fall asleep in different circumstances. The available data do not allow a direct test of this alternative; however, one of the questions on the napping questionnaire asked, "Do most of your naps occur accidentally or involuntarily (e.g., while reading, watching T.V., etc.)?" On a four-point rating scale only 26 of the 259 nappers answered "definitely yes," while 91 answered "definitely no." The mean HGSHS:A score did not differ between the involuntary nappers and those who felt that they had control over when they napped. However, compared to the majority of nappers who felt that they decided when to nap, the involuntary nappers who were overwhelmed by sleep reported (p < .05, two-tailed t-tests) that they typically fell asleep faster when they napped compared to other nappers who had more control of the napping process, that they enjoyed the nap less, and that they found it less likely to improve their work and concentration. Unlike most nappers, they would not be likely to take a nap if they had time; their naps bore little relation to when they felt tired, and they were less able to fight off sleep if they had slept less the night before.

In addition, unlike this small group of involuntary nappers, people who nap typically report they can choose to stay up later on some occasions at night because they realize they have the ability to nap to make up for lost sleep if they find they need it the next day. Consequently, the time at which they go to bed at night is more variable than for both involuntary nappers and habitual nonnappers.

Thus, while additional data will be required to clarify the nature of the control mechanism, for the majority of subjects being studied, the ease of falling asleep in different circumstances does seem to be under the direct volitional control of most subjects scoring high on the control dimension.

Control of Sleep and Hypnotizability in Nonnappers

In a separate section of the questionnaire completed only by nonnappers on their attitudes toward and reasons for nonnapping, several questions significantly differentiated between high-, medium-, and low-hypnotizable nonnappers. These data (some of which are summarized in Table 2) show that the hypnotizable nonnapper chooses not to nap primarily because he feels that he has no time to do so and that it interferes with his work and leisure. The unhypnotizable nonnapper, however, gives as a major reason for not napping that he would not be able to fall asleep.

These interesting findings (along with the related trends, indicated in the footnote to Table 2, that did not reach significance) suggest that the hypnotizable nonnapper chooses not to nap because he does not want to do so. It is likely, however, that he could nap if he chose to do so. In contrast, the unhypnotizable nonnapper probably does not nap because he does not seem to have the ability to do so even if he wanted to. In fact, differences between these two groups of nonnappers are quite analogous to findings in the previous study [24] reporting differences between habitual nonnappers who at previous times in their life did nap compared to those who never did so.

Unhypnotizable Nonnappers: Inability to Control Sleep

These findings are extended in TABLE 3. This complex table summarizes the responses on the section of the napping questionnaire completed by all subjects. Data for high- and low-hypnotizable subjects are presented in the right-hand column regardless of their napping classification. In the middle column the results are broken down into high- and low-hypnotizable nappers. In the left-hand column the high and low hypnotizable nonnappers are summarized.§

There are several interesting aspects of these data. It is clear that hypnotizability is an important variable related in a moderator-variable fashion to nonnapping, but not to napping. Only two of the fifteen comparisons

TABLE 2

DIFFERENT REASONS FOR NOT REGULARLY NAPPING AS A FUNCTION OF SUSCEPTIBILITY TO HYPNOSIS AMONG NONNAPPERS †

Reason for Not Napping (5=definitely applies)	HGSHS:A			F	t (High vs. Low)
	High	Medium	Low		
No time	3.42	3.34	2.68	3.10 **	2.31 **
Interferes with work	3.46	3.04	2.81	2.80 *	2.22 **
Not be able to fall asleep	2.48	3.12	3.16	4.73 ***	−2.23 **
Nap has unpleasant physical aftereffects	2.13	2.24	1.55	2.93 *	2.26 **
Rest more beneficial	2.56	2.31	1.90	2.44 *	2.22 **

† *p < .05; ** p < .025; *** p < .01. In general, for categories marked$^\phi$, high subjects endorsed the statement more strongly than mediums, both of whom did so more than lows; for statements marked*, similarly insignificant trends were noted in which highs least often endorsed the statement as applicable on the following questions: Reasons for not napping that do not discriminate levels of susceptibility include: no need to nap,$^\phi$ interferes with leisure,$^\phi$ would not feel better afterwards,$^\phi$ would not feel less tired afterwards, would not be able to sleep at night,$^\phi$ get enough sleep now,$^\phi$ napping is a sign of laziness,* napping is an unpleasant experience,* and napping has unpleasant mental consequences.*

between hypnotizable and unhypnotizable nappers are of borderline significance. However, there are significant differences between high- and low-hypnotizable nonnappers that for the most part relate to those several questions that are concerned with the ability to control sleep in a variety of unusual circumstances. Thus, highly hypnotizable nonnappers claim they can fall asleep

§ The fact that the mean questionnaire responses of medium hypnotizability (HGSHS:A scores of 6 to 8 inclusive) tend to fall in the middle in these and subsequent comparisons is a minor, but important, finding. One of the problems of previous studies seeking correlates of hypnotic susceptibility is that subjects of medium levels of susceptibility typically do not fall in the middle of high- and low-hypnotizable subjects on the relevant variable.

TABLE 3

THE MODERATING EFFECTS OF BEING A NAPPER (N=259) OR NONNAPPER (N=210) ON THE RELATIONSHIP BETWEEN HYPNOTIC SUSCEPTIBILITY (HGSHS:A—HIGH=9-12; LOW=0-4) AND SUBJECTIVE SLEEP QUESTIONS INDICATING SKILL IN CONTROLLING SLEEP †

Sleep Item (Nap Questionnaire)	Nonnappers			Nappers			All Ss		
	High 67	Low 31	t	High 85	Low 36	t	High 152	Low 67	t
Could sleep now (Yes=1)	.63	.42	1.99**	.79	.92	2.08**	.72	.69	—
Min. usually to fall asleep	19.2	28.8	1.90*	18.6	19.2	—	18.9	26.4	2.42***
Time usually to bed (a.m.)	00:41	01:18	1.97*	00:36	00:55	—	00:38	01:06	2.12**
Hr. sleep regularly	7:15	7:37	1.95*	7:17	7:22	—	7:16	7:30	—
Fall asleep easily	3.64	3.13	2.56***	3.81	3.64	—	3.74	3.40	2.76***
Wake up nights	2.52	2.26	2.21**	2.67	2.72	—	2.61	2.51	—
Difficulty falling asleep	2.33	3.00	3.47****	2.34	2.47	—	2.34	2.72	2.94***
Do you fall asleep:									
Reading book	2.48	1.90	3.07***	2.75	2.97	—	2.63	2.48	—
Studying	2.40	1.94	2.29**	2.64	2.89	—	2.53	2.43	—
Play or theater	1.64	1.23	3.17****	1.73	1.78	—	1.69	1.52	—
Plane or train	2.54	1.90	2.84****	2.86	2.86	—	2.72	2.42	1.92*
Movies	1.97	1.48	3.12****	2.18	2.06	—	2.09	1.79	2.58****
Stress	1.79	1.58	—	2.18	1.86	1.66*	2.01	1.73	2.00**
Lectures, speeches	2.22	2.81	2.35***	2.44	2.61	—	2.34	2.24	—
Watching TV	2.64	2.13	2.17**	2.85	2.61	—	2.76	2.39	3.34*****
No. of 10 sit. always diff.	2.45	4.65	3.99*****	1.46	1.58	—	1.89	3.00	3.14*****
Sleepwalk	1.28	1.16	—	1.32	1.08	3.15****	1.30	1.12	2.88***
Sleeptalk	2.12	1.97	—	2.22	2.00	—	2.18	1.99	1.48

† * p < .05; ** p < .025; *** p < .01; ***** p < .001 (all one-tailed values).

easily at night and can readily fall asleep while reading a book, while studying, at a play or theater, or on a train or plane, at the movies, at a lecture, and while watching television. In fact, of the ten comparisons made concerning the conditions under which they can fall asleep readily, hypnotizable nonnappers answered "never," to only an average 2.45 of the 10, compared to 4.65 "never" responses of the unhypnotizable nonnappers ($p < .00001$).

It is also of some importance to note that on all of these questions, regardless of their hypnotizability, nappers score significantly higher than nonnappers. Indeed, almost all these questions have means that have the same rank order: both high- and low-hypnotizable nappers score higher than either of the nonnapper groups. Thus, our previous finding that nappers have greater voluntary control over sleep than nonnappers is not violated by these results. The new finding is that although nonnappers generally have less control over sleep than habitual nappers, this difference is moderated by hypnotic responsivity. Those nonnappers who have the ability to experience

TABLE 4

$\overline{X}$ Response to Question: Do You Fall Asleep Readily? †
In Nappers and Nonnappers in Relation to Their Susceptibility to Hypnosis

| | HGSHS:A | | |
	High (9–12) (N=152)	Low (0–4) (N=67)	All Ss (N=219)
Napper (N=121)	3.81	3.64	3.76
Nonnappers (N=98)	3.64	3.13	3.48
	3.74	3.40	3.63

† 5=always, 1=never.
F (Napper vs. nonnapper=7.55, $p < .005$; F (High vs. low hypnosis)=7.68, $p < .005$; F (Interaction: Hypnotizability vs. nap type) =1.87, n.s.; χ^2 (Comparing 4 subgroup N's) =0.02, n.s.

hypnosis also have greater control over sleep processes than the unhypnotizable nonnappers.

The nature of this relationship is summarized in TABLE 4, which tabulates the mean responses of nappers and nonnappers classified by hypnotizability on the question that perhaps measures the Control of Sleep dimension best: "Do you fall asleep readily?" It is clear from the analysis of variance that the difference between nappers and nonnappers is significant ($p < .001$). The difference between high- and low-hypnotizability levels is also significant ($p < .001$). However, the interaction between the propensity for napping and hypnotizability is quite insignificant. Indeed, the frequency distribution of hypnotizability among nappers and nonnappers is identical ($\chi^2 = .02$; n.s.).¶

¶ Of some passing interest is that highly hypnotizable subjects more frequently report walking in their sleep than do unhypnotizable subjects ($p < .01$). They similarly tend to talk in their sleep more often, but partly because of the low incidence of sleep-talking, high- and low-hypnotizable subjects do not differ on this variable.

INDIVIDUAL DIFFERENCES IN THE VOLUNTARY CONTROL OF ALTERED STATES

In summary, then, it appears that the ability to achieve deep hypnosis and the ability to fall asleep easily and virtually at will share some common mechanism. It is hypothesized that this mechanism involves individual differences in the ability to maintain control over the level of functioning or state of consciousness that seems appropriate to the person at the time. This control mechanism apparently involves the ability to change readily from one kind of psychological state or activity to another: or to maintain a flexibility in changing psychological sets.

The control system that allows a person to choose and initiate entry into hypnosis or into sleep, and presumably other states, may be a very general ability possessed by some people, and it may manifest itself in any of a number of circumstances. The person who possesses this ability may develop a variety of skills or coping styles to handle situations in everyday life when it is beneficial to function at different levels of consciousness. It is interesting in this regard that EEG delta sleep has been observed during the meditation periods of experienced meditators.[25, 26] Similarly, hypnotizable subjects were reportedly able to learn meditation techniques faster than insusceptible subjects.[27]

Of course, which of a number of possible and relevant states of consciousness that an invidual can readily decide to enter will depend on other capacities that he may or may not possess. Most individuals have the capacity to sleep, although there are many who do not have the necessary control of the sleep mechanisms to achieve it as readily as, for example, the habitual napper. Individuals with a well-developed control mechanism of this kind can fall asleep almost anywhere and any time they choose. They could nap if they felt it beneficial to do so, and they would be unlikely to have serious insomnia problems. Those less fortunate individuals in whom this control mechanism is less well developed may have more difficulty in achieving sleep (within the limits set by extreme fatigue) and indeed may need a variety of rituals and a rigidity of time schedules, or may need to depend on the timing of circadian rhythms to maximize the likelihood of obtaining needed sleep without disrupting other activities. On the other hand, the capacity to experience the hypnotic state is probably much less widespread. The fact that an individual may have a flexibility in achieving different states and changing psychological sets would be irrelevant if he did not also possess whatever other prerequisite skills are necessary to enter hypnosis, or even if he did not have the motivation to experience hypnosis. If a person can readily experience hypnosis, this suggests evidence that he potentially has well-developed control mechanisms, and consequently could fall asleep easily (and nap if he chose to) whenever this was appropriate. However, the person who possesses the necessary control to nap may or may not have the prerequisite capacity to experience hypnosis. In short, it is not being suggested that sleep and hypnosis are interchangeable or functionally equivalent, but rather that (providing the necessary capacities exist for the individual) the ability to *achieve* either state is subsumed under the same control mechanisms—involving the capacity to change psychological sets, attentional states, and altered states of awareness.

This hypothesis has several interesting clinical implications. For example, it suggests that most patients with insomnia are probably relatively unresponsive to hypnosis. If, however, there were some people with sleep-onset insomnia who could experience hypnosis, then this implies that the individual has the necessary control mechanism, and therefore it should be possible to teach the person to fall asleep easily. A recent unpublished study by Graham provides partial support of this possibility. The responses of 20 insomniac patients with sleep-onset insomnia differed significantly on the Control of Sleep factor from 20 control subjects (p < .01 for five of the six defining items). However, following short-term counseling, using a self-hypnosis relaxation procedure, six months after the treatment period the insomniac students had improved in their ability to exert voluntary control over sleep (p < .001) on all the criterion questions. The change was accompanied by reports of significantly improved daily sleep patterns. Unfortunately, the relationship between the amount of improvement and the level of hypnotic responsivity was not reported.

It appears, then, that the ability to control a variety of states of consciousness may vary widely among individuals, but for those who possess appropriate control capacity, other abilities and situational factors will determine which states will be chosen by an individual. Some people may choose to nap, but only if their schedules allow it; others may choose to enter a trancelike state, or become totally absorbed in specific tasks, or become oblivious of other surrounding activities;[28, 29] some may be able to meditate; others, like the executive who takes a short time out with his feet on the desk, may rest; still others may choose to escape into fantasy. There are undoubtedly other altered states that can easily be substituted by the person who has the capacity to experience them; indeed, some may have negative implications, like the phobic states that are more likely to occur in hypnotizable patients.[30] However, which of these coping styles an individual uses may depend on a variety of factors, one of which may be the appropriate opportunity to use the common control mechanism to learn the particular skill involved in the coping style he may prefer. In any case, how effectively the various altered states can be used will be determined within the limits imposed by his capacity to control states of consciousness.

Regardless of whether these hypotheses are confirmed in subsequent studies, it does appear that hypnotizable subjects have the ability to fall asleep easily and in a wide variety of circumstances. While this finding does not imply any basic similarity of sleep and hypnosis, it does indicate that there may be a common underlying mechanism involved in the capacity to experience hypnosis and the ability to fall asleep easily and maintain control of basic sleep processes.

ACKNOWLEDGMENTS

I wish to thank R. Lynn Horne, Betsy E. Lawrence, Pamela A. Markowsky, Emily Carota Orne, Martin T. Orne, Helen M. Pettinati, Joanne Rosellini, Anthony Van Campen, William M. Waid, and Stuart K. Wilson for their helpful comments during the preparation of this report, and Jeremy DeLong, Eileen Grabiec, James Hamos, Alexander Myers, and Neal Shore for their technical assistance.

REFERENCES

1. EVANS, F. J. 1972. Hypnosis and sleep: Techniques for exploring cognitive activity during sleep. *In* Hypnosis: Research Developments and Perspectives. E. Fromm & R. E. Shor, Eds. : 43–83. Aldine-Atherton. Chicago, Ill.

2. RECHTSCHAFFEN, A. & A. KALES, Eds. 1968. A Manual of Standardized Terminology, Techniques and Scoring System for Sleep Stages of Human Subjects. National Institutes of Health Publication No. 204. Washington, D.C.

3. LONDON, P., J. T. HART & M. P. LEIBOVITZ. 1968. EEG alpha rhythms and susceptibility to hypnosis. Nature 219: 71–72.

4. EDMONSTON, W. E., JR. & W. R. GROTEVANT. 1975. Hypnosis and alpha density. Amer. J. Clin. Hypn. 17: 221–232.

5. ENGSTROM, D. R. 1973. The effects of observationally presented information on hypnotizability: The physiology of enhanced hypnotic susceptibility. Paper presented at the 81st Ann. Convention Amer. Psychol. Assn. Montreal, P.Q., Canada.

6. MORGAN, A. H., H. MACDONALD & E. R. HILGARD. 1974. Lateral asymmetry related to task, and hypnotizability. Psychophysiology 11: 275–282.

7. TEBECIS, A. K., K. A. PROVINS, R. W. FARNBACH & P. PENTONY. 1975. Hypnosis and the EEG: A quantitative investigation. J. Nerv. Ment. Dis. 161: 1–17.

8. ULETT, G. A., S. AKPINAR & T. M. ITIL. 1972. Hypnosis: Physiological, pharmacological reality. Amer. J. Psychiat. 128: 799–805.

9. ULETT, G. A., S. AKPINAR, T. M. ITIL & T. FUKUDA. 1971. The neurophysiological basis of hypnosis–objective techniques. Folia Psychiat. Neurol. Jap. 25: 203–211.

10. PASKEWITZ, D. A. This volume.

11. ORNE, M. T., F. J. EVANS, S. K. WILSON & D. A. PASKEWITZ. 1975. The potential effectiveness of autoregulation as a technique to increase performance under stress. Report to the Advanced Research Projects Agency of the Department of Defense, Office of Naval Research, Contract no. N00014–70–C–0350.

12. ORNE, M. T. & S. K. WILSON. 1976. Alpha, biofeedback and arousal/activation. *In* Biofeedback and Behavior. J. Beatty, Chairman. Symposium presented at meeting NATO. Munich, Germany.

13. EVANS, F. J., L. A. GUSTAFSON, D. N. O'CONNELL, M. T. ORNE & R. E. SHOR. 1969. Sleep induced behavioral response. J. Nerv. Ment. Dis. 148: 467–476.

14. EVANS, F. J., L. A. GUSTAFSON, D. N. O'CONNELL, M. T. ORNE & R. E. SHOR. 1970. Verbally induced behavioral responses during sleep. J. Nerv. Ment. Dis. 150: 171–187.

15. EVANS, F. J. & W. ORCHARD. 1969. Sleep learning: The successful waking recall of material presented during sleep. Paper presented at the Ann. Mtg. Assn. Psychophysiological Study of Sleep. Boston, Mass.

16. Braid, J. 1852. Magic, Witchcraft, Animal Magnetism, Hypnotism and Electrobiology. 3rd edit. Churchill. London, England.

17. MESMER, F. A. 1774. Mémoire sur la découverte du Magnétisme Animal. Geneva, Switzerland.

18. KRATOCHVIL, S. 1970. Prolonged hypnosis and sleep. Amer. J. Clin. Hypn. 12: 254–260.

19. ORNE, M. T. 1959. The nature of hypnosis: Artifact and essence. J. Abnorm. Soc. Psychol. 58: 277–299.

20. ORNE, M. T. & F. J. EVANS. 1966. Inadvertent termination of hypnosis with hypnotized and simulating subjects. Int. J. Clin. Exp. Hypn. 14: 61–78.

21. EVANS, F. J. & M. T. ORNE. 1971. The disappearing hypnotist: The use of simulating subjects to evaluate how subjects perceive experimental procedures. Int. J. Clin. Exp. Hypn. 19: 277–296.

22. EVANS, F. J. In press. The subjective characteristics of sleep efficiency. J. Abnorm. Psychol.

23. SHOR, R. E. & E. C. ORNE. 1962. Harvard Group Scale of Hypnotic Susceptibility, Form A. Consulting Psychologists Press. Palo Alto, Calif.

24. EVANS, F. J., M. R. COOK, H. D. COHEN, E. C. ORNE & M T. ORNE. 1976.
Sleep patterns in replacement and appetitive nappers. *In* Who Needs a 24-
Hour Day? Efficiency of Napping and Fragmented Sleep. H. L. Williams,
Chairman. Symposium presented at 84th Ann. Convention Amer. Psychol.
Assn. Washington, D.C.

25. PAGANO, R. R., R. M. ROSE, R. M. STIVERS & S. WARRENBURG. 1976. Sleep during transcendental meditation. Science **191:** 308–310.

26. YOUNGER, J., W. ADRIANCE & R. J. BERGER. 1975. Sleep during transcendental
meditation. Percept. Mot. Skills **40:** 953–954.

27. RIVERS, S. M. 1976. Hypnosis and meditation. Paper presented at the 84th
Ann. Convention Amer. Psychol. Assn. Washington, D.C.

28. SHOR, R. E. 1960. The frequency of naturally occurring "hypnotic-like" experiences in the normal college population. Int. J. Clin. Exp. Hypn. **8:** 151–163.

29. TELLEGEN, A. & G. ATKINSON. 1974. Openness to absorbing and self-altering
experiences ("absorption"), a trait related to hypnotic susceptibility. J. Abnorm. Psychol. **33:** 268–277.

30. FRANKEL, F. H. & M. T. ORNE. 1976. Hypnotizability and phobic behavior.
Arch. Gen. Psychiat. **33:** 1259–1261.

A COMPARISON OF HYPNOSIS, ACUPUNCTURE, MORPHINE, VALIUM, ASPIRIN, AND PLACEBO IN THE MANAGEMENT OF EXPERIMENTALLY INDUCED PAIN *

John A. Stern,† M. Brown,‡ George A. Ulett,§ and
Ivan Sletten ‡

† Behavior Research Laboratory
Washington University
St. Louis, Missouri 63104
‡ Missouri Institute of Psychiatry
St. Louis, Missouri 63139
§ Deaconess Hospital
St. Louis, Missouri 63139

Hypnosis, acupuncture, morphine, and aspirin are reasonably widely used analgesic "agents." The question of whether the effects of such agents are in whole or in part a function of suggestibility or hypnotizability has been debated in the literature, with suggestibility given as perhaps a major component of placebo effects. It has been suggested by some that acupuncture effects are mediated principally through suggestibility and/or hypnosis.[1] Certainly most of the anesthetic and analgesic effects claimed for acupuncture stimulation can be equally well demonstrated with hypnosis. Whether the same can be said of acupuncture "tonification" procedures in the treatment of more-or-less specific physical illnesses is not known, since acupuncture treatment for symptoms other than the relief of pain, and the production of analgesia/ anesthesia have not enjoyed much popularity in Western medicine, and little or no investigative effort has been expended on such research in the English-speaking countries.

Of the many possible phenomena demonstrable under conditions of hypnosis or acupuncture, the reduction of experimentally induced pain is perhaps one of the simplest for research purposes. The effectiveness of hypnosis in reducing such pain has been well documented.[2] Additionally, pain may be alleviated pharmacologically. Whether it is, in fact, pain that is reduced or anxiety associated with such pain that is affected by analgesics will not be debated here. Whatever it is that is reduced causes subjects to emit statements suggesting reduction in discomfort. These statements are our data base.

This study explored the analgesic effects of acupuncture, hypnosis, and a number of pharmacological agents in human subjects. The experiment was designed to answer the following questions: 1) Is the analgesic effect of acupuncture on experimentally induced pain attributable to suggestibility or to hypnotizability? 2) Is induced analgesia by acupuncture stimulation dependent on stimulation at specified acupuncture points or is random-site stimulation equally effective in reducing pain? 3) Are there differences in the analgesic effects of acupuncture compared to hypnoanalgesia and chemically induced

* This work was supported by a research grant (1–R01–GM–20621–01) from the National Institutes of Health, Bethesda, Md.

175

analgesia (via drugs), in terms of (a) pain sensation and/or (b) the responses to pain of certain physiological systems?

METHODS

Twenty normal, healthy Caucasian males, ages 18–30 years ($\bar{x}$ 22 years) volunteered as paid subjects.

Seven challenging agents were employed, each with two types of experimentally induced pain: 1) hypnosis; 2) stimulation of acupuncture points; 3) stimulation of nonpoints; and the following four drugs: 4) morphine, 5) aspirin, 6) diazepam, and 7) a placebo. The two procedures for inducing experimental pain were: ice-water bath (cold-pressor pain) and tourniquet-induced pain (ischemia).

Thus, each subject participated in 14 experimental sessions: seven sessions with ice water and seven with ischemic pain. In each session the subject was exposed twice to the painful stimulus, once under control and once under the experimental condition. Order of challenging agent and the two pain-induction procedures were randomized.

Six physiological variables were sampled to evaluate changes in response under the various conditions:

1) EEG: recorded from bilaterally symmetrical skull sites: frontal, parietal (F-P), and occipital leads (P-O);
2) EGK: precordial to right ear-lobe leads;
3) EMG: from frontalis muscles (electrodes centered over left and right eyebrow);
4) skin temperature: recorded from dorsal surfaces of right and left forearms;
5) peripheral vascular activity from a sensor encircling the middle finger of the right hand;
6) respiration: a pneumograph belt (Stoelting) encircling the chest and attached to a Statham pressure transducer.

Due to restriction of space and lack of definitive results from these measures, we will not present these results here.

The hypnosis induction was achieved by means of a standardized video tape-recording viewed by the subject on a television monitor.

The electrical stimulation through the acupuncture needles utilized a Grass Model S–4 Stimulator. A common electrode (EKG plate) was placed with a rubber strap on the subject's left inner wrist. The characteristics of the electrical stimulation were: frequency 130 Hz; current output 10 milliamperes maximum; pulse duration 0.1 millisecond. Duration of stimulation through needles was standardized at 50 minutes.

Acupuncture true loci and the random false loci were determined by the skin potential method described in detail elsewhere.[3] A reference electrode was placed on a skin-drilled, inactive area on the volar surface of the right forearm about 5 cm from the elbow crease along the inner edge of the forearm. A silver bar rounded to 1–2 millimeters at the tip was used as a probe to locate both true and false loci on the left arm. Both reference and active electrodes were connected to a Grass 7 Pl preamplifier in the polygraph recorder. The existing skin potential of the subject was balanced out and subsequently the probe was passed lightly over the skin surface. A deflection of the pen on the recorder indicated a change in skin potential toward lesser negativity, signaling the location of a true acupuncture site. In turn, no deflection indicated an electrically silent area that was utilized for false-locus stimulation (placebo site).

Half-inch, 34-gauge stainless-steel acupuncture needles were used.

In the acupuncture true-site stimulation sessions, four needles were inserted at specific loci in the left arm as recommended by Chinese medicine for analgesia of the hand and arm: Hoku (Large Intestine (LI 4)) in the web of the hand between the thumb and index finger; LI 11 on the outer forearm at the elbow; LI 14 on the lateral surface of the upper arm near the "V" of the deltoid muscle: LI 15 between the acromium and the greater tubercle of the humerus and the middle of the upper deltoid muscle.

In the selection of acupuncture false loci for stimulation, several criteria were used: the area had to be electrically silent, with respect to potential difference; the areas should avoid falling on any "meridian" or any recognized acupuncture point, according to available charts; the areas selected should avoid major blood vessels, bones, scar tissue, or skin sores. As nearly as possible, the same placements were used for all subjects, as follows: 1) the knuckle area between the index and third finger; 2) 3 cm on the forearm toward hand from LI 11; 3) 3.5 cm to the outside of the arm directly across from LI 14; 4) 6 cm down and 2.5 cm to outside of arm from LI 15.

The water-bath (hereafter referred to as bath) pain was produced by means of a six-gallon refrigerated bath maintained at 0° C. A plastic sheet placed across the surface of the water permitted the subject's left forearm to remain dry, yet be in contact with the cold water. Only the length of the fingers were immersed in the water. The intensity of cold experiences was thus considerably less than that found in the standard cold-pressor test.[2]

The pressure pain (hereafter referred to as cuff) was produced by means of a Baum Sphygmomanometer, attached to a blood-pressure cuff placed around the subject's left arm (biceps) with the cuff inflated to 300 mm Hg and held steady at that level by a clamp.

All recording equipment was in a room adjoining the shielded room where the subject sat. An intercom system permitted voice communication between the subject and the experimenters. Continuous visual monitoring of the subject was possible both via a large one-way window and by video monitor.

Subjective Pain Rating Scale

At each 15-second interval during the five-minute pain periods, for both bath and cuff pain, the subject was asked to signal, via a finger switch connected to a channel of the polygraph, his rating of the degree of pain experienced, using a five-point scale: 0 = no pain; 1 = mild pain; 2 = moderate; 3 = severe; 4 = pain stopped at subject's request when no longer tolerable. If the pain stimulus was stopped, a score of 4 was entered for each 15-second interval of the time remaining in the five-minute pain period.

Hypnosis Screening

Since the effects of suggestibility were of major interest in this investigation, we screened all volunteers prior to their first experimental session by means of

Form A of the Harvard Group Scale of Hypnotic Susceptibility (HGSHS). Groups of volunteers were tested by this scale until we accumulated a sample of 20 subjects.

To ensure that our study population was in good health, prior to participating in the experiment, each volunteer underwent a physical examination, including EKG, and blood/urine analyses. Next, he was scheduled for the HGSHS test.

Two subjects did not pass the physical examination: one "used" drugs and one was taking a number of prescribed medications; several subjects withdrew as candidates after the HGSHS test; several subjects participated in a number of sessions but failed to complete all sessions. None of the data from any of these subjects was used. The results reported from this investigation are based on 20 volunteers who completed all 14 experimental sessions and met the other criteria of the study design.

The 14 trials involving seven challenging agents (1 hypnosis, 2 acupuncture, and 4 drugs) presented under both pain conditions were assigned in random order to all subjects. For any subject, at least three days intervened in the scheduling of injections of morphine or diazepam or between acupuncture trials (both true- and false-site stimulations), to avoid possible carryover effects contaminating the results.

The subjects were advised on a preceding trial when a drug trial was scheduled and were asked to eat only a light meal prior to the drug trial. They were also asked not to smoke, drink alcohol, or use any drugs during the eight hours preceding any of the trials. Since most sessions were run in the morning, these abstentions occurred during the usual hours of sleep and caused no problem for most subjects.

The drug dosages used were: morphine intramuscularly (i.m.) in right arm, 10 mg per 70 kg of body weight. A standard dose of diazepam, 10 mg in 2-ml solution, was injected i.m. in the same arm of all subjects. The other two drugs were administered orally: 2 tablets (5 grains each) of aspirin: 2 small white capsules resembling Darvon® but containing milk sugar constituted the placebo. At the time subjects were recruited as volunteers into the project, they were informed of the identity of the drugs to be used in the investigation; however, subjects remained naïve with respect to the identity of the drugs at the time of administration, with the exception of aspirin because of its common use as a household medication.

PROCEDURE

When the subject arrived in the laboratory, the sensors required to record the physiological variables were applied.

On trials involving acupuncture, the subject was first subjected to an acupuncture site location procedure (true or false) using the technique developed by Brown et al.[3] In the search for true acupuncture sites, the areas of each of the four sites were probed sequentially until each site was located, and lines with a felt-tip pen were placed on either side of the site for future identification for needle insertion. When the trials involved acupuncture false-site placement, the same probing of true sites was carried out, but the probing continued in a nearby area at a specific distance from the true sites. When this new location yielded an electrically silent site, pen markings on the skin identified these false site areas.

When the probing was completed, the subject went to the adjoining experimental room where the necessary sensors were applied for the recording of physiological variables, after which the experiment began. The subject lay almost supine in a comfortable reclining chair, in a dimly lit room.

The format of the trials was similar for the three types of challenging agents: hypnosis, acupuncture, and drugs, but the time interval between onset of agent intervention and later testing for analgesic effects of each of the three types of agents differed somewhat.

Morphine i.m. reaches peak analgesic effectiveness in the body approximately one hour after injection. At the moderately strong dosage used, we could expect the peak effects of diazepam to last for at least one hour, and one hour would ensure that oral aspirin would have been absorbed into the system. Thus, the analgesic effects of all drugs were tested one hour after administration. Acupuncture analgesia was tested after 50 minutes of electrical stimulation. This duration was selected for two reasons: it approached the duration used with the drugs, and in the scant literature available, we could find no established required duration of stimulation to produce acupuncture analgesia. Hypnoanalgesia trials had the shortest duration before testing of effects, 35 minutes from the start of induction, but the duration of the total session was similar to that of the other agents: after the experimental pain test, there was a five-minute period of trance reinduction followed by a ten-minute period in which the depth of trance was rated on the objective portion of the Barber Suggestibility Scale (BSS)[4] by the experimenter; the hypnotic trance was then ended and the subjective part of the BSS test was rated by the subject. In an effort to reduce temporal order effects on hypnosis trials, half the subjects were randomly assigned to receive the bath control pain immediately following the initial ten-minute rest period; the other half received the bath control pain after hypnosis had ended and following the subjective ratings of the BSS test. This order was reversed for the two groups on the cuff-pain trials. Thus, each subject experienced both orderings of the control rest and control pain trials for hypnosis sessions (see TABLE 1). The session for all Ss ended with the subject completing a self-rating questionnaire regarding his hypnotic experience.

TABLE 1 illustrates the procedures followed with each of the three types of challenging agents.

In the acupuncture trials just before needle insertion in the left arm and hand, the experimenter explained the procedure to S as follows: one needle at a time would receive the stimulating current. The needle placements were identified to S as "shoulder" (LI 15), "biceps" (LI 14), "elbow" (LI 11), and "hand" (LI 4). The subject was asked to indicate the threshold levels of stimulation. E recorded the current intensity at this point. Following this, S was told that stimulus intensity would be slowly increased to the highest level he could comfortably tolerate. He was encouraged to experience a "good, strong" sensation at the site; not painful, but strong. When this level was reached, current intensity was again recorded. After all four needles were thus activated, S was told that if the sensation seemed to become weak at any site during the 50 minutes of stimulation, he was to inform E, and the stimulation would be increased until a strong level was again felt by S. S was told that adaptation to the stimulus was a common experience and that it was important to the investigation that he keep E informed when a site no longer felt strongly stimulated. All Ss were cooperative and attended to this task with little need of prompting.

The pattern of stimulation was similar for true- and false-site trials, in that

TABLE 1

SCHEMATIC REPRESENTATION OF THE EXPERIMENTAL PROGRAM

Hypnosis Sessions A — N=10, Total Time 85 min

Control		Experimental								
10 min control rest	5 min control pain	25 min hypnotic induction	5 min rest (prepain) hypnosis	5 min pain continues	5 min trance deepening	10 min depth of trance tests (Objective BSS) hypnosis ends	5 min (Subjective BSS)	10 min resting recording	5 min hypnosis self-rating questionnaire	end of session

Hypnosis Sessions B — N=10, Total Time 85 min

Control		Experimental					Control			
10 min baseline recording	25 min hypnotic induction	5 min rest (prepain) hypnosis	5 min pain continues	5 min trance deepening	10 min depth of trance tests (Objective BSS) hypnosis ends	5 min (Subjective BSS)	5 min control pain	10 min control rest	5 min hypnosis self-rating questionnaire	end of session

Acupuncture Sessions True and False sites — N=20, Total Time 85 min

Control		Experimental						
10 min rest	5 min pain	3 min needles inserted	45 min electro-stimulation of needles	5 min stim. cont'd. rest (prepain)	5 min stim. cont'd. pain	2 min stim. stopped needles withdrawn	10 min final rest	end of session

Drug Sessions — N=20, Total Time 90 min.

Control		Experimental					
10 min rest	5 min pain	drug given	55 min drug absorption	5 min rest (prepain)	5 min pain	10 min final rest	end of session

stimulation began with the hand locus and progressed up the arm, ending with the shoulder locus (LI 15). There were five false-site trials and six true-site trials that were stimulated in the reverse order (shoulder to hand), and no differences in maximum current values were observed. The range of the maximum stimulating current tolerated by all subjects at the four true and four false needle loci was 0.8 ma–7.8 ma).

FIGURE 1 shows the threshold, maximum, and mean current values used during acupuncture trials for both true and false sites. Since no significant differences in current values were found when bath and cuff trials were compared, the mean of the two trials was used and is depicted for each needle locus in FIGURE 1.

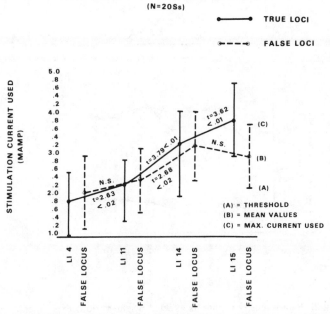

FIGURE 1. Threshold, average, and maximum current intensities used in the stimulation of acupuncture point. Values are the x̄ of bath and cuff trials combined, since no significant differences were found between them.

For true acupuncture loci, the mean stimulating current used was significantly higher (P < .02–<.01) at each ascending site from hand to shoulder (LI 4 to LI 15). The data suggest a decreasing sensitivity to stimulation as one moves from distal to proximal sites, when true sites are electrically stimulated. The shoulder site (LI 15) tolerated more than twice the amount of current used at the hand site.

The results were somewhat different for false-site stimulation: when the level of current required was compared between successive loci, only one significant difference (P < .02) was found, the elevated mean current at the upper arm equivalent to locus LI 14 compared to the forearm area, equivalent to

LI 11. A comparison of the mean current used for true and false loci at each of the sites yielded only one significant difference (<.02): true acupuncture loci tolerated higher stimulating currents compared to false loci at the shoulder site, LI 15. There was no significant difference between true and false loci at the other three sites, in the amount of current used.

RESULTS

Subjective Pain Ratings: Total Group

FIGURE 2 shows the mean pain ratings for five minutes of pain under both control and experimental conditions for each of the seven challenging agents.

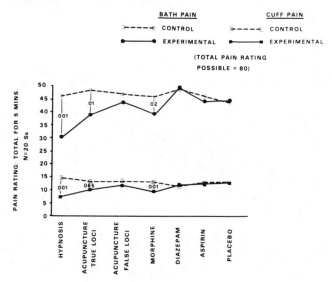

FIGURE 2. Pain-intensity ratings as affected by the various experimental treatments.

The upper two curves of the graph represent the scores for Bath trials; the lower two curves are the scores for Cuff trials. The higher mean scores on the Bath trials reveal it to be a more painful experience than the occlusion Cuff.

The *t* tests of the difference between control and experimental pain scores yielded the following significant results (FIGURE 2): hypnosis provided the most effective analgesia on both types of pain (bath: $\bar{x}$ difference = 16.00, t = 3.91, p < .001; cuff: $\bar{x}$ difference = 6.43, t = 4.56, p < .001). Morphine produced significant analgesic effects on both types of pain (bath: $\bar{x}$ difference = 7.05, t = 2.63, p < .02; cuff: $\bar{x}$ difference = 3.38, t = 4.28, p < .001). Acupuncture stimulation at true loci was an effective pain reliever for bath pain ($\bar{x}$ difference = 9.00, t = 3.59, p < .01) but failed to reach the .05 level of significance on cuff pain trials ($\bar{x}$ difference = 2.72, t = 2.01, p < .065). None of the other four pain challengers (acupuncture false loci, Diazepam, aspirin,

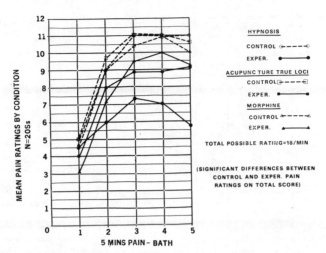

FIGURE 3. Minute-by-minute pain ratings for the hypnosis, acupuncture true points, and morphine experiences with cold-pressor pain.

or placebo) showed effectiveness as pain relievers, as shown by the pain scores in FIGURE 2.

The subject's perception of pain, reflected in his mean ratings, minute by minute, over the five-minute pain period, is illustrated in FIGURES 3–5. FIGURES 3 (bath) and 4 (cuff), reveal the ratings for the three conditions that were found to provide significant pain relief when control pain was contrasted with

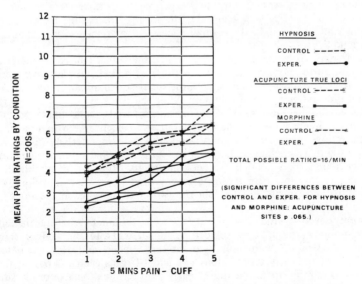

FIGURE 4. Minute-by-minute pain ratings for the hypnosis, acupuncture true points, and morphine experiences with ischemic pain.

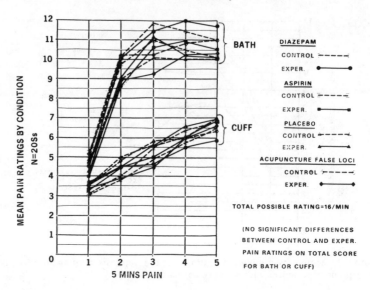

FIGURE 5. Minute-by-minute pain ratings for the diazepam, aspirin, placebo, and acupuncture false-point stimulation experiences with cold-pressor and ischemic pain.

experimental pain (this latter involving the effect of the challenging agent). FIGURE 5 illustrates the data for the four conditions that failed to provide significant pain reduction, when control and experimental periods were compared.

On cuff trials (FIGURES 4 and 5), the mean pain ratings for both control and experimental periods show small successive increments over time for all seven conditions.

Bath trials (FIGURES 3 and 5) do not display this consistent pattern: all conditions, during both control and experimental periods, display increased pain ratings for the first three minutes, with the steepest rise in pain ratings occurring between the first and second minutes. After the third minute, the pain ratings vary by condition (FIGURE 3). On experimental trials (solid lines) beyond the first minute, hypnosis shows the lowest ratings at each of the minute intervals and the ratings decline at the fourth and fifth pain minutes; morphine ratings remain essentially unchanged between the third and final minutes; acupuncture true-loci ratings show a small rise between the fourth and fifth minute of pain. Acupuncture true-loci pain ratings are somewhat lower than morphine ratings at the third and fourth minutes, but the two conditions reach the same rating level by the fifth minute.

Twenty-seven of the 280 pain trials were terminated before the end of the five-minute period. Five subjects terminated before the end of the five-minute period on 27 pain trials; two subjects (nos. 9 and 10) accounted for 23 (85%) of the early terminations (11 and 12 trials each). Four of the five subjects, accounting for 26 of the 27 early pain terminations, were classified as "Good Hypnotic Subjects," based on their high scores on the HGSHS test.

Subjective Pain Ratings: Good Hypnotic vs. Poor Hypnotic Subjects

Subjects were dichotomized into Good and Poor hypnotic groups. We segregated groups on the basis of subject scores falling into the upper and lower segment of the scores on the Harvard Group Scale of Hypnotic Susceptibility. Highly susceptible subjects (Good) scored between 8 and 11 on the HGSHS, while subjects of low susceptibility (Poor) scored either 2 or 3 on HGSHS; six subjects fell into each group. We compared the pain ratings for subjects in these two extreme groups.

FIGURE 6 displays the results of the total pain ratings for subjects of high (Good) and low (Poor) hypnotic susceptibility on control pain trials and on experimental pain trials during cold-pressor (bath) and ischemic (cuff) pain sessions for all seven pain-challenging agents. Student *t*-test analyses for correlated means were computed between control and experimental pain trials for Good subjects and for Poor subjects.

On both bath- and cuff-pain trials, Good subjects were afforded significant pain reduction by hypnosis and morphine, compared with control pain sessions. On bath trials only, Good subjects also reported less pain after diazepam, compared with control pain sessions. Acupuncture true-site stimulation did not quite achieve a significant difference between control and experimental pain sessions for Good Ss on bath pain trials ($t = 2.33$), although pain scores were lower on experimental trials. On cuff trials, however, Good Ss did achieve significantly lower pain scores after acupuncture true-site stimulation as well as with hypnosis and morphine, when compared to control pain sessions.

Poor hypnotic subjects reported significantly less pain with only one agent—morphine—compared to control pain on cuff pain trials only; bath-pain trials

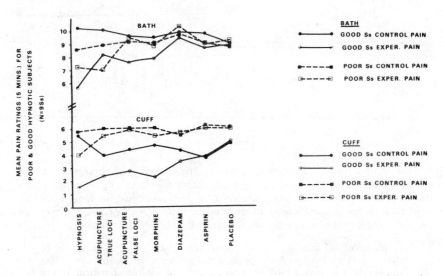

FIGURE 6. Pain-intensity ratings under the various experimental conditions for groups of subjects identified as "good" and "poor" hypnotic subjects.

yielded no significant differences between control and experimental pain sessions for Poor Ss with any of the seven agents.

Difference scores between control minus experimental pain ratings were calculated for Good and for Poor hypnotic Ss on bath- and cuff-pain trials over all seven pain-challenging agents. Analyses of these difference scores using *t* tests were computed between Good and Poor Ss (see FIGURE 7).

On bath-pain trials only, hypnosis and Diazepam provided significantly more protection from pain for Good Ss than for Poor Ss when compared with control pain sessions. On hypnotic trials, both Good and Poor Ss reported less pain with hypnosis than on control pain sessions, but scores of Good Ss were significantly lower than those of Poor Ss.

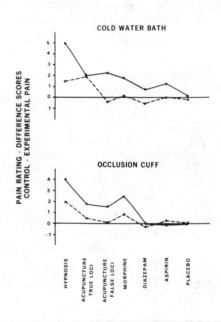

FIGURE 7. Comparison of pain-rating difference scores (control pain-experimental pain) for "good" and "poor" hypnotic subjects.

DISCUSSION

The verbal report of subjects regarding the intensity of their experienced pain provided our most consistent and significant effects throughout the experiments. The physiological measures were far less rewarding in their contributions to a better understanding of our independent variables and their effects on pain. Hilgard and Hilgard [2] speak knowledgeably on this issue:

> The physiological measures, which seem more objective and less subject to individual whim than verbal reports, turn out to be less satisfactory than what the subject says about his pain . . . the physiological indicators are affected indiscriminately by so many influences other than pain. . . . As a consequence, no single physiological measure provides an infallible indicator of felt pain.

Our study confirms these statements. We further confirm their observation that the reports of pain for a given subject are relatively consistent from one repetition of the pain experience to another. This is true for both the cold-pressor and ischemic pain. The correlation for control pain experiences across days ranged from 0.55 to 0.79. We further confirmed their observations of "reasonable" reliability of pain ratings. Coefficients of correlation for pain ratings across days for the control pain experience ranged from .55 to .79. Within-day correlations were somewhat larger. For example, for the placebo condition, the correlations were .86 for cold pressor and .73 for ischemic pain. For aspirin the respective correlations were .72 and .96, the latter being the highest correlation obtained. By far the lowest correlations were obtained between the rest and hypnosis conditions (−.01 and .15).

Hypnosis

With both types of pain, the greatest protection from pain was afforded by hypnotic suggestion of analgesia (FIGURE 2). The effectiveness of hypno-analgesic suggestions in pain reduction with susceptible Ss is well established.[2] We dichotomized our group of volunteers to obtain populations of Good and Poor hypnotic Ss. The most suggestible and least suggestible Ss (ranking in the upper and lower third with respect to scores on the HGSHS suggestibility scale) were selected for this analysis. (We found it necessary to select the extreme scores (8–11 = Good, and 2–3 = Poor) for analysis, because our data did not produce clear-cut results when Ss were included whose HGSHS scores fell in the middle of the scale. Apparently, this has been the experience of others who use such scales, since populations are described as "highly susceptible" and "least susceptible" in a number of studies. Consonant with the reports from these and other studies, we found that the group of Good hypnotic Ss (as opposed to Poor hypnotic Ss) accounted for much of the significant lowering of pain ratings with hypnoanalgesia with both types of pain conditions (see FIGURE 7).

Acupuncture

Before we discuss our data on acupuncture analgesia, perhaps a few remarks are in order regarding acupuncture points *per se*. Currently, there is still debate as to the existence of acupuncture loci, to say nothing of the skepticism regarding the utility of acupuncture stimulation as a therapeutic tool. In addition to our earlier work, we have confirmed in this present study on a different group of volunteers that there are sites on the skin of decreased potential difference when compared with adjacent skin sites that conform reasonably well to the location of traditional acupuncture points, and, just as important, there are extensive skin areas that produce no such potential differences. A recent study employing careful exploratory techniques and controls by Reichmanis and colleagues[5] lends support to our work. They found that, with respect to surrounding tissue, the electrical resistance of acupuncture points is significantly lower. At the 1974 Federated Proceedings, Wheeler *et al.*[6] reported replication of Chinese charts mapping acupuncture points on animals by the skin-resistance method. Roppel and Mitchell,[7] using resistance measurements on humans and rats, contended that acupuncture points require some form of stimulation for detection, and that if sufficient stimulation was applied, active points could be discriminated from the neutral surrounding tissue. It is our contention that such stimulation is not necessary for the location of acupuncture points.

Let us now turn to our data relating to the Ss' verbal report of pain before and during acupuncture stimulation. Acupuncture stimulation of true sites significantly (P < .01) reduced the pain induced by cold-pressor stimulation when compared to control trials with no acupuncture (see FIGURE 2). Ischemic pain trials demonstrated marginal (P = .06) pain reduction resulting from acupuncture true-site stimulation (FIGURE 2). Ko and colleagues,[8] using the Smith method to evoke ischemic pain, measured changes in pain threshold before and after 40 minutes of acupuncture electrostimulation and reported a 72% increase in pain threshold in 80% of their Ss (12 of 15 male volunteers). Smith et al.[9] also studied the effectiveness of acupuncture (both true site and placebo site) stimulation on ischemic pain, using the technique developed by Smith. They reported a trend toward increased pain tolerance during true-site stimulation as compared to placebo-site stimulation, but the differences were not statistically significant. In discussing their results, they commented on the possible adverse effect in their procedure of beginning acupuncture stimulation after the termination of exercise in the occluded arm, when pain was already present and increasing for most subjects. In addition, acupuncture stimulation to produce analgesia had only a 20–30-minute duration, since trials were terminated at this time when "unbearable" pain was reported by Ss. They suggested the need for further study with earlier initiation of acupuncture stimulation (before the onset of pain) and longer duration of stimulation to achieve maximum analgesic effects. Another recent study by Anderson et al.[10] also compared acupuncture stimulation of true site, false site (Placebo II), and no acupuncture (Placebo I) on pain ratings, with pain invoked by the cold-pressor test. They stimulated for 15 minutes, removed the needles, and several minutes later began the cold-pressor test. The bath trial lasted 60 seconds (less if subject withdrew hand), with pain ratings obtained every ten seconds. Both stimulated (right) and control hand (left) were so tested, with three minutes' intertrial interval. They report a significant (P < .01) reduction in pain ratings with acupuncture true-site stimulation, compared to both placebo groups. The untreated left hand did not yield pain ratings different from the placebo group.

When our data for acupuncture true-site stimulation during cold-pressor pain was analyzed for the dichotomized Good and Poor hypnotic groups, to determine the effect of suggestibility on pain ratings, no significant differences in the pain ratings were found between the two groups. This lack of a difference between Good and Poor Ss was maintained even when the population was restricted to highest and lowest susceptible subjects on the HGSHS scale.

An analysis of pain ratings between Good and Poor hypnotic subjects during both cold pressor and ischemic pain yielded no significant differences between the groups for either the total group dichotomy or the smaller groups of highest and lowest susceptibility to hypnosis on HGSHS scores (FIGURE 7). Thus, hypnotic susceptibility does not appear to be a major determiner of acupuncture effects.

We have found no controlled experimental study in the literature to date that compared the effectiveness of acupuncture analgesia with that of hypnosis on pain. Yang and Clark [11] utilizing the Hardy et al.[12] radiant heat method of pain induction compared pain ratings based on the arm having acupuncture stimulation with the untreated control arm in 12 volunteers who were classified as to hypnotizability by means of the Spiegel Eye Roll Levitation Method. Their data were analyzed with the use of Signal Detection theory. As in our findings, they concluded that there was no evidence that hypnotizability was related to the raised thermal pain threshold following acupuncture stimulation. In another paper, Clark and Yang [13] stated that acupuncture decreased the proportion of withdrawals and reports of pain, suggesting production of analgesia. However, sensory decision theory analysis of the data indicated that the decrease was due to the S's raised criterion for reporting pain in the acupuncture arm. Criticisms and rebuttals of this study appeared in a later issue of *Science*.

In a recent paper, Chaves and Barber [1] proposed six factors that they suggest may be associated with the effectiveness of hypnotic and other procedures in achieving analgesia during surgery. The six operative factors they propose are: patient selection; preoperative education of patient; adjunctive use of drugs; suggestions of analgesia; distracting stimuli; and patient-physician relationship (rapport). All but the last factor is implicated in the reported success of acupuncture analgesia in surgical pain reduction. Those who are familiar with the literature of the last few years relating to hypnosis research are well aware of the ongoing debate among certain investigators, of whom Barber and Hilgard are representative of opposing points of view, as to whether or not there exists an hypnotic state which differs importantly from the normal waking state. Our study does not address itself to the merits of such issues, but the suppositions of Chaves and Barber,[1] in their recent article comparing hypnoanalgesia and acupuncture analgesia, are relevant and invite comment, albeit their focus relates to surgical pain.

1. *Selection of Subjects.* The severe pain induced by the cold-pressor test was significantly reduced for those subjects who were most susceptible to hypnosis compared to those who were least susceptible, during hypnosis trials.

On the other hand, hypnotic susceptibility does not account for the pain reduction of the cold-pressor test when acupuncture analgesia was employed (compared FIGURE 2 with FIGURE 7). Thus, if subject selection contributes to the success of acupuncture analgesia, our data suggest that such selection does not depend on hypnotic susceptibility.

2. *"Education"of Subject.* Our subjects were informed of the procedures to be used, and that the purpose of the study was to compare the effects of a variety of agents on two types of pain. This information was contained in a written document as part of the Consent Form required by the Human Rights Committee. All of the Ss received the same objective information, which contained no suggestion of a commitment on our part regarding the efficacy of any agent in affecting pain. Our Ss, the majority of whom were college students, gave no evidence of opinions for or against a belief in the effectiveness of any of the procedures at the start of the trials, but did volunteer an intellectual curiosity, particularly regarding hypnosis and acupuncture, which would be new experiences for most of them. We feel it safe to judge that monetary return was the primary motivation for their participation in the study. The hypnosis trials did present a four-minute filmed introduction that discussed some popular misconceptions and fallacies about hypnosis and attempted to remove any anxiety the Ss might have regarding such ideas. We are indebted to Dr. T. X. Barber, who wrote the script we used for this purpose. During acupuncture stimulation, our Ss were instructed only with regard to the mechanical procedures to be used and what was expected of them regarding maintenance of

electrical stimulus levels based on their reported sensations to the operator of the equipment (MLB). The same procedure was used for both true- and false-site acupuncture trials.

3. *Absence of Adjunctive Drugs.* No adjunctive drugs were used with any of the seven experimental agents.

4. *Suggestion.* Suggestion of analgesia was a vital part of the hypnosis trials, and such suggestions were given toward the end of the hypnotic induction phase for five minutes prior to the experimental pain onset, as well as continuously during the five minutes of pain. Hilgard [2] has cited studies indicating that analgesia suggestions included in hypnotic induction are more effective in increasing pain tolerance, as compared to hypnosis without such suggestions or compared to such suggestions excluding hypnotic induction. However, such suggestions were principally effective in our study of good hypnotic Ss. No suggestions of analgesia were made to our Ss on acupuncture trials, nor were they interrogated regarding the presence or absence of feelings of analgesia in the experimental arm.

5. *Distraction.* During the experimental pain trials with hypnosis, the continuous suggestions of analgesia used in the procedure may have had a distracting influence on our Ss, but, if so, were effective in reducing pain largely for the Good hypnotic Ss. Additionally, our Ss were mentally engaged in providing estimates of pain levels at 15-second intervals, using a four-digit scale throughout the pain trials; this activity, likewise, could afford distraction from the pain, but, again, the evidence indicates that it was effective in reducing pain for Good hypnotic Ss primarily, and then only on experimental pain trials and not on control pain trials. For acupuncture trials (as well as with other agents) the possible distracting influence of making pain-rating judgments at 15-second intervals during the five minutes of pain is acknowledged, but, again, such distraction was apparently not effective during control pain trials.

On the basis of our data, a parsimonious explanation dictates that where significant pain reduction occurred, it was due to the effect of the intervention of the agent (in some manner as yet unknown), rather than to extraneous and/or concomitant factors as suggested by Chaves and Barber [1]).

Our data on acupuncture false- (placebo) site stimulation yielded results quite different from those with true-site stimulation. No significant pain relief derived from stimulation of acupuncture false sites when compared to control trials for either cold pressor or ischemic pain (FIGURE 2). The verbal reports from some of our Ss regarding their sensations associated with electrical stimulation revealed differences during false-site as compared to true-site trials. Spontaneous complaints regarding the pain felt at needle insertion into the tissue occurred occasionally with false-site placement but *never* with true-site placement; the sensation caused by electrical stimulation of the placebo-site needles was often described as unpleasant, irritating, or painful, or a feeling different from that experienced with true-site stimulation. Subjects frequently remarked that the sensation with stimulation of true sites was pleasant, even enjoyable, like a gentle massage. It should be remembered that the Ss were naïve with respect to true- and false-site placements, and this fact was confirmed by frequent comments such as "It feels different from last time—it's really nice," or "I don't like it as much as I did the other day—it throbs instead of a nice feeling," or "I hope you put them in the right place—they don't feel the same as last time—they hurt."

When the sample of 20 Ss was divided into Good and Poor hypnotic Ss and compared on acupuncture false-site trials, Good hypnotic Ss had significantly greater reduction in pain during false-site stimulation than did Poor hypnotic Ss, when experimental vs. control pain was compared (P < .04) for cold pressor trials. Ischemic pain produced no significant differences between Good and Poor hypnotic groups.

In two investigations cited previously, acupuncture true-site and false-site stimulation were compared. One study employed cold pressor pain and reported that true-site stimulation produced significantly lower pain ratings compared to the placebo sites and also compared to a second placebo trial of no acupuncture. The other study utilized ischemic pain and reported longer tolerance time after true-site stimulation compared to false sites, but the difference was not statistically reliable. The problems in methodology in this study were discussed above in relation to acupuncture true-site data. It is interesting, however, that this latter study was conducted by Smith,[9] using his method for producing ischemia, which is definitely superior to the procedure we used, and yet his results, like ours, failed to yield significant differences for true or false acupuncture site stimulation. There were, as noted earlier, problems with his procedure. One cannot, however, discount the possibility that acupuncture is effective with cold pressor pain and not with ischemic pain. Further study is necessary before this issue is resolved.

Morphine

Morphine (10 mg i.m./70 kg B.W.) was the second most effective analgesic for the relief of pain with both cold pressor and ischemic stimulation (see FIGURE 2).

When we compared the results of the Good and Poor hypnotic Ss on morphine trials, the data, although not statistically significant, suggest that for both cold pressor and ischemic pain, the greatest reduction in pain ratings were found in those Ss who were classified as Good hypnotics. This finding, of course, does not mean that morphine has no organic basis for pain reduction; it does indicate that Ss who were susceptible to hypnosis also obtained the greatest relief from two very different types of experimental pain when a therapeutic dose of morphine was administered. This result may have some bearing on the evidence from Beecher[14] that morphine administered for postsurgical pain brought relief to one third of the patients beyond that obtained with a placebo; one third gained the same relief from placebo as from morphine; the final third received little relief from morphine or placebo.

Other Drugs

None of the other three chemical agents—aspirin, diazepam and placebo—produced any significant reduction in pain when control and experimental trials were compared for cold pressor or ischemic pain (FIGURE 2). When Good and Poor hypnotic Ss (for the total population) were compared, no significant difference in pain scores between control and experimental trials were found for the two groups with any of the three chemical agents. When high-low hypnotic quartiles of susceptibility were compared (FIGURE 7), the most susceptible Ss accounted for significantly lower cold-pressor pain ratings with diazepam. What is of interest is that those Ss with lowest hypnotic susceptibility experienced more pain on experimental trials, after diazepam. This latter finding indicates that for nonsuggestible Ss, the pain was not relieved, but was exacerbated by diazepam. On ischemic trials, half of the highest susceptible Ss also gave lower pain ratings during control, compared to experimental pain after diazepam. For aspirin and placebo trials, no significant differences were found between the total group of Good and Poor Ss' pain ratings on cold pressor or ischemia pain trials or on the high-low quartile analysis (FIGURE 7). Some highly susceptible Ss as well as those of low susceptibility gave lower pain scores on control pain compared to experimental pain trials with both aspirin and placebo. In fact, on ischemic trials, more Ss in the high hypnotic group gave lower control than experimental pain scores to placebo than did those Ss of low susceptibility (see negative scores on TABLE 2). These facts certainly invite the conclusion that suggestion played a negligible role in the effects of these three agents.

Lasagna et al.,[15] using the exercise-tourniquet method of ischemia, reported that 600 mg p.o. of aspirin did not delay the appearance of pain, but increased significantly the amount of work done by Ss. Smith stated that in an unpublished study with Beecher in 1958, they found pain reduced by 600 mg of aspirin p.o., using the ischemia pain method. A study by Hardy et al.[12] reported no significant pain reduction to cold pressor pain by 1 gm of aspirin, p.o., but noted that a considerably lower pain threshold was found for the aspirin group as compared to placebo group, even though the difference failed to achieve significance. Benjamin [16] employed, among other painful techniques, both cold pressor and an exercise-tourniquet method of ischemia in pain trials with aspirin. He found that because of great variability in method, only the ischemic pain method showed aspirin to be superior to placebo in amount of work done and duration of performed work. Schelling [17] reported negative results with the ischemic pain method, finding that subjects showed no pain reduction with 10 mg morphine i.m. or 600 mg of aspirin, p.o., compared to placebo.

What general conclusions can we come to on the basis of these investigations? We conclude that hypnosis and suggestions of analgesia, morphine, and acupuncture stimulation (of LI 4, 14, and 15 on the arm exposed to painful stimulation) are effective in reducing experimentally induced pain. This is true for both a cold pressor pain-induction procedure and an ischemic pain-induction procedure. Hypnotic suggestibility does not account for the effectiveness of acupuncture stimulation, though good hypnotic Ss show better protection against pain with hypnotic suggestion and morphine.

Good hypnotic Ss experience more pain than is true for Poor hypnotic Ss when exposed to the same pain-induction procedure. The effect is more marked for the cold-pressor than the ischemic pain procedure. Good hypnotic Ss are more responsive—i.e., show greater reduction in pain perception—to drugs and intervention procedures that produce significant subjective sensations (morphine and diazepam) than is true of Poor hypnotic Ss. This is not true for aspirin and placebo. Last, but not least, Ss low in hypnotic susceptibility tend to perceive painful stimuli as more painful when under the influence of diazepam as compared to the nondrug condition.

REFERENCES

1. CHAVES, J. F. & T. X. BARBER. 1976. Hypnotic procedures and surgery: A critical analysis with applications to "acupuncture analgesia." Amer. J. Clin. Hypn. **18:** 217–236.
2. HILGARD, E. R. & J. R. HILGARD. 1975. Hypnosis in the Relief of Pain. Wm. Kaufmann, Inc. Los Altos, Calif.
3. BROWN, J. L., G. A. ULETT & J. A. STERN. 1975. Acupuncture loci: Techniques for location. Amer. J. Chinese Med. **2:** 67–74.
4. BARBER, T. X. 1965. Measuring "hypnotic-like" suggestibility with and without "hypnotic" induction: Psychometric properties, norms and variables influencing response to the Barber Susceptibility Scale (BSS). Psychol. Rep. **16:** 809–844.
5. REICHMANIS, M., A. MARINO & O. BECKER. 1975. Electrical correlates of acupuncture points. IEEE Trans. Biomed. Eng. Nov.. : 533–535.
6. WHEELER, A. J., D. C. BEITZ, C. S. SWIFT & A. D. McGILBARD. 1974. Animal acupuncture: Mapping and electro-analgesia. Presented at Fed. Proc. Personal communication.
7. ROPPEL, R. M. & F. MITCHELL, JR. 1975. Skin points of anomalously low electrical resistance: Current-voltage characteristics and relationships to peripheral stimulation therapies. J. Amer. Osteopath. Assoc. **74:** 877–878.
8. KO, W. H., K. Y. LIN & I. S. CHOI. 1974. Effects of acupuncture of pain threshold. Presented at ACEMB Meetings, Philadelphia, Pa. Oct. 6–10. Personal communication.
9. SMITH, G. M., H. T. CHAING, R. J. KITZ & A. ANTOON, Eds. 1974. Acupuncture and experimentally induced ischemia pain. Adv. Neurol. **4:** 827–834.
10. ANDERSON, D. S., J. L. JAMIESON & S. C. MAN. 1974. Analgesic effects of acupuncture on the pain of ice-water: a double-blind study. Rev. Canad. Psychol. **28:** 239–244.
11. YANG, J. C. & W. C. CLARK. 1974. Relationship of acupuncture analgesia and hypnotizability: An evaluation by Sensory Decision Theory on Thermal Pain. Presented at ASA Mtg. Oct. 15. Personal communication.
12. HARDY, J. D., H. G. WOLFF & H. GODELL. 1940. Studies on pain, a new method for measuring pain threshold: Observations on spatial summation of pain. J. Clin. Invest. **19:** 649–1940.
13. CLARK, W. C. & J. C. YANG. 1975. Acupuncture analgesia evaluation by the signal detection theory. Science **184:** 1096–1097.
14. BEECHER, H. K. 1968. The measurement of pain in man. *In* Pain. A Soulairae, J. Cahn and J. Charpentier, Eds. : 207. Academic Press. New York, N.Y.
15. LASAGNA, L., L. TETREAULT & N. E. FALLIS. 1962. Analgesic drugs and experimental ischemia pain. Fed. Proc. **21:** 326.
16. BENJAMIN, F. B. 1958. Effect of aspirin on supra-threshold pain in man. Science **128:** 303–304.
17. SCHELLING, J. J. 1968. Evaluation of the analgesic effect and the antialgic effect in man. *In* Int. Symp. Pain. Univ. of Paris. 1967. A. Soulairae, J. Cahn, and J. Charpentier, Eds. Academic Press, N.Y.

INCONGRUITY IN TRANCE BEHAVIOR:
A DEFINING PROPERTY OF HYPNOSIS? *

Peter W. Sheehan

Psychology Department
University of Queensland
St. Lucia, Queensland 4067
Australia

Contemporary research in hypnosis has come to focus importantly on the inner subjective processes of the hypnotized subject. Investigators analyze in detail, for example, the various functions of imaginative processes,[1, 13, 14, 23] and the processes of dissociation [10, 11, 33] and delusion.[19, 31] In researchers' attempts to account for both individual differences in susceptibility and the meaning of subjects' testimonies regarding their altered experience, the thrust of their studies has been clearly cognitive in direction. For some (e.g., Ref. 30), this movement in research has meant that contrasting viewpoints are no longer argued as distinct; state and nonstate theories have been seen, for example, to converge upon the relevance of substantially the same kinds of cognitive processing in accounting for hypnotic and nonhypnotic behavior. For others, however (e.g., Ref. 28), the convergence is viewed as more apparent than real, and the performance of hypnotic and nonhypnotic subjects can be seen to be influenced by the operation of possibly related but distinct processes of cognition. One such process of cognition that has long been argued as peculiar to hypnosis is the hypnotized subject's tolerance of paradoxical, or incongruous response.

Binet [3] captures the essential nature of the phenomenon in the following example, which he cites: "Let us put a key, a piece of coin, a needle, a watch into the anaesthetic hand, and let us ask the subject to think of any object whatsoever; it will happen . . . that the subject is thinking of the precise object that has been put into his insensible hand." (p. 28) Other instances of incongruity can readily be cited. In age regression, for example, Orne [19] recognized the apparent stupidity of the hypnotized subjects who fail to see the obvious inconsistencies in their adult attempts to convincingly take the role of a child. Most recently, we have observed quite striking paradoxes in subjects' analgesic reports. For some subjects, reports of little pain and suffering may be followed immediately by a "hidden observer" report of pain and (depending on how the reports are collected) suffering that is similar to the kind of reports associated with nonhypnotic analgesia conditions.[12] The incongruity gathered from these and other sources of evidence emphasizes the fact that features of reality are effectively registered by the hypnotized subject without being actually consciously perceived. The phenomenon of trance logic perhaps exemplifies the process most clearly. Certainly, history has focused on this particular phenomenon as representative.

In trance logic, hypnotic subjects appear distinctively able to combine

* The research on which this paper is based was funded in part by the Australian Research Grants Committee.

perceptions derived from reality with logically contradictory ones that stem from the hypnotist's suggestions or instructions, the subject implementing them through the processes of his own imagination. The major measures that illustrate the phenomenon are positive reaction to test of double hallucination, and spontaneous report of transparency of perception of an hallucinated stimulus.

In all but one of the major studies of trance logic completed to date— Johnson et al.,[15] McDonald and Smith,[16] Orne,[17] Peters,[22] and Sheehan et al.[27]—the appropriate double-hallucination response has been cued or suggested by the procedures investigators have used; yet contemporary theorizing about the process is heavily reliant on the assumption that paradoxical response in hypnosis is not dependent for its occurrence either on cues supplied by the hypnotist or existing in the stimulus setting. Close analysis of studies shows that procedures have almost uniformly conveyed the desired response to subjects in relatively clear and structured fashion. When double hallucination was tested, subjects typically hallucinated a person in the room at the hypnotist's request and were routinely asked to turn around and confront the same person seated behind them. Johnson et al. asked, "Tell me, who is that behind you?" Peters pointed to the person behind and asked subjects directly who it was; and McDonald and Smith asked their subjects, "Can you see him in the chair?" In every one of these instances (see also Ref. 17), the hypnotist highlighted his expectation that the person behind should be acknowledged, and so enhanced the probability of a trance logic response being observed. As Orne and Hammer [20] stated, the theoretical meaning of the phenomenon is really preserved only if it is tested "without being especially cued." (p. 138)

This paper attempts to explore some of the theoretical implications of subjects' tolerance for logical incongruity by looking closely at several of the major factors that affect trance logic response. The program of work to be discussed attempts to establish the conditions for *optimal* test of the phenomenon (i.e., by establishing minimal cuing) and to explore the claim that tolerance of incongruity is a defining property of hypnosis. The first phase of the program explores the impact of cue structure on susceptible subjects' incongruous response. The second phase tests the relevance of ability for trance to the occurrence of the phenomenon both inside and outside the hypnotic setting.

STUDY 1

The Impact of Cue Structure on Incongruity Response

In the first of the two studies,[27] trance logic was investigated in two contexts. One was similar to that provided in other experiments (high-cue condition) where the hypnotist structured subjects to report the object behind them after they had hallucinated the same stimulus previously. In a second context (low-cue condition), subjects were tested for trance logic in a situation that minimally cued them that the hypnotist expected them to see the stimulus object that they had hallucinated before. Cue structure was varied only for test of double hallucination. No procedures were instituted to elicit transparency report in any way. The real simulating model was applied in both contexts, and two specific predictions were made. It was hypothesized that double hallucination will occur among both real and simulating subjects in the high-cue condition but that the two groups would be distinct in the low-cue condition. The assumption was that if double hallucination is a truly defining property of hypnosis, then real hypnotic subjects alone will show tolerance of incongruity when the expectation of paradoxical behavior is not specifically conveyed or encouraged by the hypnotist. Following past evidence, it was further predicted that transparency report would be distinctively evident among real hypnotic subjects.

Method

Subjects. Fifty-eight real, susceptible subjects (42 females and 16 males) and 49 simulating, insusceptible subjects (27 females and 22 males) were selected as the most extreme scorers from a sample population of 928 subjects who were tested on the Harvard Group Scale of Hypnotic Susceptibility, Form A (HGSHS:A; see Ref. 29). In the 2×2 factorial design (Subject Grouping $\times$ Cue Structure), real and simulating subjects were allocated to a low- or high-cue structure condition, allocation being random except that numbers of subjects hallucinating the particular stimulus on which trance logic was tested were equally distributed across the two contexts of testing. Twenty-five simulators and 35 reals were tested in the high-cue condition, and 24 simulators and 23 reals were tested in the low-cue condition.

Procedure. Subjects were met initially by an experimenter (E_1) who instructed them prior to hypnotic testing. The hypnotic testing was conducted by a second experimenter (E_2), who was blind to the identity of subjects, real or simulating. Simulators were especially motivated for their task of deception by receiving the standard set of instructions laid down for them by the real-simulating model.[18]

Each subject was administered nine items on a modified version of the Stanford Hypnotic Susceptibility Scale, Form C (SHSS:C, see Ref. 32). Trance logic was tested at the end of the scale prior to awakening and involved the hallucination of an Easter tree, which was especially constructed for the experiment. The object in question was minutely structured: seven colored eggs hung by gold thread from colored branches on the tree, and the tree itself measured 40 cm in height and stood in a copper vase 27 cm high. Subjects were asked to hallucinate the tree and describe their hallucination in detail. After hallucinating, those in the high-cue condition were asked to "turn around and tell me [the hypnotist] what is that on the stool there behind you?" (The real tree had been placed behind the subject during an earlier item on the hypnotic scale.) Subjects in the low-cue condition were asked simply to "look around the room. Describe whatever you see, anything at all, whatever you see."

Following SHSS:C testing, subjects were taken to the experimenter who instructed them initially, and she conducted a detailed inquiry into their perceptions of the study and their responses to the test of trance logic, in particular. The procedures for the inquiry are reported in detail elsewhere.[27]

Results

Of 59 reals, 19 hypnotic subjects indicated they saw the Easter tree on one of the trials the item was tested. The results for these 19 subjects con-

TABLE 1

FREQUENCY OF DOUBLE HALLUCINATION RESPONSE AMONG REAL AND
SIMULATING SUBJECTS *

Subject Grouping	Cue Condition	Hallucination Present	Hallucination Absent
Real	high	3	6
	low	2	8
Simulating	high	12	11
	low	6	17

* Adapted from Sheehan et al.[27] Only the results for those subjects who hallucinated the Easter tree in the first instance are considered in this table.

stitute the main hypnotic data for the experiment with respect to analysis of trance logic. In contrast to hypnotic behavior, faking response in the study was almost entirely uniform; the demand characteristics for the hallucination item were explicit, and 46 of the 49 simulating subjects reported seeing the Easter tree. The relative paucity of positive hallucination response among hypnotic subjects can be attributed to the special difficulty of the item. A very marked degree of susceptibility to hypnosis was required for subjects to accept the hypnotist's suggestion that the tree was present when, in fact, it was not.

TABLE 1 sets out the incidence of double-hallucination (DH) response for real and simulating subjects tested in the two cue conditions. A positive DH response was indicated if subjects said they saw two Easter trees at the same time when confronted by the hypnotist. TABLE 2 sets out the response of subjects to the hypnotist's question regarding the (real) tree behind them and specifically provides close analysis of the direct impact of cue structure on both susceptible and insusceptible subjects' response. The results in TABLE 1 show that the double hallucination measure did not differentiate subjects when there were no especially strong cues for appropriate response: The two

TABLE 2

INCIDENCE OF RESPONSE BY REAL AND SIMULATING SUBJECTS TO E₂'S INQUIRY
CONCERNING THE (REAL) TREE BEHIND THEM *

Subject Grouping	Cue Condition	Ignored Tree on Stool	Acknowledged Tree on Stool
Real	high	0	9
	low	5	5
Simulating	high	2	21
	low	15	8

* Adapted from Sheehan et al.[27] As for TABLE 1, results relate only to those subjects who originally passed the hypnotist's formal test of hallucination.

groups of subjects (real and simulating) behaved comparably. Data from TABLE 2 show that cue structure closely determined whether subjects reported the second tree behind them; an appreciable effect for cue structure (p < .001) indicated that subjects acknowledged or ignored the real tree according to the cue structure of the condition in which they were placed.

TABLE 3 sets out the incidence of cases where subjects spontaneously reported a lack of solidity, or transparent quality to their original hallucination. A substantial number of hypnotic subjects reported transparency of hallucination either to the hypnotist or to E_1 in the inquiry, while no simulator reported similarly; for test of the significance of the differences between groups, $\chi^2(1) = 20.78$, p < .001. For both double-hallucination and transparency report, incidence of positive response was not related in any meaningful way to variation in the degree of susceptibility that existed among the real subjects.

Close analysis of the data, however, showed that subjects differed in the nature of their original hallucination reports. Scrutiny of original descriptions

TABLE 3

INCIDENCE OF TRANSPARENCY RESPONSE AMONG REAL AND SIMULATING SUBJECTS *

Subject Group	Transparency Response	
	Present	Absent
Real	8 (3)	12 (2)
Simulating	0	46 (18)

* Adapted from Sheehan et al.[27] Scores in brackets represent the number of subjects in each group who also reported a DH response. The number of reals represented here (N=20) is more than the number of subjects who reported to E_2 that they hallucinated the tree originally (N=19). The anomaly is due to the fact that one subject indicated to E_1 in the postexperimental inquiry that she had seen a tree, but because it was so different from the real one she decided not to mention the experience to the hypnotist who was testing her. This subject demonstrated a transparency response, and her data are therefore included in this table.

given to the Easter tree indicated distinct differences in the kinds of hallucinations reported by the real and simulating subjects. All descriptions were analyzed in terms of the reality, color, form, and distortion of the object that was described. The percentage frequency of response occurring in each of the categories was then examined and checked with use of multiple raters. Simulators uniformly reported hallucinations that were reality-oriented, strong in color, and sharply outlined, and showed hardly any evidence of distortion. On the other hand, real subjects who behaved incongruously in the setting reported hallucinations that did not closely parallel objects in the real world and were colored, but vague in outline and distorted. The Easter tree was obviously altered by real subjects who hallucinated it in ways that insusceptible subjects did not simulate. The pattern of findings suggests that behavior illustrating tolerance of incongruity may well be stimulus-bound in the sense that it is tied to the kinds of hallucinations subjects demonstrate in the first instance.

The problem with results so far is that we know nothing about how much aptitude for trance *per se* is related to the phenomenon or how much tolerance of incongruity expresses a stable characteristic that manifests itself across different tasks or settings. Clearly, further data are needed to help define the major parameters affecting the operation of the incongruity process; these were provided by the second of the two studies.

STUDY 2

The Relevance of Ability for Trance and Generalizability Across Tasks to Incidence of Incongruity Response

"Tolerance of incongruity" is said to characterize the behavior of deeply entranced subjects and is not dependent on suggestion (explicit or implicit) for its occurrence. From the results of the last study, it appears that double hallucination is subtly cued, since simulators show the phenomenon when tested optimally, but that transparency report is a valid discriminative measure. We should determine, however, the extent to which tolerance of incongruity is manifest among nonfaking subjects motivated to respond in the normal waking state. Current theorizing would lead us to expect that aptitude for trance is important and that tolerance for incongruity will not be readily manifest among waking control subjects. In this second and as yet unpublished study,[34] three separate groups of subjects (of High, Medium, and Low aptitude for trance) were tested under either hypnotic induction instructions or standard waking instructions to imagine effects as they were happening. The prediction was made that incongruity would characterize the performance of hypnotic subjects distinctively, especially those who have a marked degree of aptitude for hypnotic response; further, if a durable trait is at issue, then paradoxical behavior should generalize across tasks.

Procedure

A range of tests that illustrated "tolerance of incongruity" was adopted to investigate the extent to which this process variable could yield stable, consistent effects. Seven different measures were selected from surveys made of incongruity tasks discussed in the hypnotic literature (e.g., Refs. 9, 17, 22).† Independent sets of 12 subjects were allocated to each of the three aptitude groupings and the two instruction conditions (N = 72). Highly susceptible subjects were those who passed 9–12 items on the HGSHS:A, and medium- and low-aptitude subjects were those who passed 5–7 and 0–3 items on the HGSHS:A, respectively.

---

† The seven tests of incongruity that were conducted were as follows: The Missing Watch Hand;[9] Problem Solving with Blocking for the Number 6;[6] Age Regression;[22] Negative Visual Hallucination;[22] Double Hallucination;[9,17] Transparency Report;[17] and Negative Auditory Hallucination (devised by the author, but influenced by Bernheim[2]).

TABLE 4

FREQUENCY OF DOUBLE HALLUCINATON RESPONSE

Subject Group	Susceptibility Level	Criterion for Scoring Item *		Incongruity Response	
		Pass	Fail	Present	Absent
Hypnotic	high	7	5	4	3
	medium	5	7	2	3
	low	0	12	0	0
Imagination	high	11	1	5	6
	medium	6	6	1	5
	low	3	9	1	2

* The criterion for considering subjects on this item was the reported presence of the hallucinated Easter tree following suggestion by the hypnotist.

Results

TABLES 4 and 5 illustrate the frequency of double-hallucination and transparency response tested under the same optimal (i.e., low-cue) conditions as adopted in Study 1 for both groups of hypnotic and imagination subjects, divided according to their aptitude for trance. Data once again challenged the validity of double hallucination as a discriminative index. Ability was clearly relevant to the phenomenon as predicted, but waking imagination subjects displayed instances of tolerance of incongruity. And, as before, transparency response proved much the more discriminative index; only hypnotic subjects illustrated this response when there were no obvious attempts to cue its appropriateness in the test situation.

TABLES 6 and 7 illustrate the data for a third measure of incongruity. This test presented subjects with the suggestion they would not see a wastepaper basket that was placed directly in front of them. For subjects passing

TABLE 5

FREQUENCY OF TRANSPARENCY RESPONSE TO THE EASTER TREE

Subject Group	Susceptibility Level	Criterion for Scoring Item *		Incongruity Response	
		Pass	Fail	Present	Absent
Hypnotic	high	7	5	2	5
	medium	5	7	0	5
	low	0	12	0	0
Imagination	high	11	1	0	11
	medium	6	6	0	6
	low	3	9	0	3

* The criterion for considering subjects on this item was the reported presence of the hallucinated Easter tree following suggestion by the hypnotist.

TABLE 6

FREQUENCY OF INCONGRUITY RESPONSE FOLLOWING TEST OF NEGATIVE
VISUAL HALLUCINATION

Subject Group	Susceptibility Level	Criterion for Scoring Item *		Incongruity Response	
		Pass	Fail	Present	Absent
Hypnotic	high	3	9	2	1
	medium	3	9	1	2
	low	4	8	4	0
Imagination	high	7	5	7	0
	medium	5	7	3	2
	low	1	11	1	0

* The criterion for this item was the reported absence of the wastebasket following negative hallucination suggestion by the hypnotist.

the negative hallucination item, data were scored for those who, when asked to move across to a table in front of which the basket was placed, walked around instead of into the object. This test is regarded as a classic demonstration of tolerance of incongruity and is said to illustrate clearly what Bowers [4] terms registration without perception (p. 104)—an essential identifying feature of trance-logic behavior. TABLE 6 demonstrates no distinctiveness for the hypnotic group at all on the item. Both hypnotic and imagination subjects acknowledged the negatively hallucinated tree by walking around it; even ability was not specifically related to the phenomenon, suggesting that the test is a poor measure of the process being analyzed. TABLE 7 presents a fascinating finding, however, which unexpectedly emerged during the session and which has, I believe, important theoretical implications for understanding subjects' tolerance of logical incongruity. Two nonhypnotic subjects reported transparency of the wastepaper basket. To my knowledge, their responses are the first reported instances of unsolicited transparency response given by subjects who had not been hypnotized and for whom the behavior was not

TABLE 7

FREQUENCY OF TRANSPARENCY RESPONSE TO THE WASTEBASKET

Subject Group	Susceptibility Level	Incongruity Response	
		Present	Absent
Hypnotic	high	1	11
	medium	0	12
	low	0	12
Imagination	high	2	10
	medium	0	12
	low	0	12

explicitly cued.‡ Transparency has always been tied to the behavior of hypnotized, entranced subjects—never to the performance of nonhypnotic subjects, unless the response in question has been clearly suggested.[15]

TABLE 8 looks across all of the measures of tolerance of incongruity and illustrates a distinct patterning in subjects' behavior. It lists the frequencies of subjects scoring from 0 to 7 on the battery of items that were used to measure the process. Leaving aside complexities in the scoring process, several conclusions can be drawn from the data. The greatest incidence of response was associated with a high degree of aptitude for trance, there being no real distinction apparent in the patterning of data for hypnotized and unhypnotized subjects; low ability was also clearly associated with near-zero incidence of response. Behavior illustrating tolerance of logical incongruity demands ability for trance, and it can obviously be demonstrated both inside and outside the hypnotic setting somewhat more frequently than the literature has led us to expect. The ability to tolerate incongruence, though, does not

TABLE 8

FREQUENCY OF COMPOSITE "TOLERANCE OF LOGICAL INCONGRUITY" SCORES FOR SEVEN TEST TASKS *

Subject Group	Susceptibility Level	Tolerance of Logical Incongruity Score							
		0	1	2	3	4	5	6	7
Hypnotic	high	4	2	3	2	1	0	0	0
	medium	8	2	0	2	0	0	0	0
	low	8	4	0	0	0	0	0	0
Imagination	high	2	4	4	1	1	0	0	0
	medium	9	0	1	2	0	0	0	0
	low	10	2	0	0	0	0	0	0

* Bracketed entries represent similar score patterns for hypnotic and nonhypnotic subjects.

appear to generalize across tasks that have been presented previously in the literature as measuring the process in question. Sixteen hypnotic and fifteen imagination subjects displayed some form of incongruity in the session, and only two of these 31 subjects scored more than three out of seven on the battery of incongruity tasks. Analysis of the total set of data and the "spread" of scores through the high category suggests that subjects' capacity

‡ Subsequent to the work reported here, instances did occur in our laboratory where a simulating subject atypically offered a transparency report. The behavior, however, occurred in a situation that was heavily conflictual (where the hypnotist deliberately suggested that opposing responses were legitimate). Transparency report obviously demonstrated a "compromise" response, given to resolve the uncertainty that the subject was experiencing in a very ambiguous testing situation. It is interesting to note that the response was described by the subject herself as "not very convincing."

to tolerate incongruity expressed itself quite variably across different test situations—assuming, of course, that the tasks in question actually did measure the same process, as those who constructed them intended.§

DISCUSSION

The process labeled here as "tolerance of incongruity" embodies the notion that a person can register information at one level of cognitive functioning that remains unappreciated at other levels, and it appeals strongly to the existence of multiple, quasi-independent levels of informational processing.[4] Theorizing about the process argues unequivocally that it is not just an anomaly of behavior that is involved; a peculiar quality of consciousness is at issue that is said to be related to trance depth and hypnotic involvement.

One of the primary attributes of this construct, viewed as an internal process variable, is that logical faculties are assumed to be in abeyance. This is really why, for instance, waking simulating subjects working rationally on a task are said to be unable to duplicate incongruity of behavior. Many theorists make this essential point in their own particular way. Hilgard,[9] for instance, talks of selective inattention which we can link with his concept of dissociation; Gill and Brenman [8] talk of adaptive regression of the ego where there is a subsidence of planning function and change in the processes of thought functioning; and Bowers [4] focuses directly on registration without perception and theorizes that "effortful, actively directed attention seems to be precisely what the high-susceptible subjects do *not* engage in." (p. 138) These various viewpoints substantially overlap. Bowers argues, for instance, that it could be the seemingly effortless attention to the task at hand that is permitted and preserved by the highly susceptible subject's talent for dissociation. The notion, however, that there is a qualitative shift in thought process from a sharp, critical attitude to an uncritical and diffuse one is clearly a common one in contemporary theorizing about hypnosis.

I believe the data from the work I have described challenge this assumption of lack of cognitive effort on the part of the deeply susceptible subject. The evidence is consistent with the notion that some hypnotic subjects (as do nonhypnotic subjects) respond to suggestion by working to structure the test situation in a way that renders it compatible with the communication that has been presented. The data tell us, for example, that cues existing in the test setting are enormously influential on subjects, and subjects obviously take effort

§ There are indications elsewhere in the data, however, indicating that hypnosis may have enhanced the occurrence of subjects' tolerance of incongruity on certain kinds of incongruity tasks. If one considers just those items which illustrated the phenomenon for high-aptitude subjects—i.e., excluding any item that was passed by a low-aptitude subject (either hypnotic or nonhypnotic)—the data suggest a superiority for the hypnotic group. For the five tests that satisfied this stringent ability criterion (Age Regression, Problem Solving, Missing Watch Hand, Transparency Report, and Negative Auditory Hallucination) there was a substantial increase in frequency of trance-logic behavior associated with the hypnotic as compared with the imagination condition. Looking just at the data for these particular ability-demanding items, and scoring specifically for paradoxical response, 55% of all instances where incongruity was tested in hypnosis yielded positive evidence for tolerance of incongruity, whereas only 18% of instances tested in the waking imagination condition did so.

both to detect and to process them. I would like to highlight this point by drawing attention to the incidence of transparency response that was observed in the research I have just described and ask the question why nonhypnotic subjects spontaneously reported transparency in this program of work. The unexpected emergence of this response in the waking group suggests that we should analyze the cognitive components of test situations very closely to try to understand the exact nature of incongruity behavior in hypnosis.

The suggestion for negative hallucination of the wastebasket could have subtly indicated to subjects that a transparency report was legitimate, and the involvement of some subjects was effortful enough for them to process the cue implications of the test suggestion and respond appropriately. As the object faded, as it were (following the influence of the hypnotist's communication that the wastebasket would disappear), it wasn't simply a matter of blocking out the relevant stimulus. For some subjects, selective inattention could have been accompanied by a gradual cognitive construction of the absence of the stimulus; in this sense, a transparent wastebasket response emerged, not as an unsuggested effect of hypnosis, but as a partial blocking response—the result of stimulus reality being actively, cognitively assimilated with the nature of the hypnotist's suggestion. When we look on subjects' cognitive processing in this way, transparency behavior can be seen as quite consistent with the total stimulus nexus operating at the time. In a different but related sense, hypnotic subjects could have given a transparency response in the first study because it was compatible with the kind of stimulus features that individually characterized their particular hallucinations of the Easter tree (and which were perfectly permissible within the framework of suggestion that was supplied).

Theorizing to date has asserted that subjects' tolerance of incongruity illustrates a nonsuggested attribute of hypnotic behavior, a quality of consciousness unrelated either to setting characteristics or cues from other sources. The data here quite strongly militate against the generality of such an account, but this assertion is intended in no way to detract from the genuineness of the phenomenon. It appears that the elicitation of most incongruity behavior—e.g., double hallucination and even transparency report—is quite compatible with the kinds of communication offered by the hypnotist. Cues for paradoxical response are inherent in the stimulus situation and may be actively processed by hypnotic subjects. The evidence suggests that it is more legitimate to view incongruity behavior as a predictable outcome of such processing rather than as a spontaneously occurring, unsuggested attribute of hypnosis. The hypnotic subject is quite definitely not a victim of mechanical suggestion. As Field [7] implies, we should take considerable care not to intellectualize the test situation and downgrade the hypnotic subject's higher mental processes. Suggestion appears to be, as he terms it, hinting and intimating rather than directing, and the evidence suggests that some hypnotic subjects are especially alert to detect and process, in their own individual way, subtle cues that point them toward, or are consistent with, appropriate response—cues or messages that simulators may miss because of the absence of their genuine involvement in trance events.[27] ¶

¶ Data relating to the influence of uncanceled suggestion serve to reinforce the point. The evidence that is available indicates that cuing (of a more direct kind than that associated with transparency report) is positively related to the extent to which hypnotized subjects will continue to respond after other subjects have assumed that a suggestion has been terminated.[21] Here, also, as with the data on transparency report, simulators miss the kinds of cues that hypnotic subjects register and process.

Search for the presence of unique behavior among hypnotized subjects is no longer a credible goal. We now seek only to establish distinctive patterns of response to support our theoretical concepts. I would argue that the subtle communication aspects of the test situation that appear to determine distinctive patterns of incongruous response derive from subjects' motivated involvement in trance events, and the data suggest that we should attend more to the motivated cognitive planning functions of hypnotic subjects than to the seemingly uncritical and passive nature of their acceptance of what the hypnotist says.

Process variables illustrated by tolerance of incongruity do not operate in isolation; they clearly interact with aptitude for trance, orientation to the task, and the network of stimulus features existing in the situation, in order to determine actual behavioral outcomes. Data coming from several sources, however, suggest that there are different types of susceptible subjects whose behavior illustrates contrasting cognitive and motivational orientations to their tasks. For example, some but not all good hypnotic subjects interpret hypnotic events in a way that leads them to counter previously held preconceptions about appropriate patterns of responding;[24] and only a minority of susceptible subjects will continue to respond to unterminated suggestions,[21] and override the cognitive influence of previous perceptions.[26] It is significant to note that the incongruity data appear to highlight just this pattern of differentiation. Some susceptible subjects respond incongruously; others do not. And we know that depth of trance offers too simplistic—and inaccurate—a solution.|| The mediating process, which I am suggesting helps account for the variability in the data, is the motivational commitment of the hypnotic subject. In particular, the hypnotized person is motivated in such a way that he detects and processes cues stemming from his involvement that other (nonhypnotic) subjects miss. And he plays altogether too active and too discriminating a part to be regarded as an automatic, effortless responder.**

Predictions about hypnotic subjects' motivated involvement may, in fact, very strongly assist us to separate out those who will accept the hypnotist's suggestions literally and routinely from those who will cognitively work his communications through to satisfy their own personal commitment to the hypnotic events that they are experiencing. It is the activity-passivity dimension of subjects' involvement in trance events that really appears to be at issue; and a considerable body of data argues its relevance.[5, 25] ††

In conclusion, hypnotic analgesia, age regression, aspects of negative hallucination, and trance logic clearly share in common the possibility that stimuli as suggested by the hypnotist will be registered without perception. The more intriguing question, however, is why it is that stimulus events in the trance

---

|| Appeal to aptitude for trance is obviously insufficient to account for the data. Results from this program of work, for example, demonstrated that transparency was not reliably reported when double hallucination was present, and apart from the fact that susceptible subjects could illustrate either of these two forms of behavior, it was definitely not the most susceptible of the high group of subjects who evidenced both.

** Long ago, White[33] made the same point when he argued cogently that subjects respond to suggestions in ways that are consonant with their strivings, but that their response should be regarded as effortful.

†† The problem, however, can be conceptualized in other ways. Considering regression theory (e.g., Ref. 8), for instance, one could ask why the executive functions of the ego are laid aside less readily for some subjects than for others, quite independently of the subjects' level of susceptibility to hypnosis.

setting are cognitively processed much more distinctively by some hypnotic subjects than by others. The evidence has accumulated to suggest that tolerance of incongruity is a defining property of hypnosis, but not quite in the ways that the literature has led us previously to suspect.

ACKNOWLEDGMENTS

The author wishes to thank Isolde Obstoj, Kevin McConkey, and Robyn Dolby for their help in gathering the data on which this paper is based.

REFERENCES

1. BARBER, T. X., N. P. SPANOS & J. F. CHAVES. 1974. Hypnosis, Imagination and Human Potentialities. Pergamon Press. New York, N.Y.
2. BERNHEIM, H. 1890. Suggestive Therapeutics. Trans. by C. A. Herter. Pentland. Edinburgh, Scotland.
3. BINET, A. 1905. On Double Consciousness: Experimental Psychological Studies. Open Court Publishing Co. Chicago, Ill.
4. BOWERS, K. S. 1976. Hypnosis for the Seriously Curious. Brooks-Cole. Monterey, Calif.
5. DOLBY, R. & P. W. SHEEHAN. 1977. Cognitive processing and expectancy behavior in hypnosis. J. Abnorm. Psychol. In press.
6. EVANS, F. J. 1972. Posthypnotic amnesia and the temporary disruption of retrieval processes. Paper presented at Symposium on Amnesia, Annual Conf. Amer. Psychol. Assoc. Honolulu, Hawaii. September.
7. FIELD, P. B. 1972. Humanistic aspects of hypnotic communication. In Hypnosis: Research Developments and Perspectives. E. Fromm & R. E. Shor, Eds. Aldine Atherton. Chicago, Ill.
8. GILL, M. M. & M. BRENMAN. 1961. Hypnosis and Related States. International Universities Press. New York, N.Y.
9. HILGARD, E. R. 1965. Hypnotic Susceptibility. Harcourt Brace & World. New York, N.Y.
10. HILGARD, E. R. 1973. A neodissociation interpretation of pain reduction in hypnosis. Psychol. Rev. 80: 396–411.
11. HILGARD, E. R. 1974. Toward a neodissociation theory: Multiple cognitive controls in human functioning. Perspect. Biol. Med. 17: 301–316.
12. HILGARD, E. R. & J. R. HILGARD. 1975. Hypnosis in the Relief of Pain. William Kaufmann. Los Altos, Calif.
13. HILGARD, J. R. 1970. Personality and Hypnosis: A Study of Imaginative Involvement. Univ. Chicago Press. Chicago, Ill.
14. HILGARD, J. R. 1974. Imaginative involvement: Some characteristics of the highly hypnotizable and nonhypnotizable. Internat. J. Clin. Exp. Hypn. 22: 138–156.
15. JOHNSON, R. F., B. A. MAHER & T. X. BARBER. 1972. Artifact in the "essence of hypnosis": An evaluation of trance logic. J. Abnorm. Psychol. 79: 212–220.
16. McDONALD, R. D. & J. R. SMITH. 1975. Trance logic in tranceable and simulating subjects. Internat. J. Clin. Exp. Hypn. 23: 80–89.
17. ORNE, M. T. 1959. The nature of hypnosis: Artifact and essence. J. Abnorm. Soc. Psychol. 58: 277–299.
18. ORNE, M. T. 1971. The simulation of hypnosis: Why, how, and what it means. Internat. J. Clin. Exp. Hypn. 19: 183–210.

19. ORNE, M. T. 1974. On the concept of hypnotic depth. Paper presented at the 18th Internat. Conf. Applied Psychol. Montreal, Canada. August.
20. ORNE, M. T. & A. G. HAMMER. 1974. Hypnosis. In Encyclopaedia Britannica: 133–140. William Benton. Chicago, Ill.
21. PERRY, C. W. 1976. Uncancelled hypnotic suggestions: The effects of hypnotic depth, hypnotic skill, and interpersonal effects on their post hypnotic persistence. Unpublished paper. Concordia Univ. Montreal, Canada.
22. PETERS, J. E. 1973. Trance logic: Artifact or essence in hypnosis? Unpublished Doctoral Dissertation. Pennsylvania State University, University Park, Pa.
23. SARBIN, T. R. 1972. Imagining as muted role-taking: A historical-linguistic analysis. In The Function and Nature of Imagery. P. W. Sheehan, Ed. Academic Press. New York, N.Y.
24. SHEEHAN, P. W. 1971. Countering preconceptions about hypnosis: An objective index of involvement with the hypnotist. J. Abnorm. Soc. Psychol. Monog. 78: 299–322.
25. SHEEHAN, P. W. & L. BOWMAN. 1973. Peer model and experimenter expectancies about appropriate response as determinants of behavior in the hypnotic setting. J. Abnorm. Psychol. 82: 112–123.
26. SHEEHAN, P. W. & R. DOLBY. 1975. Hypnosis and the influence of most recently perceived events. J. Abnorm. Psychol. 84: 331–345.
27. SHEEHAN, P. W., I. OBSTOJ & K. McCONKEY. 1976. Trance logic and cue structure as supplied by the hypnotist. J. Abnorm. Psychol. 85: 459–472.
28. SHEEHAN, P. W. & C. W. PERRY. 1976. Methodologies of Hypnosis: A Critical Appraisal of Contemporary Paradigms of Hypnosis. Erlbaum. Hillsdale, N.J.
29. SHOR, R. E. & E. C. ORNE. 1962. The Harvard Group Scale of Hypnotic Susceptibility, Form A. Consulting Psychologists Press. Palo Alto, Calif.
30. SPANOS, N. P. & T. X. BARBER. 1974. Toward a convergence in hypnosis research. Amer. Psychol. 29: 500–511.
31. SUTCLIFFE, J. P. 1961. "Credulous" and "skeptical" views of hypnotic phenomena: Experiments in esthesia, hallucination, and delusion. J. Abnorm. Soc. Psychol. 62: 189–200.
32. WEITZENHOFFER, A. M. & E. R. HILGARD. 1962. Stanford Hypnotic Susceptibility Scale, Form C. Consulting Psychologists Press. Palo Alto, Calif.
33. WHITE, R. W. 1941. A preface to the theory of hypnotism. J. Abnorm. Soc. Psychol. 36: 477–505.
34. OBSTOJ, I. & P. W. SHEEHAN. Aptitude for trance, task generalizability, and incongruity response in hypnosis. J. Abnorm. Psychol. To be published.

EXPERIENCED INVOLUNTARINESS AND RESPONSE TO HYPNOTIC SUGGESTIONS

Nicholas P. Spanos, Steven M. Rivers, and Stewart Ross

Department of Psychology
Carleton University
Ottawa K1S 5B6, Ontario, Canada

Since the last century, it has been commonly observed that good hypnotic subjects typically report that their overt response to motoric suggestions are experienced as involuntary occurrences.[1,2] These responses feel as if they "happened to" the subject, rather than feeling like self-initiated, self-guided acts. Our paper addresses itself to this phenomenon. The first part reviews theoretical approaches and empirical findings associated with the problem of *experienced involuntariness*. The second presents an experiment aimed at clarifying some of the methodological issues raised by previous research.

APPROACHES TO THE PROBLEM OF EXPERIENCED INVOLUNTARINESS

Traditional Formulations: Two Types of Behavior

Most attempts to explain reports of response to suggestion being experienced as involuntary have been based on the assumption that there exist two fundamentally different types of skeletal motor behavior. The first type consists of so-called "voluntary" actions carried out in everyday life. These actions are conceptualized as being planned, goal-directed strivings regulated by conscious awareness. The second type consists of complex but nonetheless "involuntary" or automatic movements. These actions are thought to be produced by rather esoteric psychological processes and restricted to unusual situations like hypnosis, or to unusual people like hysterics. When carrying out "involuntary" behavior, the person is no longer conceptualized as an active, planning, self-directed being. Instead, he is conceptualized as an automaton. His motor behavior occurs independently of his plans as a set of automatic responses to certain mental events.

One well-known formulation based on the above dichotomy was proffered by Pierre Janet.[1,2] Janet suggested that "involuntary" motor responses resulted from ideas that were "dissociated" or "split off" from normal consciousness. For Janet, the "hypnotized" subject experienced his behavior involuntarily because it was, in fact, automatic. It occurred despite the subject's wishes as a function of dissociated ideas over which he could exercise no conscious control.

Implicit in Janet's formulation was the notion of ideomotor action. According to this notion, ideas—dissociated ideas in Janet's case—lead directly to corresponding actions. A variant of the ideomotor action notion was also used by Magda Arnold to account for "involuntary" motor responses.[3] Arnold argued that:

> . . . every attempt to imagine a movement results in minimal nervous excitation in peripheral muscle groups concerned in that movement . . . such

minimal nervous excitation in effector organs, originating in the subject's imagining a movement, can become intensified until actual movement results. (p. 111)

In short, Arnold postulated that "involuntary" motor responses occur automatically whenever the subject vividly imagines the movement in question.

Hypotheses that posit two types of motor behavior are associated with a number of difficulties. Oftentimes they are untestable because objective means for assessing esoteric theoretical constructs such as "dissociated ideas" are unavailable. When based on the notion of ideomotor action, these hypotheses become embroiled in the thorny philosophical problem of explaining how images can cause action.[1] Moreover, the notion that vividly imagining a movement invariably produces that movement seems to contradict everyday experience. For instance, vivid daydreamers do not invariably enact their imagings. The fact that they do not indicates that any relationship between imagery and the simultaneous enactment of overt behavior is probably moderated by variables such as situational demands concerning the "appropriateness" of the overt enactment. In part because of difficulties such as these, hypotheses postulating two types of motor behavior have generated relatively little empirical research.

An Alternative Formulation: Involuntariness as an Attribution

We believe that investigators have been seriously misled by the assumption that reports of involuntariness imply the existence of a special type of corresponding motor mechanism. This assumption is simply unnecessary. What needs explanation is not subjects' motor behavior, but instead, the attributions of causality that they apply to their behavior. This perspective generates questions of the following type:

1) What variables lead subjects to develop the expectation that their motor behavior is to be experienced as involuntary?
2) How regularly do subjects define their response to suggestion in that manner?
3) What variables enable some subjects to succeed in defining their response as involuntary?

Expectations for Involuntary Behavior

The hypnotic situation contains an abundance of cues informing subjects that their behavior is to occur involuntarily. First, hypnosis is still associated with the image of a passive subject acted upon and controlled by a powerful hypnotist.[5] Traditional hypnotic induction procedures do nothing to dispel this image. Instead, they reinforce the notion of involuntariness by implicitly informing subjects that various effects are happening *to* them rather than being produced *by* them (e.g., you are becoming relaxed; your eyes are closing). Thus, the popular image of hypnosis, reinforced by the structure of the typical hypnotic encounter, generates strong expectations that hypnotic behavior is *not* self-generated.

A more specific generator of expectations for involuntariness is the structure of the suggestions used in hypnosis research. Motoric suggestions invariably contain two directives. First, they instruct subjects to perform some simple overt behavior such as lifting or lowering the arm. Second, subjects are implicitly instructed to experience their overt behavior as involuntary (e.g., "your arm is rising" as opposed to "raise your arm"). These suggestions further imply that the overt behavior is to occur only if subjects can succeed in defining their response as involuntary.[5, 6]

In short, the hypnotic situation in general and hypnotic suggestions in particular are structured to convey the expectation that responses are to be experienced as occurring involuntarily. It becomes important, therefore, to determine how regularly subjects do, in fact, meet this expectation.

Overt Behavior and Experienced Involuntariness

A great deal of research in hypnosis is based on the assumption that subjects' overt response to suggestion accurately reflects the degree to which they have defined their response as involuntary. If subjects "pass" a suggestion, it is typically assumed that they experienced their response as involuntary. If they "fail," it is assumed that they were unable to experience their behavior as involuntary. This assumption is oversimplified.[7] Subjects' overt response may fail to correspond to the suggestion's directive concerning involuntariness in at least two ways. Subjects may "fail" a suggestion while defining their response as at least in part involuntary, or they may "pass" a suggestion while defining their behavior as volitional. The first of these cases is illustrated by subjects who "fail" challenge suggestions but later report that they met the challenge only by exerting great effort. For instance, such a subject given an arm-rigidity suggestion might report that his arm involuntarily became very stiff, but by dint of great effort be managed to bend it. The second case is more common. Subjects may "pass" the suggestion while defining their act as more or less voluntary compliance.

In order to assess the correspondence between subjects' overt response to suggestion and their experience of responding involuntarily, we reanalyzed data that were originally gathered by Spanos et al.[8] In that study subjects rated their response to an arm-rigidity suggestion on a five-point continuum ranging from completely voluntary (I could have easily bent my arm) to completely involuntary (my arm was completely unable to bend). Overt response (bending or failing to bend the arm when challenged) was assessed by the experimenter. We dichotomized subjects' ratings into those indicating primarily involuntary experiences and those indicating that the response was experienced as equally or more voluntary than involuntary. TABLE 1 presents the relationship between subjects' dichotomized ratings of involuntariness and their overt response to the suggestion. This table shows that there is a discrepancy between overt response to suggestion and experienced involuntariness of response for a substantial proportion of subjects. In fact, almost half (45%) of the subjects who passed the suggestion *failed* to define their response as being a primarily involuntary occurrence. If nothing else, these data indicate rather forcefully that overt response to suggestion does not always accurately reflect subjects' experiences. Therefore, in order to avoid ambiguity, studies aimed at delineating variables that effect experienced involuntariness should include a measure of that dimension which is independent of motor performance.

Variables Associated with Defining Response as Involuntary

Several years ago it was hypothesized that subjects tend to define their overt response to suggestion as involuntary when they become absorbed in a pattern of imaginings called goal-directed fantasy (GDF).[6] GDF's are defined as imagined situations which, if they were to actually occur, would be expected to lead to the involuntary occurrence of the motor response called for by the suggestion. For instance, subjects administered the suggestion that their arm is unable to bend are scored as showing GDFr (i.e., reported goal-directed fantasy) if they report such events as imagining a cast on their arm, or imagining that their arm has been transformed into a piece of steel.

Absorption or involvement refers to the intensity and consistency with which subjects attend to a situation. Individuals can become involved in covert (i.e., imagined) situations as well as in external situations.[9, 10] Thus, the subject highly involved in GDF is attending fully to his imaginings while ignoring or reinterpreting information that contradicts the "reality" of his imaginings.[11]

The GDF hypothesis can be illustrated with a concrete example. Suppose a subject given an arm-rigidity suggestion tenses his arm and simultaneously

TABLE 1

NUMBER AND PROPORTION OF SUBJECTS PASSING OR FAILING AN ARM-RIGIDITY
SUGGESTION AND DEFINING THEIR BEHAVIOR AS INVOLUNTARY OR VOLUNTARY *

	Passed	Failed
Involuntary	21 (.33)	2 (.03)
Voluntary	17 (.21)	24 (.37)

* Reanalysis of data gathered by Spanos *et al.*[8]

becomes absorbed in imagining his arm held tightly in a cast. According to the GDF hypothesis the subject is likely to attribute the tension in his arm to his imaginings rather than to a volitional decision to tense the arm. Once again, it should be noted that GDF is not hypothesized as causing the motor behavior (arm-tensing). The hypothesis deals instead with the subject's attribution of causality to his own behavior.

GDFr-Experienced Involuntariness Ratings and Motor Behavior. Several studies have administered one or more motoric suggestions and assessed both experienced involuntariness of response and GDFr.[5, 8, 12, 13] These studies have yielded consistent results. In all of them, subjects who showed GDFr rated their response as more involuntary than those who failed to show GDFr. The relationship between involuntariness ratings and GDFr held within subjects as well as between subjects. Thus, subjects who showed GDFr in response to one suggestion but not to another indicated greater involuntariness when they exhibited GDFr than when they did not.[13]

A number of studies have assessed the relationship between GDFr and overt response (passing or failing) to motoric suggestions.[5, 6, 8, 12-15] The results of these studies have been inconsistent. Some found a relationship between GDFr and "passing" suggestions.[6, 13] However, others failed to find such a relationship or found it only for some suggestions and not others.[8, 12, 14, 15] These findings are not particularly surprising in light of what was said earlier about the rather tenuous relationship between subjects' overt behavior and ratings of involuntariness. Unfortunately, some of these studies assessed only overt behavior, and therefore their relevance to the GDF hypothesis is difficult to assess. Several of these studies, however, assessed both overt response and involuntariness ratings.[8, 12, 13] They found GDFr to be associated with relatively high involuntariness scores even when it was unrelated to overt response to suggestion.

Suggested GDF and Response to Suggestion. Many motoric suggestions explicitly ask subjects to carry out a GDF (GDF-suggestions). For instance, the arm-lowering suggestion of the Stanford Hypnotic Susceptibility Scale Form C asks subjects to imagine holding a heavy weight in their hand.[16] Several studies have compared the efficacy of GDF-suggestions with suggestions that do not include a GDF. None of them found that GDF-suggestions consistently enhanced overt response to all suggestions.[8, 12-14] Three of these studies also assessed experienced involuntariness of response. GDF-suggestions enhanced ratings of experienced involuntariness in two of those studies,[8, 12] but not in the third.[13]

It is important to keep in mind that some subjects administered a GDF-suggestion fail to actually show GDFr. Furthermore, many subjects given non-GDF-suggestions devise and carry out their own GDFr's.[13] Thus, one study found that GDFr was related to experienced involuntariness ratings even though these ratings were unrelated to whether or not the suggestions had provided a GDF.[13]

Involvement in GDF and Response to Suggestion. A number of investigators from differing theoretical backgrounds have stated or implied that experiential response to suggestion is facilitated by the extent to which subjects become involved in suggestion-related imaginings.[6, 9-11, 17] Although relatively little work has focused on subjects' degree of involvement in specific suggestions, what has been done is consistent with the involvement hypothesis.

One study found that high- and medium-susceptible hypnotic subjects failed to differ in their overt response to an arm-rigidity suggestion.[5] Nonetheless, the high susceptibles were more likely than the medium susceptibles to become involved in GDFr, rate their response as involuntary, and ascribe reality status to their imaginings. A similar study found that involvement in imaginings generated by a GDF suggestion was correlated with rated involuntariness and degree of reality status ascribed to imaginings.[18] This study also demonstrated that subjects' involuntariness ratings could not be accounted for in terms of their self-observation of having passed or failed the suggestion.

The results discussed above may be summarized as follows. Experienced involuntariness is not strongly related to subjects' passing or failing suggestions. It has been found consistently that subjects who show GDFr are more likely than those who do not to define their response to suggestion as an involuntary occurrence. Findings concerning a relationship between GDFr and overt response have been less consistent. Some studies found that GDFr was associated with passing suggestions, but others found no relationship between these variables. Suggested GDF's enhance ratings of involuntariness when they first enhance GDFr. These suggestions, however, do not always enhance GDFr. Finally, subjects who become involved in GDFr are more likely than those who do not become involved to experience their response as an involuntary occurrence.

The studies on which these conclusions are based have all employed the same basic methodological procedures. Subjects were administered one or more suggestions. Following their overt response and subjective ratings, they were asked a series of questions aimed at assessing if they experienced GDF while they were responding. These procedures raise a number of methodological issues which have yet to be adequately resolved. The second part of this paper outlines these issues and presents the results of an experiment aimed at addressing them.

METHODOLOGICAL ISSUES IN THE ASSESSMENT OF GDF
Experimenter Bias

In all GDFr studies reported to date, subjects' experiences were assessed by the same experimenter who administered the suggestion and observed subjects' overt response and subjective ratings. This procedure leaves the studies open to a criticism of experimenter bias. Since the experimenters knew how subjects had responded to the suggestions, they may have inadvertently provided cues concerning the kinds of subjective testimony expected.[19] In short, the relationship between GDF and involuntariness of response obtained in previous studies may be an artifact generated by the transmission of expectations for different types of subjective reports to subjects who passed or failed suggestions. The present study assess this hypothesis. All subjects were administered the same suggestion. The experiences of half the subjects were assessed by the same experimenter who administered and observed their response to the suggestion. The experiences of the remaining subjects were assessed by a different experimenter, who was unaware of how subjects had responded to the suggestion.

Oral vs Written Testimony

Most studies have assessed GDFr on the basis of subjects' oral testimony to verbal queries concerning their experiences.[5, 6, 12, 14, 15] However, two studies have asked subjects, in writing, to write descriptions of their experience.[8, 13] Oral transactions between subject and experimenter probably provide more cues for ferreting out an experimental hypothesis than do written transactions. Therefore, these two modes for eliciting and gathering subjects' testimony were compared. Half the subjects in this study responded orally to verbal inquiries, while the other half responded in writing to written questions.

Interview Demands and Subjects' Testimony

Most studies have assessed GDF either with semistructured interview procedures or with a single but highly leading question. Only one study assessed the effects of using standardized but increasingly specific questions to elicit subjects' testimony.[13] In that study subjects were first asked a relatively general question about their experiences during the suggestion period. This was followed by a highly specific question that included an example of GDF and asked subjects if they had a similar experience. A substantial proportion of subjects who had not shown GDFr to the general inquiry reported it to the specific question. However, even the general inquiry used in that study asked subjects to report everything that they had *imagined* during the suggestion. Use of the word *imagined*, even in the absence of more specific information, may have cued some subjects about the experimenter's hypothesis.

The present study attempted to minimize cues that could lead subjects to assume that the experimenters were particularly interested in assessing one aspect of their experience. Subjects were administered an arm-catalepsy suggestion that did not contain a GDF. The word *imagine* was not used in the suggestion, and descriptive terms such as "stiff," "rigid," and "solid," that might lead subjects to guess that certain imaginings were required, were also avoided. The suggestion simply informed subjects repeatedly that their arms would be unable to bend. Following the suggestion, subjects were administered a very general inquiry that did not employ the word *imagine*. Subjects were simply asked to honestly report everything they had experienced (Low Cue inquiry). This was followed by a more specific question asking them about what they had thought about and imagined (Medium Cue inquiry). Finally, they were given an example of a GDF and asked if they had had similar experience (High Cue inquiry).

Subjects administered general questions often give general answers that contain nothing about GDF.[13] Their answers become increasingly likely to indicate a GDFr as the questions they are asked become more specific. One hypothesis that may account for these findings can be summarized as follows: Subjects' experiences are quite complex, and they tend to initially report what is most compelling to them. Because their interests may not correspond to what the experimenter is assessing, a general inquiry may do a poor job of tapping the specific experiences he is interested in. As questions become more specific, subjects report honestly about facets of their experience they previously failed to mention. Subjects for whom GDFr was a compelling and highly absorbing experience are likely to report it with minimal cuing. Those for whom GDFr was less absorbing show it only after some cuing.

This hypothesis predicts that there are positive correlations among (1) the point at which subjects first show GDFr (Low, Medium or High Cue inquiries), (2) reported involuntariness of responding, and (3) degree of absorption in the suggestion. The present study tested these predictions.

Other Facets of Subjects' Experiences

The time between the initial administration of a suggestion and its termination is usually less than a minute. Despite such a short duration, subjects typically report a complex flow of experiences. In one study, some reported carrying on an internal dialogue. Some reported that before being challenged to do so, by the experimenter, they told themselves that they knew they would be able to bend their arms. Others indicated being uncertain as to how they were going to respond when challenged, and some reported nothing about these issues. The latter subjects tended to indicate, instead, that they focused on their sensations and imaginings and were not concerned with other issues. Subjects also differ in the elaborateness with which they describe their experiences. Some report a variety of sensations accompanying their responding (e.g., stiffness, numbness, tingling), while others report few if any such sensations.

In the present study, subjects were never asked if they had wondered about how they would respond. They were also never specifically asked to report sensations that they had experienced. Unsolicited reports of this kind may reflect differences in subjects' levels of absorption in the suggestion. Therefore, subjects were divided on the basis of their postsuggestion testimony into those who reported (1) unequivocally knowing they would bend their arm before being challenged, (2) being uncertain as to how they would respond, and (3) nothing about this aspect of their experience. Furthermore, the number of terms used by subjects to describe sensations associated with their arm (e.g., numb) were counted. It was predicted that these dimensions would be correlated with Cue level at which GDF was first reported, experienced involuntariness, and ratings of absorption in imaginings.

Method

Subjects

Twenty-four male and 48 female undergraduates at Carleton University (ages 18–24) volunteered to participate in a hypnosis experiment. Subjects received course credit for their participation. None had been previously hypnotized in our laboratory.

Procedure

Subjects were seen individually in a single 20-minute session. All subjects were initially seen by the same male experimenter (SMR). Immediately after being seated, subjects were informed that they would be hypnotized, administered a single standard suggestion, and subsequently questioned about their experiences. After being assured that no personal or embarrassing questions would be asked, they were asked to close their eyes and were administered a seven-minute hypnotic induction procedure via tape-recording. The voice on the tape was that of the experimenter. The hypnotic induction procedure was based on one frequently employed by Barber and consisted of interrelated suggestions that the subject was (1) becoming drowsy and sleepy, (2) entering hypnosis, and (3) able to respond easily to suggestion.[20]

Immediately following the hypnotic induction procedure, each subject was asked to hold his right arm straight out at shoulder height. He was then administered a 40-second arm-catalepsy suggestion taken verbatim from Spanos and McPeake.[13] The suggestion simply informed the subject repeatedly that he would be unable to bend his arm even when challenged to try to do so. Three seconds after presentation of the suggestion, the experimenter said "Try and bend your arm." After five more seconds the subject was informed that he could now easily bend his arm. Next, the subject was asked to open his eyes and complete a five-point Likert-type scale (taken verbatim from Spanos and McPeake, Note 1) that assessed the extent to which his arm-catalepsy was experienced as an involuntary occurrence. The alternatives on this scale ranged from "(a) I did not experience my arm being *unable* to bend. That is, I felt as though I could easily bend it." (scored 0), to "(e) I experienced my arm as *completely unable* to bend. That is, I did not feel as though I could bend it." (scored 4).

At this point subjects were randomly assigned to one of the four cells of a 2×2 factorial design (1 experimenter/2 experimenters $\times$ Oral presentation/ Written presentation) with the single restriction of an equal number of males (6) and females (12) assigned to each cell.

Experimental Treatments. For half the subjects, all postsuggestion inquiries were conducted by the initial experimenter. For the other hand, inquiries were conducted by a second experimenter. The first experimenter excused himself from the room. The second experimenter (SR) entered immediately and carried out the postsuggestion inquiries. The second experimenter was unaware of subjects' overt or subjective response to the suggestion.

Half the subjects assessed by each experimenter were orally asked a series of three standardized inquiries. These subjects also responded orally and had their answers tape-recorded. The remaining subjects were administered the same inquiries in writing. They wrote their answers to each inquiry, and had to complete their response to one inquiry before proceeding to the next.

Postsuggestion Inquiries and Scoring. After responding to the Experienced Involuntariness Scale, each subject was administered three standardized questions about his experiences. The first question asked him to give a complete description of everything he experienced from the time he was first told that his arm would be unable to bend until he was told that he could bend it easily (Low Cue inquiry). The second question reiterated the first, but added that the experimenter was interested in discovering everything that the subject had thought about, imagined, or pictured during the suggestion period (Medium Cue inquiry). The third question informed the subject that some people imagine various things related to their arm's being unable to bend. He was further informed that subjects sometimes imagine a cast on their arm, or imagine that the arm had been transformed into a solid piece of wood or metal. The subject was then asked if he had imagined anything related to his arm's being unable to bend. If he answered affirmatively, he was asked to give a complete description of what he imagined (High Cue inquiry).

Subjects' oral and written testimony was transcribed. It was scored for GDFr by an investigator (NPS) who remained blind to subjects' experimental treatment or response to suggestion. The level of inquiry at which subjects' first exhibited GDFr was also scored. GDFr to the Low Cue inquiry was scored 3; to the Medium Cue inquiry, 2; to the High Cue inquiry, 1. The absence of GDF was scored 0.

Subjects' testimony was also scored for reports of knowing that the arm would bend before being challenged to bend it. Reports in which the subject explicitly stated that he knew he could bend his arm were scored 0. Testimony indicating uncertainty as to whether the arm could bend was scored 1. Testimony in which this issue was simply not addressed was scored 2. Two judges independently rated subjects' testimony on this dimension. Interrater reliability was high ($r = .84$).

The number of sensations that each subject reported experiencing in his arm were also scored. Included as sensations were the terms solid, rigid, numb, tingling, painful, heavy, stiff, detached, light, and floating. The number of sensations were summed to yield a single score for each subject.

Immediately following the Low Cue inquiry, the subject was administered a five-point Likert-type scale (modified from Spanos [5]) which assesed the extent of his absorption in the arm-catalepsy suggestion. The alternatives on the scale ranged from (a) I was *completely* absorbed in thinking about and/or imagining that my arm was unable to bend (scored 4), to (e) I was *not at all* absorbed in thinking about and/or imagining that my arm was unable to bend (scored 0).

Finally, the first experimenter instructed each subject to "awaken" from hypnosis, answered any questions he had about the experiment or about hypnosis in general, asked him not to discuss the experiment with others, thanked him for his participation, and dismissed him.

RESULTS

Overall Analyses

Separate 2×2 factorial analyses of variance were computed on the five dependent variables: Experienced Involuntariness, Inquiry Level of First GDFr Absorption in the Suggestion, Expectancy of Arm Bending, and Number

TABLE 2

ANALYSES OF VARIANCE FOR THE FIVE DEPENDENT VARIABLES

Source	DF	F	F	F	F	F
Experimenter Number (A)	1	<1	<1	1.25	<1	<1
Mode of Testimony (B)	1	<1	<1	<1	<1	5.00*
A × B	1	<1	<1	<1	<1	<1
Error	68					

$p < .05$.

of Sensations. Since all subjects were administered and Experienced Involuntariness Scale by the same experimenter, the analysis of this variable merely served as a check on the randomization of subjects. As TABLE 2 indicates, no significant main effects or interactions emerged for this variable. This indicates that subjects in the four treatments reported equal levels of Experienced Involuntariness. TABLE 1 further indicates that all of the analyses yield only one significant effect. Subjects exposed to only the first experimenter reported a somewhat greater number of sensations in their arm ($X = 3.0$) than did subjects questioned by the second experimenter ($X = 1.8$).

Level of First Reported GDF, Experienced Involuntariness and Experimenter Effects

TABLE 1 indicates that the two experimenters did not differ in the overall amount of GDFr that they elicited. This does not, however, mean that they failed to differentially influence the point at which GDFr was first elicited. For instance, one experimenter could have elicited a good deal of GDFr on the first inquiry, but little on the remaining two. The other experimenter could have elicited no GDFr on the first inquiry but a moderate amount on one or both of the other two. In order to assess such a possibility, the inquiry level at which each experimenter first elicited GDF was computed. As TABLE 3 indicates, the inquiry levels at which the two experimenters first elicited GDFr do not differ significantly ($X^2 = < 1$, df 3).

The experimenter-bias hypothesis predicts that GDFr and Experienced Involuntariness will be correlated when these variables are assessed by the same experimenter, but uncorrelated when assessed by different experimenters. This pattern of results is possible despite the fact that the two experimenters elicited the same amounts of GDFr. The hypothesis was tested by computing the correlations between Inquiry Level of First GDFr and Experienced Involuntariness separately for the two experimenters. Both correlations differed significantly from zero (Experimenter 1, $r = .37$, $p < .05$; Experimenter 2, $r = .69$, $p < .01$). However, these two correlations did not differ significantly from one another ($z = 1.91$, $p > .05$).

TABLE 3

NUMBER AND PROPORTION OF SUBJECTS TESTED BY EACH
EXPERIMENTER SCORING AT EACH GDFr INQUIRY LEVEL *

| | GRFr Inquiry Level Score | | | |
	3	2	1	0
Experimenter 1	6 (.17)	8 (.22)	6 (.17)	16 (.44)
Experimenter 2	4 (.11)	8 (.22)	8 (.22)	16 (.44)

* GDFr exhibited on the first, second, or third inquiry was scored 3, 2, and 1, respectively. Absence of GDFr was scored 0. Numbers in parentheses are proportions for each row.

In order to illustrate more clearly the relationship between Level of First GDF and Experienced Involuntariness, subjects were divided into those who reported high levels of Experienced Involuntariness (scores of 4 and 3) and those who reported low levels of Involuntariness (scores of 1 and 0). Subjects who exhibited moderate levels of Involuntariness (scores of 2) were dropped from the analysis. High Involuntariness subjects showed GDFr to earlier inquiries than did low Involuntariness subjects (high Involuntariness; GDFr Level $X = 1.8$; low Involuntariness: GDFr Level $X = .6$; $t = 14.5$, $p < .001$). The relationship between First GDFr and Experienced Involuntariness is shown in TABLE 4. As this table indicates, 64% of the high Involuntariness subjects showed GDFr on either the first or second inquiry. On the other hand, only 18% of the low Involuntariness subjects showed GDFr on these inquiries. A Chi Square performed on these data indicated a significant association between level of first GDF and ratings of involuntariness ($X^2 = 15.35$, df 3, $p < .01$).

TABLE 4

NUMBER OF SUBJECTS SCORING AT EACH GDFR INQUIRY LEVEL WHO DEFINED
THEIR RESPONSE AS VOLUNTARY OR INVOLUNTARY *

Definition	GDFr Inquiry Level Score			
of Response	3	2	1	0
Voluntary	1 (.03)	6 (.15)	10 (.26)	22 (.56)
Involuntary	6 (.35)	5 (.29)	2 (.12)	4 (.24)

* Numbers in parentheses are proportions for each row.

Correlational Analyses

TABLE 5 shows the correlations among the five dependent variables collapsed across treatment conditions. Only two of the variables failed to correlate with one another; Expectancy of Arm Bending did not correlate with Number of Senations. A multiple regression analysis was carried out in order to assess the extent to which Experienced Involuntariness was predicted by the other four variables contained in TABLE 5. This analysis was significant ($R^2 = .45$, $F = 13.3$, $p < .001$), indicating that the four variables accounted for 45% of the variance in Experienced Involuntariness scores.

DISCUSSION

This study replicated previous findings which indicated that GDFr was related to subjects' tendency to define their overt response to suggestion as an involuntary occurrence.[5,8,12,13] Thirty-five percent of the subjects who experienced their response as highly involuntary showed GDFr to a very general inquiry that provided no cues concerning the types of experiences that the experimenter was interested in. On the other hand, only one subject (out of 39) who experienced his response as voluntary showed GDFr to this inquiry. Furthermore, the relationship between GDFr and experienced involuntariness was found when subjects' testimony was obtained by an experimenter who was

TABLE 5

CORRELATION MATRIX FOR THE FIVE DEPENDENT VARIABLES

	Experienced Involuntariness	GDF	Absorption	Expectancy
GDF	.52 **			
Absorption	.44 **	.31 **		
Expectancy	.46 **	.23 *	.26 *	
Adjectives	.23 *	.31 **	.27 *	.22

* <.05.
** <.01.

unaware of how they had responded to suggestion. GDFr was also unaffected by the mode through which subjects' testimony was obtained (oral vs. written). These results suggest that previous findings of a relationship between GDFr and response to suggestion were not simply experimenter-produced artifacts.

The fact that subjects reported more sensations in their arm, when questioned by the first experimenter, is open to several interpretations. It is unlikely that the experimenter was consciously or unconsciously biasing the subjects in this regard, simply because Number of Sensations was not a variable he was interested in assessing. He was not even informed that this aspect of subjects' experience was to be looked at until after the study was over. The result may simply indicate that subjects felt more comfortable and freer to respond with the first experimenter, since he had administered both the hypnotic induction procedure and the suggestion. At any rate, it should be kept in mind that this was the only significant finding to emerge from five analyses of variance and may therefore simply represent a chance finding.

The inquiry level at which subjects first showed GDFr, their experienced involuntariness, and the extent that they reported becoming absorbed in the suggestion, correlated with one another. One parsimonious interpretation of these interrelationships is that the point at which most hypnotic subjects first show GDFr is, at least in part, a function of the salience which that experience held for them. This interpretation obviously does not exclude the possibility that some subjects simply fabricated their reports in order to please the experimenter. Such an interpretation may, in fact, be applicable to some of the subjects who exhibited GDFr only after being given an explicit example of the phenomenon. It is difficult, however, to see how this interpretation could parsimoniously account for the results of subjects who exhibited GDFr to the more general inquiries.

The degree of rated absorption in the suggestion correlated both with subjects' expectancy of arm bending and with the number of sensations they reported in their arm. The latter two types of report were spontaneously offered by subjects, and the fact that they correlated with absorption helps to buttress the construct validity of that notion. These facts further indicate that attempts to quantify other unsolicited aspects of subjects' reported experiences may yield fruitful results.

REFERENCES

1. JANET, P. 1924. The Major Symptoms of Hysteria. Macmillan. New York, N.Y.
2. JANET, P. 1925. Psychological Healing. Vol. 1. Macmillan. New York, N.Y.
3. ARNOLD, M. B. 1946. On the mechanism of suggestion and hypnosis. J. Abnorm. Soc. Psychol. 41: 107–128.
4. PYLYSHYN, Z. W. 1973. What the mind's eye tells the mind's brain: A critique of mental imagery. Psychol. Bull. 80: 1–24.
5. SPANOS, N. P. 1973. Hypnosis: A Sociological and Phenomenological Perspective. Unpub. Doctoral Dissertation. Boston University. Boston, Mass.
6. SPANOS, N. P. 1971. Goal-directed fantasy and the performance of hypnotic test suggestions. Psychiat. 34: 86–96.
7. TELLEGEN, A. & G. ATKINSON. 1976. Complexity and measurement of hypnotic susceptibility: A comment on Coe and Sarbin's alternative interpretation. J. Pers. Soc. Psychol. 33: 142–148.

8. SPANOS, N. P., J. SPILLANE & J. D. MCPEAKE. 1976. Cognitive strategies and response to suggestion in hypnotic and task-motivated subjects. Amer. J. Clin. Hypn. **18:** 254–262.
9. SARBIN, R. R. & W. C. COE. 1972. Hypnotic Behavior: The Psychology of Influence Communication. Holt. New York, N.Y.
10. SHOR, R. E. 1970. The three factor theory of hypnosis as applied to the book reading fantasy and to the concept of suggestion. Internat. J. Clin. Exper. Hyp. **18:** 89–98.
11. SPANOS, N. P. & T. X. BARBER. 1974. Toward a convergence in hypnosis research Amer. Psychol. **29:** 500–511.
12. SPANOS, N. P. & T. X. BARBER. 1972. Cognitive activity during "hypnotic" suggestibility: Goal-directed fantasy and the experience of non-volition. J. Pers. **40:** 510–524.
13. SPANOS, N. P. & J. D. MCPEAKE. 1976. Cognitive strategies, reported goal-directed fantasy, and response to suggestion in hypnotic subjects. Carleton University. Ottawa, Ontario, Canada. (mimeo)
14. BUCKNER, L. G. & W. C. COE. In press. Imaginative skills, wording of suggestions and hypnotic susceptibility. Internat. J. Clin. Exper. Hypn.
15. COE, W. C., J. L. ALLEN, W. M. KRUG & A. G. WURZMAN. 1974. Goal-directed fantasy in hypnotic responsiveness: Skill, item wording, or both? Internat. J. Clin. Exper. Hypn. **22:** 157–166.
16. WEITZENHOFFER, A. M. & E. R. HILGARD. 1962. Stanford Hypnotic Susceptibility Scale, Form C. Consulting Psychologists Press. Palo Alto, Calif.
17. HILGARD, J. R. 1970. Personality and Hypnosis. University of Chicago Press. Chicago, Ill.
18. SPANOS, N. P. & J. D. MCPEAKE. 1974. Involvement in suggestion-related imaginings, experienced involuntariness, and credibility assigned to imaginings in hypnotic subjects. J. Abnorm. Psychol. **83:** 687–690.
19. ROSENTHAL, R. 1966. Experimenter Effects in Behavioral Research. Appleton-Century-Crofts. New York, N.Y.
20. BARBER, T. X. 1969. Hypnosis: A Scientific Approach. Van Nostrand Reinhold. New York, N.Y.

HYPNOSIS: AN INFORMATIONAL APPROACH *

Kenneth S. Bowers

Department of Psychology
University of Waterloo
Waterloo, Ontario, Canada N2L 3G1

It is an historical truism that hypnosis has generally been received with a certain amount of skepticism by the medical and scientific community—skepticism ranging from bemused tolerance to venomous opposition. An important reason for this skepticism might be phrased as follows: "How can mere words, uttered by a hypnotist to a patient, have such profound effects as its apologists claim? How can words minimize or eliminate pain, relieve or even cure various diseases, recover early memories, and so on?" The gap between the presumed cause (i.e., words) and the dramatic effects claimed for them is simply too large to be accommodated by many disinterested persons. A backdrop to skepticism of this sort is the notion that somehow, dramatic effects require correspondingly dramatic causes. This sort of thinking is surely one reason why Mesmer produced his theory of animal magnetism, which was as singular and striking in its own way as the mesmeric crises it purportedly explained.

The implicit assumption that large effects require great causes overlooks the role of receiver characteristics as an important variable in the understanding of hypnotic phenomena. The one fact that everyone working in the field of hypnosis agrees on is that there are important individual differences in hypnotic ability. In effect, these differences in hypnotizability can be conceptualized as differences in receiver characteristics that differentially amplify, distort, filter, and transduce information. It is largely these receiver characteristics of high-hypnotizable persons that account for most of the dramatic effects classically associated with hypnosis.

A considerable portion of this paper will establish, via a review of the literature, that persons high and low in hypnotizability do in fact process information differently, that these differences are very important vis-à-vis the hypnotic treatment of various disorders, and that the greater treatment success of hypnosis with high susceptibles is not a placebo effect, nor is it due solely to the undoubted ability of hypnosis to relax and emotionally stabilize them. The upshot of these findings will establish the plausibility of an informational view of hypnosis. This view holds that suggestions delivered to deeply hypnotized subjects (Ss) can be transduced into information that is somatically encodable, thereby producing a selective and specific impact on body function and structure.

SUSCEPTIBILITY DIFFERENCES IN INFORMATIONAL PROCESSING

The first set of studies I wish to discuss are those by Fred Evans and his associates.[23-26] These investigators have shown in several replicated studies that

* Partly supported by grants-in-aid-of-research from the Spencer Foundation of Chicago and the Banting Foundation of Toronto.

persons respond about 20% of the time to specific suggestions administered in alpha-free, Stage I sleep. Even more interesting for present purposes is this: the correlation between such sleep-administered suggestions and hypnotic susceptibility ranges as high as .64. In other words, high-susceptible Ss are responding in their sleep far more often than low susceptibles; the latter Ss, in fact, tend to awaken when presented with sleep suggestions. This finding with sleep suggestibility seems to indicate that high-susceptibles are more able than low-susceptibles to register and effectively process information at a level they do not consciously notice; [10, 11] or, to put it another way, highly susceptible Ss are more able to *dissociate* certain information from conscious awareness.[44, 45, 63] In his recent work, Hilgard [39, 41] has justifiably invoked such dissociative processing of information as one key feature of hypnotic phenomena.

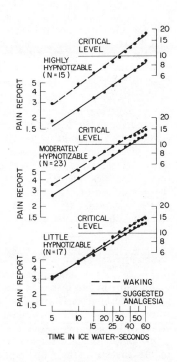

FIGURE 1. Cold pressor pain in normal waking and hypnotic analgesia for subjects differing in measured hypnotic susceptibility. The upper curve of each pair is normal waking pain, the lower following attempted hypnotic induction with analgesia suggestions. (By permission of Elsevier-North Holland Biomedical Press, Amsterdam, The Netherlands, publisher of Reference 40.)

Such dissociative abilities can have considerable practical significance. It has been demonstrated both clinically [17, 18] and experimentally [49] that surgical patients under general anesthesia can register the often ominous chatter of the attending surgical team. After the patient is awake, the emotionally painful but dissociated information can cause inexplicable distress. Whether such hazards are greatest with highly hypnotizable Ss has not yet been established, but it seems likely.

Quite another sort of observation, this one from work on the hypnotic control of pain, also suggests important differences in the receiver characteristics of subjects varying in hypnotic susceptibility. FIGURE 1 presents the data of interest, as graphically presented by Hilgard.[38, 40] High-, medium-, and low-hypnotizable persons are each seen twice, once under ordinary waking conditions, and then under hypnotic conditions in which suggestions for pain analgesia are given. Pain ratings are given on the ordinate, and the amount of time a person's hand and forearm is immersed in ice water is given on the absicssa, with the data plotted on log-log paper. Notice that the lines within each level of hypnotizability are more or less parallel, and that the upper dotted (waking condition) line is at about the same height for all levels of susceptibility. It is the lower line, representing the pain reports in the hypnotic analgesia condition, that shifts down, especially in the highly hypnotizable Ss. Indeed, it is in this condition only that Ss never reach a pain rating of 10, the so-called critical level at which Ss would prefer to terminate their participation in the experiment. As Hilgard notes:

> the general parallelism of the normal and reduced curves suggests that the pain reduction acts as if a filter were placed somewhere between the painful stimulation and the registration of pain, for the parallel lines mean that the reduction bears in each case a constant ratio to the original height of the pain at that time. (Ref. 38, p. 573)

Clearly, the receiver characteristics of high hypnotizables are especially effective at filtering and attenuating pain.

A lingering suspicion entertained by many people about hypnotic phenomena, such as suggested analgesia, is that they represent placebo effects. Several lines of inquiry testify against this interpretation. One study simply correlated placebo responsiveness and hypnotic suggestibility, and found essentially a zero relationship.[4] Jerome Frank,[28] reviewing evidence from his laboratory, concludes that "the extent of response to a placebo depends primarily on the interaction of the patient's state at a particular time with certain properties of the situation." (p. 147) By contrast, hypnotic suggestibility is a relatively enduring characteristic of a person,[10, 37] showing far more stability than placebo responsiveness.

The most vivid demonstration of the difference between placebo and hypnotic responsiveness, however, derives from the Hilgards' reanalysis (Ref. 42, p. 75) of data initially presented by McGlashan et al.[59] In this study 12 high- and 12 low-hypnotizable Ss were seen in an initial base-line condition, then in a hypnotic analgesia, and finally, in a placebo condition. During each of the three conditions, the dependent variable was the amount of time S could do work with his hand before the pain—caused by a blood pressure cuff on his arm—simply made it impossible for S to continue. FIGURE 2 shows the results of this investigation. Low-hypnotizable Ss showed a similarly small degree of improvement over base line in both the placebo and hypnotic analgesia conditions. This pattern of data suggests that whatever help the low-susceptibles achieve in the hypnotic analgesia condition is due primarily to placebo factors. It is quite otherwise for the high hypnotizable Ss, who show a rather dramatic increase in pain tolerance in the hypnotic analgesia condition, whereas they show a slightly reduced tolerance for pain in the placebo condition.

The data from this last study clearly indicates that under conditions of hypnotic analgesia, certain receiver characteristics of high-hypnotizable Ss somehow attenuate or filter pain, and in ways not attributable to placebo responsiveness. The exact mechanism by which this attenuation is accomplished is not clear, but there is no disputing the fact that hypnotic analgesia is effective, and the more so in Ss highly susceptible to hypnosis.

The Importance of Hypnotic Depth for Therapeutic Effectiveness

Although the dimension of hypnotic susceptibility clearly reflects important receiver characteristics, it seems to be generally accepted by many clinicians that *"there is no correlation between the depth of hypnosis obtainable in a patient and the therapeutic result."* (Ref. 31, p. 333) This characterization may be valid for many problems that a psychotherapist ordinarily sees in private practice. However, it seems far less true when hypnosis is employed in the treatment of various physical disorders. It seems clear, for example, that the hypnotic alleviation of clinical pain is often more successful in persons of high hypnotic ability.[42] Butler,[15] for example, presented 12 cases suffering from terminal cancer and commented as follows:

> Hypnotic techniques as used in this study did reduce pain, allay anxiety, and aid in organ function; but the results were proportional to the depth, and only five of these selected 12 cases, who were somnambulistic, can be said to be unequivocally benefited by this therapy. (p. 12)

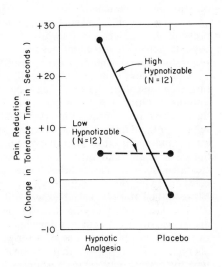

Figure 2. Differential effect of hypnotic analgesia and placebo on subjects susceptible and not susceptible to hypnosis. High values of tolerance time refer to successful pain reduction. (By permission of William Kaufmann, 1 First Street, Los Altos, Calif., 94022, publisher of Reference 42.)

Even apart from the pain literature, one cannot help being struck by various authors' repeated referrals to the importance of trance depth in the successful hypnotic treatment of various psychosomatic disorders. Seldom are these avowals supported by hard data, but I would like to mention three studies in which there is at least some systematic evidence in favor of this claim.

Asher[1] saw 33 successive patients who were suffering from multiple warts. Each patient was seen for ten weeks or less, and under hypnosis, was given suggestions for the warts to go away. Fifteen of the 33 patients were completely cured, but as Table 1 shows, the cure rate is by far the highest among persons capable of deep hypnosis. Among the eight unhypnotizable Ss there were no remissions at all. Incidentally, such a clear association of treatment effectiveness with hypnotic ability is one sort of evidence that spontaneous remission of warts is an unlikely explanation for the success rate obtained.

Another study, by Collison,[20] looks at the effectiveness of hypnosis in the

TABLE 1

RELATIONSHIP BETWEEN HYPNOTIC DEPTH AND SUCCESSFUL REMOVAL OF WARTS
BY SUGGESTION [1] *

Hypnotic State	Improvement		
	Cured	Improved	No Change
Deep	11	4	2
Light	4	0	4
Unhypnotized	0	0	8

* $N=33$; $\chi^2=18.95$; d.f.$=4$; $p \leq .001$.

treatment of asthma. In a study of patients seen over a ten-year period, Collison provided hypnotherapy that involved (1) ego-enhancing suggestions, (2) discussion under hypnosis of patients' problem areas, and (3) emotional abreaction of repressed experiences. Of the 121 patients in this sample, 25 showed "excellent results," 40 showed "good results," and 56 Ss showed poor or no improvement. The criteria for these ratings was clearly specified. For example, patients achieving excellent results had complete remission of asthma, with respiratory function studies giving results within normal limits.

Collison also allocated his patients into three groups according to "the depth of trance typically achieved," i.e., light, medium, or deep. When the data is cast into the resulting 3×3 configuration, TABLE 2 is the result. Again, it is clearly the case that for asthma sufferers, the effectiveness of hypnotic therapy is closely related to the depth of trance S can achieve. There are many other quite interesting findings in this exemplary clinical study that we must simply ignore. Suffice it to say that other factors, especially age, correlated (inversely) with treatment success. Nevertheless, when age was partialled out of the relationship between hypnotic susceptibility and treatment effectiveness, the correlation between the latter two variables was still a quite respectable .41.

The last study showing a fairly clear relationship between hypnotic depth and successful treatment is somewhat different in character from the preceding two. Stephen Black,[6] in one of a series of provocative articles on hypnosis and allergic reactions, showed that certain selected Ss could inhibit their immediate-type hypersensitivity (skin) responses to various allergens as a result of receiv-

TABLE 2

RELATIONSHIP BETWEEN HYPNOTIC DEPTH AND SUCCESSFUL TREATMENT
OF ASTHMA BY SUGGESTION [20] *

Hypnotic State	Improvement		
	Cured	Improved	No Change
Deep	19	17	7
Light	6	21	20
Unhypnotized	0	2	29

* $N=121$; $\chi^8=51.91$; d.f.$=4$; $p \leq .001$.

ing appropriate direct suggestions under hypnosis. Twelve Ss selected for their allergic and hypnotic responsiveness were given skin tests, once in a waking condition, and once after being hypnotized with direct suggestions to inhibit their typical allergic responses. "Of the eight subjects showing evidence of inhibition six were deep-trance subjects and two were medium-trance subjects. . . . Of the four subjects who failed to show evidence of inhibition three were medium-trance subjects and one was a deep-trance subject." (p. 926) In another paper by Black,[7] a similar relationship was found between hypnotic depth and inhibited skin responses, but the relationship was less clear in a third paper.[9] All these papers and a variety of others by this British investigator are engagingly reviewed in Black.[8]

Mason [58] sharply criticized Black's [6] study, especially for his use of a somewhat problematic criterion of hypnotic depth. Actually, all the studies cited in this section can be faulted on somewhat similar grounds: either the criterion for trance depth is not specified clearly, or the criterion that is specified leaves something to be desired. Nevertheless, trance depth was never inferred from treatment effectiveness, but was established independently on clinical grounds, an assessment technique that often correlates with standardized scales of hypnotic ability (e.g., Ref. 68). Thus, despite the somewhat inexplicit standards of hypnotic depth employed by these studies, a strong relationship seems indicated between depth of hypnosis on one hand and the efficacy of hypnotic treatment on the other.

GENERAL AND SPECIFIC FACTORS IN HYPNOTIC TREATMENT

It is often supposed that the effects of hypnosis are essentially due to profound relaxation that can be achieved in deep hypnosis. Indeed, there is every reason to believe that teaching a person deep-relaxation techniques, by whatever means, can have salutory consequences. For example, in a fascinating and unusual study, Lucas and his associates [51-53] employed hypnotic techniques on hemophiliacs who were having sundry teeth extracted. Although hypnotic suggestions for anesthesia were administered, "a completely relaxed individual [was] . . . the main reason for using hypnosis," (Ref. 53, p. 471) since hemostasis is facilitated by a confident, emotionally stable individual. Together with some specialized surgical techniques employed by these investigators, such hypnotic relaxation permitted the extraction of 110 teeth from 24 hemophiliacs without the need of a single transfusion, an outcome highly discrepant from that of conventional dental methods employed with patients of this sort.

Although the relaxing effects of hypnosis are doubtlessly important for many of its therapeutic successes, other investigations show that more specific effects can be induced by hypnotic suggestion. This specificity is most easily seen when such suggestions have a simultaneous but differential impact on different parts of the body. Perhaps the best known example of such an effect involves the ability of highly selected, well-trained hypnotic subjects to increase the temperature of one hand, while reducing the temperature in the other,[54, 64] and to do so in response to specific hypnotic suggestions. Not everyone in these experiments was successful in demonstrating this effect, but one S demonstrated a maximum difference in hand temperature of $9.2°$ C, a very considerable temperature differential indeed.

This S was later investigated more closely for the study of just how this feat was accomplished. "When the subject decreased temperature in the monitored hand, blood flow was almost completely cut off except during the suppressed arterial pulse. When the subject increased temperature in the hand, an accelerated pulse and blood flow was detected." (Ref. 64, p. 168) I have elsewhere reviewed the clinical potential of such vascular control.[10] What is important for present purposes is that achieving temperature differentials in the two hands simultaneously is not easily explained by generalized autonomic and/or emotional factors; something much more specific and selective seems to obtain.

Some indication of this selectivity of suggested effects is evident in an old report of Delboeuf, as reported by Bramwell (Ref. 13, p. 84). After obtaining the woman's consent for this rather arduous experiment, Delboeuf hypnotized the subject and suggested that her right hand would be insensible to pain. The normal and the anesthetized arms were then each "burnt with a red-hot bar of iron, 8 millimeters in diameter, the extent and duration of its application being identical on both." The burns were bandaged and examined the next day. The burn on the normally sensitive hand had a wound three centimeters in diameter with an outer circle of inflamed blisters; on the anesthetized hand there was only a scab the exact size of the iron, without inflammation or redness.

A modern experiment [16] also demonstrated that hypnotic suggestions selectively modified the magnitude of vascular response and the degree of tissue damage in the skin following noxious stimulation. The investigators demonstrated this selectivity by inducing "a state of moderate to deep hypnosis" in the 13 adult Ss they employed, and by giving suggestions for one arm to be either normal or anesthetic, while suggesting that the other arm was "painful, burning, damaged, and exceedingly sensitive, i.e., 'vulnerable'." (p. 121) Both arms were then burned by a standard intense-light source. The inflammatory reaction and tissue damage that ensued was then variously determined over a considerable period of time. In 20 of 27 such experiments, inflammation of the burn on the anesthetized arm was less than it was on the vulnerable arm. In one S, the investigators went another step and perfused the tissues around the burn area in both the anesthetized and vulnerable arm. A powerful vasodilator was far more evident in the perfusate extracted from the flare zone of the vulnerable arm than from a corresponding area on the anesthetized arm. In addition, the skin temperature and pulse amplitude was much lower in the anesthetized than in the vulnerable arm. What is especially interesting from our current perspective is that within a particular S, the underreactivity of the burn zone on the anesthetized arm was contemporaneous with the overreactivity of the burn zone of the vulnerable arm. Consequently, the suggestions were highly selective and local in their effects, which are therefore not easily attributed to some generalized alteration in autonomic arousal.

In a very brief comment on a procedure not employing a burn stimulus, Mason [57] reports that he hypnotically and selectively inhibited the reaction of a tuberculin skin test in one arm of a Mantoux-positive patient, while the other arm showed a typical allergic response. Some weeks later, he performed the same test on the same subject, but reversed the arms displaying the allergic and the inhibited reaction. Again, on both trials, the disparate results in the two arms were achieved simultaneously, which argues against some generalized bodily response as mediating the effect of the hypnotic suggestion.

There is additional evidence for selective effects of hypnotic suggestions in the clinical literature. Perhaps the most cited study of this sort is the one reported by Sinclair-Gieben and Chalmers.[72] These investigators gave 14 Ss hypnotic suggestions to the effect that warts on one side of the body would disappear. Of the ten subjects judged to be adequately hypnotized, nine were either completely free of warts or almost so between five weeks and three months after treatment began. However, the cure was limited to the treated side of the body; there was virtually no improvement on the untreated half of the body. It is true that attempts to replicate this study have been less success-ful.[74, 75] However, it seems more likely that these replicative efforts somehow failed to mobilize important variables in the healing process than to assume that the initial one-sided cure of warts was fortuitous.

Moreover, there is evidence of a related kind that strongly implies the selec-tivity of hypnotic suggestions. In a classic study published in 1952, Mason[55] reported considerable success in the hypnotic treatment of a sixteen-year-old boy suffering from congenital ichthyosiform erythroderma. This hereditary problem, commonly called fishskin disease, was extensively distributed on the patient's body. The skin was covered with papillae varying in size from two to six millimeters above the skin's surface—and the skin between was black, horny, and fissured. The skin was very inelastic, with attempts to bend it resulting in cracks that would ooze blood-stained serum. The patient's schooling was in-terrupted because the other pupils and teachers objected to his smell.

Attempts to transplant normal skin from the patient's chest to affected areas resulted in the graft's becoming indistinguishable from its papilliferous sur-round. When hypnotic treatment was begun, ameliorative suggestions were limited to the patient's left arm. "About five days later the horny layer softened, became friable, and fell off. The skin underneath was slightly erythematous, but normal in texture and color. . . . At the end of 10 days the arm was com-pletely clear from shoulder to wrist." (Ref. 55, p. 422) The right arm was successfully treated in turn, and then finally, the legs and trunk. In other words, healing of a particular body area did not occur until its improvement had been specifically suggested.

In a later report, Mason[56] presented the photographs in FIGURE 3 to show the patient's skin condition before treatment and four years after treatment termination. As can be seen, the improvement was considerable. Indeed, the patient's skin had continued to improve over the interim period with no further treatment of any sort.

Although this first case study by Mason is by far the most carefully executed and reported, I have found four more reports [5, 46, 66, 78] of at least partial success in the hypnotic treatment of seven additional cases of ichthyosis. In addition, a related congenital skin disorder (*Pachyonicia congenita*) was considerably improved by hypnotic suggestions.[60] In one of these case reports,[78] the improve-ment of the skin progressed in a manner that corresponded at least roughly with suggestions for a particular part of the body to heal. (Evidently, none of the other investigators utilized this staged approach to healing.)

The fact that successful hypnotic treatment of a congenital skin disorder can proceed in a somewhat predictably piecemeal fashion argues against a generalized reduction in bodily stress as a likely explanation of improvement. On the basis of his treatment of two ichthyosiform patients, Kidd[46] came to much the same conclusion on somewhat different grounds. He maintained that "emotionally stable [ichthyosis] patients have as good an outcome as the emo-tionally unstable, [so] it seems that emotional factors are not a primary influ-ence in determining outcome of treatment by hypnosis." (p. 104) Rather, im-provements of congenital skin disorders by hypnotic suggestion imply "the

influence of a psychological process acting directly on local tissue metabolism."
(Ref. 78, p. 742)

AN INFORMATIONAL INTERPRETATION OF HYPNOSIS

When a psychological treatment clearly and positively affects a physical
disorder, it is often assumed that the extent of symptom remission represents
the degree to which psychic factors were responsible for the disorder in the

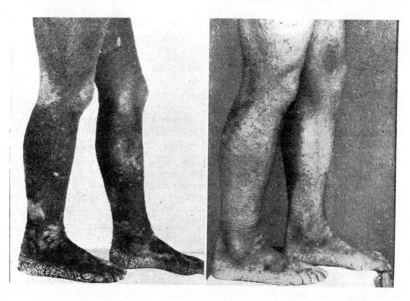

FIGURE 3. Patient before (left) and four years after hypnotic treatment for congenital ichthyosiform erthyroderma. (By permission of the British Medical Journal,
London, England, publisher of Reference 55.)

first place. For example, in summarizing his own and others' treatment of
ichthyosis and related disorders by hypnosis, Mason[57] argued as follows:

> if a psychogenic process like hypnosis affects a symptom complex, then it
> is psychogenic elements of this complex which are being affected. One must
> therefore infer that as certain allergic symptoms are affected by hypnosis,
> psychogenic factors have played a part in the production of those symptoms.
> (p. 337)

However much this point of view implicitly or explicitly dominates medical
thinking, I submit that it is very misleading. In the first place, it is simply
incorrect to infer the etiology of a disorder from remedies that successfully
combat it: headaches are not caused by the lack of aspirin. More importantly,

the tendency to split etiological factors of disease into either psychic or somatic components, though heuristic for many purposes, nevertheless perpetuates, at least implicitly, a mind-body dualism that has defied rational solution for centuries. Perhaps what we need is a new formulation of this ancient problem, one that does not presuppose a formidable gap between the separate "realities" of mind and body.

One way of reformulating the question involves the concept of information. The entire human body can be viewed as an interlocking network of informational systems—genetic, immunological, hormonal, and so on.[8] These systems each have their own codes, and the transmission of information between systems requires some sort of transducer that allows the code of one system, genetic, say, to be translated into the code of another system—for example, immunological.

Now, the mind, with its capacity for symbolizing in linguistic and extra-linguistic forms, can also be regarded as a means for coding, processing and transmitting information both intra- and interpersonally. If information processing and transmission is common to both psyche and soma, the mind-body problem might be reformulated as follows: How is information, received and processed at a semantic level, transduced into information that can be received and processed at a somatic level, and vice versa? That sounds like a question that can be more sensibly addressed than the one it is meant to replace. And some knowledgable people are beginning to ask it. For example, in a discussion section of the New York Academy of Science's Second Conference on Psychophysiological Aspects of Cancer, Jonas Salk commented on a stimulating paper by Shands[67] as follows: "Human language is a specialized form of communication. You then jumped to the molecular level, and I was glad you did that, because there are parallels in that both express forms of communication. The code needs to be translated. . . ." (Ref. 65, p. 588)

Unfortunately, we are a long way from being able to understand the complex mechanisms that help to transduce information from a semantic to a somatic level, but some such mechanisms surely exist, since, as we have seen, the selective and specific impact of suggestion on body structure and functioning seems very well supported indeed. And I would like to suggest that the capacity for deep hypnosis is an important variable in this transduction process. We have already shown that the healing potential of suggestions seems to be maximized in persons capable of deep hypnosis, and it is helpful to examine briefly why this might be so.

Good hypnotic Ss seem to be very talented in achieving what Deikman[22] has termed a *receptive* mode of attention. Basically, this attentional mode has a suspended, effortless quality, in which the S is not trying to *do* anything except to receive sensory-perceptual information without critically analyzing it. Freud, although puzzled by hypnosis, recognized the importance of this suspended state of mind for a precursor of the free association technique he substituted for it. He comments as follows:

I am rather of opinion that the advantage of the procedure lies in the fact that by means of it I dissociate the patient's attention from his conscious searching and reflecting—from everything, in short, on which he can employ his will—in the same sort of way in which this is effected by staring into a crystal ball, and so on. (Ref. 30, p. 355)

Russian investigators have had similar insights. Platanov,[62] for example, remarks:

> Verbal influence perceived critically *cannot be suggested*, because it is perceived consciously, actively. On the other hand, verbal influence perceived passively, without criticism, may easily become *suggested*, even though it may contradict past experience and be severed from present reality. (p. 34)

Research by Van Nuys [77] certainly confirms that high susceptibles are better than their low-susceptible counterparts at receptively and uncritically attending to sensory information without distraction or interruption. And my own research [12] indicates that high hypnotizables in receipt of pertinent posthypnotic suggestions subsequently process some forms of information more passively, automatically, and efficiently than they do under normal waking conditions. Somehow, information is simply more direct and immediate in its impact when a person's critical faculties are suspended, an insight by no means novel.[44, 69] The quality of receptive attention or "suspended absorption," vis-à-vis intra- and interpersonal communications seems to characterize deep hypnosis, and is arguably an initial step in the transduction of semantic information into a form that is somatically encodable. Unfortunately, I am not at this time able to trace the transduction process any deeper into the organism. There is, however, growing reason to believe that "hypnotic susceptibility and its correlates are deeply embedded in a person's biological organization." (Ref. 10, p. 128)

HYPNOSIS AND CANCER

The informational view of hypnosis suggests certain treatment possibilities that might otherwise seem implausible. If it is true that semantically received information can be somatically encoded, especially under conditions of deep hypnosis, the possibility exists that some forms of cancer might be helped by hypnotic techniques.[19] Because the previous sentence will undoubtedly cause some eyebrows to rise, let me juxtapose it with the following assertion: To my knowledge, there is not a scintilla of direct scientific evidence that hypnosis can reverse the course of cancer. Moreover, although there are many reports in the literature in which hypnosis successfully alleviated the *pain* of cancer,[14, 15, 21, 61] there are virtually no claims that the malignancy itself remitted. In fact, death is the almost universal outcome of even extraordinarily successful use of hypnosis as an analgesic for cancer patients. A search of the literature, by no means exhaustive, unearthed only one case in which an apparently permanent remission of cancer at least temporally coincided with the use of hypnosis (Ref. 47, p. 247)

Given this rather bleak evidential state of affairs, why even articulate the controversial proposition that hypnosis might be helpful in at least some forms of cancer? Basically, the reason for doing so derives from several considerations that indirectly suggest the possibility. In the first place, there is a plethora of literature [e.g. 2, 3, 48, 73, 76] that strongly implies a psychosomatic aspect to cancer. For example, the probability of developing cancer increases considerably after a significant interpersonal loss, a stressful time when there is a lowered resistance to disease generally. The possibility of mobilizing and strengthening the cancer patient's internal resources via hypnotic techniques should therefore not be discounted. For example, one of Collison's [20] strategies in the treatment of asthmatics by hypnosis was to utilize ego-strengthening procedures and suggestions originally employed by Hartland.[34, 35]

Another line of indirect evidence derives from the well-known fact that spontaneous remissions of cancer do take place, although such occurrences are rare. Everson and Cole[27] presented 182 documented cases of such remissions that they were able to glean from the medical literature published since 1900. The existence of such remissions was, until recently, the best available evidence that immunological considerations played an important role in cancer.[32] In effect, it was argued that belated immune reactions to the cancer caused its remission. This explanation of spontaneous remission is consistent with the fact that road-accident victims evidently have a much higher incidence of (previously undetected) cancer than exists in the population at large. The implication of this finding is that the immune system effectively prevents the vast majority of new malignancies from becoming clinically established.[50] The details of the immunological surveillance system that blocks or even reverses the growth of cancer is beyond the scope of this paper. What is interesting is that immunological factors causing certain *allergic* responses are "amenable to psychological control [via hypnosis] even under the most stringent experimental controls." (Ref. 8, p. 243) So the principle of psychological control over immunological responses seems established. There are, of course, important differences in inhibiting an allergic reaction produced by one antibody,[33] and enhancing the effectiveness of yet another antibody to destroy malignant cells. The apparent effectiveness of hypnosis in the treatment of warts does suggest, however, that immunological efficiency vis-à-vis benign, virally induced tumors can be psychologically enhanced.

The last sort of indirect evidence regarding the possible relevance of hypnosis to cancer involves sundry claims made regarding the nonmedical healing of various diseases, including cancer. It is, of course, important to view such assertions with extreme caution, since they are often exaggerated, virtually never flow from a critical examination of available evidence, and have little regard for the incidence of failure. It is unwise, however, to dismiss all such claims as fallacious simply because the advocates themselves are frequently incautious. Recall, for example, that unsophisticated "primitives" discovered the cure for malaria; medical science simply isolated quinine from the bark of the cinchona tree.

Consider, then, the recent claims for a psychological approach to the treatment of cancer proffered by a radiologist, Carl Simonton, and his wife, Stephanie.[70, 71] Although providing their patients with conventional medical treatment for cancer, they also invite patients to participate in a program of psychotherapy aimed at ameliorating their malignant status. Part of the therapeutic procedure involves exploration of a patient's emotional problems, but there is in addition strong emphasis on getting the patient to relax, to meditate, and to visualize the tumor being defeated by the conventional treatment and by the body's natural defenses. Patients are instructed to engage in this meditative visualization three times a day.

The Simontons claim that a very high percentage of patients who follow this unconventional treatment regimen undergo remission, and some of the anecdotally presented case studies are indeed quite dramatic. So were the initial results of Arden Hedge,[36] who employed various psychological techniques, including hypnosis, to help treat cancer patients. Nevertheless, within a year's time, virtually all Hedge's patients had succumbed to the disease. Thus, long term follow-up data by the Simontons seems absolutely necessary before their claims of success can be taken too seriously. Even their short-term successes are difficult to appraise, since (1) the patients received conventional medical treatment as well as meditative visualization, and (2) the patients participating in the latter procedure were highly self-selected. Indeed, up to 90% of the Simontons' patients refuse to have anything to do with the psychological aspect of the treatment, or are simply not diligent in the practice of it. There are undoubtedly defensive reasons for this state of affairs, since the Simontons apparently oblige their cancer patients to assume responsibility for becoming ill in the first place, and do so in a manner that almost guarantees adding insult (in the form of guilt) to injury.

But there may be quite another reason for the high holdout rate. The Simontons do not specifically invoke hypnosis in their work, but the imagery procedures they do use closely resemble those frequently employed by hypnotherapists for other physical disorders. My feeling is that a high percentage of cancer patients who *do* cooperate in this unorthodox venture are also hypnotically talented and find such a procedure psychologically congenial. Conversely, I would guess that the holdouts are relatively less hypnotizable and find the process of meditative visualization difficult. In other words, the 10% of patients who involve themselves in this visual-meditative approach to the treatment of cancer may be a subset of the population who are most hypnotizable. This is only a hunch, of course, but one that is coherent with everything we know about the imaginative abilities of high hypnotizable persons.[43]

At the very least, the possibility that some cancer victims can be helped by hypnotic and hypnotic-like techniques seems a hypothesis worth exploring systematically. Even if hypnotic procedures proved effective in only a very small percentage of (high-hypnotizable?) cancer patients, it would be reason enough to include such a treatment strategy as one line of attack on this dread disease. Moreover, even such limited success in practical terms would have profound implications for the view that semantic information can somehow be transduced and somatically encoded.

It must be admitted that scientifically proving the case for the effectiveness of hypnosis as a treatment for cancer would be a logistic nightmare, involving subject selection with respect to both hypnotizability and type of cancer, random allocation of Ss to treatment and nontreatment conditions, and following up the patients for an extended period of time—say, five years. As always, there is a huge gap between stating the hypothesis and establishing its warrant. Even if the difficulties were met head-on and the project were seen through to its conclusion, Jerome Frank's [29] assessment of the role of psychotherapy in medical disorders will doubtless still stand:

> by and large psychotherapy will probably prove to be an adjunct to conventional medical and surgical treatments for such illnesses, rather than a major treatment method. (p. 200)

Such a judicious appraisal from one of the world's foremost authorities on psychotherapy should be etched in the mind of anyone who boldly offers the hope of relief from physical disorders by any psychological means whatsoever—including hypnosis.

REFERENCES

1. ASHER, R. 1956. Respectable hypnosis. Br. Med. J. Feb. **11:** 309–313.
2. BAHNSON, C. B., Ed. 1969. Second Conf. Psychophysiological Aspects of Cancer. Ann. N.Y. Acad. Sci. **164**(2): 307–634.
3. BAHNSON, C. B. & D. M. KISSEN, Eds. 1966. Psychophysiological Aspects of Cancer. Ann. N.Y. Acad. Sci. **125:** 773–1055.
4. BENTLER, P. M., J. W. O'HARA & L. KRASNER. 1963. Hypnosis and placebo. Psychol. Rep. **12:** 153–154.
5. BETHUNE, H. C. & C. B. KIDD. 1961. Psychophysiological mechanisms in skin diseases. Lancet **11:** 1419–1422.
6. BLACK, S. 1963. Inhibition of immediate-type hypersensitivity response by direct suggestion of hypnosis. Br. Med. J. April 6 : 925–929.
7. BLACK, S. 1963. Shift in dose-response curve of Prausnitz-Kustner reaction by direct suggestion under hypnosis. Br. Med. J. April 13 : 990–992.
8. BLACK, S. 1969. Mind and Body. William Kimber. London, England.
9. BLACK, S., J. H. HUMPHREY & J. S. F. NIVEN. 1963. Inhibition of Mantoux reaction by direct suggestion under hypnosis. Br. Med. J. June 22 : 1649–1652.
10. BOWERS, K. S. 1976. Hypnosis for the Seriously Curious. Brooks-Cole. Monterey, Calif.
11. BOWERS, K. S. 1976. Listening with the third ear: On paying inattention effectively. Paper delivered 7th Int. Congr. Hypnosis and Psychosomatic Medicine. Philadelphia, Pa. July 2.
12. BOWERS, K. S. & H. A. BRENNEMAN. 1976. Listen, hear. Posthypnotic responsiveness to attended and unattended auditory information. Paper presented Mtg. Soc. Clinical and Experimental Hypnosis. Philadelphia, Pa. June 30.
13. BRAMWELL, J. M. 1930. Hypnotism: Its History, Practice and Theory. 3rd edit. J. B. Lippincott. Philadelphia, Pa.
14. BUTLER, B. 1955. The use of hypnosis in the care of the cancer patient. Part 2. Br. J. Med. Hypnotism **6:** 2–12.
15. BUTLER, B. 1955. The use of hypnosis in the care of the cancer patient. Part 3. Br. J. Med. Hypnosis **6:** 9–17.
16. CHAPMAN, L. F., H. GOODELL & H. G. WOLFF. 1959. Augmentation of the inflammatory reaction by activity of the central nervous system. Arch. Neurol. **1:** 113–128.
17. CHEEK, D. E. 1959. Unconscious perception of meaningful sounds during surgical anesthesia as revealed under hypnosis. Am. J. Clin. Hypn. **1:** 101–113.
18. CHEEK, D. B. 1966. The meaning of continued hearing sense under general hemoanesthesia: A progress report and report of a case. Am. J. Clin. Hypn. **8:** 275–280.
19. CLAWSON, T. A. & R. H. SWADE. 1975. The hypnotic control of blood flow and pain: The cure of warts and the potential use of hypnosis in the treatment of cancer. Am. J. Clin. Hypn. **17:** 160–169.
20. COLLISON, D. R. 1975. Which asthmatic patients should be treated by hypnotherapy? Med. J. Australia **1:** 776–781.
21. CRASILNECK, H. B. & J. A. HALL. 1975. Clinical Hypnosis: Principles and Applications. Grune & Stratton. New York, N.Y.
22. DEIKMAN, A. J. 1971. Bimodal consciousness. Arch. Gen. Psychiat. **25:** 481–489.
23. EVANS, F. J. 1972. Hypnosis and sleep: Techniques for exploring cognitive activity during sleep. In Hypnosis: Research Developments and Perspectives. E. Fromm & R. E. Shor, Eds. : 48–83. Aldine-Atherton. Chicago, Ill.
24. EVANS, F. J., L. A. GUSTAFSON, D. N. O'CONNELL, M. T. ORNE & R. E. SHOR. 1966. Response during sleep with intervening waking amnesia. Science **152:** 666–667.

25. EVANS, F. J., L. A. GUSTAFSON, D. N. O'CONNELL, M. T. ORNE & R. E. SHOR. 1969. Sleep induced behavioral response. J. Nerv. Ment. Dis. **148:** 467–476.
26. EVANS, F. J., L. A. GUSTAFSON, D. N. O'CONNELL, M. T. ORNE & R. E. SHOR. 1970. Verbally induced behavioral responses during sleep. J. Nerv. Ment. Dis. **150:** 171–187.
27. EVERSON, T. C. & W. H. COLE. 1966. Spontaneous Regression of Cancer. Saunders. Philadelphia, Pa.
28. FRANK, J. D. 1973. Persuasion and Healing: A Comparative Study of Psychotherapy. Johns Hopkins Univ. Press. Baltimore, Md.
29. FRANK, J. D. 1975. Psychotherapy of bodily diseases: An overview. Psychother. Psychosom. **26:** 192–202.
30. FREUD, S. & J. BREUER. 1974. Originally published in English in 1955. Studies on Hysteria. Pelican. Harmondsworth, England.
31. GILL, M. M. & M. BRENMAN. 1959. Hypnosis and Related States: Psychoanalytic Studies in Regression. International Universities Press. New York, N.Y.
32. GOODFIELD, J. 1975. The Siege of Cancer. Dell. New York, N.Y.
33. HAMBURGER, R. N. 1976. Allergy and the immune system. Am. Scientist **64:** 157–164.
34. HARTLAND, J. 1965. The value of "ego-strengthening" procedures prior to direct symptom removal under hypnosis. Am. J. Clin. Hypn. **8:** 89–93.
35. HARTLAND, J. 1971. Further observations on the use of "ego-strengthening" techniques. Am. J. Clin. Hypn. **14:** 1–8.
36. HEDGE, A R. 1960. Hypnosis in cancer. Br. J. Med. Hypn. **12:** 2–5.
37. HILGARD, E. R. 1965. Hypnotic Susceptibility. Harcourt, Brace & World. New York, N.Y.
38. HILGARD, E. R. 1971. Hypnotic phenomena: The struggle for scientific acceptance. Am. Scientist **59:** 567–577.
39. HILGARD, E. R. 1973. A neo-dissociation interpretation of pain reduction in hypnosis. Psychol. Rev. **80:** 396–411.
40. HILGARD, E. R. 1975. The alleviation of pain by hypnosis. Pain **1:** 213–231.
41. HILGARD, E. R. 1976. Neodissociation theory of multiple cognitive control. *In* Consciousness and Self-Regulation. G. E. Schwartz & D. Shapiro, Eds. Vol. I. Plenum Press. New York, N.Y.
42. HILGARD, E. R. & J. R. HILGARD. 1975. Hypnosis in the Relief of Pain. William Kaufmann. Los Altos, Calif.
43. HILGARD, J. R. 1970. Personality and Hypnosis: A Study of Imaginative Involvement. Univ. Chicago Press. Chicago, Ill.
44. JANET, P. 1901. Mental State of Hystericals. G. P. Putnam's Sons. New York, N.Y.
45. JANET, P. 1965. Second edition originally published in 1929. Major Symptoms of Hysteria. Hafner. New York, N.Y.
46. KIDD, C. B. 1966. Congenital ichthyosiform erythroderma treated by hypnosis. Br. J. Dermatol. **78:** 101–105.
47. KROGER, W. S. 1963. Clinical and Experimental Hypnosis. Lippincott. Philadelphia, Pa.
48. LESHAN, L. 1959. Psychological states as factors in the development of malignant disease: A critical review. J. Nat. Cancer Inst. **22:** 1–18.
49. LEVINSON, B. W. 1967. States of awareness during general anesthesia. *In* Hypnosis and Psychosomatic Medicine. J. Lassner, Ed. : 200–207. Springer-Verlag. New York, N.Y.
50. LEWIN, R. 1974. In Defense of the Body. Anchor Press/Doubleday. New York, N.Y.
51. LUCAS, O. N. 1965. Dental extractions in the hemophiliac: Control of the emotional factors by hypnosis. Am. J. Clin. Hypn. **7:** 301–307.
52. LUCAS, O. N., A. FINKELMAN & L. M. TOCANTINS. 1962. Management of tooth extractions in hemophiliacs by the combined use of hypnotic suggestion, protective splints and packing of sockets. J. Oral Surg. **20:** 487–500.

53. LUCAS, O. N. & L. M. TOCANTINS. 1964. Problems in hemostasis in hemophilic patients undergoing dental extractions. Ann. N.Y. Acad. Sci. **115**(1): 470–480.
54. MASLACH, C., G. MARSHALL & P. H. ZIMBARDO. 1972. Hypnotic control of peripheral skin temperature: A case report. Psychophysiology **9**: 600–605.
55. MASON, A. A. 1952. A case of congenital icthyosiform erythroderma of Brocq treated by hypnosis. Br. Med. J. Aug. 23 : 422–423.
56. MASON, A. A. 1955. Icthyosis and hypnosis. Br. Med. J. July 2 : 57–58.
57. MASON, A. A. 1960. Hypnosis and suggestion in the treatment of allergic phenomena. Acta Allergol. (Kbh.) (Suppl.) **VII**: 332–338.
58. MASON, A. A. 1963. Hypnosis and allergy. Br. Med. J. June 22 : 1675–1676.
59. McGLASHAN, T. H., F. J. EVANS & M. J. ORNE. 1969. The nature of hypnotic analgesia and the placebo response to experimental pain. Psychosom. Med. **31**: 227–246.
60. MULLINS, J. F., N. MURRAY & E. M. SHAPIRO. 1955. Pachyonychia congenita: A review and a new approach to treatment. AMA Arch. Dermatol. Syphilol. **71**: 265–268.
61. MUN, C. T. 1968. The use of hypnosis in the management of patients with cancer. Singapore Med. J. **9**: 211–214.
62. PLATONOV, K. 1959. The Word as a Physiological and Therapeutic Factor. Foreign Languages Publishing House. Moscow, USSR.
63. PRINCE, M. 1915. The Unconscious. Macmillan. New York, N.Y.
64. ROBERTS, A. H., D. G. KEWMAN & H. MacDONALD. 1973. Voluntary control of skin temperature: Unilateral changes using hypnosis and feedback. J. Abnorm. Psychol. **82**: 163–168.
65. SALK, J. 1969. Immunological Paradoxes: Theoretical Considerations in the Rejection or Retention of Grafts, Tumors, and Normal Tissue. Ann. N.Y. Acad. Sci. **164**(2): 365–380.
66. SCHNECK, J. M. 1954. Icthyosis treated with hypnosis. Dis. Nerv. Syst. **15**: 211–214.
67. SHANDS, H. C. 1969. Integration, discipline, and the concept of shape. Ann. N.Y. Acad. Sci. **164**(2): 578–587.
68. SHOR, R. E., M. T. ORNE & D. N. O'CONNELL. 1966. Psychological correlates of plateau hypnotizability in a special volunteer sample. J. Pers. Social Psychol. **3**: 80–95.
69. SIDIS, B. 1902. Psychopathological Researches: Studies in Mental Dissociation. G. E. Stechert. New York, N.Y.
70. SIMONTON, C. 1975. The role of the mind in cancer therapy. Paper presented Dimensions of Healing Symp. UCLA. Los Angeles, Calif. Oct. 7.
71. SIMONTON, O. C. & S. S. SIMONTON. 1975. Belief systems and management of the emotional aspects of malignancy. J. Transpers. Psychol. **7**: 29–47.
72. SINCLAIR-GIEBEN, A. H. C. & D. CHALMERS. 1959. Evaluation of treatment of warts by hypnosis. Lancet Oct. 3 : 480–482.
73. SOLOMON, G. F. & R. MOOS. 1964. Emotions, immunity and disease. Arch. Gen. Psychiat. **11**: 657–674.
74. SURMAN, O. S., S. K. GOTTLIEB, T. P. HACKETT & E. SILVERBERG. 1973. Hypnosis in the treatment of warts. Arch. Gen. Psychiat. **28**: 439–441.
75. TENZEL, J. H. & R. L. TAYLOR. 1969. An evaluation of hypnosis and suggestion as treatment for warts. Psychosomatics **10**: 252–257.
76. THOMAS, C. B. & K. R. DUSZYNSKI. 1974. Closeness to parents and the family constellation in a prospective study of five disease states: Suicide, mental illness, malignant tumor, hypertension and coronary heart disease. Hopkins Med. J. **134**: 251–270.
77. VAN NUYS, D. 1973. Meditation, attention, and hypnotic susceptibility: A correlational study. Int. J. of Clin. Exp. Hypn. **21**: 59–69.
78. WINK, C. A. S. 1961. Congenital ichthyosiform erythroderma treated by hypnosis: Report of two cases. Br. Med. J. Sept. 16: 741–743.

HYPNOTHERAPY: PATIENT-THERAPIST RELATIONSHIP

Harold Lindner

Washington, D.C.

That hypnosis is a heightened form of interpersonal relationship, which, like all other relationships, is also an experience in "sharing"—that is, one in which both persons (hypnotist and subject) share an emotional satisfaction, cannot be denied. Previously there had been serious insistence that the hypnotic experience was not a "shared" one; that is, it represented a singular experience for the subject willing to "submit" to the "dominant will" of the hypnotist. This ancient shibboleth has long been laid to rest. Today all serious investigators and practitioners of this modality of treatment and research recognize the indisputable fact that the one-on-one as well as the group utilization of this technique is a manifestation of an interaction between the persons involved, and therefore interpersonal in character.

In an earlier paper [1] I discussed the Shared Neurosis of the hypnotist and subject. I pointed then to the potential danger of the hypnotist-psychotherapist not sufficiently in touch with his own unconscious needs to inflict upon his patient those powerful libidinal forces unworked-through within him. I described the phenonemon of the quasitherapeutic situation in which the psychotherapist could use hypnosis as a means of expressing his own omnipotent and controlling demands on the unsuspecting patient under the guise of "a therapy"; in which case we must ask: therapy for whom?

It would be sheer folly to ascribe such a situation, even today, as rare or so uncommon as to be unworthy of the attention of well-trained personnel in this field. Unhappily, it is probably more common, perhaps ubiquitious, than we are willing to believe. As we all know, hypnosis is a modality of great convenience and easy access in the arsenal of psychiatric, psychological, medical, and dental practice. Training facilities abound in today's marketplace of Continuing Education, many superficial and financially rewarding to the purveyors of this skill; many, but not nearly enough, designed with great skill, offering scientifically sound and experimentally expert in thoughtful design and development combining sufficient talent devoted to teaching, practicum, and follow-up under superior professional competency. However, no matter how proficient the neophyte may become as a result of even the most superior training facilities with the most talented and dedicated instructors, unless that student is well rooted in the learnings of his own discipline, he should be denied the right to practice hypnotherapy of any variety. But even more importantly, even that above-mentioned hypothetical superb training facility is not equipped to examine the student's personal psychodynamics or his freedom from the defensiveness and ego-states that would serve to minimize the possibility of his projecting his own needs on his patient. Needless to state here, this is a concern that all psychotherapies share. Hypnosis is not alone with this problem. It is essential, however, to appreciate two additional dangers that the hypnotic modality exacerbates and does not share in common with the others: (1) hypnosis is a technique that, as already indicated, is readily accessible to anyone wishing to make even the most modest investment of time and interest in learning how to use it; and (2) because of the rapid, dramatic, and, at times, seemingly magical qualities of its use, professionals are often sorely tempted to use it when their needs for therapeutic results are expected but thwarted by more traditional modalities; and patients, due to media and parlor influences as well as their natural desire for "the quick fix," request and even demand its use. It becomes increasingly clear as one reflects on these considerations how tremendous can be the pressure placed on a therapist to use the technique. This is why this therapeutic procedure requires more than ordinary professional judgment, so that patient selectivity (and therefore therapeutic gain and not harm) is maintained within the proper confines of the therapist's discipline's diagnostic and therapeutic capacities without being taxed by unresolved psychodynamic problems arising from within his own person.

To further illustrate and emphasize the premise that hypnosis is a shared relationship, like any other multiple-person situation, and one in which both the hypnotist and the subject share in common an emotional satisfaction through this heightened interpersonal relationship, I offer a few clinical examples of the kind of problem situation one must consider before commencing hypnotherapy.

On referral from a distinguished psychiatric colleague a few years ago, I met an attractively pleasant woman of 26 years, single, gainfully employed, articulate, and, so it almost immediately seemed to me then, obsequiously fawning and complimentary about the wonderful things the psychiatrist had told her about my work with hypnosis in psychotherapy. Her presenting complaint over the telephone had been severe despair over her lifelong battle with weight control and compulsive eating. In person, I greeted a beautifully attired woman who obviously invested a great deal in her wardrobe and appearance, and, most shockingly to me because of my private expectation of viewing a terribly obese person, was slim, very chic, with no apparent evidence of excess body fat or figure distortion at all. She immediately stated that she was so very pleased to have learned of my work because she had had much too much of "that psychoanalytic stuff," having been in intensive dynamic therapy for more than six years without much consequence or symptom-relief. She stated she now wanted someone to hypnotize her ("like I read in the newspaper a couple of weeks ago") and teach her hypnosis so that she would not eat so much anymore. I encouraged her to talk. Through her statements I learned that what she described over the telephone as "compulsive eating" was indeed compulsive, but was a nocturnal compulsion to awaken, nightly, in a state of severe anxiety suffering an overwhelming thirst and feeling that she was suffocatingly dry. She would hasten to the kitchen of her apartment and in what was described as a fugue state, compulsively engorge herself with soft drinks and enormous amounts of foods, indiscriminately chosen, until she felt nauseous and began to regurgitate, thus vomiting the contents of her stomach. In her judgment the vomiting was responsible for the happy fact that she never gained weight from the voracious, gluttonous overindulgence. She also described a lifestyle that was excessively isolated, depending mainly on family and a few office associates for her only social relationships. She said she found it incredibly difficult to meet new people, was terrified of men and had never had any sexual experiences, was shy and withdrawn in male company, felt that people didn't like her, and was despairing of ever having a comfortable relationship outside her family circle. I could continue to describe the dynamics inherent in this serious situation, but that is not the immediate purpose of this illustration. I list it here to emphasize the importance of good initial history superimposed upon professional competency within one's discipline in order to achieve adequate diagnostic and therapeutic prognostication. Clearly this woman, who very well might be helped symtomatically, had far vaster difficulties than she expressed in her telephone request for hypnosis and a significant psychopathology that demanded psychotherapy of a more intensive perspective than one limited to the so-called "weight control" problem. In this case I explored the various dynamics of her distress with her, and, following a few consultations, we agreed to commence a hypnoanalytic therapy that we successfully pursued for about two years primarily devoted to her resolving her psychosexual oedipal difficulties, working through her anxieties about her rage and the passive-aggressive components of her dependency needs, forging an adequate identity, and only within the process of therapy achieving symptom control and relief. Had there been a primary concern with symptom removal, it is unlikely that meaningful clinical results would have been accomplished. More importantly, however, the woman would have left therapy as impoverished emotionally as she had appeared initially, with the probability of further life problems predictable. Parenthetically, although hypnosis was used in this treatment, principally as an aid in uncovering and exploring fantasies and dreams, there was nothing that could not have been done just as satisfactorily without hypnosis. The hypnosis merely served as an agent for working more rapidly in therapy and thus reducing the length of time required.

In that earlier paper on the Shared Neurosis I reported a case that so cogently illustrates the viewpoint I have concerning the pitfalls of working with an inappropriate frame of reference in the hypnotic modality that I now share this material with you. I must stress that I do so for convenience, and not because this represents a singular example serving to reinforce the viewpoint related to the "shared" emotional investment which the participants experience in hypnotherapy.

A physician from whom I often receive referrals recently called to ask whether I could arrange an immediate consultation with a patient who was in a state of acute anxiety. I agreed; and that evening, following my last patient, met a highly distraught young man of 32 years who was severely depressed and suicidal. In a rapid and not too coherent manner he told me that he had been seeing a doctor who had been offering him hypnosis for the relief of severe stuttering which had always interfered with scholastic and social satisfactions. He said that the doctor had been teaching him auto-suggestion and had been hypnotizing him for about 2 months duration in what I gathered was a combination of hypnotic relaxation and sophomoric psychotherapy. The immediate situation was brought on by the temporary removal of stuttering along with uncontrolled probing of psychological factors relevant to the man's feelings of hostility and aggression (which the stuttering had served to deny). As any experienced psychotherapist knows, in such cases, the symptom should not have been superficially disturbed until the underlying psychopathology was properly worked-through and all the dynamics understood. In this case, the loss of the ego-defense without proper integration of the dynamics, ruptured the psychological homeostasis and led to an almost break with realistic thinking into depression.

I asked my physician friend about the hypnotist (whom I didn't know) and learned that he was a physician who used hypnosis on the suggestive level for symptomatic removal; that he had had no particular training in psychological theory: and that he was more physiological than psychological in professional viewpoint. He described him as a dogmatic and over-bearing person whose approach to patients was authorative.

During one of my ensuing sessions with the patient, I asked him to describe his hypnotist and to relate how their relationship developed. He told me that when he first met the doctor he was impressed with the man's manner in that it suggested great certainty and skill. He also felt the doctor had treated him with a curious mixture of condescension and friendliness, having given him the impression that were he to follow his instructions all would be well. He also said that hypnosis was suggested to him as a method of relaxation and for purposes of posthypnotic suggestion to remove the stuttering and related tension. He felt he was grasping at a straw in agreeing to this and did so rather reluctantly. When I inquired why he agreed to something he did not trust, he replied that he felt it was important not to reject the doctor's advice so that he would not lose someone who had become important to him and towards whom he had felt a great deal of respect.

It thus became clear that the patient was responding to his feelings about the doctor. Technically, he was caught in a dependency relationship in which he parataxically transferred to the doctor feelings which were originally reserved for his own father.

I asked him how the doctor had conducted the hypnotic relationship and whether he knew how his doctor had felt about his hypnotizability. To this he replied with evident pride: his doctor had made it quite clear that he was an exemplary patient, that hypnosis and its desired depth of attainment was most important and that through this means he could remedy the patient's serious personal and social problems. With every successful hypnotic session he would be complimented by the doctor, who, he said, revealed pleasure in the success and obviously took pride in his work. As the patient revealed anxiety about his loss of stuttering and of the emotional revelation made under hypnotic probing, the doctor assumed a cold and demanding authority and threatened to cancel further appointments unless the patient agreed to "calm down" and "appreciate the value of these results."

Here, then, we find a situation in which *both* the hypnotist and his subject were caught in a shared neurosis: the hypnotist neurotically impressed with his strength and the subject neurotically impressed with his capacity to satisfy his hypnotist's neurosis. A shared hypnotic neurosis. To verify my impression that the hypnotist was sharing a neurotic experience with his subject some assumptions were postulated about the relationship and the probable satisfactions which were in it for the hypnotist. By evaluating the subject's description of the hypnotist and comparing it with the reliable report of my physician-friend, it was possible to assume that the relationship was one in which the hypnotist was able to flatter his authoritative, patriarchal feelings of omnipotence and indulge in the "hypnotic phantasy" of power.[1]

A patient who had been seeing me for a number of months and who was a practicing dentist specializing in anesthesiology spoke to me about obtaining training in hypnosis for use in dental surgery. Obviously this was a legitimate question for one like him, who was interested in expanding his professional competency. He was, however, extremely schizoid, with borderline ego-status, and used anesthesia because he could not tolerate the overwhelming anxieties he experienced when working with patients, but could tolerate them when he had the patient asleep and thus was in control and felt dominant. I advised him to delay such training until his emotional state was more integrated. Obviously, he wanted still another sedating technique to exploit, and it was really in the service of meeting his own neurotic needs than for good dentistry.

Now, although hypnosis is a many-faceted tool in the hands of the psychotherapist, it also carries with it the danger of either overutilization or erratic selectivity in its application to a wide variety of clinical problems. The danger of the practitioner's being caught in his own fantasies of power (which I have characterized as a megalomanic and omnipotent sort of daydream, evoked in the hypnotist on infantile levels below consciousness and serving to flatter his ego through the successful utilization of a "power tool" such as hypnosis represents) [2] has been explicitly defined. The problem of overutilization falls into another category, but one that has parameters of proximity to that already described one of "fantasy." Because the nature of the hypnotic model is so temptingly simple and often expediently useful, one might be naïvely tempted to extend its use beyond the limits of generally accepted psychotherapeutic practice in order to achieve the "quick fix" or the sometimes startling progress in alleviating symptoms of distress by undercutting defenses without the difficult and painstaking efforts of working-through. A well-trained therapist knows the dangers inherent in that practice; and therefore diagnostic selectivity is of paramount importance when one faces the decision of what treatment modality to consider when treating an emotional problem. Obviously, not all good treatment is psychodynamic intensive therapy. Nor is the psychoanalytic model advisable for every clinical problem. There are many conditions that respond better to other psychotherapies. Some conditions mandate behavior modification, symptom removal, crisis intervention, amelioration from depressive syndromes, chemical and psychologic therapy of psychotic episodes, and many others. The critical importance of well-grounded theoretical and skillfully trained professionalism represents the key to making the correct diagnostic decision, and from it the therapeutic prognostications in which the therapeutic model to be used is determined. The best protection for the neophyte or the experienced therapist is based on these solid and proven understandings. It is when one ignores these that trouble might ensue—and this is probably no different in hypnosis than in the other psychotherapies, with the *caveat* that hypnosis, being so incisive an instrument, bears more cautious and complete self-awareness than perhaps many of the other psychotherapies require.

It is incumbent upon us now to examine some of the more positive aspects of the hypnotic relationship lest one conclude that there are only negative and threatening ones. The very character of the hypnotic collaboration by definition dictates a close, syntonic bond between the persons involved. There is a heightened awareness of each other's persona. There is an intense perception of each other's demeanor. There is an intimacy that resembles the dimensions of love and care inherent in the mother-child protective relationship wherein the hypnotist lovingly takes the patient through the progressions of hypnotic trance in a manner that is so nonthreatening as to be felt safe and secure by the patient. In this posture there is no domination of will, no power hungry effort to overwhelm, no Svengali. The relationship is fully collaborative. The attitude is permissive and reassuring. The security of strong safety in passage is comforting. A true hypnotic relationship represents the essence of togetherness in its most positive sense. Induction is a cooperative experience. There is no hypnosis without cooperation, but indeed there are different levels of psychological cooperation. Lest the inexperienced exaggerate the fear of its inducing too much dependency, it is necessary to note that as with all other psychologic factors in the experience, they are attended to and worked with so that they do not superimpose additional problems on or in replacement of others. Just as there is no growth without risk, so there is no movement toward health in therapy without risk. The experienced psychotherapist will be able to work effectively with these whether in the hypnotic situation or in any other. Truly, in the hypnotic relationship there is that symbiosis that arouses infantile and often long-repressed needs and drives—but so is that true of the analytic couch, the doctor's societal status, and numerous other affectations in our world. We do not counsel spilling out the baby with the bath water in hypnosis any more than we do in any of these other processes. Rather, we try to comprehend the mechanisms and treat them constructively.

In more than 25 years of experience as an observer, researcher, teacher, and practitioner in hypnosis, I have never known anything to happen under hypnosis that did not have a similar potential without hypnosis. I have also come to know that there is nothing one can accomplish with hypnosis that could not similarly be done without it; only it often takes longer without it. There is no "magic" in hypnosis. There is only that heightened focus that permits a more expeditious exploration of the depths of consciousness and unconsciousness. In consequence of the incredible proximity of hypnotist and patient, the hypnotherapist must exercise even more care and perspicacity than therapists who practice other techniques. To the patient the therapist using hypnosis instantly assumes the identity of an authority figure with unsurpassed strengths and powers. This transference phenomenon, the key to any psycho-therapeutic value, instantly aroused by the unique relationship between hypnotist and patient, conveys all the intensity of the Oedipal situation, which is the dynamic most essential to psychotherapy. In the person of the hypnotist, the patient finds that terrifying figure whom he both loves and hates, fears and admires, desires and rejects. The enormity of the seemingly mystical experience arouses in the hypnotic patient those elementary anxieties through his projections of omnipotence on the therapist. He easily identifies the hypnotherapist with all those longings that have for him so distorted his life and dictated his very being without any rationality of awareness. The hypnotherapist can now offer that "great giving," that total love concomitantly with the power and strength of the authority who "cures" *within* the confines of a cooperative (shared) therapeutic relationship. But also concomitantly, the patient soon realizes his own powers within the relationship to thwart the hypno-therapist. As is well known either party can contribute to the furtherance of hypnosis or terminate it. Cooperatively they can proceed within it to produce the therapeutic gains synonymous with personal growth or terminate the process by resistance and avoidance and denial and thus punish the other one (real and imagined-symbolic). Either a folie-à-deux might ensue in which each party proceeds to activate ancient Oedipal longings, or a successfully collaborative therapeutic milieu might be built in which both relate to the therapeutic goals of growth and health.

Precisely because *both* hypnotherapist and patient can obtain satisfactions of their own psychosexual needs through the shared hypnotic fantasy, hypnosis is so longingly sought an experience for so many people, even though filled with anxiety, terror, and fear. My thesis rests upon the psychoanalytic theoretical position that we are all entrenched in our roles in the Oedipal struggle, even though below conscious awareness, and hypnosis represents one of the most commonly perceived ways of expressing our deepest feelings about this ancient struggle for freedom within an expressly defined sublimated activity that, though so disguised, nevertheless touches those precise emotional chords that scream for expression in all neurotic characters. In this dyad the hypnotherapist is free to explore his own unconscious in the ambience of the "professional healer": the patient makes the final achievement of his ancient longings for the "good father" with all the security of knowing that, at his own discretion, he can, by resistance of various forms, terminate any threat in the encounter, thus either proving that he is truly the more invincible of the two or the more loving because he trusts (e.g., loves so true), all without fear of any punishment because of the established safeguards of the therapeutic alliance. Again we see that in this powerful experience we call hypnosis lies fertile territory for the growth of the hypnotic phantasy which, if enacted, would defeat therapy.

The responsibility for making treatment growth-enhancing rather than destructive is always with the therapist. Not only, as in all therapies, are the transferences critical to emotional growth, but equally dynamic and worthy of consideration are those ubiquitous countertransference issues [3] that, as in all therapies, crop up between hypnotist and patient. Within the hypnotic process these latter are, as for transferences, exacerbated by the very nature of the relationship. One must be wary of so-called "transference cures" where behavior and symptom changes are transient at best and often mask severe pathology at worst. Hypnosis, in unskilled hands, might encourage patient performances of acting-out an assumed restored state of health while being basically unchanged or even more disturbed in order to satisfy the unspoken demands of the therapist (or his own fantasies that such demands exist) that he respond to the treatment modality or suffer its withdrawal. Unless the psychotherapist who uses hypnosis in therapy is fully in touch with his own unconscious processes and maintains a constant vigil on his own countertransference feelings, his patient could easily suffer destructive therapeutic manipulations. The erudite Adlai Stevenson once observed in the heat of political battle that "everyone is against sin." Likewise, every psychotherapist is against wild therapy. However simplistic may be the righteousness of such proclamations, unless one's training included a personal therapy as well as the appropriate didactic study, it is unlikely that one has the insight into oneself to successfully abort countertransference interferences. One therapist in memory once observed that he hated his work because he spent it with sniveling, angry, bitchy people who were so self-absorbed that they belied the state of humanity. He said he wished he had become an entertainer rather than a doctor, because everyone loves an entertainer whose life is full of fun and games. Clearly, that man would not be my choice of personal therapist, and even more clearly, I would not like him to be my hypnotherapist! Yet he practices with an exhausting patient-load obviously oblivious to the potential for harm that his feelings suggest. Another colleague said he can only prescribe psychotropic medications because he can't abide the emotional strains of interpersonal relationships in psychotherapy. He at least understands enough of himself so that he does not impose his personal difficulties on others who seek his professional help.

In the hypnotherapeutic experience the ambience is such that the delicate nature of the interpersonal relationship between therapist and subject reaches levels of intensity so rapidly that one must be constantly alert to all the nuances and variances of associative recall, dreamwork, mood swings, compliant and aggressive expressive feeling, and ideation. There is no opportunity to relax one's vigil. It taxes the resources and enervates even experienced therapists using hypnosis. With hypnosis there is no rest or respite for the therapist. His major task in facilitating the therapeutic process is the ever-present demand that he know himself. This might appear to be a clarion call for the psychoanalysis of all hypnotherapists. It is not, although it is my belief that that would be optimal. Rather, it is an emphasis on the necessity of personal therapy for all potential hypnopsychotherapists to ensure, as much as possible, that he be in touch with his own unconscious to remain acutely aware of those psychodynamic and psychosexual forces which of necessity intrude in any psychotherapy, especially in the intensification of the relationship in hypnosis. Unless the hypnotherapist who practices psychological treatment has worked through his own infantile distortions to reach genital maturity and thus knows his unconscious and can keep abreast of his own personal intrusions into the patient's life (and, of course, keep out of them), he cannot possibly conduct the treatment course with the economy and positive progress that his patients rightfully expect from him. Not all therapies can be curative, but every therapy must be predicated on the therapist's person and the training that makes relief a reasonable potential. The therapist who does not prepare himself to conduct potentially curative therapy is a miscreant. This is true of all therapies and includes all psychotherapies, and certainly hypnotic therapy as well.

A 26-year-old, extremely well-nourished white male requested a consultation because of feelings of anxiety and tensions in his continuously difficult relationships with fellow graduate students and faculty. A physically strong man with a surprisingly whining, nasal quality to his voice, he told me that he was a painfully lonely person who found that although he desperately wanted to form close friendships, he was repeatedly unsuccessful because people, soon after having a few experiences with him, made it plain that they wished to avoid him. He said he was a trustworthy person and was always willing to be helpful to others. He also complained of moderate insomnia and difficult weight control, and said that he was worried about his future because he was only skimming through school with no real motivation to study, even though success was extremely important to him. Tangentially and with embarrassment, he mentioned that in the gym where he worked out daily, he increasingly noticed that he had become possessed with comparing his genital organ size with those of others there, and the resultant fantasies were making him insufferably anxious at times, verging on panic. Clinical evaluation indicated an obsessive-compulsive neurosis in an extremely aggressive person who was frightened of his angers and had erected defensive postures to sublimate, displace, deny, and project his hostilities within the framework of a passive-aggressive personality pattern. Psychosexually, he was struggling with an Oedipal conflict that he experienced in low self-esteem, overwhelming dependency needs, and fears concerning sexual potency. He was the older of two children, his sister being four years younger. The family economic position was secure. They were striving, upward mobile people, primarily devoted to their flourishing retail business, a liquor store in the seedy part of a city, and to their country club membership. The father was described as a blunt, uneducated, unemotional person of powerful physical dimensions, who largely ignored the family and communicated only sparsely, who worked from dawn until late at night every day. The mother was described as a woman who spent her time at their country club, was overly protective of the children, lavished her attentions on her appearance, and seemed cathected to her Cadillac automobile.

A hypnoanalytic program was agreed upon, and we proceeded with three sessions each week. He proved to be a difficult hypnotic subject, not being able to achieve anything deeper than a light hypnoidal state. After about six months, when his neurosis became less fixed, he allowed himself to trust me enough to minimize the obsessive control and thus reach somewhat deeper levels of hypnotic trance. Therapy was without incidence for almost three months. He found introspection and rumination difficult. He intellectualized and repeatedly denied feeling recognition. Through the training in hypnosis, he was beginning to get relief from his insomnia and was sleeping more regularly. Otherwise, he began to complain that although he was working very hard in therapy, nothing was changing, and he was growing disenchanted with me. Other than for those hypnotic sessions we had when he knew I was "really working" with him, he questioned my participation, because all I did was "listen" and rarely speak to him, stating that he could just as well talk to himself for all the good he was getting from me. And most importantly, he complained, he was spending an enormous amount of his parent's money on treatment, and "when in the hell are you going to do something to earn it . . .?" I encouraged him to talk about his feelings toward me. He continued to complain about my being "a cold fish," not even willing to smile or joke with him. He said he was telling me everything about himself but he knew nothing about me, and although I had become so important to him, he doubted that I even cared for him but probably viewed him as a convenient weekly paycheck and was probably relieved when he wasn't in my office and certainly never thought of him between sessions. I encouraged him to articulate his conjectures about me to the fullest. Under hypnoidal status he described an idyllic life-style for me and obviously projected omnipotency onto me. I induced a deeper hypnosis and offered a posthypnotic suggestion that he dream about me, and that through his reporting the dream to me and analyzing it he would become more aware of his true feelings about me and why he had them.

At the next session he said that although he knew I had asked him to dream, he had not done so; furthermore, he questioned whether he should continue seeing me, because he needed someone who could help him and not just "listen to me spill my guts back there where for all I know you could be sleeping but sure as hell are not interested in me . . . and as far as this hypnotic stuff, I'm beginning to think it's a bunch of bullshit. . ." He proceeded to rant about my failure to be helpful to him; he was doing his share but I was not; perhaps he should see someone else; he wasn't getting any place with me because he still had faith in therapy but not in me. He continued with vituperations, alternating with remarks to mollify me. ("I really like you," "You have a good reputation," "You're a nice guy," "I must admit I sleep better now."). He left the office saying he would have to think about whether he would be returning for his next appointment. I did not comment then, as I had not commented during the session.

He returned for his next appointment 15 minutes late, storming into the office without his usual amiability. He said he didn't know why he had decided to return and that he wasn't sure he would again, but that he hated to see "so much of my folks' money go down the drain," and so he would try a little longer—but "only if you start doing something for me. . . . Can't you see I need help? Don't you care? Why won't you talk to me? Say something. . . . I feel as if I'm going nuts. . . . Aren't you human? . . . Don't you know how much I want us to be friends? . . . Please . . . help me . . . please.". Then ensued a paroxysm of uncontrolled crying and hyperventilation, terminated by a burst of coughing. I asked him if he would like to relax through hypnosis, and suggested he try to do so. When his composure and breathing-rate indicated he was hypnoidal, I asked whether he had any dream to report. He replied he wasn't sure, but that he thought he had dreamt that he received a telephone call from his mother telling him that his father had been in a fight with a drunk in their store and that she needed him to come home for a week because she couldn't handle things alone and that only he could be relied upon, because there was no one else and the employees would steal them broke and only he was trustworthy. His associations to the dream were:

> My father is so strong. He frightens his employees and me too; I once saw my father beat up a drunk who tried to steal a bottle of wine; my mother and father used to argue and scream at each other all the time; she complained that he was not doing enough for her and he would yell that all she wanted was his money and that she didn't give a damn for him and that besides he got better sex from the whores on the streets than from her and for a hell of a lot less money too; my mother used to make me have milk and cookies every afternoon, telling me that I needed to grow strong and healthy; she would sit with me and tell me how much she loved me and that only because of me was she putting up with my father who was only in love with his business; sometimes she would lie next to me in my bed and tell me stories and I would fall asleep in her arms; she told me how handsome a boy I was and what a good-looking man I was going to be and that she was sure I would eventually leave her for some "pretty thing" and then she would miss me so much but she would be happy because she would know I was happy; when I was 6 I wanted to "love" my baby sister but mother would warn me not to hurt her because she was just a little girl-baby; I used to jerk-off and once I tried to suck my penis to see what it was like but I couldn't reach it and I was afraid my mother would come in.

He showed abreactive anxiety at that last association, and I interrupted then to suggest relaxation and amnesia for all that had transpired. I told him he would regain full alertness and that he could retain whatever of his recalls he wished, but that anything he preferred to not remember, he would not. He started talking immediately upon opening his eyes and said that he felt much better than when he first came into the office; that he wasn't sure what he had been saying, because he could only remember a few of the things he had recalled, but that he didn't feel so angry now; that he somehow felt that I really did care for him enough to accept his anger and did not reject him for being so hostile to me; he knew that I wouldn't punish him for being so vicious, and that I really did want to work with him. He added that he would like to continue in therapy if it was agreeable to me. I suggested that we still had a great deal to learn together about him and that we both, being human, might say things that upon further reflection we might regret, but that our mistakes, our loves, and our hates were only human-sized and therefore tolerable, and that if we courageously pursued them to break through our defenses they could provide great insight and understanding and lead to authenticity. I recommended that we now try to correlate the material he had exposed that day with the rest of his feelings about himself and the other significant people in his life, including me. We spent the next few weeks working on these various associations to the dream, which gave us more understanding of the powerful forces that impelled him to test himself and others within the passive-aggressive character posture and the ways in which his Oedipal needs affected the neurotic development of his narcissistic ego.

Since it is not our purpose in this paper to examine the intricacies of psychodynamics with this case but to only use it to exemplify the hypnotic patient-therapist relationship in the workings of psychotherapy, let us turn our attention to some of the factors implied in this case illustration.

This clinical sequence, experientially for me, renewed my conviction that the patient-therapist relationship is the critical element in the hypnotherapeutic process. Of primary interest to this investigator is the importance in this case report of the way in which a therapist can become trapped by his unconscious needs to be dominant and powerful under the provocation of the patient who both demands and rejects, for neurotic needs, such reactions from his therapist. In the above, the patient acted as though he were demanding proof of omnipotency and power from his therapist. In point of fact, had the therapist been caught in his own fantasy of grandeur—especially with the potency of the hypnotic tool at his disposal—he would have misread the dynamic at play there. In any attempt to cater to the hysterical pressure to "perform," he would have reinforced the ego-defense. By encouraging repression and denial in aiding the patient to avoid confronting his own acting out he would prevent him from uncovering the dynamics motivating such behavior and the therapeutic opportunity to work through them and move constructively toward more integration. Any fear on the part of the therapist, any anxiety concerning hostility or aggression, any acceptance of the threat of rejection of him as a worthwhile person and therapist, any deviation from the therapeutic course in the face of the assault, would only have given the patient more reason to hate himself and to bolster the guilt and infantile sexual distortions about his own potency-impotency conflict. By being aware of his own feelings and addressing the adequacies in the patient and thus respecting those ego-strengths that propel the therapeutic alliance, the therapist made a major communication to the patient that supported the man's growth potential without inflicting further hurt on an already impoverished self-esteem and frightened person who experienced his angers as intolerable and destructive. Here it was the strong but quiet acceptance of him by the therapist that signaled to him that it was safe to proceed to study himself and to learn from his feelings rather than remain so afraid of them that they had to continue either to be denied or repressed, only to wreck havoc interminably in the disassembling of his capacity to form worthwhile interpersonal relationships.

Certainly in all of the preceding there is nothing that the hypnotherapist, as different from any other psychotherapist, must not know and practice. Both must be trained to practice good psychotherapy. In the methodology of hypnotherapy the prevalence of seduction by the neurotic fantasy of power through the power-tool of hypnosis is different only in that the temptation "to do something" is more enticing because the technique can more rapidly open up the dynamic through a seemingly innocuous short cut to "progress." It is only by being secure in one's authenticity as a person and as a therapist that one is protected from the devestation to self and patient that such deviations from well-supported theory and practice might cause. By being well-entrenched in one's own understandings of oneself, by being free of those defenses that cause and encourage emotional blindness and deafness, by having achieved and personally integrated one's own freedom, by being whole and psychosexually genital, and by being human and real, one can, with comfort and safety and assuredness, be the true therapist to those who seek one's professional resources in their quest for an emotionally healthy life and love of people and living.

REFERENCES

1. LINDNER, H. 1960. The shared neurosis: hypnotist and subject. Int. J. Clin. Exp. Hypn. : 62–64.
2. LINDNER, H. 1963. Hypnotherapy: patient-therapist reactions. J. Psychother. 10(1): 66–70.
3. LINDNER, H. 1965. I and me: the psychotherapist's narcissism. Voices: J. Art Sci. Psychother. 1(1): 83–84.

THE ROLE OF HYPNOSIS IN BEHAVIOR THERAPY

L. Michael Ascher

Department of Psychiatry
Temple University School of Medicine
Philadelphia, Pennsylvania 19129

Hypnosis has been employed by proponents of many psychotherapeutic approaches in an effort to facilitate the effectiveness of their therapy. As might be expected, it has been most closely associated with those psychotherapeutic systems whose characteristics are most relevant to, and best complimented by, the hypothesized properties of hypnosis. Consideration of the characteristics or the definition of hypnosis, by those interested in this psychotherapy-hypnosis association, is, of course, influenced by their relevant theoretical conceptions. In the majority of cases, it is the traditional view of hypnosis that is espoused, i.e., the "trance state" position. A theme central to this view is the assumption that an individual experiences an "altered state of consciousness" as a consequence to the administration of a hypnotic induction procedure. It then follows that the properties of the "trance" are enlisted to enhance aspects of a specific relevant therapeutic system. For example, Wolberg [1] uses hypnosis within a psychoanalytic context to facilitate efforts in uncovering difficult unconscious material; another use of hypnosis for Wolberg is the dissolution of defensive blocks that the patient might employ in order to impede therapy. Whether hypnosis actually facilitates the course of psychoanalytic psychotherapy is difficult to determine, since psychoanalytic psychotherapy itself eludes efforts to operationalize its significant components and adequately measure therapeutic outcome.

The situation with hypnosis and behavior therapy is slightly different. While the traditional view of hypnosis dominates even in the behavioral context, behavior therapy is more available to objective testing and thus to the assessment of the effectiveness of such ancillary variables as hypnosis. The present paper examines the role of hypnosis in behavior therapy. First, the traditional "state" conception of hypnosis will be described along with its implications for behavior therapy. This will be followed by a critical review of the logical and empirical basis of the trance state in behavior therapy. Finally, the "nonstate" conception of hypnosis will be briefly described and its potential contributions for behavior therapy outlined.

THE "STATE" VIEW OF HYPNOSIS

The traditional view of hypnosis suggests that, under most circumstances, the hypnotic process begins with verbal instructions presented by the hypnotist to the subject. Although variations of these verbal directions called the "hypnotic induction" procedure may diverge drastically from one another, the information transmitted typically contains five components: defining the situation as hypnosis; suggestions of relaxation, drowsiness, and sleep; instructions to the subjects to close their eyes; instructional statements designed to enlist cooperation and maximal performance; and finally, statements that subjects will find it easy to respond to further test suggestions and to experience suggested effects.[2-5]

It is hypothesized that the administration of hypnotic-induction instructions results in a trance state or an altered state of consciousness. This trance state is assumed to mediate a number of changes in the subject,[5] including enhanced responsiveness to such suggestions as limb rigidity, deafness, visual or auditory hallucination, amnesia, age regression;[6, 7] hypnotic appearance;[8-10] reports of unusual experiences;[8, 9, 11] and subjective statements of having been hypnotized.[7, 12] This altered state of consciousness is viewed as resembling sleep or, more accurately, "the state in which the sleep walker finds himself."[13]

The trance-state formulation of hypnosis has been the basis of a number of articles that espouse the position that hypnosis can facilitate various aspects of behavior therapy. These papers can generally be classified within two categories. Some authors, largely from a hypnosis or hypnotherapy context, propose that the effectiveness of behavior therapy can be explained by postulating the development of the trance state during the administration of certain imaginal behavioral techniques (e.g. References 14–18).

Others, mostly behavior therapists or those primarily interested in behavioral techniques, propose the use of hypnosis by behavior therapists suggesting that hypnosis enhances various behavioral procedures. The literature abounds with illustrations of the enhancement by hypnosis of relaxation (e.g., Todd and Kelley,[19] Rothman et al.,[20] Scott[21]), vividness of imagery (Rubin,[22] Glick,[23] Bell[24]), reduction of anxiety (Perin,[25] Moorefield[26]), increased motivation (Wickramasekera[27]), even of behavior therapy when applied to the general academic difficulties of students (Krippner[28]). Many of these clinicians also point to the potential of the posthypnotic suggestion[25, 26, 28] and the hypnotic trance to facilitate the behavior therapy process in general. Most authors of relevant articles seem to agree that whatever else its properties, hypnosis can enhance the effectiveness of behavior therapy because of its ability to promote a deeper state of relaxation and a greater degree of vividness of imagery than can be achieved without its use.[29-32]

CRITIQUE OF THE STATE POSITION

Barber[5] has criticized the trance-state formulation of hypnosis on logical grounds. For example, a major implication of the state position suggests that the hypnotic-induction procedure is instrumental in producing the above-mentioned changes in the behavior of the hypnotized subject (e.g. enhanced responsiveness to suggestions, hypnotic appearance). It is assumed that this functional relationship is mediated by the hypothetical trance state. To test this, suggestions similar to those included in the Barber Suggestibility Scale[33] are administered following the hypnotic-induction procedure. Subjects who score high on the test items are then assumed by those who accept the trance theory to be responding under the influence of a hypnotic state.

From the trance-state position, an analysis of the relationship of the independent variables (e.g. the hypnotic-induction procedure) through the intervening variable, (i.e. hypnotic trance) to the dependent variables (e.g. enhanced responsiveness to the suggestions of the Barber Suggestibility Scale) reveals some circularity. The circular reasoning results from the need both to account for the enhanced suggestibility by hypothesizing the trance state and to support the existence of the trance state by demonstrating heightened suggestibility.[5] To avoid this circularity, evidence for the existence of this state must be obtained that is independent of the behavior supposedly resulting from the trance state.

Toward this end, physiological data have been sought in an effort to differentiate hypnotized subjects from nonhypnotized subjects. No physiological index has been obtained that permits reliable discrimination of those in whom a trance state is assumed to exist from those subjects not hypothesized to be in a trance state.[34, 35] Therefore, if all that remains to support the existence of the trance state is the behavior it is hypothesized to produce, then a circular relationship exists between the dependent and the intervening variable.

Similar criticism can be directed at the remaining indices of the trance state; for example, the "state" has been inferred from a trance-like appearance (e.g., psychomotor retardation, limpness, fixed facial expression).[10] Barber,[5] however, suggests that the components of this trance-like appearance are responses made to direct requests contained in the context of the hypnotic-induction procedure; in addition, the behaviors that compose the trance-like appearance can be viewed as responses to other implicit and explicit demands of the hypnosis situation. As was the case with enhanced responsivity to suggestions, trance-like appearance is assumed to result from the trance state but is also employed to demonstrate the existence of that state.

Finally, the trance state has been inferred from subjects' reports of having been hypnotized or having undergone unusual experiences. Barber[5] has shown that such subject reports can be modified by observable variables that are independent of the hypnotic induction procedure. For example, some subjects' reports of being hypnotized are dependent upon the degree to which they responded to the test suggestions. In such cases, circular reasoning is again involved in then inferring the existence of the trance state from such subject reports.

In sum, one major difficulty with the trance-state concept is the tendency to infer the existence of this state by the same behaviors for which it acts as an explanatory construct.[5, 36-38] The attempt to undermine this circularity by proposing independent physiological indices or converging behaviors, has failed. In the case of a physiological index, none has been demonstrated to differentiate reliably between the "hypnotized" and "nonhypnotized" subject. Behaviors that are purported to be indicants of the hypnotic trance are either uncorrelated with each other, can be modified by manipulating variables unrelated to the hypnotic-induction procedure, or are circularly related to the trance construct.

In addition to logical considerations, Barber has criticized the trance-state conception of hypnosis on the basis of empirical data. Specifically, he has suggested that behaviors that are assumed to necessarily accompany the hypnotic trance are not invariably present following a hypnotic-induction procedure.[5, 37] Thus, aspects of the experimental situation not necessarily related to hypnosis, e.g. the wording of postexperimental questions[39] or the tone of the experimenters voice,[40] can significantly influence the degree to which subjects report having experienced various hypnotic phenomena.

A second empirical difficulty for the trance state theorists is the frequent finding that behaviors assumed to denote the existence of the trance (e.g., hypnotic appearance, reports of experiencing hypnosis, enhanced responsiveness to tests of suggestibility) do not typically co-vary; that is, the low correlation usually obtained among these behaviors can account for only a small percentage of the variance. The remainder of the variance of these classes of trance behavior are independent of each other. In practical terms, this means that some subjects may be highly responsive to test suggestions but may not report that they were hypnotized or display a hypnotic appearance; or subjects may not respond to test suggestions or display the hypnotic appearance but may report having experienced hypnosis. This poses a difficulty for those who hypothesize that a unitary underlying construct can account for these relatively independent categories of behavior; rather, it becomes implausible that such is the case.[5, 37]

Further, the low correlation that has been demonstrated can be attributed to some subjects employing responsivity in one category to influence responsivity in another category. Thus, subjects who perform well on tests of suggestibility following the administration of a hypnotic-induction procedure may assume that this performance results from having been hypnotized; their report of having experienced "hypnosis" is then due not to some altered state of consciousness but directly to another set of dependent behaviors. Correlations produced in this manner, of course, do not support the existence of an underlying construct independently producing both sets of behaviors.

Finally, even the analogy the trance state theorists have adopted, i.e., the somnambulist, is suspect.[41] There are several aspects of the behavior labeled "sleepwalking" that differentiate it from other similar behaviors. They include an EEG pattern that denotes sleep (at stages 3 or 4); a difficulty in awakening; when awakened, an inability to recall the incident; rigidity of movement, locomotion in a shuffling manner, a low level of motor skill, and a blank stare; and reduced awareness of the surroundings (e.g. a lack of response when spoken to).

By contrast, the hypnosis subject displays markedly different behavior.[41] For example, Barber[5] points out that the EEG profile of hypnotized subjects when compared with those of subjects who are asleep or sleepwalking is quite disparate. On the other hand, there is no difference between the EEG of a group of "hypnotized" subjects and "awake" control subjects. Barber et al.[41] suggest that, in contrast to sleep walkers, "hypnotized" subjects readily "awaken" when instructed to do so. Barber[42] and Barber and Calverly[43] have demonstrated that hypnotized subjects are able to recall every detail of events occurring during the hypnosis session when suggestions for posthypnotic amnesia are not specifically administered. Finally, Barber et al.[41] note that although the behavior of the hypnosis subject may appear to resemble that of the somnambulist (e.g. blank stare) as a result of suggestions to relax, feel drowsy and sleepy, such behavior can be easily changed by appropriate alternative suggestions (e.g., "although in a deep trance I want you to appear to be wide awake and alert"). Therefore, there appears to be little similarity between the significant aspects of behavior that denote somnambulism and those of the "hypnotized" subject.

CRITIQUE OF THE TRADITIONAL VIEW OF THE ROLE OF HYPNOSIS IN BEHAVIOR THERAPY

In detailing the implications of the trance-state view of hypnosis for behavior therapy, it was suggested that hypnosis is assumed to facilitate the application of behavioral techniques by increasing the depth of relaxation and by enhancing the vividness of imagery. The fact that the theoretical basis of this hypothesis has been questioned does not preclude the possibility that the hypothesis may nevertheless be correct. Two areas of investigation in hypnosis seem most relevant to a test of the traditional view of the role of hypnosis in behavior therapy. First are those studies which explore the effects of the hypnotic-induction procedure on relaxation. Second are experiments that focus on hypnotically induced "hallucination." The inclusion of this second group is based on the assumption that the role of hypnosis in enhancing the experience of suggested visual or aural stimuli for experimental subjects is similar to that of enhancing the imaginal component of systematic desensitization, covert conditioning, or flooding for the behavior-therapy client. This research will be reviewed in the following two subsections.

Hypnosis and Relaxation Procedures

An experiment by Barber and Hahn [44] was concerned with the relative effectiveness of a hypnotic-induction procedure to produce relaxation. A group of subjects that had been administered a hypnotic induction was compared with a control group that was simply told to sit quietly for twenty minutes. Relaxation was defined by such physiological measures as frontalis muscle tension, heart rate, respiratory rate, and skin conductance. Although the hypnotic-induction procedure was effective in producing some measure of relaxation, it was no more effective than was the control procedure. In fact, there were certain periods during the middle of the session when the hypnosis group actually showed increased heart rate and muscle tension. By contrast, the control group exhibited continual decrement in all physiological measures throughout the session. Barber and Hahn [44] concluded that their "data offer no support to the hypothesis that a 'hypnotic induction' focusing on suggestions of relaxation, drowsiness, and sleepiness is more effective than the single instruction to sit quietly in producing 'relaxation' " (p, 110). Later investigations [45, 46] provided data that supported Barber and Hahn's [44] conclusion.

The aforementioned experiments were conducted by researchers interested in the area of hypnosis *per se.* Another small group of studies has been conducted by clinicians associated with behavior therapy. The general purpose of these investigations was to determine the effectiveness of a hypnotic-induction procedure in enhancing conventional behavioral relaxation procedures and, in some cases, the total systematic desensitization program.

In an early analog study, Lang [47] compared a group receiving a hypnotic induction plus desensitization with a group receiving the desensitization procedure alone. He failed to find any significant differences between the two groups. This study would seem to have implications for the hypothesis that hypnosis augments the effectiveness of systematic desensitization (either as the result of increasing the depth of relaxation and/or enhancing the vividness of imagery).

Marks *et al.*[48] compared a group that received a hypnotic induction followed by direct suggestions of fear reduction with a group that received a modified desensitization procedure. The desensitization group demonstrated greater fear reduction than did the hypnotic-induction group. Of course, this was not necessarily a fair test of hypnosis, since the two procedures differed on a number of aspects that may have been related to fear reduction.

Paul [48] compared groups receiving either an abbreviated form of progressive relaxation, hypnotic induction emphasizing direct suggestions relevant to relaxation, or control instructions in which the subject was asked to sit quietly and relaxed for a period equal to that required for the remaining two procedures. Physiological measures of relaxation included muscle tension, heart rate, skin conductance, and respiratory rate. The data indicated that the progressive relaxation and hypnotic-induction groups demonstrated a greater degree of relaxation than did the control group, as measured by the physiological systems, which were specifically monitored by Paul; in addition, the progressive relaxation group yielded significantly greater effects than did the hypnotic-induction group on several of these measures. Paul [48] concludes that "progressive relaxation training is more effective than hypnotic suggestion in producing desired physiological changes, whether considered in terms of efficiency, intensity or extent." (p. 434)

In a second study, Paul [49] compared the effectiveness of progressive relaxation training with a hypnotic-induction procedure in reducing the physiological excitation resulting from stressful imagery. After providing appropriate training to each of the two experimental groups and the self-relaxation control, subjects were instructed to think of imaginal scenes previously established to be anxiety-provoking. "Relaxation" associated either with progressive relaxation training or with a hypnotic induction produced significantly greater inhibition of the physiological response to stressful imagery when compared with the self-relaxation control. Although the progressive relaxation training group demonstrated greater inhibition of this response than did the hypnotic induction group, the difference was not significant.

McAmmond et al.[50] investigated the relative effectiveness of progressive relaxation training and a hypnotic induction procedure in reducing self-report and physiological responses to stress related to dental procedures. Unfortunately, the study contained several methodological flaws, not the least of which was an inadequate control group. Even more damaging was the fact that the administration of the training instructions to the relaxation group was accomplished by means of a single sixteen-minute tape recording repeated during seven sessions. By contrast, the hypnotic-induction procedure was administered to the hypnosis group by the dentist who later carried out the dental procedure with all subjects.

At least three general difficulties result from these differences. First, the hypnosis group receives live instructions from an individual who, one may assume, is sensitive to the requirements of these subjects and changes his instructions accordingly; as the subjects move in the desired direction, the experimenter modifies the induction material and applies social reinforcement. The relaxation group, however, has little preexperimental contact with the investigators, and they receive the *same* instructions on each occasion. These instructions are not responsive to the needs and developing skills of the subjects and, as Paul and Trimble [51] have shown, will produce results inferior both to a live presentation of relaxation instructions or a hypnotic-induction procedure. Second, Barber et al.[52] demonstrated that successive presentations of the same hypnotic-induction procedure resulted in decreasing effectiveness when compared with the same number of presentations of alternative hypnotic-induction procedures. They hypothesized that these results may have been due to boredom resulting from multiple presentations of the same material. Third, Barber [5] would predict superior performance for the hypnosis group as a result of the differences in their attitudes, expectancies, and motivations that resulted from receiving extensive pretreatment hypnotic-induction training directly from the individual who later administered the experimental procedure. By contrast, the relaxation group had no contact with the experimenter until the experimental procedure was administered. However, notwithstanding the advantages with which the hypnosis group was provided, the investigators failed to find any significant differences between the self-report and physiological measures of these two groups in response to the experimentally administered dental procedure.

Two studies (Gibbins et al.[53] and Woody and Schaube[54]) presented data that seemed to indicate that desensitization plus a hypnotic-induction procedure resulted in greater fear reduction than desensitization alone. However, an analysis of the procedures employed suggests that the conclusion may be unwarranted, or at least premature. Both studies confound the hypnotic induction with added elaboration of desensitization scenes, as well as additional direct fear-reduction suggestions. In addition, Gibbins et al.[53] further confounded their study by placing good hypnosis subjects into the hypnotic-induction group as opposed to the desensitization or control groups. Barber[5] has pointed out that the type of method that Gibbins et al.[53] employed in subject assignation, as opposed to random assignment, results in the inability to control for such things as previous experience, the relationship of the subject with the experimenter, and the differential effects of these factors on the subject's attitudes, expectancies, and motivation.

The data presented in this section suggests that "relaxation" related to a hypnotic-induction procedure is, at worst, no more effective than that related to the suggestion merely to "sit quietly."[44] At best, it is no more effective than the experimental analogues of progressive relaxation.[48, 50] These experimental analogues can provide only a pale representation of the progressive relaxation procedure that is actually administered in a clinical setting. Thus, in the McAmmond et al. study,[50] it would seem fair to assume that if conditions were optimal for the presentation of progressive relaxation, as they were for the administration of hypnosis, relaxation resulting from the progressive relaxation procedure may have been substantially more effective than that resulting from a hypnotic induction.

"Hypnotically" Suggested "Hallucinations"

In addition to increasing the depth of "relaxation," those who hold the "trance state" view of hypnosis and adhere to the traditional role of hypnosis in behavior therapy suggest that hypnosis can enhance the effectiveness of certain behavioral techniques by intensifying the vividness with which the necessary images are experienced. The research that most closely explores this hypothesized characteristic of the hypnotic induction focuses on "hypnotically" induced "hallucinations." That is, subjects are instructed to experience visual or aural stimuli as clearly as possible that are not presently in the subject's environment. It is assumed that following hypnotic-induction procedure, subjects are more capable of experiencing such stimuli and the imaginal stimuli are perceived with greater clarity. For example, Erikson[55] suggests that hypnotically induced visual hallucinations have all the characteristics of the actual stimuli they represent and are thus perceived by "hypnotized" subjects as being identical to physically tangible objects.

In a study by Barber and Calverly,[56] subjects, in a base-level test, were asked to imagine a specific condition and a visual stimulus. Each subject was then assigned randomly to one of three groups. One group received short task-motivation instructions," a second received a standard hypnotic-induction procedure; and the third, a control group, received no specific instructions.

Barber and Calverly [56] demonstrated that nearly 50% of unselected, uninstructed subjects reported that they clearly heard a suggested auditory stimulus, and nearly 33% clearly saw a suggested visual stimulus. This finding, later corroborated by Spanos and Barber [57] and supported to some extent by Bowers,[58] suggests that a greater percentage of individuals than was previously thought could clearly experience imaginal auditory and visual stimuli without any special introduction or training. Barber [59] points out that these data cast some doubt on the findings of earlier hypnotic hallucination studies (e.g. References 60, 61) that failed to include an independent uninstructed control group.

A second important finding of the Barber and Calverly study [56] indicated that subjects who received either task-motivation or hypnotic-induction instructions reported that they experienced the suggested imaginal stimuli more clearly than they did during the base-level condition; this was not the case for the control group. Further, there was no significant difference in the reported experience of the imaginal stimuli following the hypnotic-induction procedure as compared with the task-motivation instructions. These data were extended by Spanos and Barber [57] to show that the subjective report of "hallucination" following the task-motivation or hypnotic-induction instructions was raised only slightly above the base-level response to the suggested auditory and visual stimuli. In other words, the total percentage of the variance of the posttreatment response to the hallucinated stimuli contributed by the task-motivation and hypnotic induction procedures was very small (6%); in contrast, the contribution of the base-level response to the total posttreatment self-report variance was considerably higher (64%). This suggests that previous studies that employed only a hypnotic-induction condition in demonstrating the ability of hypnotized subjects to hallucinate should be reexamined. There is a distinct possibility that such results could have been obtained without the use of a hypnotic-induction procedure.

The data reviewed in this section suggests that "hypnosis" can produce little increase in the vividness of imagery when compared to the base-level response. Any increment obtained following a hypnotic induction can be equaled by the administration of short task-motivational instructions. It thus seems logical to hypothesize that the essence of such instructions is presented by the behavior therapist when administering an imaginal behavioral technique. If this is the case, then there is no reason to believe that the occurrence of a hypnotic induction prior to the presentation of an imaginal behavioral assignment can provide any additional benefit.

The Role of the "Trance" in Behavioral Techniques

Finally, some individuals writing from the context of hypnotherapy, have suggested that the effects of specific imaginal behavioral techniques may be due to the possible existence of hypnosis or the trance state unwittingly incorporated into these behavioral procedures.[14-16] The difficulties of such a position have been addressed by Barber,[5] Cautela,[62, 63] Johnston and Donaghue,[64] Spanos,[65] Spanos *et al.*,[66] Spanos and Barber,[38] and Weitzenhoffer,[17] among others. The following, as a group, have pointed out the difficulties inherent in the position that certain procedures, not otherwise associated with hypnosis, may nevertheless result in the production of a "trance state" in susceptible subjects (Barber,[5] Chaves,[37] and Spanos[65]) have delineated the differences between hypnosis and various behavioral procedures (Cautela,[62, 63] Spanos *et al.*,[66] and Spanos and Barber[38]); and have presented strong arguments for suggesting that the effectiveness of hypnotherapeutic techniques are due to the inclusion of components of desensitization in the procedure rather than to the induction of a "trance." [17, 63, 64]

IMPLICATIONS OF THE "STATE" POSITION FOR BEHAVIOR THERAPY:
A SUMMARY STATEMENT

The "trance state" conception of hypnosis has been criticized on both logical and empirical bases. The outstanding logical flaw of this position results from the failure to extract physiological variables that could serve to reliably denote the existence of the hypnotic trance. As a consequence of their inability to obtain an independent referent, those who support this position have been forced to demonstrate the existence of the trance state by pointing to changes of responses in several classes of behaviors traditionally associated with hypnotic induction. Unfortunately, these behavioral changes are also explained by hypothesizing an "altered state of consciousness." The circularity that is the outcome of such reasoning precludes the utility of the "trance state" as an explantory construct.

Empirically, the trance state conception is also permeated with basic difficulties. One problem again arises from the need to find some referent that uniquely defines and denotes the hypnotic "trance." Proponents suggest that following the administration of a hypnotic induction, and as a direct result of the consequent "trance state," there are predictable changes in four classes of behavior that converge to uniquely denote the existence of a "trance." The data, however, do not support this contention. In fact, there is very little correlation among these four classes of behavior, indicating that the classes are probably independent of each other and not readily explainable by a single hypothetical construct. Much of Barber's work poses another empirical problem for the "trance state" position. Barber has demonstrated that the behavioral interaction labeled "hypnosis" can be explained with use of the same empirically based concepts that are employed to explain other behavioral interactions. He has thereby obviated the explanatory function of the "trance" construct.

A large body of literature has accumulated in an effort to support the hypothesis that the trance state conception of hypnosis can enhance the effectiveness of behavior therapy. Although the methods for attaining this enhancement are varied (e.g., time distortion, age regression), the two hypothesized characteristics of "hypnosis" whose enhancement effects find the greatest consental support are the capability of the subject "under hypnosis" of attaining deeper levels of "relaxation" and imagining scenes with greater clarity than is possible without hypnosis. A review of the relevant hypnosis literature indicated that hypnotic-induction procedure was typically no more capable of increasing the level of "relaxation" or of enhancing the vividness of imagery than were direct instructions aimed at producing these behavioral changes. Further, support was sought from studies of the effects of hypnosis on various behavioral procedures; these generally failed to demonstrate significant differences between subjects who received a hypnotic induction plus a behavioral procedure and subjects who received the behavioral procedure alone. It can therefore reasonably be concluded that the traditional "state" view of the role of hypnosis in behavior therapy is simply not valid. The concept of "hypnosis" as enhancing behavioral procedures by increasing the level of "relaxation" or the clarity of images is not generally supported in the experimental literature. Recently, however, Barber [5] has presented an alternative view of "hypnosis" that has important implications for behavior therapy.

THE "NONSTATE" VIEW OF HYPNOSIS

Barber [5] has suggested that a majority of previous investigators in postulating a "trance state" have been forced to make unwarranted assumptions that have served to reduce the value of their findings and theoretical formulations. That is, the "hypnotic trance" is considered to be different from other phenomena studied by psychologists, and, as such, its special properties preclude the use of conventional experimental methods more suitable to ordinary variables. As a result, studies of hypnosis often fail to meet even the most basic criteria of the psychological experiment. Barber questions the need to postulate the trance state, or invest the interaction labeled "hypnosis" with special attributes, in studying and explaining behavior relevant to the hypnosis situation. Rather, hypnosis is conceived of as a behavioral interaction that can be described in terms previously employed with all similar interactions. There are at least two advantages resulting from the position that hypnosis is similar to other behavioral interactions. First, the use of accepted, conventional approaches to psychological experimentation may now be applied in studying hypnosis. Second, variables that have been found useful for the analysis of other behavioral interactions can be utilized in facilitating an understanding of the hypnosis interaction. Because Barber [5] makes the assumption that there is little which distinguishes the "hypnosis" interaction from other human interactions, he has been able to analyze this interaction employing the same scientific method that is the basis for all psychological inquiry. Initially, he operationalized the hypnosis situation in terms of denotable independent and dependent variables. These above-mentioned dependent variables are contained in four categories: response to test suggestions, hypnotic appearance, reports of unusual experiences, and testimony of having felt hypnotized. The independent variables also can be classified into four groups: procedural variables, subject variables, experimenter variables, and subject-experimenter interaction variables. Barber next concerned himself with determining the significant empirical relationships between the independent and dependent variables in an extensive series of studies.[5] The results of his investigations led him to tentatively propose a set of empirical generalizations to serve as the basis for a cognitive-behavioral system.

A summary conclusion that Barber and his co-workers have recently drawn from numerous experimental investigations suggest that "subjects carry out so-called 'hypnosis' behaviors when they have positive attitudes, motivations, and expectations toward the test situation which lead to a willingness to think and imagine with the themes that are suggested." (Ref. 41, p. 6) His analogy is that of the reader of a novel, or a member of the audience at a movie. "The processes involved in responding to suggestions in a hypnotic situation resemble those found when a person is experiencing sadness, happiness . . . and a variety of other emotions as he reads an interesting novel or observes a motion picture. In each of these instances—when responding to suggestions in a hypnotic situation, when reading a novel, or when observing a movie— the person who has positive attitudes, motivations, and expectancies toward the situation thinks and imagines with the communications he is receiving." (Ref. 41, p. 13)

Recognition both by proponents of "state" and "nonstate" views of hypnosis, that these two determinants of good "hypnosis" subjects—willingness to cooperate (based upon positive expectancies, attitudes, and motivation) and the ability to become involved in one's imagery—are perhaps the most significant indicators of such subjects is an important area of agreement between two otherwise diametrically opposed positions.[67] Because the "hypnosis" situation has a number of aspects in common with the administration of imaginal behavioral therapy techniques, it is possible that procedures which enhance responsiveness to the imaginal hypnosis test suggestions might also be effective in augmenting involvement in the imaginal component of the behavioral techniques.[38, 66]

Thus, Barber[5] summarizes an extensive series of studies that demonstrate the importance of a procedure designed to enhance subjects' motivation to cooperate with the experimenter. This short verbal instruction, which Barber has labled "task motivational," served to amplify subjects' responses to a variety of suggestions. Mere motivation is not sufficient to enhance performance, but, as Barber et al.[41] have shown, directing cooperative subjects to attempt cognitive strategies congruent with the performance of overt hypnosis behavior enhances the responsivity of such subjects to suggestions. It is this cognitive structuring which Spanos labels "goal-directed fantasy"[68] and Barber designates as "think with" instructions[69] that is proposed as the necessary preparation for a good "hypnotic" performance.

Similarly, there is general agreement that motivation to change and cooperation with the treatment program proposed by the therapist are important factors in determining the outcome of the endeavor of any therapeutic approach. In the case of behavior therapy, a large number of the techniques in the therapist's repertoire contain a significant imaginal component. Therefore, Spanos and Barber[38] suggest that some of the cognitive strategies which they employ to enhance hypnosis behavior could be used by behavior therapists to augment their clients' responsivity to the imaginal components of various relevant behavioral techniques (e.g. systematic desensitization, covert conditioning, flooding).

REFERENCES

1. WOLBERG, L. R. 1954. The Technique of Psychotherapy. Grune and Stratton. New York, N.Y.
2. BARBER, T. X. 1965. Experimental analysis of "hypnotic" behavior: a review of recent empirical findings. J. Abnorm Psychol. 70: 132–154.
3. BARBER, T. X. & D. S. CALVERLY. 1965. Empirical evidence for a theory of "hypnotic" behavior: effects on suggestibility of five variables typically included in hypnotic induction procedure. J. Consult. Psychol. 29: 98–107.

4. BARBER, T. X. & W. DEMOOR. 1972. A theory of hypnotic induction procedures. Am. J. Clin. Hypn. **15:** 112–135.
5. BARBER, T. X. 1969. Hypnosis: A Scientific Approach. Van Nostrand Reinhold Company. New York, N.Y.
6. HILGARD, E. R. 1965. Hypnotic susceptibility. Harcourt, Brace, and World. New York, N.Y.
7. HILGARD, E. R. & C. T. TART. 1966. Responsiveness to suggestions following waking and imagination instructions and following induction of hypnosis. J. Abnorm. Psychol. **71:** 196–208.
8. ORNE, M. T. 1959. The nature of hypnosis: artifact and essence. J. Abnorm. Social Psychol. **58:** 277–299.
9. GILL, M. M. & M. BRENMAN. 1959. Hypnosis and related states. International Universities Press. New York, N.Y.
10. WEITZENHOFFER, A. M. 1957. General Techniques of Hypnotism. New York, N.Y.
11. ORNE, M. T. 1966. Hypnosis, motivation, and compliance. Am. J. Psychiat. **122:** 721–726.
12. TART, C. T. 1972. Measuring the depth of an altered state of consciousness, with particular reference to self-report scales of hypnotic depth. In Hypnosis: Research Development and Perspectives. E. Fromm and R. E. Shor, Eds. Aldine-Atherton. Chicago, Ill.
13. HILARD, E. R. 1969. Altered states of awareness. 1969. J. Nerv. Ment. Dis. **149:** 68–79.
14. LITVAK, S. B. 1970. Hypnosis and the desensitization behavior therapies. Psychol. Rep. **27:** 787–794.
15. MURRAY, E. J. 1963. Learning theory and psychotherapy: biotropic versus sociotropic approaches. J. Counseling Psychol. **10:** 250–255.
16. WOODY, R. H. 1973. Clinical suggestions and systematic desensitization. Am. J. Clin. Hypn. **15:** 250–257.
17. WEITZENHOFFER, A. M. 1972. Behavior therapeutic techniques and hypnotherapeutic methods. Am. J. Clin. Typn. **15:** 71–82.
18. DEVOGE, S. 1975. A behavioral analysis of a group hypnosis treatment method. Am. J. Clin. Hypn. **18:** 127–131.
19. TODD, F. J. & R. J. KELLY. 1970. The use of hypnosis to facilitate conditioned relaxation responses. Behav. Ther. Exp. Psychiat. **1:** 295–298.
20. ROTHMAN, I., M. L. CARROLL & F. D. ROTHMAN. 1976. Homework and self-hypnosis: the conditioning therapies in clinical practice. In Hypnosis and Behavior Therapy. E. Dengrove, Ed. Charles C Thomas. Springfield, Ill.
21. SCOTT, D. L. 1970. Treatment of a severe phobia for birds by hypnosis. Am. J. Clin. Hypn. **12:** 146–149.
22. RUBIN, M. 1972. Verbally suggested responses for reciprocal inhibition of anxiety. J. Behav. Ther. Exp. Psychiat. **3:** 273–277.
23. GLICK, B. S. 1972. Aversive imagery therapy using hypnosis. Am. J. Psychother. **26:** 432–436.
24. BELL, G. K. 1972. Clinical hypnosis: warp and woof of psychotherapies. Psychotherapy: Theory, Research and Practice. **9:** 276–280.
25. PERIN, C. T., Jr. 1968. The use of substitute response signals in anxiety situations. Am. J. Clin. Hypn. **10:** 207–208.
26. MOOREFIELD, C. W. 1971. The use of hypnosis and behavior therapy in asthma. Am. J. Clin. Hypn. **13:** 162–168.
27. WICHRAMASEKERA, I. 1974. Hypnosis and broad spectrum behavior therapy for blepharaspism: a case study. Int. J. Clin. Exp. Hypn. **22:** 201–209.
28. KRIPPNER, S. 1971. Hypnosis as verbal programming in educational therapy. Academic Ther. **3:** 5–12.
29. FUCHS, K., Z. HOCH, E. PALDI, H. ABRAMOVICI, J. M. BRONDES, I. TIMOR-TRITSCH & M. KLEINHOUS. 1973. Hypno-densensitization therapy of vaginismus: Part

I. "In vitro" method. Part II. "In vivo" method. Int. J. Clin. Exp. Hypn. **21:** 144–156.

30. DENGROVE, E. 1973. The uses of hypnosis in behavior therapy. Int. J. Clin. Exp. Hypn. **21:** 13–17.

31. DENGROVE, E. 1976. Hypnosis. *In* Hypnosis and Behavior Therapy. E. Dengrove, Ed. Charles C Thomas. Springfield, Ill.

32. ASTOR, M. H. 1973. Hypnosis and behavior modification combined with psychoanalytic psychotherapy. Int. Clin. Exp. Hypn. **21:** 18–24.

33. BARBER, T. X. 1965. Measuring "hypnotic-like" suggestibility with and without "hypnotic induction"; psychometric properties; norms, and variables influencing response to the Barber Suggestibility Scale (BSS).

34. BARBER, T. X. 1961. Physiological effects of "hypnosis." Psychol. Bull. **58:** 390–419.

35. BARBER, T. X. 1965. Physiological effects of "hypnotic suggestions": a critical review of recent research (1960–64). Psychol. Bull. **63:** 201–222.

36. BARBER, T. X. "Hypnosis" as a causal variable in present-day psychology: a critical analysis. *Psychological Reports,* 1964b, **14:** 83–84.

37. CHAVES, J. F. 1968. Hypnosis reconceptualized: an overview of Barber's theoretical and empirical work. Psychol. Rep. **22:** 587–608.

38. SPANOS, N. P. & T. X. BARBER. 1976. Behavior modification and hypnosis. *In* Progress in Behavior Modification Vol. 3 M. Hersen, R. M. Eisler, and P. M. Miller, Eds. Academic Press. New York, N.Y.

39. BARBER, T. X., H. S. DALAL & D. S. CALVERLY. 1968. The subjective reports of hypnotic subjects. Am. J. Clin. Hypn. **11:** 74–88.

40. BARBER, T. X. & D. S. CALVERLY. 1964. Effect of *E*'s tone of voice on "hypnotic-like" suggestibility. Psychol. Rep. **15:** 139–144.

41. BARBER, T. X., N. P. SPANOS & J. F. CHAVES. 1974. Hypnosis, Imagination, and Human Potentialities. Pergamon Press. Elmsford, N.Y.

42. BARBER, T. X. 1962. Toward a theory of hypnosis: posthypnotic behavior. Arch. Gen. Psychiat. **7:** 321–342.

43. BARBER, T. X. & D. S. CALVERLY. 1966. Toward a theory of "hypnotic" behavior: experimental analysis of suggested amnesia. J. Abnorm. Psychol. **71:** 95–107.

44. BARBER, T. X. & K. W. HAHN, JR. 1963. Hypnotic induction and "relaxation": an experimental study. Arch. Gen. Psychiat. **8:** 295–300.

45. DUNWOODY, R. C. & W. C. EDMONSTON, JR. 1974. Hypnosis and slow eye movements. Am. J. Clin. Hypn. **16:** 270–274.

46. EDMONSTON, W. E., JR. 1972. Relaxation as an appropriate experimental control in hypnosis studies. Am. J. Clin. Hypn. **14:** 218–228.

47. LANG, P. J. 1965. The mechanism of fear: a laboratory analysis of desensitization therapy. Paper read at Am. Psychol. Assoc. Chicago, Ill. September.

48. MARKS, I. M., M. G. GELDER & G. EDWARDS. 1968. Hypnosis and densensitization for phobias: a controlled prospective trial. Br. J. Psychol. **114:** 1263–1274.

48a. PAUL, G. L. 1969. Physiological effects of relaxation training and hypnotic suggestion. J. Abnorm. Psychol. **74:** 425–437.

49. PAUL, G. L. 1969. Inhibition of physiological response to stressful imagery by relaxation training and hypnotically suggested relaxation. Behav. Res. Ther. **7:** 249–256.

50. McAMMOND, D. M., P. O. DAVIDSON & D. M. KOVITZ. 1971. A comparison of the effects of hypnosis and relaxation training on stress reactions in a dental situation. Am. J. Clin. Hypn. **13:** 233–242.

51. PAUL, G. L. & R. N. TRIMBLE. 1970. Recorded as "live" relaxation training and hypnotic suggestion: comparative effectiveness for reducing physiological arousal and inhibiting stress response. Behav. Ther. **1:** 285–320.

52. BARBER, T X., L. M. ASCHER & M. MOVROIDES. 1970. Effects of practice on hypnotic suggestibility: a re-evaluation of Hull's postulates. Am. J. Clin. Hypn. **14:** 48–53.
53. GIBBONS, D., L. KILBOURNE, A. SOUNDERS & C. CASTLES. 1970. The cognitive control of behavior: a comparison of systematic desensitization and hypnotically induced "directed experience" techniques. Am. J. Clin. Hypn. **12:** 141–145.
54. WOODY, R. H. & P. G. SHAUBE. 1969. Desensitization of fear by video tapes. J. Clin. Psychol. **25:** 102–103.
55. ERICKSON, M. H. 1958. Deep hypnosis and its induction. *In* Experimental Hypnosis. L. M. LeCrone, Ed. MacMillan. New York, N.Y.
56. BARBER, T. X., & D. S. CALVERLY. 1964. An experimental study of "hypnotic" (auditory and visual) hallucinations. J. Abnorm. Soc. Psychol. **63:** 13–20.
57. SPANOS, N. P. & T. X. BARBER. 1968. "Hypnotic" experiences as inferred from subjective reports: auditory and visual hallucinations. J. Exp. Res. Personality **3:** 136–150.
58. BOWERS, K. S. 1967. The effect of demands for honesty on reports of visual and auditory hallucinations. Int. J. Clin. Exp. Hypn. **15:** 31–36.
59. BARBER, T. X. 1964. Toward a theory of "hypnotic" behavior: positive visual and auditory hallucination. Psychol. Rec. **14:** 197–210.
60. ERICKSON, M. H., S. HERSHMAN & I. I. SECTOR. 1961. The Practical Application of Medical and Dental Hypnosis. Julian Press. New York, N.Y.
61. HALPERN, S. 1961. On the similarity between hypnotic and mescaline hallucinations. Int. J. Clin. Hypn. **9:** 139–149.
62. CAUTELA, J. R. 1966. Hypnosis and behavior therapy. Behavior Res. Ther. **4:** 219–224.
63. CAUTELA, J. R. 1966. Desensitization factors in the hypnotic treatment of phobias. J. Psychol. **64:** 277–281.
64. JOHNSTON, E. & J. R. DONOGHUE. 1971. Hypnosis and smoking: a review of the literature. Am. J. Clin. Hypn. **13:** 265–274.
65. SPANOS, N. P. 1970. Barber's reconceptualization of hypnosis: an evaluation of criticisms. J. Res. Personality **4:** 241–258.
66. SPANOS, N. P., W. DeMOOR & T. X. BARBER. 1973. Hypnosis and behavior therapy: common denominators. Am. J. Clin. Hypn. **16:** 45–64.
67. SPANOS, N. P. & T. X. BARBER. 1974. Toward a convergence in hypnosis research. Am. Psychol. **29:** 500–511.
68. SPANOS, N. P. 1971. Goal-directed fantasy & performance of hypnotic test suggestions. Psychiatry **34:** 86–96.
69. BARBER, T. X. This volume.

VARIABLES INFLUENCING THE POSTHYPNOTIC PERSISTENCE OF AN UNCANCELED HYPNOTIC SUGGESTION *

Campbell Perry †

Department of Psychology
Concordia University
Montreal, Quebec, H3G 1M8 Canada

A fundamental belief about hypnosis is that any suggestion that is administered to the hypnotized S should be clearly and unambiguously canceled during hypnosis. It is believed that if the hypnotist does not do this, the suggestions will persist posthypnotically, and in some cases will have quite profoundly disruptive effects upon the hypnotized person's subsequent behavior posthypnosis. The basis for this belief is entirely anecdotal.

Weitzenhoffer,[1] for instance, administered a posthypnotic suggestion that the S would be unable to stand up at the end of hypnosis session until the hypnotist clapped his hands. Following hypnosis, the S was asked to stand up, and, as expected, was unable to. He was still unable to, however, when the hypnotist clapped his hands, and the experimenter (E) became concerned that he had inadvertently triggered off a hysterical paralysis. The S was rehypnotized, and it transpired that as the E was canceling the suggestion, a power lawn mower outside the experimental room had drowned out his voice just as he was describing the hand-clap condition. The S remained unaware that the suggestion had been canceled, and it remained in force.

Evans,[2] likewise suggested amnesia to the number 6 to a group of Ss. He intended the amnesia to last for the duration of the session, but one S misunderstood the instruction to mean that the amnesia for the number 6 was to last until a later scheduled session. The S was a high school mathematics teacher, who proceeded to experience great teaching difficulty in the classroom during the interim.

In another such incident,[3] Schultz placed a coin on the back of a S's hand, and suggested the coin was red hot and would burn the hand without causing pain. There was no trace of a burn when the coin was lifted, but two weeks later the S reported that every morning since the session he had awakened with a painless blister on the very same spot on the back of his hand; the blister had proceeded to subside during the course of the day. Schultz then remembered that he had forgotten to cancel the suggestion, and proceeded to do so. From there on, the man's daily blister ceased.

There are at least 20 other examples like this known to the author, but they are all likewise anecdotal and may thus overestimate the incidence of the phenomenon. There may be many instances where the hypnotist fails to cancel the suggestion and the S suffers no posttrance sequalae. Such cases, by their very nature, would tend to go unreported. Only one report known to the present

* The first two studies in this series were supported by National Research Council of Canada, grant no. APA 0344, and the third study by a University of Queensland Post Doctoral Research Fellowship for 1975–76.

† Reprint requests to: Campbell Perry, Department of Psychology, Sir George Williams Campus, Concordia University, Montreal, Quebec, H3G 1M8, Canada.

investigator indicates that some hypnotic Ss cancel an uncanceled suggestion themselves. M. Bowers [4] was demonstrating hypnotic induction procedures to a group of students, one of whom later pointed out that she had not canceled a specific hypnotic item. Bowers immediately realized that she had forgotten, but the S quickly interceded on her behalf by saying that he had realized during hypnosis that she was no longer interested in the hypnotic item in question and so had canceled it himself.

When the present investigator first became interested in this phenomenon, no laboratory study of it had ever been undertaken. Thus there was no preexisting model to indicate what the parameters of the phenomenon might be. The closest available model comes from experimental studies of posthypnotic suggestion. These indicate a compulsive, quasiautomatic quality to posthypnotic response,[5] rather similar to that already noted for uncanceled suggestions. Other studies, however, have shown that the carrying out of posthypnotic suggestion is affected also by the hypnotized person's perceptions of the hypnotist's expectations.[6,7] Further, the work of Sheehan [8] indicates that the hypnotized person may give special meaning to the hypnotist's communication, to the extent of countering a preconception about hypnosis if it conflicts with the hypnotist's implied intent.

The report summarized five experiments that have sought to follow this model derived from our rather limited knowledge of the parameters affecting response to posthypnotic suggestion and apply it to uncanceled suggestions.

EXPERIMENTS ONE AND TWO

The first two experiments [9] can be summarized briefly. Both use the real-simulating design of Orne,[10] where the simulators are used to check for the possibility that the response of Ss is merely a matter of implicit cues in the experiment's design and/or procedure. This model uses Ss insusceptible to hypnosis who are instructed to fake hypnosis before a hypnotist who is unaware that they are simulating. If high-susceptible Ss in hypnosis behave in the same way as insusceptible simulating Ss, all that can be concluded is that the particular item of behavior under examination is not crucial for differentiating trance from nontrance behavior. It does mean that the hypnotic item in question is not subjectively real to the hypnotized S; for instance, just about anyone can simulate an hypnotic hallucination. That does not mean that the hypnotized S is not experiencing something different in his/her ongoing experience; only that the verbal and behavioral data from a truly hypnotized person cannot be distinguished from that of a play actor on a particular hallucination item.

Differences between real and simulating Ss are argued by Orne [10] to indicate something unique to hypnotic experience that cannot be duplicated by waking role players. As Barber [11] has argued, where differences between reals and simulators are obtained, they may be due to different preexperimental instructions given to the respective groups. To control for this possibility, all experiments reported in this series utilized a group of medium-susceptible Ss in addition to the high-susceptibles and the insusceptible simulators. Such medium-susceptible Ss act as a conventional control group. They receive the same preexperimental instructions as highs and differ only in terms of their degree of hypnotizability.

In all experiments, Ss were screened for susceptibility by the HGSHS:A [12] in order to obtain groups of high-, medium-, and low-susceptible Ss.

Experiments 1 and 2 used three such groups, each containing six Ss. In Experiment 1, the item left uncanceled was a delusion of a missing number. The Ss were instructed to visualize the digits from 0 to 9 on a hallucinated TV screen with eyes closed. When S reported being able to see all the digits, the E suggested that the number 5 was fading and would disappear completely, so that S would no longer be able to visualize 5, write it, say it, or think about it at all. Then Ss were tested on this item with three long-division problems, two of which involved the number 5. When Ss stopped trying to solve the problems, E said, "Good. Now I'll take the pad and pencil and you can close your eyes and relax. Just relax and remain deeply hypnotized." In other words, there was no explicit attempt to cancel the suggestion, and E proceeded with the next hypnotic item.

Of the 18 Ss in Experiment 1, only 1 S, a highly hypnotizable S, showed posthypnotic persistence. Prior to hypnosis, she had completed 30 arithmetic items and got two wrong, neither of which involved the number 5. Posthypnotically, she completed seven items, getting four wrong. Two of the first seven problems involved the number 5, and she got both wrong. In the postexperimental inquiry, she reported feeling very anxious about something but could not say what. Of course, we restored the number 5 after testing her on the arithmetic problems.

Experiment 2 followed from Experiment 1. The low incidence of uncanceled suggestions persisting posthypnotically could have been due to any of the following reasons: (1) the difficulty of the delusion of the missing number item, which, during hypnosis was passed only by the highly susceptible Ss; (2) the fact that Ss were screened for hypnotizability by HGSHS:A,[12] a very effective screening device but rough; and (3) that although we made a serious effort not to cancel the delusion of the missing item explicitly, we may have canceled it implicitly by saying, "Just close your eyes and relax."

In Experiment 2, we chose a paralysis of the body from the waist down as the item to be left uncanceled. To test it in hypnosis, we asked the S to stand up and walk two feet and pick up a vase of paper flowers after the leg paralysis had been induced. In an attempt to avoid implicit cancellation, the E said, after S had tried and failed to get up, "O.K., now stop trying to reach for the flowers, and lean back in the chair. Just let your eyes close." In other words, we terminated the instruction to reach for the flowers, but did not cancel the leg-paralysis item. To make the determinations of hypnotizability more stringent, we screened Ss both on HGSHS:A [12] and on SHSS:C.[14] Again, we used six highs, six mediums, and six insusceptible simulators. To test for posthypnotic persistence of the leg paralysis, we asked Ss, after hypnosis had been terminated, to get up and walk six feet to a table in order to complete the cognitive tests used in Experiment 1, on which, once again, Ss had been pretested.

Despite the greater care taken to control the variables I have already described, we did even worse than in Experiment 1. Not one S manifested the phenomenon; all Ss were able to get up and walk to the table after hypnosis had been terminated. Further, the effect of screening Ss more stringently appeared to work against us. Three of the insusceptible simulators reported in the postexperimental inquiry that the leg paralysis had not been canceled, an effect that seemed to be related to their getting two hypnotic screening sessions prior to the main experiment. It was clear, however, that they had not sensed the experiment's hypothesis, since they all got up and walked to the table without difficulty when requested to in the posthypnotic period.

EXPERIMENT THREE

Recent research has indicated that many hypnotic Ss show a special wish to please the hypnotist. The work of Sheehan [8] indicates that the hypnotist's communication may have a special importance in the trance setting. This motivational and possibly transference aspect of the hypnotic interaction may be tapped by including a suggestion—not utilized in the first two studies—that the S will experience all effects suggested for *as long as the hypnotist asks him to experience them*. Such a communication conveys, in an indirect fashion, the hypnotist's wish that the S should respond to a suggestion indefinitely, in a quasi-automatic fashion.

This study utilized 20 Ss: seven highs, six mediums, and seven insusceptible simulators. The hypnotic induction was on videotape, and Ss were told that this was for standardization purposes. They were told, however, that one item could not be standardized in this manner, and that when the induction came to that point, the E would turn off the video and administer the item personally. This item, which was the item to be left uncanceled, involved an analgesia of the right hand and arm. It was used both because high- and medium-susceptible Ss are capable of good analgesia, and because it gave me a chance to quantify the effect of the uncanceled suggestion by obtaining some pain ratings.

In order to distract Ss from the fact that the analgesia was left uncanceled, a new procedure was introduced, adapted from Binet.[15] After the E had administered and tested the analgesia by pinching both hands, the E introduced a Thought Reading task. The E said:

> Now listen to me very carefully. Your probably know that when you're hypnotized you can quite often do things that you might have great difficulty doing when not hypnotized . . . things that you might not even be able to do at all when not hypnotized. One of these abilities I am very interested in is your ability while hypnotized to tell what another person is thinking about, just by concentrating on that other person's thought. I want to see if you can do that. . . . Right now I am thinking about a number—it's a number somewhere between 1 and 10. I wonder if you can tell me what it is? It's a number that I have clearly in my mind . . . etc."

Following this, the E tapped the analgesic hand three times with a pencil and asked the S what number he was thinking of. Regardless of S's response, he was always told that the number had been "3." The video was then turned on again to complete the session.

The rationale of this procedure had been developed in a pilot study involving 13 insusceptible simulators who had perceived the tapping on the hand as an attempt to trick them into denying that the hand was analgesic. They were put in the position of doing what the E expected—that is, to say "3"—at the expense of denying the reality of their reported analgesia. In this way it was hoped that none of the Ss would notice that the analgesia item was not removed, since the E then turned the video back on and the induction continued.

This time, of 20 Ss, three reported an analgesic hand and arm posthypnotically. These three Ss constituted three of the seven highly susceptible Ss employed in this study. The way that these reports were elicited was as follows. After hypnosis was terminated, the E conducted an amnesia inquiry to ascertain what Ss recalled during hypnosis. The amnesia was then lifted by a prearranged cue and Ss were questioned further as to what they could recall. At some point the Ss recalled the analgesia item, and after they had described how it felt, E casually asked them how the hand felt then. If they reported that it felt numb, the E said that he had forgotten to remove the analgesia, and then said he thought he should test the analgesia to make sure that it had completely dissipated. He proceeded to pinch the skin on both hands, and the S was asked to rate how painful each pinch felt on a pain scale from 1 to 10, where 1 = completely painless and 10 = extremely painful. These Ss gave the following ratings: S_1 rated the analgesic hand as 4 on the control hand as 8–9, S_2 gave ratings of 4 and 8, and S_3 gave ratings of 2–3 and of 5–6, respectively. One of the other high-susceptible Ss reported that he had canceled the analgesia himself at the time at which the taste hallucination item (which immediately succeeded the analgesia) was canceled. It could not be ascertained what had happened with the uncanceled suggestion for the other three highly susceptible Ss. One of them continually massaged the arm throughout the amnesia and postexperimental inquiries, while steadfastly denying that the arm felt any different other than that it was feeling a little tired. This she attributed to having spent the previous afternoon in the gymnasium. None of the medium susceptible Ss and simulating Ss reported any such persistence of analgesia beyond the hypnotic induction into the posthypnotic period.

EXPERIMENT FOUR AND FIVE

The final two experiments had a dual purpose. The evidence of Experiment 3 indicated that the phenomenon of uncanceled analgesia persisting posthypnotically was confined to a minority of highly susceptible Ss. Although it was clear that the set induced in that experiment (that S was to respond for as long as E asked him to) had a bearing on the phenomenon's occurrence, it was thought that the Ss who manifested it might have greater hypnotic skill than those who did not. Specifically, it was predicted that the Ss for whom analgesia persisted posthypnotically would report better analgesia during hypnosis, and would also manifest greater hypnotic depth throughout the hypnosis session and during the analgesia item.

A second hypothesis was derived from McConkey and Sheehan,[16] who found that there was no difference in hypnotic performance between Ss tested in a collaborative as opposed to a contractual context of testing. Both Experiments 4 and 5, however, involved contractual testing; the Ss were recruited to fulfill requirements of a course in Introductory Psychology. In Experiment 4, the hypnotic induction was presented on videotape, as in the previous experiment, so that interaction between hypnotist (H) and S was minimal. In Experiment 5, an almost identical induction was used, except that it was carried out personally by the hypnotist, who made a major effort to vary his procedures to suit the S in an attempt to maximize the S's experience of the subjective effects of hypnosis. It was predicted, following McConkey and Sheehan,[16] that there would be no difference in the incidence of uncanceled suggestions carrying over into the posthypnotic period.

Each experiment involved 24 Ss, consisting of eight Highs, eight Mediums, and eight Insusceptible simulators. As well as the 48 Ss tested in the 2 experiments, ten pilot Ss were run, four of whom were highly susceptible.

The experiments followed the format of Experiment 3, but an attempt was made to clean up the pain stimulus used in that experiment. Instead of pinching the hands, where the E might inadvertently pinch with differential strengths, an electrical stimulus was used to test analgesia. It consisted of a prod device, powered by an Eveready 9-volt transistor battery, which was applied standardly to a point immediately behind the third knuckle of each hand.

The results can be summarized quickly. Two Ss in experiment 4 and one S in experiment 5 showed posthypnotic persistence of uncanceled analgesia. One of the four Ss in the pilot study also manifested the effect. It was thus clear that the interpersonal effects had little effect on the phenomenon's occurrence, although they did have other effects that go beyond the scope of the present paper.

The fact that only four highly susceptible Ss out of 20 tested over the two experiments and pilot study manifested the phenomenon meant that I had to pool data to test the first hypothesis. The pooling was justified on the grounds that there were no significant differences between the 16 highly susceptible Ss in the two experiments in terms of analgesia, depth during analgesia, depth

TABLE 1

HYPNOTIC SUSCEPTIBILITY, HYPNOTIC DEPTH AND HYPNOTIC ANALGESIA FOR SS
WHO DID, AND DID NOT MANIFEST POSTHYPNOTIC PERSISTENCE OF AN
UNCANCELED SUGGESTION

		Uncanceled Suggestion Persisted Posthypnotically (N=4)	No Uncanceled Sugggestion (N=16)	
HGSHS: A score	M	11.25	11.13	42
	Range	10–12	10–12	
Intensity of analgesia	M	1.38	3.34	9 *
	Range	1–2	1–6	
Difference between left and right	M	3.87	3.25	20.5
hand during analgesia	Range	2–6	1–8	
Depth during analgesia	M	8.88	7.16	11 *
item	Range	7–10	5–10	
Average depth during	M	8.20	6.69	11 *
hypnosis	Range	7–9.7	4.9–8	

*=p < .05; Mann Whitney U test.

across the session, and HGSHS:A score, and the pilot study was identical in format to Experiment 4.

In confirmation of the first hypothesis, it was found that the Ss manifesting the phenomenon had significantly better analgesia during hypnosis than the 16 who did not. They reported significantly greater depth on a 10-point scale where 1 = not at all hypnotized and 10 = as deeply hypnotized as they felt they ever could be. The depth reports of the Ss manifesting the phenomenon were significantly greater, both when averaged across the whole session and during the analgesia. The superiority of this group can be seen from a retrospective analysis; the four Ss for whom analgesia persisted posthypnotically all rated their analgesia as 2 or less on the 10-point pain scale and their average depth on the 10-point depth scale was 7 or greater. Only 3 of the remaining 16 high-susceptibles performed comparably ($X^2 = 6.64$, df = 1, p < 0.01, corrected for continuity). The data for these 20 Ss are summarized in TABLE 1.

The data for all Ss participating in Experiments 4 and 5 are summarized in TABLE 2.

It is interesting to note what happened to the uncanceled suggestion for the 16 Ss not manifesting the phenomenon. Five of them canceled it themselves, six reported that the arm was still numb posthypnotically, but that it wore off while talking to the E, four had no analgesia posthypnotically and had no awareness of when the analgesia had ceased, and for one S the analgesia ceased when the E tapped his hand with the pencil during the Thought-Reading item. The subjective reports of Ss for whom analgesia persisted posthypnotically are interesting, and tend to be of two kinds. About half of them treated the post-hypnotic persistence in a matter-of-fact, unconcerned way, as if posthypnotic analgesia was a commonplace occurrence of hypnosis. When E said he could remove the analgesia, some even informed him that the effect would wear off

TABLE 2

HYPNOTIC SUSCEPTIBILITY, HYPNOTIC DEPTH, AND HYPNOTIC ANALGESIA FOR HIGH, MEDIUM, AND INSUSCEPTIBLE SIMULATING Ss ACROSS THE TWO EXPERIMENTS

		Highs (N=16)	Mediums (N=16)	Simulators (N=16)
HGSHS: A score	M	11.00	8.63	0.06 *
	Range	10–12	8–9	0–1
Intensity of analgesia	M	3.13	3.72	2.26
	Range	1–6	1–8	1–5
Difference between left and right hands during analgesia	M	3.14	3.34	4.25
	Range	1–8	1–9	1–8
Depth during analgesia item	M	7.31	7.13	2.13
	Range	5.10	3.5–10	1–5
Average depth during hypnosis	M	7.00	6.22	1.81
	Range	4.9–9.7	3.1–8.9	1–3.7

$* = p < .05$: Kruskal-Wallis one-way analysis of variance.

by itself, and that he need not take the trouble. By contrast, others registered amazement that such an effect could persist so intensely following hypnosis.

One S (who reported the right hand as 2 and the left hand as 8 during hypnosis, gave corresponding ratings of 2 and 9 posthypnosis), when asked how the right hand felt during the amnesia inquiry, said: "It feels funny. I can't feel my fingers moving. I'm moving them, but I can't feel them. When I do this (moves fingers of the left hand) I can feel them move. But I can't feel them in the right. I know I'm moving them because I can see it."

A second S (right hand = 1, left hand = 5, during hypnosis; corresponding ratings posthypnosis = 3 and 7), was even more intrigued; she could not believe that the electrical stimulus had been applied to the right hand during hypnosis. She described the removal of the analgesia by the E after hypnosis in the following manner during the postexperimental inquiry: "After I woke up, the hand was still very sleepy, and then he made me close my eyes and he moved his pencil along it. And it just woke up. It's absolutely incredible."

By contrast, a third S (right hand = 1–2, left hand = 5, during hypnosis; ratings of 2 and 5, respectively, posthypnosis), when told that E would remove the analgesia, said: "Don't bother, it will go away, but it *does* feel heavy." She said of the shock to the right arm posthypnosis that she could feel it "more than last time (during hypnosis) but it's not very much." By contrast, the left hand jumped when tested both during and subsequent to hypnosis. A final S (1 and 3 during hypnosis, 2 and 3 posthypnosis) said that her right hand and arm had changed color following hypnosis, and held it up for the E's inspection. The E offered to remove the analgesia, and like the previous S, she insisted that it would wear off with time. The E removed the analgesia for both Ss notwithstanding. This latter S explained the low pain ratings in the left hand as due to having caught the hand in the wringer of a washing machine years earlier, but reported that both during and posthypnosis, the two hands felt distinctively different.

DISCUSSION

The following conclusions can be drawn from this series of studies, even though they must be somewhat tentative, since the program of research on this phenomenon is ongoing.

1. A comparison of the first two experiments with the last three indicates that part of the effect is due to the hypnotist implicitly cuing the S that he expects all suggested effects to persist indefinitely. This point has been made independently by Weitzenhoffer,[1] and the present pattern of results supports his observation. The cue used in Experiments 3–5 was fairly subtle though it could be made into a subject preconception about hypnosis following the procedures of Sheehan.[8] It should be noted, however, that the first two experiments were conducted in Montreal, and the next three in Australia. These differences in results could therefore be due to differences in motives, attitudes, and sets about hypnosis held by these respective national groups. This possibility will soon be checked out.

2. The posthypnotic persistence of an uncanceled suggestion appears to be confined to a minority of highly susceptible Ss; it is much more common for Ss to cancel the effect themselves, or for the effect to persist posthypnotically, and wear off on its own during the posthypnosis period. Again, this may reflect the relative subtlety of an instruction that suggested effects will persist for as long as the hypnotist requests it. Conversely, it may mesh with a lot of other data that has accrued about very difficult hypnotic items.

3. Highly hypnotizable Ss are selected on the rather demanding criteria of being able to have suggested posthypnotic amnesia, and to carry out a posthypnotic suggestion. But it has been shown in recent years that only a small percentage of such highly susceptible Ss manifest Hilgard's hidden-observer effect,[17] counter a preconception about hypnosis as demonstrated by Sheehan,[8] report a double hallucination,[10, 18–22] and carry out a posthypnotic suggestion beyond the experimental context.[5] This lack of homogeneity among highly susceptible Ss has led investigators such as Hilgard to speak of the hypnotic virtuoso, Orne to speak of the top 5% of hypnotically responsive individuals, and Speigel to speak of Grade 5 hypnotizable syndrome. In all cases the emphasis is on a small percentage of highly hypnotizable Ss who seem to have special hypnotic skills over the above mere amnesia and posthypnotic suggestion—which themselves are extremely difficult hypnotic items. The evidence

of the Experiments 4 and 5 was that the Ss manifesting the phenomenon during hypnosis had significantly better analgesia during hypnosis and reported feeling more deeply hypnotized throughout. Perhaps these kinds of subjective reports—which need to be checked further—are pointing in the same direction, that only a small percentage of highly hypnotically skilled individuals are able to maintain an analgesia posthypnotically, under conditions where the E implicitly communicates his expectation that such will occur. For the majority, the effort and concentration of maintaining a hypnotic analgesia during hypnosis may be so great that once the hypnotist passes onto another item, either the Ss remove it themselves, or else it fades gradually with time.

ACKNOWLEDGMENTS

I am indebted to Ernest R. Hilgard and Peter W. Sheehan for their constructive suggestions, which were instrumental in developing the procedures used in Experiments 3–5. I wish to thank also Candace Riguet, who performed the SHSS:C sessions of Experiment 2; Bruce Duncan, who acted as E1 in Experiments 1–2; Rosemary Nordin, who acted as E2 in Experiment 3; and Michele Waldron, who acted as E2 in Experiments 4–5. Special thanks go to Oscar Rudzitis for constructing the shock apparatus used in Experiments 4–5 and to David Perry, Video Artist in Residence, Griffiths University, Brisbane for technical assistance in preparing the videotaped induction of Experiments 3 and 4.

REFERENCES

1. WEITZENHOFFER, A. M. 1957. General Techniques of Hypnotism, Grune and Stratton. New York.
2. EVANS, F. J. 1971. Recent studies in post-hypnotic ammesia. Paper to 23rd Ann. Mtg. Soc. Clin. Exp. Hypn. Chicago, Ill.
3. LINDEMANN, H. 1973. Relieve Tension the Autogenic Way. Peter C. Wyden. New York, N.Y.
4. BOWERS, M. K. 1956. Understanding the relationship between the hypnotist and his subject. In A Scientific Report on "The Search for Bridey Murphy." Milton V. Kline, Ed. : 83–128. Julian Press. New York, N.Y.
5. ORNE, M. T., P. W. SHEEHAN AND F. J. EVANS 1968. Occurrence of posthypnotic behavior outside the experimental setting. J. Personality Soc. Psychol. 9: 189–196.
6. FISHER, S. 1954. The role of expectancy in the performance of posthypnotic behavior. J. Abnorm. Soc. Psychol. 49: 503–507.
7. SHEEHAN, P. W. & M. T. ORNE. 1968. Some comments on the nature of posthypnotic behavior. J. Nerv. Ment. Dis. 146: 209–220.
8. SHEEHAN, P. W. 1971. Countering preconceptions about hypnosis: An objective index of involvement with the hypnotist. J. Abnorm. Psychol. Monogr. 78: 299–322.
9. DUNCAN, B. & PERRY C. 1977. Uncanceled hypnotic suggestions: Initial studies. Am. J. Clin. Hypn. 19: 166–176.
10. ORNE, M. T. 1959. The Nature of hypnosis: Artifact and essence. J. Abnorm. Soc. Psychol. 58: 277–299.
11. BARBER, T. X. 1969. Hypnosis: A Scientific Approach. Van Nostrand. New York, N.Y.
12. SHOR, R. E. & C. ORNE. 1962. The Harvard Group Scale of Hypnotic Susceptibility Form A. Consulting Psychologists Press. Palo Alto, Calif.

13. FRENCH, J. W., R. S. EKSTROM & L. S. PRICE. 1973. Manual for Kit of Reference Tests for Cognitive Factors. Educational Testing Service. Princeton, N.J.
14. WEITZENHOFFER, A. M. & E. R. HILGARD. 1962. Stanford Hypnotic Susceptibility Scale, Form C. Consulting Psychologists Press. Palo Alto, Calif.
15. BINET, A 1905. On Double Consciousness. The Open Court Publishing Co. Chicago, Ill.
16. McCONKEY, K. & P. W. SHEEHAN. 1976. Contrasting interpersonal orientations in hypnosis: collaborative versus contractual modes of response. J. Abnorm. Psychol. 85: 390–397.
17. HILGARD, E. R. 1974. Neodissociation theory in relation to the concept of state. Paper to the 26th Ann. Mtg. Soc. Clin. Exp. Hypn. Montreal, Canada.
18. HILGARD, E. R. 1972. A critique of Johnson, Maher and Barber's artifact in the "essence of hypnosis: An evaluation of trance logic, with a recomputation of their findings. J. Abnorm. Psychol. 79: 221–233.
19. JOHNSON R. F., B. A. MAHER & T. X. BARBER. 1972. Artifact in the "essence of hypnosis": An evaluation of trance logic. J. Abnorm. Psychol. 79: 212–220.
20. McDONALD, R. D. & J. R. SMITH. 1975. Trance logic in tranceable and simulating subjects. Int. J. Clin. Exp. Hypn. 23: 80–89.
21. PETERS, J. E. 1973. Trance logic: Artifact or essence in hpnosis. Unpublished doctoral dissertation. Pennsylvania State Univ. University Park, Pa.
22. SHEEHAN, P. W., I. OBSTOJ & K. McCONKEY. 1976. Trance logic and cue structure as applied by the hypnotist. J. Abnorm. Psychol. 85: 459–472.

PERCEPTUAL PROCESSES AND HYPNOSIS: SUPPORT FOR A COGNITIVE-STATE THEORY BASED ON LATERALITY

Kenneth R. Graham

Department of Psychology
Muhlenberg College
Allentown, Pennsylvania 18104

Hypnosis is characterized by perceptual and cognitive distortions that take place as the result of suggestion. Perceptual effects may take two forms: positive effects in which the person experiences something he has not previously experienced and for which there may be no physical basis of perception; and negative effects in which the person fails to experience something, even in the presence of an appropriate stimulus. When a hypnotized person reports that he sees someone in a chair which is actually empty, he is said to be experiencing a positive, visual hallucination. When he fails to report a ticking clock held next to the ear, assuming that his hearing is otherwise normal, he is said to be experiencing a negative, auditory hallucination.

Perceptual effects have been of interest since the beginning of the modern study of hypnosis. According to Ellenberger,[1] one of Mesmer's most celebrated cases involved his attempt to restore the sight of a blind, eighteen-year-old girl. After several sessions she declared that she was seeing, but these claims occurred only when Mesmer was present. Eventually a conflict arose between Mesmer and her family, and she lost her sight again for good. Mesmer was apparently convinced that she had achieved some measure of sight, and suggested that she and her family did not really want her cured, because she would have lost her fame as a blind musician as well as the financial support of the Empress.

During the past two hundred years, researchers have extensively investigated the effects of hypnotic suggestions on perceptual reports. The purpose of this paper is to review selected studies of visual and auditory perception, and to summarize the theoretical contributions made by them. One point often overlooked is that such studies may reveal as much about perceptual and cognitive processes as they do about hypnosis.

In recent years there has been a revival of interest in the study of cognition. This revival has grown out of the gestalt tradition, which views thought as an active, generative process rather than the result of the passive accumulation of associations. In perception this means that an observer interprets sensory events through an active process of construction and matching. One theory, proposed by Neisser,[2] refers to the process as *analysis by synthesis*. At times the synthetic process may result in perception when sensory evidence is contrary or lacking. Almost everyone has had the experience of getting into the shower and then hearing the telephone ring, especially when one was expecting a call. One turns off the water and jumps out of the tub, only to find that the phone was not ringing. We can think of this as a case in which the constructive process resulted in perception in the absence of an external, sensory input. We can think of the result as a positive, auditory hallucination. One way to manipulate and study such constructive processes is through hypnosis. Some people when hypnotized are able to experience hallucinations repeatedly, in a controlled manner that is difficult to duplicate by any other method.

274

Some hypnotized subjects readily report visual hallucinations when instructed to do so, but it is difficult to show that they are not faking or pretending to see the suggested stimulus. One attempt to establish the validity of hypnotic hallucinations was made by Underwood.[3] He used three optical illusions in which the background disorted a superimposed figure. The purpose of his experiment was to see if the same effect would be reported when the background was hallucinated and not physically present. Some figure distortion was produced by positive hallucinations of the background in very deeply hypnotized subjects, but not in others. While the use of an unfamiliar illusion lessened the chances that the subject was guessing, rather than really hallucinating, a great deal of information about the experimenter's expectations was transmitted through the instructions. Weitzenhoffer and Moore[4] reported similar results when subjects "negated" the ground of the same illusion by means of a negative hallucination. Sarbin and Andersen[5] repeated the Underwood experiment without hypnosis and got similar results. They explained their findings in terms of subject selection and differences in base-rate performance. Although they found that perceptual alterations could occur without hypnotic induction, they also gave their subjects detailed instructions about what they wanted them to see.

Brightness Contrast by Hypnotic Hallucination

One method for reducing experimenter bias was suggested by Leuba's[6] study of conditioned hallucinations. He reported several experiments in which mental images or hallucinations were conditioned under hypnosis to auditory or tactile stimuli. This procedure was used by Graham[7] in an experiment involving brightness contrast. It was predicted that two gray circles hallucinated on a black and white background would appear to be of different shades, corresponding to the usual contrast effects.

The subjects were 11 junior and senior high school students chosen from a pool of more than 200 volunteers who were highly susceptible to hypnosis. During Stage I of the experiment, the subject was hypnotized and given ten conditioning trials. On each trial, a plain white card with two gray circles on it was paired with a buzzer for five seconds. The subject was then aroused from hypnosis and given ten test trials. On these trials, a plain white card was presented as the buzzer was sounded, to show if the subject would hallucinate the circles. Stage II immediately followed the first test session. The subject was rehypnotized and given ten additional conditioning trials followed by a test for the hallucinated contrast. In this test, the plain white background card and a second card, which was half black and half white, were randomly presented a total of 30 times.

The results showed that although the circle hallucination tended to fluctuate greatly, the expected responses were reported on a majority of trials. That is, subjects tended to report that one circle looked darker than the other in accordance with the usual contrast effect, when the black and white card served as the background, whereas the circles were reported as looking the same when the plain card was used. This pattern of responding was significantly different from that of a control group of 12 additional subjects who were not hypnotized but who were asked to respond as if they had been.

Although this experiment provides evidence for the perceptual reality of hallucinations, many other studies involving illusions have proved negative. In one recent study, Miller *et al.*[8] attempted to develop an objective measure of hypnotic perception, using the Ponzo illusion. They induced a negative hypnotic hallucination to ablate the radiating lines of the illusion and then measured its effect. They found that the suggested hallucination did not affect susceptibility to the illusion, and that certain highly susceptible hypnotic subjects were more susceptible to the Ponzo illusion than were less hypnotic subjects under all experimental conditions.

A number of investigations by T. X. Barber and his associates has shown that subjects may report hallucinatory experiences after task-motivating instructions, without any hypnotic induction. Ham and Spanos[9] administered auditory and visual hallucination suggestions to two groups of subjects following either task-motivating instructions or hypnosis. The task-motivated subjects scored higher than hypnotic subjects on both auditory and visual hallucination measures. The majority of subjects in both treatments also reported some visual imagery in response to the auditory hallucination suggestion and described their experiences as imagined, rather than seen or heard. Ham and Spanos concluded that this "supports the hypothesis that hallucinatory experiences involve the constructive synthesis of diverse imaginal information. The positive correlations obtained between auditory and visual hallucination measures, for both hypnotic and task-motivated subjects, are consistent with the notion of a generalized cognitive ability underlying the performance of suggested phenomena." (p. 100)

Eye Movements as a Criterion of Hypnotic Hallucinations

Because some experiments have shown that hypnotic hallucinations have a degree of perceptual reality that is different from ordinary imagining, a few attempts have been made to study the degree of veridicality by observing whether or not certain eye movements, which are presumed to be involuntary, occur during hallucinations. Several of these have involved the pattern of eye movements known as optokinetic nystagmus. The term refers to a class of oscillatory eye movements induced whenever a nonhomogeneous visual field is moved continuously past an observer. A common example is "train nystagmus," in which rhythmic oscillations of the eyes occur when one gazes at stationary objects from the window of a moving train. The eye-movement pattern that results is characterized by a series of alternate pursuit movements and rapid saccadic returns.

Although it may be affected by nonstimulus factors,[10] optokinetic nystagmus is believed to be an involuntary reaction to an appropriate stimulus.[11] For this reason, Brady and Levitt[12] suggested that the occurrence of optokinetic nystagmus, in the absence of the stimulus, might serve as a criterion of hypnotic hallucinations. They found that hypnotized subjects who were asked to hallucinate a rotating striped drum demonstrated nystagmus but that they and other control subjects were unable to produce nystagmus voluntarily in the waking state.

Graham[13] replicated and extended the Brady and Levitt experiment. It was assumed that eye-movement differences between actually looking at a moving stimulus and imagining it would be most apparent in the pursuit component of each nystagmus oscillation. Consequently, a slowly moving stimulus was used, so that the purusit component would be quite long.

It was also hypothesized that the background present during imagery may influence eye movements. It might be possible, for example, to produce nystagmus-like movements when a complex background is present, providing successive fixation points even in the absence of vivid imagery. To test this hypothesis, a plain white background screen and a screen with a grid of diagonal stripes superimposed were used.

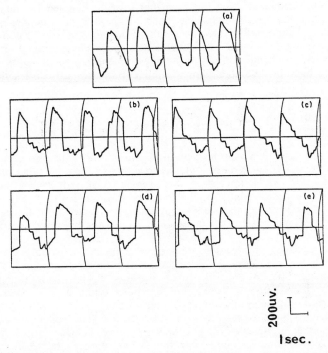

FIGURE 1. Electrooculogram recordings of eye movements. (a)-actual observation; (b)-waking imagery, plain background; (c)-waking imagery, grid background; (d)-hypnotic hallucination, plain background; (e)-hypnotic hallucination, grid background. (By permission of the publisher of J. Nerv. Ment. Dis.[13])

Eye movements were recorded from 12 subjects who were asked first to observe a slowly moving stripe and then to image it, both in the waking state and in hypnosis. The results showed that an oscillatory pattern of left- and right-eye movements occurred in all conditions of observation and imagery (FIGURE 1), but there were significant differences among the patterns.

Although some subjects had particularly good hypnotic hallucinations, close examination of the records revealed that not a single subject showed nystagmus during imagery that was identical with the eye-movement pattern of actual observation. In another study of eye movements, Evans and associates [14] found that some subjects were able to produce optokinetic nystagmus voluntarily, but such control was not a function of either hypnosis, vivid and real hallucinations, or vividness of imagery.

In summary, highly susceptible hypnotized subjects may report vivid, visual hallucinations that are subjectively real and that may be indistinguishable from ordinary percepts. The proportion of subjects capable of such hallucinations, however, is quite small. According to Hilgard,[15] only about 3% of unselected subjects experienced the visual hallucination item on an advanced test of hypnotic susceptibility with eyes open. Moreover, as Bowers [16] pointed out, hallucinations do not follow optical laws. This fact was first noted almost 100 years ago by Bernheim,[17] who observed that a prism doubled the image of a real object but not of a hallucinated one. Experimental evidence suggests that hypnotic hallucinations are the result of higher level cortical processes that do not interact with the subcortical control of visual system. Subjectively real and veridical hallucinations may be extreme cases on a continuum of imagining which involves the basic cognitive processes of construction and synthesis.

AUDITORY PERCEPTION

As in the case of visual perception, hypnotic investigations of auditory phenomena have primarily been attempts to establish the perceptual reality of suggested effects. Much interest in this area has centered around the study of suggested deafness. Many studies reported profound changes in hearing when the subject's verbal responses were used as the criterion of deafness, but the results were inconsistent when responses to various objective criteria were examined.

Positive evidence of suggested deafness was found in several experiments in which hearing was tested by means of a conditioning technique.[18-21] On the other hand, little or no evidence of suggested deafness was found when hearing was tested more directly. For example, Kline et al.[22] used verbal performance during delayed auditory feedback as the criterion of deafness and reported that hypnotized subjects performed better than nonhypnotized subjects, but neither group performed as well as control subjects who were truly deaf. Using the same technique, Sutcliffe [23] and Barber and Calverly [24] reported no evidence for enhanced performance during hypnosis.

The inconsistency of objective and subjective data makes it difficult to interpret the positive cases. In most, evidence for impaired hearing is confounded with the effects of situational factors that may have biased the subject's verbal responses. For that reason, Graham and Schwarz [25] attempted to separate sensory effects from response bias effects by the method of signal detectability. This method allows the subject's response in a psychophysics task to be converted into a sensitivity measure (d') and a separate response criterion measure, beta (β).

In this experiment, seven highly susceptible hypnosis subjects and seven nonsusceptible simulating control subjects were chosen on the basis of scores obtained from a standard test of hypnotic susceptibility. All subjects performed a signal-detection task that required them to report each time they heard a faint 1200-Hz tone imbedded in white noise. On some trials the tone was actually presented, and on others it was not. This enabled the experimenter to characterize the subject's performance in terms of two ratios representing "hits" (correct acceptances) and "false alarms" (false acceptances), and these are the basis for calculating d' and β. After one complete series involving 120 presentations of the tone, the subject was hypnotized and given suggestions for impaired hearing. The effect of the suggestions was measured by asking the subject to report whether or not he could hear a clock that the experimenter held in his hand. Deafness suggestions were continued until the subject reported hearing the ticking no farther than half the distance it was perceived prior to the suggestions.

Subject's "yes" and "no" responses were converted into detectability scores (d') and response criterion scores (β). Ordinarily, several such determinations are made to produce what is known as a receiver-operating characteristic. In this experiment we used a simpler procedure, which involved calculating mean d' and β scores for the two groups, and then performing t tests. There were significant changes within each group following hypnotic suggestions for diminished hearing. d' scores, that is, those which presumably indicate true changes in sensitivity, decreased significantly for the highly susceptible subjects, whereas there was no significant change for the simulators. On the other hand, there was a marginally significant increase in β scores, those which presumably reflect response bias tendencies rather than sensitivity for the simulators, but not for the highly susceptible subjects. Although subjects in both groups reported substantial hearing impairment as measured by the clock test, only the highly susceptible subjects showed a significant decrease in sensitivity.

The results do not contradict earlier studies [23, 24] which reported that hypnotic suggestions did not produce deafness when hearing was tested according to clinical criteria. Apparently, hypnotic suggestions do not result in hearing impairment that is comparable to true deafness. Nevertheless, the present experiment shows that hypnotic suggestions can result in sensory changes as opposed to changes in verbal response patterns, among susceptible subjects.

LATERALITY AND HYPNOSIS

Although perceptual studies have long been part of hypnosis, their relation to theory has generally been tangential. Various attempts to account for hypnotic behaviors have stressed other factors, such as psychopathology, the physiological state of the brain, the personality of the subject and the hypnotist, dissociation, role-playing, and the effect of situational and motivational factors. Studies of perceptual distortions have often been used in attempts to confirm the existence of hypnosis as a separate and identifiable "state," but not to define the nature of that state.

Recent studies of lateral brain functioning, however, suggest a central role for perceptual processes in defining hypnosis. These studies support the view that hypnotic effects may be a function of right-hemisphere activity in most right-handed and in some left-handed people. The nondominant hemisphere is the right hemisphere for most right-handed people and for left-handers whose speech center is located on the left side of the brain. This group encompasses all but about five percent of the population, since about 90 percent of all people are right-handed and about half the left-handers are also thought to have their speech centers on the left side.

Language, a left-hemisphere function, is time-ordered and sequential. Hypnosis, on the other hand, is characterized by distortions of time perception and the sequencing of events,[26] a dramatic example of which is posthypnotic amnesia. Recent research on amnesia by Evans and Kihlstrom [27] has shown that when instructions are given for subjects to recall everything, thereby terminating the amnesia, highly susceptible subjects recall events significantly out of order, compared to less susceptible subjects. In other words, "for the hypnotizable subject, posthypnotic amnesia is characterized primarily by a disruption or disorganization of part of the recall process, leaving other aspects of memory processing relatively unimpaired." (p. 317) The right hemisphere, on the other hand, has a major role in visuospatial and nonverbal auditory perception,[28] and is involved in emotional expression.[29] Hypnosis is used to stimulate the recall of repressed emotional experiences and often involves distortions of spatial and auditory perception.

Beyond these analogies are experimental data that suggest a relationship between hypnosis and the nondominant hemisphere. Bakan [30] reported a significant positive correlation between hypnotic susceptibility and right-hemisphere functioning, using lateral eye movements as a measure of laterality. He found that persons who gazed consistently to the left, thereby revealing right-hemisphere activity, were more hypnotizable than those who gazed consistently to the right. Gur and Gur [31] confirmed and extended Bakan's results in an experiment that involved handedness, sex, and eyedness as moderating variables. They found a significant negative correlation between hypnotic susceptibility and number of eye movements to the right for right-handed males, and a significant positive correlation for left-handed females. In other words, their results were consistent with the belief that hypnosis is a right-hemisphere function for those who are strongly right-handed, and a left-hemisphere function for those who are strongly left-handed.

Although studies show a relation between the nondominant hemisphere and hypnotic susceptibility,[30, 31] there is little *direct* evidence of differences in hemispherical activity between persons who are hypnotized and those who are not. Morgan et al.[32] recorded occipital EEG alpha separately from the right and left hemispheres of subjects during analytical, spatial, and musical tasks administered during the waking state, and during a test of hypnotic susceptibility. Highly hypnotizable subjects showed significantly more alpha activity than low hypnotizables in both the waking and hypnotic conditions. There were no significant differences, however, between high- and low-hypnotizable subjects in EEG laterality.

Laterality, Hypnosis, and the Autokinetic Effect

Recent experimental evidence, based on perceptual data, reveals a clear difference in lateral activity between hypnotized and nonhypnotized subjects. Graham and Pernicano [33] studied changes in lateral brain functioning as the result of hypnosis by means of the autokinetic effect. The effect involves the apparent motion of a stationary point of light in totally dark surroundings. It was hypothesized: (1) that hypnotized subjects would report more autokinetic movement to the left than waking subjects, reflecting greater use of the right hemisphere, and (2) that since no attempt was made to differentiate among highly lateralized and less lateralized left-handers, the effect would be most pronounced for right-handed subjects.

The experiment was conducted in two one-hour sessions, held within a few days of one another. The first was a test of hypnotic susceptibility. In the second session, half of the left-dominant and half of the right-dominant subjects observed the autokinetic light while hypnotized. The rest of the subjects made their observations in the waking state. The autokinetic testing was performed by an experimenter who was unaware of the subject's handedness and hypnotic susceptibility score.

It was hypothesized that hypnosis would result in greater apparent movement to the left, especially for right-handers. This hypothesis was supported by the data. Subjects who were not hypnotized, whether left- or right-handed, reported a relatively small proportion of autokinetic movement to the left, averaging about 33%. Subjects who were hypnotized showed substantially more apparent movement to the left, averaging 54%. The proportion of left movement was greater during hypnosis for both left- and right-handed subjects, but the difference was statistically significant only for right-handers. Although sex was not a variable manipulated in this experiment, there was some evidence that the effect observed was attributable more to males than to females.

The results support the hypothesis that hypnosis, as induced by a standard test of hypnotic susceptibility, involves greater activation of the right hemisphere for most subjects. It is not a complete test of the hypothesis that hypnosis is a function of the nondominant hemisphere, because no attempt was made to distinguish among left-handers. It is not easy to determine conclusively where the speech center is situated. In this experiment it was simply hypothesized that because some highly lateralized left-handers might respond in a way opposite to the others during hypnosis, differences between waking and hypnotic performance for left-handed subjects would not be as great as for right-handed subjects.

A Laterality Theory of Hypnosis

The results have important theoretical implications. They support the point of view that hypnosis involves a cognitive change of state and suggest that hypnotic phenomena cannot be explained entirely in terms of motivational variables. Further, they suggest a theory of hypnosis based on lateral brain functioning. From this point of view, the term *hypnosis* is a construct that involves a number of nondominant hemisphere functions. Similar distortions of perceptual and cognitive functions may occur in everyday life, but they are unrewarded and discouraged, and generally do not occur systematically. One purpose of a hypnotic induction is to define the setting as an acceptable place for such behaviors to occur. It may also provide time for the subject to engage in more spatial-imaginative and less verbal-sequential thought. From this point of view it is not surprising that other techniques, such as task-motivating instructions, may produce similar results. The ability to experience hypnotic effects must then be a partial function of genetic factors which govern lateral dominance, and, if that is true, there should be some genetic component to hypnotic susceptibility. Morgan [34] demonstrated that there is such, in an investigation of hypnotic susceptibility in twins.

Laterality theory also helps to account for the fear and rejection that have often accompanied hypnosis. In his classic paper on the implications of handedness, Hertz[35] noted that attitudes toward the left and right hands represent an embodiment of the polarity between good and evil which exists in virtually every culture. In view of recent research, it seems plausible that sinistrality and hypnosis have both been widely rejected because they are manifestations of right-hemisphere thinking. To the extent that use of the right hemisphere diverts the thinker from using language, man's chief mechanism for adapting to the environment, it is nonadaptive and potentially dangerous. Trance states and imagery are practiced in some cultures as part of religious ceremony, but even then are restricted to certain individuals or to certain times.

Although there is some experimental support for a cognitive state theory based on laterality, many questions remain unanswered. There is a distinction, for example, between the general activation of the right hemisphere and specific functions for which it is dominant. If hypnosis is related to some sort of general activation, one would expect to find evidence in electroencephalographic records. So far, that has not been the case.[32] If, on the other hand, hypnosis refers to a specific set of right-hemisphere abilities, one might expect a hypnotized person to perform relatively better on visuospatial and tonal perception tasks than on verbal tasks, when compared to a similar test conducted in the waking state. There is not yet conclusive evidence on this point, either. Whatever the outcome of future investigations, perceptual studies are likely to play a major role in hypnosis research during the years to come.

REFERENCES

1. ELLENBERGER, H. F. 1970. The Discovery of the Unconscious. Basic Books. New York, N.Y.
2. NEISSER, U. 1967. Cognitive Psychology. Appleton-Century-Crofts. New York, N.Y.
3. UNDERWOOD, H. W. 1960. The validity of hypnotically induced visual hallucinations. J. Abnorm. Soc. Psychol. 61: 39–46.
4. WEITZENHOFFER, A. M. & R. K. MOORE. 1960. Influence of certain hypnotic suggestions upon a type of visual illusion: Preliminary report. Percept. Motor Skills 11: 137.
5. SARBIN, T. R. & M. L. ANDERSEN. 1963. Base-rate expectancies and perceptual alterations in hypnosis. Br. J. Soc. Clin. Psychol. 2: 112–121.
6. LEUBA, C. 1940. Images as conditioned sensations. J. Exp. Psychol. 26: 345–351.
7. GRAHAM, K. R. 1969. Brightness contrast by hypnotic hallucination. Int. J. Clin. Exp. Hypn. 17: 62–73.
8. MILLER, R. J., R. T. HENNESSY & H. W. LEIBOWITZ. 1973. The effect of hypnotic ablation of the background on the magnitude of the Ponzo perspective illusion. Int. J. Clin. Exp. Hypn. 21: 180–191.
9. HAM, M. W. & N. P. SPANOS. 1974. Suggested auditory and visual hallucinations in task-motivated and hypnotic subjects. Am. J. Clin. Hypn. 17: 94–101.
10. BACKUS, P. S. 1962. An experimental note on hypnotic ablation of optokinetic nystagmus. Am. J. Clin. Hypn. 4: 184.
11. DAVSON, H. 1963. The Physiology of the Eye. Little, Brown & Co., Inc. Boston, Mass.
12. BRADY, J. P. & E. E. LEVITT. 1964. Nystagmus as a criterion of hypnotically induced visual hallucinations. Science 146: 85–86.
13. GRAHAM, K. R. 1970. Optokinetic nystagmus as a criterion of visual imagery. J. Nerv. Ment. Dis. 151: 411–414.

14. EVANS, F. J., L. H. REICH & M. T. ORNE. 1972. Optokinetic nystagmus, eye movements, and hypnotically induced hallucinations. J. Nerv. Ment. Dis. **152:** 419–431

15. HILGARD, E. R. 1965. Hypnotic Susceptibility. Harcourt, Brace & World, Inc. New York, N.Y.

16. BOWERS, K. S. 1976. Hypnosis for the Seriously Curious. Brooks/Cole Publishing Co. Monterey, Calif.

17. BERNHEIM, H. 1964. Hypnosis and Suggestion in Psychotherapy: The Nature and Uses of Hypnotism. University Books. New York, N.Y. Originally published in English in 1888 under the title Suggestive Therapeutics.

18. LUNDHOLM, H. 1928. An experimental study of functional anesthesias as induced by suggestion in hypnosis. J. Abnorm. Soc. Psychol. **23:** 337–355.

19. ERICKSON, M. H. 1938. A study of clinical and experimental findings on hypnotic deafness: II. Experimental findings with a conditioned response technique. J. Gen. Psychol. **19:** 151–167.

20. BLACK, S. & E. R. WIGAN. 1961. An investigation of selective deafness produced by direct suggestion under hypnosis. Br. Med. J. **2:** 736–741.

21. KOROTKIN, I., T. V. PLESHKOVA & M. M. SUSLOVA. 1969. Change in auditory thresholds as the result of hypnotic suggestion. Soviet Neurol. Psychiat. **1:** 33–40.

22. KLINE, M. V., H. GUZE & A. D. HAGGERTY. 1954. An experimental study of the nature of hypnotic deafness: Effects of delayed speech feedback. J. Clin. Exp. Hypn. **2:** 145–156.

23. SUTCLIFFE, J. P. 1961. "Credulous" and "skeptical" views of hypnotic phenomena: Experiments on esthesia, hallucination, and delusion. J. Abnorm. Soc. Psychol. **62:** 189–200.

24. BARBER, T. X. & D. S. CALVERLEY. 1964. Experimental studies in "hypnotic" behaviour: Suggested deafness evaluated by delayed auditory feedback. Br. J. Psychol. **55:** 439–446.

25. GRAHAM, K. R. & L .M. SCHWARZ. 1973. Suggested deafness and auditory signal detectability. In Proc. 81st. Ann. Convention Am. Psychol. Assoc. **8:** 1091–1092. American Psychological Assoc. Washington, D.C.

26. KRAUSS, H. H., R. KATZELL & B. J. KRAUSS. 1974. Effect of hypnotic time distortion upon free-recall learning. J. Abnorm. Psychol. **83:** 140–144.

27. EVANS, F. J. & J. F. KIHLSTROM. 1973. Posthypnotic amnesia as disrupted retrieval. J. Abnorm. Psychol. **82:** 317–323.

28. KIMURA, D. 1973. The asymmetry of the human brain. Sci. Am. **228**(3): 70–78.

29. SCHWARTZ, G. E., R. J. DAVIDSON & F. MAER. 1975. Right hemisphere lateralization for emotion in the human brain: Interaction with cognition. Science **190:** 286–288.

30. BAKAN, P. 1969. Hypnotizability, laterality of eye movements and functional brain asymmetry. Percept. Motor Skills **82:** 927–932.

31. GUR, R. C. & R. E. GUR. 1974. Handedness, sex, and eyedness as moderating variables in the relation between hypnotic susceptibility and functional brain asymmetry. J. Abnorm. Psychol. **83:** 635–643.

32. MORGAN, A H., MACDONALD & E. R. HILGARD. 1974. EEG alpha: Lateral asymmetry related to task and hypnotizability. Psychophysiology **11:** 275–282.

33. GRAHAM, K. R. & K. PERNICANO. 1976. Laterality, hypnosis, and the autokinetic effect. Paper presented 84th. Ann. Conv. Am. Psychol. Assoc. Washington, D.C.

34. MORGAN, A. H. 1973. The heritability of hypnotic susceptibility in twins. J. Abnorm. Psychol. **82:** 55–61.

35. HERTZ, R. 1973. The pre-eminence of the right hand: A study in religious polarity. In Right and Left. R. Needham, Ed. and Trans. Univ. Chicago Press. Chicago, Ill. First published in 1909.

MODELS OF POSTHYPNOTIC AMNESIA *

John F. Kihlstrom

Department of Psychology and Social Relations
Harvard University
Cambridge, Massachusetts 02138

The term "posthypnotic amnesia" refers to the temporary inability of the hypnotized subject to remember, after hypnosis, the events that had transpired while he or she was hypnotized. Over the years, several parallels have been drawn between posthypnotic amnesia and other disorders of memory that are observed in the psychological clinic and the experimental laboratory, and in the psychopathology of everyday life. In each case, the person finds it difficult or impossible to gain access to certain critical memories through the ordinary process of active recall. Nevertheless, it is apparent that the critical memories are stored essentially intact, because the amnesia can be lifted and accurate recall restored. Even during the amnesic period itself, the unrecalled memories can be observed to affect behavior and experience, if only indirectly. All of this takes place in the apparent absence of any defect or alteration in central nervous system functioning. These broad phenotypic similarities uniting the various *functional* amnesias may imply genotypic similarities as well. Thus, the study of posthypnotic amnesia may serve as an important avenue of approach to a variety of topics in normal and pathological memory functioning.

Since the development of standardized hypnotic procedures for laboratory use (e.g., the Stanford Hypnotic Susceptibility Scale, Forms A, B, and C; the Revised Stanford Profile Scales of Hypnotic Susceptibility, Forms I and II; and the Harvard Group Scale of Hypnotic Susceptibility, Form A), research has yielded a great deal of information concerning the major parameters of posthypnotic amnesia (see the reviews by Cooper [14] and Hilgard [32, 33]). We know, for example, that posthypnotic amnesia is temporary and can be canceled or lifted by the administration of a prearranged reversibility cue.[42, 43, 49] Furthermore, the extent of the initial amnesia and the degree to which the lost memories can be recovered after the suggestion has been canceled, are both highly correlated with hypnotic susceptibility; [32, 42, 49] factor-analytic studies suggest, in fact, that amnesia lies at the core of the domain of hypnosis.[32] Moreover, the quantitative differences in recall observed during amnesia are matched by qualitative differences between the vague and fragmentary memory of subjects with complete or partial posthypnotic amnesia and the clearly detailed memories of those who are not amnesic.[21, 40] Finally, posthypnotic amnesia must be specifically suggested to the subject: in contrast to many other functional amnesias, it rarely occurs in a truly spontaneous fashion.[35]

In attempting to understand the phenomenon of posthypnotic amnesia, a number of conceptual models of the amnesic process have been developed.

* Based on research supported in part by grant MH 19156 from the National Institutes of Health, United States Public Health Service, and in part by grants from the Institute of Experimental Psychiatry, the Harvard Graduate Society, and the Joseph H. Clark Bequest to Harvard University.

Analogies to posthypnotic amnesia have been drawn from ordinary forgetting, the withholding of secret information, the repression of unpleasant memories, and the experience of having memories "on the tip of the tongue." Whether they have been explicitly formulated or remained only implicit, these four broad models have guided the vast majority of studies of posthypnotic amnesia, and each has contributed greatly to our understanding of the amnesic process, both what it is, and what it is not. In this paper, I propose to sketch the primary features of each of these models of amnesia, summarize the major findings of the research which has ensued from them, and draw some conclusions of my own about the nature of posthypnotic amnesia.

AMNESIA AS FORGETTING

One of the most stimulating models of amnesia has been suggested by the experience of ordinary forgetting. In this model, posthypnotic amnesia is likened to the process of gradual decay or erosion of memory traces that apparently occurs in everyday life. Of course, it was recognized at the outset that the reversibility of amnesia rendered the forgetting model, in its strict sense, inappropriate. Memories that can be recovered have not been lost from storage; therefore, as Hull [38] noted (p. 132), "amnesia is not a phenomenon of retention." Moreover, recent work in normal memory has called the entire trace-decay theory of forgetting into question.[65, 78] Nevertheless, it is useful to study amnesia *as if* it were a storage problem, recognizing the limitations of the model but employing the techniques developed by those working in the classic verbal learning tradition initiated by Ebbinghaus. Despite the fact that few if any investigators have seriously proposed that amnesia involves a functional ablation of memories, the forgetting model and its associated strategies of inquiry have yielded a wealth of important information concerning the manner in which posthypnotic amnesia affects memory processes.

A good example of this sort of research is the extensive and careful investigation carried out by Williamsen *et al.*[80] In their study, subjects learned a list of six familiar words and received a number of different tests of memory. TABLE 1 presents the major results of three particularly important groups of subjects. The *amnesic* group contained highly hypnotizable subjects who learned the words during hypnosis, with memory testing carried out during suggested posthypnotic amnesia. The *simulator* group consisted of insusceptible subjects who were instructed to simulate the behavior of a deeply hypnotized subject, and who then went through the same study-test sequence as the amnesic group. The *control* subjects, while hypnotizable, did not receive an induction of hypnosis but rather carried out the learning and memory tests in the normal waking state.

For the purposes of the present discussion, the relevant comparisons are between the amnesic subjects and the controls; the behavior of the simulators will be considered later. (1) On the first test, which required the subjects to actively recall the critical material, the amnesic subjects did quite poorly relative to the controls; as expected, these hypnotizable subjects responded positively to the suggestion for posthypnotic amnesia. (2) Then the experimenters took the six critical words and six similar words that had not been presented, deleted letters so that they were difficult to decode, and showed the partial words to the subjects. Both groups had a great deal of difficulty with the new, neutral words. Despite their inability to recall the recently learned material, however, the amnesic subjects achieved almost as many solutions with the old, critical material as the control subjects, and almost as rapidly. (3) For the third test, the subjects were asked to free-associate to words that were first-associates of the six critical and six neutral words. Again despite their previous difficulty in recalling the study items, the amnesic subjects gave the critical words as associates as often, and as quickly as did the controls. (4) Then the six critical, six neutral, and six new "dummy" words were presented to the subjects with instructions for them to pick out those words that had been learned during hypnosis. The amnesia suggestion was still effective, as can be seen in the substantial difference in accuracy between the amnesic and the control subjects; it is nevertheless also apparent that for the amnesic subjects

TABLE 1

RESULTS OF VARIOUS TESTS OF POSTHYPNOTIC MEMORY *

Memory Test	Hypnotized	Group Simulator	Control
Initial Recall	1.3	0.0	5.4
Partial Words—Critical			
Correct Solutions	3.5	1.7	4.6
Time	15.7	24.4	10.5
Partial Words—Neutral			
Correct Solutions	0.9	1.2	1.0
Time	23.4	22.7	23.8
Word Associations—Critical			
Number Correct	4.8	4.6	4.6
Time	1.2	1.8	1.2
Word Associations—Neutral			
Number Correct	3.5	3.7	3.7
Time	1.1	1.2	1.1
Recognition			
Number Correct	2.9	0.0	5.5
Time	51.9	33.9	46.0
Final Recall (Postamnesia)	4.6	4.2	5.4

* Adapted from Tables 1–4 of Williamsen et al.[80] Time given in seconds.

as a group, recognition memory is clearly superior to recall memory. (5) Finally, the amnesia suggestion was canceled and at this point a recall test was given, on which the subjects in the amnesia and control groups showed equivalent levels of memory.

Other, less extensive studies lead to similar conclusions. Strickler,[72] working in Hull's laboratory, taught subjects paired-associate nonsense material during hypnosis, followed by suggestions for posthypnotic amnesia; on other trials, the same subjects learned comparable material in the normal waking state. On an initial test, the subjects recalled only about 3% of the critical material during amnesia, compared with 86% correct recall in the waking trials. However, when they were instructed to learn the material again, the amnesic group showed a savings of 48% in relearning—a considerable advantage over never having learned the material previously, though still appreciably worse than the rate of relearning observed in the waking state (98% savings). Graham and Patton [27] employed a retroactive inhibition paradigm in another experiment. All subjects learned an original list of adjectives in the normal waking state. One group also learned the interpolated list in the waking state; a second group learned the second list in hypnosis, followed by suggestions for posthypnotic amnesia; a control group did not learn the second list at all. All subjects then relearned the original list. Despite their virtually complete inability to recall the items on the interpolated list, the amnesic subjects manifested the same amount of retroactive inhibition affecting the original list as did the waking group (55% and 46% savings, respectively, compared with 87% savings for the control group).

One can succinctly summarize a wealth of literature in this area as follows: the extent of amnesia appears to vary appreciably, depending on the type of memory test that is employed. While amnesic subjects have a great deal of difficulty in recalling the critical material, recognition memory [4, 80] and relearning of the critical material [15, 72] are considerably less impaired. Tasks involving retroactive inhibition,[12, 27, 48] word associations,[71, 75, 76, 80] and psychophysiological indices of memory [6, 63] all indicate that the memories covered by the amnesia suggestions remain active within the memory system. There are, of course, some exceptions to this generalization,[50, 73] chiefly the study by Stern et al.[70] But on the whole, only certain aspects of the processing and utilization of stored information are affected by posthypnotic amnesia.

Posthypnotic amnesia also exerts a selective impact on memory recall in which certain aspects of the critical material itself, but not other aspects, can be remembered. One of the most dramatic demonstrations of this property of amnesia is observed during the deeply hypnotized subject's response to posthypnotic suggestions. Here, the subject carries out some activity in response to a prearranged cue, but when questioned about the behavior, he or she does not remember having received the suggestion.[7, 8, 16, 17] Amnesia is by no means necessary for the production of posthypnotic behavior,[24, 64] but the two phenomena are frequently associated. In these instances, the person remembers *to do something*, but does not remember *why*.

The same kind of selectivity is observed in experiments in which the amnesic subject is required to capitalize on information acquired during the previous hypnotic state. In the experiment by Strickler,[72] for example, the amnesic subjects relearned the material rather quickly, as if they were already somewhat familiar with it. Williamsen et al.[80] found, by the same token, that their amnesic subjects remained sensitized to the critical material—enough so that they had a fair amount of success in decoding the critical words when they were presented in degraded form on the partial words task. Furthermore, while the amnesia prevented the subjects from recalling words that they had just learned, it did not prevent them from employing these same words in the free-association test. Similar results have been obtained by others.[26, 45, 56] One of the most striking observations in this regard has been of posthypnotic *source amnesia*.[18, 22] In this phenomenon, the hypnotized subject is incidentally taught some obscure information while hypnotized (e.g. the color that amethyst turns when it is exposed to heat), and subsequently receives suggestions for posthypnotic amnesia. When tested later, approximately one third of otherwise completely amnesic subjects nevertheless immediately and effortlessly remember the new information which had been taught to them. When the experimenter presses further, the subjects are not able to recollect the circumstances in which they learned the facts, and may even confabulate the source of the knowledge. To paraphrase Evans: [19] the amnesic subject knows, but does not necessarily know how, why, or even what he knows.

The studies carried out under the rubric of the forgetting model of amnesia all underscore the general point that amnesia suggestions do not affect the memories themselves, but rather affect certain memory functions. The critical memory traces are not by any means dormant. Despite the failure of active recall, the amnesic subject may still gain access to the information by other means, such as recognition; and the critical material continues to intearct with other ongoing acquisition, storage, and retrieval processes. When the material can be recalled, as in free-association or the source amnesia experiments, it is frequently devoid of "autobiographical" reference to the experiential context in which it was acquired. These findings, along with the reversibility of amnesia discussed earlier, point up the *paradox of posthypnotic amnesia,* which resides in the apparent contradiction between the subject's assertion that he or she cannot remember and the objective evidence of the availability and activity of the memories. This seeming paradox is an important touchstone for all contemporary theoretical and experimental work in posthypnotic amnesia.

AMNESIA AS THE KEEPING OF SECRETS

From a social-psychological perspective, the paradox of posthypnotic amnesia can be taken to mean that the subject only appears to be amnesic but in fact does not experience any difficulty in remembering at all. The hypnotic subject, from this point of view, attempts to comply with amnesia suggestions by actively suppressing his memory for the experience, exerting insufficient effort to complete the recall task or deliberately withholding information from the experimenter. Compliant subjects alter their verbal reports in accordance with immediate situational demands and their conceptions of the wider "hypnotic role," but indirect indices of memory that are difficult to modify intentionally show that they remember the material perfectly well. Thus, the use of recognition measures, retroactive inhibition procedures, or psychophysiological tests catch the subject in a lie, as it were, and show that the expressed amnesia is not "real." When the subject feels it is legitimate to do so, as when the prearranged reversibility cue is given at some later time, he provides a complete memory report to the experimenter, thus divulging his secret. This hypothesis has also been termed *amnesia by neglect,*[44] and has been articulated in various forms.[2–5, 11, 60] Barber,[3] (pp. 130–131) for example, provides the following personal account, which he contends applies to both hypnotized subjects and nonhypnotized subjects who have positive attitudes, motivations, and expectancies concerning the experimental situation:

> Later the experimenter suggests that when the session is over I will not re-member anything that occurred. Soon afterward he states that the experi-ment is over and asks me what I remember. Since I have no reason to resist the suggestion for amnesia, I say to myself that I do not remember what occurred, I keep my thoughts on the present, I do not think back to the preceding events, and I state that I do not remember. The experi-menter subsequently states, "Now you can remember." I now let myself think back to the preceding events and I verbalize them.

On the face of it, the neglect hypothesis seems to arise from a misinterpretation of the results of studies that employed conventional memory-testing procedures to assess the extent of posthypnotic amnesia. Consider a simple experiment in normal memory, in which a subject studies a list of words and then takes recall and recognition tests of memory. It is commonly found that recognition is superior to recall under such circumstances,[46] but it does not follow that the subject is keeping a secret from the experimenter or has somehow fooled himself into believing that he cannot remember something. Rather, such an outcome is interpreted in terms of the strength of the memory trace (i.e., below the threshold for recall, but above that for recognition), or the disruption of search processes in retrieval, and so on. The same logic should apply to experiments on amnesia as well.

There is also more direct evidence regarding the "secrets" model of amnesia. One line of evidence has to do with insusceptible subjects who have been instructed to simulate deep hypnosis.[54] Simulators remember their experiences perfectly well; however, they attempt to comply with the suggestion for amnesia by deliberately withholding memory reports from the experimenter and suppressing other evidence of the critical knowledge as best they can. Thus, it should be instructive to compare those simulating hypnosis with those who have not been given simulation instructions. TABLE 1, introduced earlier, provides such a comparison for the hypnotized and simulating subjects who were run in the experiment by Williamsen et al.[80] It is apparent that the two groups performed quite differently. On the initial test of recall during amnesia, the simulators showed a significantly greater memory deficit than those who were hypnotized; the former group did not remember any of the critical material at all. On the partial words task, the simulator group achieved significantly fewer solutions and took significantly longer to perform the task than did the hypnotic group; they also showed no recognition memory for the words whatsoever and responded significantly more quickly on this test than did the other group. Note also that the recall and recognition tasks yielded identical results for the simulators, whereas the hypnotized subjects performed better on recognition testing than on the recall task. These results were largely confirmed in a subsequent study by Barber and Calverley.[4]

Other studies have provided similar evidence. Bowers[7] gave hypnotized and simulating subjects suggestions to begin sentences with the words "he" or "they" on a later Taffel task, followed by suggestions for posthypnotic amnesia. As expected, there was no difference between hypnotized subjects and simulators in performance on the Taffel task. After the task, the subjects were led to believe that the experiment was over, and were interviewed by another experimenter. All of this was intended to make the subject drop the role of "good subject" and reflect honestly on his behavior. Although the amnesia suggestion had not yet been canceled, all of the simulating subjects showed full memory for their hypnotic and posthypnotic behavior in the previous phases of the experiment; less than half of the hypnotized subjects, however, showed full memory. Under the changed experimental demands, then, the simulators showed complete memory—they divulged their "secret"; the hypnotized subjects did not. Other studies have found that simulators do not show source amnesia, although source amnesia occurs with some frequency among hypnotized subjects;[18] and simulating subjects frequently show spontaneous amnesia, which is rare among hypnotic subjects.[39] The essential point here is that simulated amnesia, in which highly motivated, compliant subjects deliberately suppress recall or withhold material from the experimenter, is quite different from the amnesia observed in hypnotized subjects. The different outcomes would seem to imply different underlying processes.

One can also assume that if social-psychological factors are of primary importance in this realm, subjects' expectations about hypnosis should be a major determinant of their actual behavior during an experimental session. Shor [66] assessed the impact of preexisting expectations on hypnotic behavior in the following manner. At the beginning of the session, the subjects received a questionnaire that listed the suggestions they would receive during hypnosis, including one for amnesia, and were asked to predict how they would respond to each item. Later a hypnotic procedure was administered, and the subjects' personal predictions, assessed prior to hypnosis, were compared to their objective scores on each item. The resulting *phi* coefficient measuring correlation with −.04 for the amnesia item, indicating no relationship between expectancies and behavior. (Interestingly, advanced knowledge of the content of the hypnotic procedure did not seem to appreciably diminish the occurrence of posthpynotic amnesia.) In a somewhat related study, Young and Cooper [82] employed a procedure introduced by Orne [52] to experimentally manipulate subjects' expectancies regarding hypnosis. Slightly different versions of a lecture on hypnosis were delivered to sections of an introductory psychology class: half the students were told that amnesia always occurred after hypnosis while the other half was told that it never occurred; otherwise, the lectures were identical. In a subsequent session, a standardized hypnotic procedure was administered to the subjects, from which the usual amnesia suggestion was deleted. On a test of posthypnotic memory the "expect amnesia" group recalled significantly fewer items than the "not-expect amnesia" group, showing some effect of the instructional conditions and thus of expectancies. However, the difference observed was very small, with the treatment conditions accounting for less than 10% of the observed variance in posthypnotic amnesia.

Finally, a more recent study [44] attempted to manipulate experimental demands during posthypnotic amnesia itself. Groups of subjects were administered a slightly modified version of the Harvard Group Scale of Hypnotic Susceptibility, Form A, including a suggestion and test for posthypnotic amnesia. Before the amnesia suggestion was lifted, however, memory was tested again, with the difference that this second test was preceded by one of four kinds of special instructions. One group was simply administered a retest of memory, with no further instructions; a second was asked to recall the suggestions in the order in which they occurred during the hypnotic procedure; the third group was asked to exert an extra degree of effort in recalling the material; and the fourth group was instructed to be completely honest in reporting those things which they actually remembered. If the subjects were responding principally to the demands contained in the experimental situation, the special instructions should have abolished the amnesia, or at least produced a significant improvement in recall on the second test over that observed in the retest condition. FIGURE 1 shows the results for those hypnotizable subjects who met a criterion for virtually complete posthypnotic amnesia on the first recall test (each of the groups contained 15–24 subjects). It is apparent that the expected effects were not observed. In no condition did the interpolated test serve to abolish the amnesia that had been observed initially; there was still a significant further recovery of memory on the third test, after the amnesia had been lifted by the reversibility cue. Moreover, the special instructions did not have differential effects on recall, either on the second test of amnesia or on the postamnesia test: the four lines are essentially parallel. In short, in this study posthypnotic amnesia was not breached despite considerable pressure placed on the subjects.

All of this research seems to converge on the conclusion that the subject who appears to be experiencing posthypnotic amnesia is not simply suppressing memory or failing to be completely candid with the experimenter. Nor does he or she appear to be simply complying with the perceived or expressed demands arising from within a particular experimental context, or behaving in accordance with some wider conceptualization of hypnosis. Rather, the amnesic subject's memory report seems to reflect a subjectively compelling internal state in which the person is trying to recall some material but finds

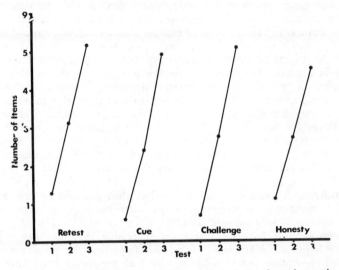

FIGURE 1. Mean number of items recalled on three tests of posthypnotic memory for hypnotizable subjects meeting a strict criterion for initial posthypnotic amnesia. Maximum recall=9 items. Tests 1 and 2 occurred during suggested amnesia, Test 2 preceded by special instructions (retest, cue, challenge, or honesty). Test 3 occurred after the reversibility cue was given to lift the amnesia. Based on FIGURE 1a of Kihlstrom et al.[44]

the process extremely difficult, inefficient, and unproductive. This means that the important sources of posthypnotic amnesia lie not so much in the subject's motivation during the recall task, nor in the particular demands placed on the subject, but rather involve other factors that interfere with the usual processes of information retrieval. These factors are described in the remaining two models that I wish to discuss.

AMNESIA AS REPRESSION

From a dynamic, intrapsychic point of view, posthypnotic amnesia may be seen as resulting from the repression of certain memories by the subject.

This hypothesis was formally proposed by Schilder and Kauders,[62] and was commented upon favorably by Rapaport [58] and Stengel,[69] among others. According to Schilder and Kauders, the motive for amnesia lies in the subject's transference relationship with the hypnotist (p. 60):

> Obviously, the hypnotized is ashamed of his infantile-masochistic adjustment and denies the hypnosis in order to conceal the adjustment. Very frequently, therefore. we find hypnotized persons indignantly denying that they have been hypnotized.

According to Rapaport (p. 176), recovery of these memories occurs when the subject accepts his masochistic relationship, an affective change that is instigated by the hypnotist's further suggestions. In many respects these notions parallel Freud's [23] account of the forgetting of dream material.

The repression hypothesis has little trouble dealing with the paradoxes of posthypnotic amnesia—after all, repressed material may be expected to "leak" into consciousness in various ways or express itself in indirect ways—but it has problems in other respects. For example, the hypnotic subject is typically aware of his loss of memories, whereas repression is usually construed as an unconscious process. Moreover, the motive to repress does not always seem to be present in amnesic subjects. Patients hypnotized in clinical settings may well experience strong transference reactions or give expression to unacceptable thoughts or impulses during hypnosis,[24, 53] but the experience of hypnosis is quite different for normal subjects participating in laboratory research. Here the hypnotist is looked upon more as a coach or a guide than as a powerful authority figure.[37] Even without the powerful transference relationship as a primary motivating source, amnesia occurs in about one third of laboratory subjects.

If posthypnotic amnesia is like repression, then it might be reasonable to expect that those who experience amnesia after hypnosis are also likely to employ repression as a defense at other times as well.[33] The idea here is that certain subjects have an ability for repression that they can capitalize on during hypnosis. Hammer [29] tested this hypothesis by administering the Jung word-association test to subjects who had previously been assessed for response to hypnosis. On the first run through the stimulus words, they were asked to respond with the first word that came to mind; on the second trial, they were asked to repeat the association that they had given the first time through the list. A repression score was computed by counting the number of errors in repeating associations to those words (one-half the list) that were emotionally provocative. Subjects who had shown posthypnotic amnesia during the earlier hypnosis session proved to show no more repression than those who had been nonamnesic. Apparently, the occurrence of posthypnotic amnesia does not depend on a generalized "talent" for repression.

Perhaps the most direct test of the repression hypothesis currently available examines the content of what is remembered and forgotten during posthypnotic amnesia. If posthypnotic amnesia is like repression, then memories of hypnosis associated with a negative affective valence should be particularly subject to the impact of amnesia suggestions. Although special techniques can be devised to examine the selectivity of amnesia,[10] the most widely used procedures have employed the standardized scales of hypnotic susceptibility. Following Zeigernik,[83] one can assume that those suggestions on which the subject fails to pass the standardized criterion (i.e., "failure" experiences) will be negatively toned, and that these items should be more strongly subject to the effects of amnesia than those which are passed—if, that is, amnesia involves repression. If the subject recalls fewer failed items than passed items, one would have evidence for a repression-like process involved in posthypnotic amnesia. Of course, some subjects cannot be considered in such an analysis, namely, those who pass or fail all the items as well as those who remember or forget all of the items. Fortunately for the method, such subjects are relatively few in number, and there is plenty of data left for analysis.

The repression hypothesis, then, predicts that during amnesia recall should favor passed (positively toned) over failed (negatively toned) items; more-

TABLE 2

SELECTIVE RECALL OF PASSED AND FAILED ITEMS DURING AMNESIA
FOR HYPNOTIZABLE AND INSUSCEPTIBLE SUBJECTS

| Study | N | Index of Selective Recall * | |
		Hypnotizable	Insusceptible
Hilgard & Hommel [36] †	124	.06	.15
O'Connell [51] †			
Sample A	100	.07	.12
Sample B	152	.11	.33
Sample C	54	.18	.40
Sample D	86	.02	.44
Sample E	94	.10	.05
Coe et al. [12] †			
Objective Pass/Fail	29	−.22	.08
Subjective Pass/Fail	29	−.08	.17
Pettinati & Evans [57] †			
Sample A	88	.09	.18
Pettinati & Evans [57] ‡			
Sample A	88	.07	.11
Sample B	108	.06	.11

* A positive index means that recall favors passed over failed items. A negative index means that recall favors failed over passed items.
† Selective Recall Index, calculated from results reported by the authors.
‡ Recall Probability Index, from Pettinati & Evans.[57]

over, this selectivity in recall should be most prominent in those subjects who are highly hypnotizable, because, after all, they are the ones who are most likely to respond to suggestions for amnesia. TABLE 2 presents the results of the four available studies. A positive "Selective Recall Index" means that subjects reported more passed than failed items; a negative index means that the subjects favored failed items in recall. Hilgard and Hommel,[36] in their original study, did find that fewer failed than passed suggestions were recalled during amnesia; however, this differential suppression of items associated with failure was more prominent among those subjects who were relatively insusceptible to hypnosis. In a later study, O'Connell [51] replicated the Hilgard-Hommel procedure in five separate samples totaling 486 subjects. Although there was some variation from sample to sample, in general he confirmed the earlier findings: relatively more recall of passed than failed items, particularly among the less hypnotizable subjects. Coe and his colleagues [13] performed a similar study and obtained somewhat different results. Using objective (behavioral) measures of success and failure, Coe *et al.* found that the selectivity of amnesia favored the recall of failed items among the hypnotizable subjects and of passed items among the insusceptible subjects. When they shifted from objective pass-fail ratings to the subjects' own impressions of whether or not an item had been successful (certainly a better approximation of the subjective feeling of failure), this tendency diminished appreciably. Finally, Pettinati and Evans [57] applied a new index of selective recall (the "Recall Probability Index") designed to eliminate the artifactual influence of the number of items remembered. In two samples totaling 196 subjects, hypnotizable and insusceptible subjects both favored the recall of passed items, regardless of the measure used, but with the improved index the difference between hypnotizable and insusceptible subjects was not significant.

Interpretation of the selective recall phenomenon is somewhat problematic because, as Hilgard and Hommel [36] pointed out, identical results could be produced by the repression of failed items and the enhancement of passed items. Whatever the source of the effect turns out to be, what is most important is that the findings of Pettinati and Evans [57] show that selective recall is not associated with depth of hypnosis. Thus the phenomenon probably does not stem from the suggestion for posthypnotic amnesia, but more likely reflects the vicissitudes of memory in general. In short, there is at present no evidence for a repression-like process operating specifically in posthypnotic amnesia.

AMNESIA AS MEMORY "ON THE TIP OF THE TONGUE"

The final mode of posthypnotic amnesia that I wish to discuss has its roots planted firmly in the information-processing theories of contemporary cognitive psychology. In this case, an analogy is drawn between posthypnotic amnesia and the experience of having memories "on the tip of the tongue" (Ref. 9 and pp. 719–721, Ref. 81), or the "feeling of knowing" something.[30, 31] Here, a person has difficulty remembering something (say, the location of the car keys or the name of a casual acquaintance), yet we know that the memory is available in storage because he will remember it eventually or recognize it when it is presented to him. Moreover, the person is able to determine with considerable accuracy that he knows the material and can correctly report some of its general characteristics. In much the same way, posthypnotic amnesia is reversible and can be breached by recognition testing; and amnesic subjects frequently offer comments such as the following: "I did some things, but I don't remember what they were—I think there was something about a mosquito, but I'm not sure."

Contemporary cognitive theorists (e.g. Anderson and Bower [1]) conceive of memory as a network of "locations" corresponding to events, concepts, and the like. Each location is associated with at least a few others and is also marked with certain "tags" that provide information about the spatiotemporal context in which the event occurred, the semantic and syntactic properties of the concept, orthographic and acoustic properties of the word, strength of the memory trace, and so forth. Retrieval of an item from memory proceeds by following associative pathways from location to location, generating likely items whose tags are then examined to determine if the candidate item is actually part of what the person is trying to remember. The search process is aided by various sorts of organizational cues and strategies by which the person can work systematically through the array of associations. Moreover, Tulving [77] has argued that there are two general types of systems into which memories are organized: "episodic" memory, which deals with personal experiences and other material with an autobiographical reference; and "semantic" memory, which represents a kind of mental encyclopedia in which knowledge about one's world and language is stored. Many memories, of course, have both episodic and semantic components. When we learn a new word, concept, or fact, its location in memory will be tagged with both information about the spatiotemporal context in which the learning occurred (episodic memory) and information about the new item's relationship to other words, concepts, or facts that are already familiar (semantic memory).

Without a sufficiently rich associational structure and without sufficient retrieval cues and an adequate plan for searching through memory, the person will not be able to gain access to material that is available in memory.[79] In this instance, there will occur a complete failure of retrieval. Or, he may be able to gain access to certain items (or certain aspects of the to-be-remembered material) but not to others. Recognition is more successful than recall, according to this account, largely because it facilitates the search through memory for candidate items. The search mechanism can go directly to the location in memory that corresponds to the presented item and proceed to test the tags against the relevant criteria.

Some of the "paradoxical" aspects of posthypnotic amnesia begin to make sense when viewed from the perspective of this theoretical account of memory retrieval. We know from studies based on the "forgetting" model that recall memory is profoundly disrupted by posthypnotic amnesia. However, recognition memory and other mnemonic processes which do not necessarily involve retrieval (such as those which generate interlist interference) are left relatively intact during amnesia. This suggests that the locus of the memory deficit lies in the organized search-and-retrieval process by which a subject gains access to stored memories. Moreover, when word lists are learned during hypnosis, amnesia does not prevent the list items from being employed in word-association tasks, and facts learned during hypnosis may be remembered in the absence of recollection about the context in which they were learned. This suggests that episodic relationships among the critical memories, but not semantic ones, are disrupted by the suggestion. Thus, the paradox of posthypnotic amnesia is not a paradox at all. The apparent contradictions in the amnesic subject's behavior stem from a selective disruption of certain access routes to memory but not of others.

Following this sort of reasoning, Evans and Kihlstrom [20] argued that if organizational cues make recall as easy, efficient, and productive as it usually is, then when recall is difficult, inefficient, and unproductive—as it is during posthypnotic amnesia—the memory deficit reflects the disorganization of the process of retrieval. Now, the organization of recall draws on many sources, including visual, orthographic, acoustic, semantic, and syntactic cues; sensory modality, frequency, and saliency; and the spatiotemporal relationships among the to-be-remembered items and their surrounding context. Formal analyses [77] indicated that temporal context cues are of overriding importance in the retrieval of episodic memories. Introspection, moreover, suggested that in retrieving the experiences of a previous hypnosis session, a prominent organizational strategy would involve the temporal sequence uniting the several events. Because amnesic subjects are trying unsuccessfully to remember a series of personal experiences, Evans and Kihlstrom proposed that posthypnotic amnesia resulted, at least in part, from a specific disruption in the temporal organization of recall.

In a first test of the disorganized retrieval hypothesis,[20] 112 subjects took part in an experiment involving three standardized hypnotic procedures, each of which contained a series of hypnotic suggestions followed by a final suggestion for posthypnotic amnesia. Those subjects who showed virtually complete amnesia in response to the suggestion were excluded from further consideration, since they recalled too few items to permit analysis of the organiza-

TABLE 3

TEMPORAL ORGANIZATION IN RECALL DURING POSTHYPNOTIC AMNESIA *

Study	N	Rho Index	
		Hypnotizable	Insusceptible
Evans & Kihlstrom [20]	112		
HGSHS:A		.67	.80
SHSS:B		.39	.58
SHSS:C		.08	.55
Unpublished Replication	107		
HGSHS:A		.61	.81
SHSS:C		.16	.68
Kihlstrom et al.[44]	488		
HGSHS:A		.68	.85

* HGSHS:A=Harvard Group Scale of Hypnotic Susceptibility, Form A; SHSS:B and SHSS:C=Stanford Hypnotic Susceptibility Scale, Forms B and C.

tion of recall. For those subjects who recalled at least three of the events and experiences of hypnosis, despite the suggestion for complete amnesia, Spearman rank-order correlation coefficients (rho) were calculated between the order in which each subject recalled those suggestions that he or she could remember and the order in which those suggestions were actually administered as part of the hypnotic procedure. By this measure, hypnotizable subjects showed significantly less temporal organization during amnesia than did the insusceptible subjects. These findings were replicated in a subsequent unpublished study involving 107 subjects who received two different hypnotic procedures and one in which 488 subjects received a single standardized procedure,[44] as well as on other occasions. TABLE 3 portrays these results, which indicate that the temporal-disorganization effect in posthypnotic amnesia is highly stable.

More detailed analyses lend further support to the conclusion that the disorganization of temporal sequencing in recall is an aspect of posthypnotic amnesia, along with reversibility and the vague and fragmentary nature of the subjects' memory reports. Despite the subject's ability to recall some of his or her experiences, these three properties may be cited in support of the conclusion that he or she is responding at least partially to the amnesia suggestion. Subsequent studies have shown that temporal sequencing in recall is unaffected when subjects are hypnotized but do not receive suggestions for amnesia, and that during amnesia hypnotizable subjects are relatively unable to arrange those items that they recall in correct temporal sequence when they are specifically instructed to do so. These findings indicate that temporal disorganization is functionally tied to the suggestion for amnesia, rather than to hypnosis alone, and does not merely reflect the subject's disinclination to organize recall in a particular way. A full account of this research is forthcoming.[11]

There are many issues that remain to be addressed. For example, we need to know what other access routes to memory are disrupted during amnesia as well as those which remain undisturbed. What techniques, aside from the administration of the reversibility cue, will serve to relieve posthypnotic amnesia? What is the function of the reversibility cue, and how does it work? What is it about hypnosis that allows posthypnotic amnesia to occur? With respect to the last question—that of mechanism—it is possible that the disruption of retrieval observed in posthypnotic amnesia reflects a dissociation of cognitive control systems,[28, 34] but final conclusions await further research on amnesia as well as further elaboration of the concept of dissociation.

The hypothesis that posthypnotic amnesia occurs through the inability of subjects to capitalize on organizational cues and strategies important to memory retrieval was originally suggested by the similarities between posthypnotic amnesia and instances of recall difficulty observed in waking life. In contrast to hypotheses generated by the "secrets" and "repression" models of amnesia, the available results are quite consistent with the notion of posthypnotic amnesia as disrupted retrieval. The initial success of the enterprise alone should be enough to justify further research efforts along these lines. Moreover, the notion that posthypnotic amnesia involves a disruption of retrieval processes gains strength from the fact that similar accounts have been sketched for a wide variety of memory failure, including ordinary forgetting,[65, 78] Korsakoff's syndrome,[59, 74] infantile amnesia in humans and in animals,[61, 68] amnesia induced by electroconvulsive shock,[46, 67] and state-dependent learning produced by alcohol, barbiturates, and other drugs.[55] Thus, the retrieval-failure approach advocated here is strongly tied to the ongoing attempt to develop a comprehensive view of both normal and abnormal memory processes within the context of contemporary cognitive psychology. It is to be hoped that the experimental study of posthypnotic amnesia will not only draw passively upon advances made in other areas, but will make its own unique contribution to the fuller understanding of the mind that we all seek.

ACKNOWLEDGMENTS

I thank Frederick J. Evans, Sharon Greene, A. Gordon Hammer, Helen M. Pettinati, Moshe Twersky, and especially Reid Hastie for their helpful comments during the preparation of this paper.

REFERENCES

1. ANDERSON, J. R. & G. H. BOWER. 1972. Recognition and retrieval processes in free recall. Psych. Rev. 79: 97–123.
2. BARBER, T. X. 1969. Hypnosis: A Scientific Approach. Van-Nostrand-Reinhold. New York, N.Y.
3. BARBER, T. X. 1972. Suggested ("hypnotic") behavior: The trance paradigm versus an alternative paradigm. In Hypnosis: Research Developments and Perspectives. E. Fromm & R. E. Shor, Eds. Aldine-Atherton. Chicago, Ill.
4. BARBER, T. X. & D. S. CALVERLEY. 1966. Toward a theory of "hypnotic" behavior: Experimental analyses of suggested amnesia. J. Abnorm. Psychol. 71: 95–107.
5. BARBER, T. X., N. P. SPANOS & J. F. CHAVES. 1974. Hypnotism, Imagination, and Human Potentialities. Pergamon Press. New York, N.Y.
6. BITTERMAN, M. E. & F. L. MARCUSE. 1945. Autonomic response in posthypnotic amnesia. J. Exp. Psychol. 35: 248–252.
7. BOWERS, K. S. 1966. Hypnotic behavior: The differentiation of trance and demand characteristic variables. J. Abnorm. Psychol. 71: 42–51.
8. BOWERS, K. S. 1975. The psychology of subtle control: An attributional analysis of behavioral persistence. Can. J. Behav. Sci. 7: 78–95.
9. BROWN, R. & D. MCNEIL. 1966. The "tip of the tongue" phenomenon. J. Verb. Learn. Verb. Behav. 5: 325–337.
10. CLEMES, S. 1964. Repression and hypnotic amnesia. J. Abnorm. Psychol. 69: 62–69.
11. COE, W. C. 1976. Posthypnotic amnesia and the psychology of secrets. Paper read at Soc. Clin. Exp. Hypn. Philadelphia, Pa.
12. COE, W C., B. BASDEN, D. BASDEN & C. GRAHAM. 1976. Posthypnotic amnesia: Suggestions of an active process in dissociative phenomena. J. Abnorm. Psychol. 85: 455–458.
13. COE, W. C., R. J. BAUGHER, W. R. KRIMM & J. A. SMITH. 1976. A further examination of selective recall following hypnosis. Int. J. Clin. Exp. Hypn. 42: 13–21.
14. COOPER, L. M. 1972. Hypnotic amnesia. In Hypnosis: Research Developments and Perspectives. E. Fromm & R. E. Shor, Eds. Aldine-Atherton. Chicago, Ill.
15. COORS, D. 1928. A determination of the density of posthypnotic amnesia for the stylus maze. Unpublished bachelor's thesis. Univ. Wisconsin. Madison, Wis.
16. DAMASER, E. C. 1964. An experimental study of long-term posthypnotic suggestion. Unpublished doctoral thesis. Harvard University. Cambridge, Mass.
17. ERICKSON, M H. & E. M. ERICKSON. 1941. Concerning the nature and character of posthypnotic behavior. J. Gen. Psychol. 24: 95–133.
18. EVANS, F. J. 1971. Contextual forgetting: A study of source amnesia. Paper read at East. Psychol. Assoc. New York, N.Y.
19. EVANS, F. J. 1972. Posthypnotic amnesia and the temporary disruption of retrieval processes. Paper read at Amer. Psychol. Assoc. Honolulu, Hawaii.
20. EVANS, F. J. & J. F. KIHLSTROM. 1973. Posthypnotic amnesia as disrupted retrieval. J. Abnorm. Psychol. 82: 317–323.
21. EVANS, F. J., J. F. KIHLSTROM & E. C. ORNE. 1973. Quantifying subjective reports during posthypnotic amnesia. Proc. 81st Ann. Conv. Am. Psychol. Assoc. 8: 1077–1078.
22. EVANS, F. J. & W. A. F. THORN. 1966. Two types of posthypnotic amnesia: Recall amnesia and source amnesia. Int. J. Clin. Exp. Hypn. 14: 333–343.
23. FREUD, S. 1900. The interpretation of dreams. In The Standard Edition of the Complete Psychological Works of Sigmund Freud. J. Strachey, Ed. Vols. 4–5. Hogarth Press. London, England. First published 1900; republished 1953.

24. GANDOLFO, R. L. 1971. Role of expectancy, amnesia, and hypnotic induction in the performance of posthypnotic behavior. J. Abnorm. Psychol. **77**: 324–328.
25. GILL, M. M. & M. BRENMAN. 1959. Hypnosis and Related States: Psychoanalytic Studies in Regression. International Universities Press. New York, N.Y.
26. GOLDSTEIN, M. S. & C. N. SIPPRELLE. 1970. Hypnotically induced amnesia versus ablation of memory. Int. J. Clin. Exp. Hypn. **18**: 211–216.
27. GRAHAM, K. R. & A. PATTON. 1968. Retroactive inhibition, hypnosis, and hypnotic amnesia. Int. J. Clin. Exp. Hypn. **16**: 68–74.
28. HAMMER, A. G. 1961. Reflections on the study of hypnosis. Austral. J. Psychol. **13**: 3–22.
29. HAMMER, A. G. 1970. Relationship of factors in hypnosis and in personality. Paper read at Am. Psychol. Assoc. Miami Beach, Fla.
30. HART, J. T. 1965. Memory and the feeling-of-knowing experience. J. Educ. Psychol. **56**: 208–216.
31. HART, J. T. 1967. Memory and the memory-monitoring process. J. Verb. Learn. Verb. Behav. **6**: 685–691.
32. HILGARD, E. R. 1965. Hypnotic Susceptibility. Harcourt, Brace & World. New York, N.Y.
33. HILGARD, E. R. 1966. Posthypnotic amnesia: Experiments and theory. Int. J. Clin. Exp. Hypn. **14**: 104–111.
34. HILGARD, E. R. 1976. Neodissociation theory of multiple cognitive control systems. In Consciousness and Self-Regulation. G. E. Schwartz & D. Shapiro, Eds. Vol. 1. Plenum Press. New York, N.Y.
35. HILGARD, E. R. & L. M. COOPER. 1965. Spontaneous and suggested posthypnotic amnesia. Int. J. Clin. Exp. Hypn. **13**: 261–273.
36. HILGARD, E. R & L. S. HOMMEL. 1961. Selective amnesia for events within hypnosis in relation to repression. J. Pers. **29**: 205–216.
37. HILGARD, J. R. 1970. Personality and Hypnosis. Univ. Chicago Press. Chicago, Ill.
38. HULL, C. L. 1933. Hypnosis and Suggestibility: An Experimental Approach. Appleton-Century-Crofts. New York, N.Y.
39. JONHSON, R. F. Q., B. A. MAHER & T. X. BARBER. 1972. Artifact in the "essence of hypnosis": An evaluation of trance logic. J. Abnorm. Psychol. **79**: 212–220.
40. KIHLSTROM, J. F. 1977. Generic recall during posthypnotic amnesia. Paper read at East. Psychol. Assoc. Boston, Mass.
41. KIHLSTROM, J. F. & F. J. EVANS. 1976. Recovery of memory after posthypnotic amnesia. J. Abnorm. Psychol. **85**: 564–569.
42. KIHLSTROM, J. F. & F. J. EVANS. 1977. The residual effect of suggestions for posthypnotic amnesia: A re-examination. J. Abnorm. Psychol. **86**:. In press.
43. KIHLSTROM, J. F. & F. J. EVANS. Memory retrieval processes in posthypnotic amnesia. In preparation.
44. KIHLSTROM, J. F., F. J. EVANS, E. C. ORNE & M. T. ORNE. Attempting to breach posthypnotic amnesia. In preparation.
45. LIFE, C. 1929. The effects of practice in the trance upon learning in the normal waking state. Unpublished bachelor's thesis. Univ. Wisconsin. Madison, Wis.
46. McDOUGALL, R. 1904. Recognition and recall. J. Phil. Sci. Methods. **1**: 229–233.
47. MILLER, R. R. & A. D. SPRINGER. 1973. Amnesia, consolidation, and retrieval. Psychol. Rev. **80**: 69–79.
48. MITCHELL, M. B. 1932. Retroactive inhibition and hypnosis. J. Gen. Psychol. **7**: 343–358.
49. NACE, E. P., M. T. ORNE & A. G. HAMMER. 1974. Posthypnotic amnesia as an active psychic process: The reversibility of amnesia. Arch. Gen. Psychiat. **31**: 257–260.
50. NAGGE, J. W. 1935. An experimental test of the theory of associative interference. J. Exp. Psychol. **18**: 663–682.

51. O'CONNELL, D. N. 1966. Selective recall of hypnotic susceptibility items: Evidence for repression or enhancement? Int. J. Clin. Exp. Hypn. **14:** 150–161.
52. ORNE, M. T. 1959. The nature of hypnosis: Artifact and essence. J. Abnorm. Soc. Psychol. **58:** 277–299.
53. ORNE, M. T. 1966. On the mechanisms of posthypnotic amnesia. Int. J. Clin. Exp. Hypn. **14:** 121–134.
54. ORNE, M. T. 1972. On the simulating subject as a quasi-control group in hypnosis research: What, why, and how. In Hypnosis: Research Developments and Perspectives. E. Fromm & R. E. Shor, Eds. Aldine-Atherton. Chicago, Ill.
55. OVERTON, D. A. 1968. Dissociated learning in drug states (state-dependent learning). In Psychopharmacology: A Review of Progress 1957–1967. D. H. Efron, J. O. Cole, J. Levine & D. H. Wittenborn, Eds. U.S. Public Health Service Publication no. 1836. Washington, D.C.
56. PATTEN, E. F. 1932. Does posthypnotic amnesia apply to practice effects? J. Gen. Psychol. **7:** 196–201.
57. PETTINATI, H. M. & F. J. EVANS. 1976. Repression or enhancement and the selective recall during posthypnotic amnesia of passed and failed experiences. Paper read at Soc. Clin. Exp. Hypn. Philadelphia, Pa.
58. RAPAPORT, D. 1942. Emotions and Memory. Williams & Wilkins. Baltimore, Md.
59. ROZIN, P. 1976. The psychobiological approach to human memory. In Neural Mechanisms of Learning and Memory. M. R. Rosenzweig & E. L. Bennett, Eds. MIT Press. Cambridge, Mass.
60. SARBIN, T. R. & W. C. COE. 1972. Hypnosis: A social-psychological analysis of influence communication. Holt, Rinehart & Winston. New York, N.Y.
61. SCHACHTEL, E. G. 1947. On memory and childhood amnesia. Psychiat. **10:** 1–26.
62. SCHILDER, P. & O. KAUDERS. 1927. Hypnosis. Nervous and Mental Disease Publications. New York, N.Y.
63. SCOTT, H. D. 1930. Hypnosis and the conditioned reflex. J. Gen. Psychol. **4:** 113–130.
64. SHEEHAN, P. W. & M. T. ORNE. 1968. Some comments on the nature of posthypnotic behavior. J. Nerv. Ment. Dis. **146:** 209–220.
65. SHIFFRIN, R. M. 1970. Forgetting: Trace erosion or retrieval failure? Science **168:** 1601–1603.
66. SHOR, R. E. 1971. Expectancies of being influenced and hypnotic performance. Int. J. Clin. Exp. Hypn. **19:** 154–166.
67. SPEAR, N. E. 1973. Retrieval of memory in animals. Psych. Rev. **80:** 163–194.
68. SPEAR, N. E. & P. PARSONS. 1976. Analysis of a reactivation treatment: Ontogeny and alleviated forgetting. In Coding Processes in Animal Memory. D. Medin, R. Davis & W. Roberts, Eds. Lawrence Erlbaum Associates. Hillsdale, N.J.
69. STENGEL, E. 1966. Psychogenic loss of memory. In Amnesia. C. W. M. Whitty & O. L. Zangwill, Eds. Butterworths. London, England.
70. STERN, J. A., W. E. EDMONSTON, G. A. ULETT & A. LEVITSKY. 1963. Electrodermal measures in experimental amnesia. J. Abnorm. Soc. Psychol. **67:** 397–401.
71. STEWART, C. G. & W. P. DUNLAP. 1976. Functional isolation of associations during suggested posthypnotic amnesia. Int. J. Clin. Exp. Hypn. **24:** 426–434.
72. STRICKLER, C. B. 1929. A quantitative study of posthypnotic amnesia. J. Abnorm. Soc. Psychol. **24:** 108–119.
73. TAKAHASHI, R. 1958. An experimental examination of the dissociation hypothesis in hypnosis. J. Clin. Exp. Hypn. **6:** 139–151.
74. TALLAND, G. A. 1965. Deranged Memory: A Psychonomic Study of the Amnesic Syndrome. Academic Press. New York, N.Y.

75. THORNE, D. E. 1969. Amnesia and hypnosis. Int. J. Clin. Exp. Hypn. **17:** 225–241.
76. THORNE, D. E. & M. V. HALL. 1974. Hypnotic amnesia revisited. Int. J. Clin. Exp. Hypn. **22:** 167–178.
77. TULVING, E. 1972. Episodic and semantic memory. *In* Organization of Memory. E. Tulving & W. Donaldson, Eds. Academic Press. New York, N.Y.
78. TULVING, E. 1974. Cue-dependent forgetting. Am. Scientist **62:** 74–82.
79. TULVING, E. & Z. PEARLSTONE. 1966. Availability and accessibility of information in memory for words. J. Verb. Learn. Verb. Behav. **5:** 381–391.
80. WILLIAMSEN, J. A., H. J. JOHNSON & C. W. ERIKSEN. 1965. Some characteristics of posthypnotic amnesia. J. Abnorm. Psychol. **70:** 123–131.
81. WOODWORTH, R. S. & S. SCHLOSSBERG. 1954. Experimental Psychology. Rev. Ed. Holt. New York.
82. YOUNG, J. & L. M. COOPER. 1972. Hypnotic recall amnesia as a function of manipulated expectancy. Proc. 80th Ann. Conv. Am. Psychol. Assoc. **7:** 857–858.
83. ZEIGARNIK, B. 1927. Das Behalten von erledigten und unerledigten Handlungen. Psychol. Forsch. **9:** 1–85.

Author Index

Ascher, L. M., 250

Barber, T. X., 34
Bowers, K. S., 222
Brown, M., 175

Coe, W. C., 2, 90

Diamond, M. J., 119

Edmonston, W. E., Jr., 1, 105
Evans, F. J., 162

Graham, K. R., 274

Hilgard, E. R., 48

Kihlstrom, J. F., 284

Levitt, E. E., 86
Lieberman, L. R., 60
Lindner, H., 238

Orne, M. T., 14

Paskewitz, D. A., 154
Perry, C., 264

Reyher, J., 69
Rivers, S. M., 208
Ross, S., 208

Sarbin, T. R., 2
Sheehan, P. W., 194
Sletten, I., 175
Spanos, N. P., 208
Spiegel, H., 129
Stern, J. A., 175

Ulett, G. A., 175

Wickramasekera, I. E., 143
Wilson, S. C., 34

Subject Index

A bsorption, *see also* Hypnotic involvement
  capacity for, 30, 109
  characterized, 211
  self-reporting and, 220
  tolerance for incongruity and, 205
Acupuncture
  analgesic effects of, 179, 182–184, 188–191
  experimental technique in, 175–176, 179, 181
  false-site-placebo stimulation, 175–177, 179–182, 187–188
  hypnotizability and, 188–191
  location of points in, 179–181, 187
  pain reduction by, 185, 188
  in specific illness treatment, 175
  true and false-site stimulation, 190, 191
Age regression, hypnotic
  as Creative Imagination Scale test suggestion, 35, 38
  hypnotized subject and simulator behavior in, 24–25
  intolerance of incongruity testing, 199n, 204n
Allergies, hypnotherapeutic treatment of, 226–227
Alpha rhythm activity
  characteristics of, 154–157
  in dominant lobe, highly suggestible subjects, 78
  individual optimum level variation, 154–155, 156
  levels of hypnotizability and, 280
  occulomotor command effects on, 155, 156
Amnesia, types of, 297; *see also* Posthypnotic amnesia, Source amnesia
Analgesia, hypnotic
  in cancer management, 232
  as counterexpectational experience, 26
  dissociation theory of, 9, 11
  distraction techniques in, 10
  dramaturgical interpretation of, 10, 11
  effects of, *see* Analgesic effects
  hypnotic suggestibility and, 49–50, 52–56, 223–224
  pain reduction reported for, 52–56, 185, 187; *see also* Pain reduction

  placebo effect and, *see* Placebo effect
  posthypnotic persistence of, 267–272
  self-induced, 50
  self-reports of, 8–9
  by waking suggestion, 51–52
Analgesic effects, *see also* Pain reduction
  of acupuncture, 175, 179, 182–184, 188–191
  of aspirin, 176, 179, 182–184, 191–192
  of diazepam, 176, 179, 182–185, 191–192
  of hypnosis and acupuncture, compared, 189–191
  in subjects rated for hypnotizability, 185–189
Analogic-synthetic mode, in suggestibility enhancement, 80
Animal magnetism, mentioned, 17, 20, 21, 163, 222
Antisocial acts, experimental
  in coercive power evaluation, 86–89
  deception in, 97–98
  ethical considerations in, 96–98
  influences of hypnosis in, 90–96, 100–101
  types of acts utilized, 93–95, 102
Anxiety, *see also* Dependency strivings
  in antisocial act demands, 101
  in hypnotic induction, 78–79, 82, 144
  suggestibility and, 79, 81, 82
Arm levitation test, 35, 37, 131
Arm rigidity test, 75, 76, 215–217
Aspirin, analgesic effectiveness versus hypnosis, 175–179, 182–184, 191–192
Asthma, hypnotherapeutic treatment of, 226
Attention, *see* Concentration
Attitude, as hypnotic-susceptibility factor, 34, 105, 122, 126, 147
Australian and New Zealand Society for the Advancement of Science, mentioned, 106
Autogenic training, 56
Autokinetic effect, 280–281
Automatic response, *see* Involuntary motor response
Automatic talking, 9, 11, 52
Automatic writing, 9, 11

303

304   Annals New York Academy of Sciences

Barber Suggestibility Scale (BSS)
  applications of, 35, 179
  hallucinatory experience as measured
    by, 56, 57
  in think-with testing, 40
Base-line performance, 124
Behavior modification, 119, 151–152; *see
  also* Susceptibility training
Behavior therapy
  hypnosis conceptualized in terms of,
    260
  hypnotic induction and relaxation
    training compared in, 254–256
  hypnotic trance-state concept and, 251–
    254, 258–260
  nontrance-state hypnosis in, 251
Believed-in imagining, hypnosis as, 20
Biofeedback
  alpha rhythm control and, 155, 157
  hypnotherapy contrasted with, 56
  in hypnotizability enhancement, 146
  in relaxation training, 150
  in susceptibility training, 119, 125
Blocked-number hallucination, 199*n*, 266
Body morphology, and hypnotizability,
    105–115; *see also* Physique
Body temperature, modification with hyp-
    nosis, 227, 228
Braid, James, 162, 163
Burn treatment, hypnotic suggestion in,
    227, 228

Cerebral-hemisphere laterality
  activity differences in, 280, 281
  affective disorders and right domi-
    nance, 138
  conceptual and perceptual roles of, 280
  as explanation of hypnosis, 280–282
  hypnotizability and, 114, 138, 279, 280
  information-processing functions of,
    69–70
  psychopathological correlations with,
    138–139
  suggestibility enhancement and, 69–72,
    80
Cerebrotonic temperament, 108, 109
Children, capacity for hypnosis of, 108
Clinical context, the
  experimental context compared with,
    119, 120, 143; *see also* Experi-
    mental context
  hypnosis in, *see* Hypnotherapy
  hypnotizability in, 143
  physiological modification in, 225–230
  think-with instructions in, 43

Coercive power
  of hypnosis, *see* Hypnotic involvement
  of personal relations and suggestion,
    compared, 90, 93–94
Cognition, 274, 276
Cognitive-behavioral theory
  evaluation of, 34–44
  postulates of, 34
  and trance-state theory compared, 40–
    44, 194
Cognitive controls
  in mentation during sleep, 164
  in hypnotizability modification, 150
  suspension of in hypnotizability, 203
  voluntary and involuntary, 58, 194
Cognitive strategies, in hypnotizability
    enhancement, 126, 260
Cold-pressor pain response, 49, 176–179,
    182, 223
Command inhibition, 75, 76
Concentration
  alpha rhythm activity in, 155
  in hypnosis, 134, 203
  hypnotizability and, 139–141, 144
  personality structure and, 139–141
  in suggestibility testing, 78
  trance state as involving, 129, 130, 134
Conditioned response, posthypnotic re-
    sponse versus, 58
Consciousness
  control over, 171, 172
  dissociation of, 48, 203; *see also* Dis-
    sociation
  multiple levels of, 48–58, 203
Contextual position, in hypnotic phe-
    nomena studies, 2–6, 18*n*
Contractual and collaborative relations,
    in testing, 268
Counterexpectational conduct, in hyp-
    nosis, 2–10
Creative Imagination Scale, 34–44
Cue structuring, *see also* Verbal prepara-
    tion
  effects on hallucinated incongruities,
    195–199, 203–204
  goal-directed fantasy reporting and,
    214–217
  in incongruity responses, 195–199
  tolerance for incongruities and, 204
  uncancelled posthypnotic-suggestion
    persistence and, 264, 271
Cuff-pain test, 176–179, 182

Deafness, hallucination of, 278, 279
Deception, as justified in antisocial act
    experiments, 97–98, 100, 102

Deep hypnosis, training for, 123
Deep relaxation techniques, see Relaxation training
Delta rhythm (EEG), 171
Delusion, references on, 194
Dependency striving(s)
  as characterizing hypnosis, 82
  interpersonal relations in, 81
  medicoclinical hypnosis and, 72
  in posthypnotic amnesia, 292
  in suggestibility enhancement, 72, 73
  in suggestibility theory, 80, 81
Depth of hypnosis
  character of, 49, 205
  napping patterns and, 166–170
  in posthypnotic-amnesia recall, 294
  self-reporting on, 94
  therapeutic affects and, 225–228
Desensitization, systematic, 254
Diazepam
  analgesic effects of, 176, 179, 182, 184, 185
  compared with hypnotic analgesia, 191–192
Disorganized recall, posthypnotic amnesia and, 28
Dissociation
  definition of, 58
  in hypnotic analgesia, 9, 11
  references on processes of, 194
  selective inattention as, 203
  in sleep, 223
  testing of, 209
Distraction
  in acupuncture, 190
  in hypnotic analgesia, 10
Double hallucination(s) (DH), 195–204
  as characteristic of hypnosis, 195
  hypnotic and waking-test responses to, 200
  positive responses of unhypnotized subjects, 197, 201, 204
  reporting of, 195–199
  tolerance of incongruity and 199n
Dramaturgical model, of hypnotic behavior, 3, 6–8
Dreams
  control of, during sleep, 164
  forgetting of, and amnesia, 292
  recall of, 164
  recall of, and hypnotizability, 166n
Drowsiness, 156, 157
Duncan Multiple Range Test, 39

Ectomorphy
  characterization of, 107, 114

hypnotizability and, 109, 113, 115
Electroencephalogram (EEG)
  characteristic of hypnosis, 253
  of hypnosis as wakefulness, 163
  laterality of, in hypnotic activity, 280
Electromyogram (EMG)
  in feedback for hypnotizability, 146–150
  in relaxation training, 146
Endomorphy, hypnotizability and, 113, 114
Ethical factors, in behavioral research with human subjects, 96–97, 100
Experienced involuntariness, 208–220
Experienced Involuntariness Scale, 216, 217
Experiential learning, in susceptibility training, 119
Experimental context, the
  applications of, in hypnosis research, 60–67
  clinical context compared with, 143; see also Clinical context
  as illusionary, 86–87
  as model of valid research procedure, 77–78
  subject-hypnotist relations in, 72; see also Subject-hypnotist relations
  subject's perception of, 87–89
  subject's role and status in, 73
Experimental methods utilized, see Methodology
Experimenter bias hypothesis, 218
Experimenter-hypnotist
  bias of, in research, 23, 218, 275
  deportment of, as research variable, 23
  dilemma of, in antisocial-act assignments, 88, 90, 92–94, 100–102
  expectations and demands of, 53–54
  in goal-directed fantasy experiments, 213–218
  in hallucinated-incongruity cuing, 195, 196
  operational instructions by, 50–51
  and physician-hypnotist, compared, 72
  presence of, and suggestibility enhancement, 79
  relations with subjects, see Subject-hypnotist relations
  stranger as, 94, 98, 102
Eye-closure test, 75, 76
Eye movements, involuntary, 276–278
Eye-roll (ER) test
  in hypnotizability, 130–132, 189
  in psychopathology diagnosis, 137–138

Faking, *see* Role enactment; Simulation
Fantasy, hypnosis and, 22, 29
Fat-type physique
  hypnotizability and, 113, 114
  suggestibility score correlations with, 110–113
Fear-reduction treatment, 254
Feedback, *see* Biofeedback
Female(s), hypnotizability in, 114
Field Scale of Hypnotic Depth, 106
Finger anesthesia, 35, 37–38
Finger-lock test, 75, 76

Gestalt, in perception, 274
Goal-directed fantasy (GDF), 211–212, 219
Good hypnotic subjects
  alpha activity laterality in, 78, 280
  behavioral criteria for, 260, 271
  cerebral hemisphere functions in, 280
  dissociation in sleep by, 223
  hallucinated incongruity tolerance of, 194, 196
  hypnotic analgesia effects in, 223–224
  information processing by, 232
  persistence of uncancelled suggestions in, 264–272
  personality traits inferred for, 78
  responsiveness to pain in, 192
  skills of, 271
  suggestibility as involuntary in, 208
  suggestibility in sleep of, 223

Hallucination(s)
  auditory, positive, 274–279
  behavioral and hypnotic methods of inducing, compared, 275
  characteristics of, 256
  as criteria of hypnotic state, 274, 279
  in hypnotic subject and simulator, distinguished, 26–27, 54
  of incongruities, *see* Double hallucination(s)
  induction of, experimental, 256–257
  involuntary eye movements in, 276
  perceptual basis of, 274–279
  response levels to, 56–57
  as test of suggestibility, 75–76
  visual, 75–76, 274–278
Hand-clasp test, 139
Hand-levitation test, 35, 37
Hand-lowering test, 75, 76
Harvard Group Scale(s) of Hypnotic Susceptibility (HGSHS)

  in analgesic-effect experiments, 178
  in antisocial-act subject selection, 91
  applicability of, 35, 73
  in cue structuring for incongruity reporting, 196
  in characterization of subject hypnotizability, 185
  eye-roll test correlation with, 131
  in heritability study, 106
  hypnotic-induction profile and, 131
  and Michigan State Suggestibility Profiles, 75
  for nappers and nonnappers, 166–170
  physique-type ratings on, 110, 111
  in posthypnotic-amnesia testing, 290
  in screening for susceptibility, 42n, 73, 91, 110, 265
  in temporal organization of recall experiments, 296
  in voluntary control of sleep scoring, 165–166
Head-fall test, 75, 76
Heritability of hypnotic affects, 106, 281
"Hidden observer"
  concept of, 9–12
  in covert hypnotic behavior reporting, 56
  non-dissociation theory and, 56
  in pain reduction assessment, 52
  in good hypnotic subjects, 271
"Hyperempiric" suggestions, 42n
Hypersuggestibility, levels of, 83
Hypnoanalgesia, *see* Analgesia, hypnotic
Hypnosis
  acupuncture and, 175, 188–191
  alpha-rhythm activity and, 78, 157, 158, 280
  as altered state of consciousness, 251; *see also* Theory (-ies) of hypnosis
  analgesic affects of, *see* Analgesia
  behavioral interaction and, 259–260
  in behavior therapy, 250–260; *see also* Behavior therapy
  body temperature modification and, 227–228
  cancer treatment and, 232–234
  capability for, *see* Hypnotizability; Suggestibility
  cerebral hemisphere functions and, 280–282
  clinical, *see* Clinical context
  cognitive falsifications in, 274, 279
  as context of procedures, 143
  counterexpectational behavior in, 2–3
  deep, training for, 123

definitions of, 14–16, 18–20, 51, 82, 130, 143, 162, 251, 274, 279
depth of, *see* Depth of hypnosis
dissociative information processing and, 223
drifting into, 51
EEG pattern in, 163, 253
etymology of term, 162
experimental psychology approach to, 9
hallucination(s) in, *see* Hallucinations
historical explanations of, 20–21
incongruity tolerance in, 194–196, 203
induction of, *see* Induction of hypnosis
induction profile of, *see* Hypnosis Induction Profile (HIP)
informational processing approach to, 222–234
involuntary behavior expected in, 209–210
measurement of, 19
misuses of, 238–239
motivation in, *see* Motivation
pain reduction by, *see* Analgesia; Pain reduction
personality and, 139–141
physiological modifications affected in, 226–228
popular notions about, 17
psychotherapeutic applications of, 238–248
reality of, 20
relaxation training compared with, 254–256
role playing in, *see* Role playing
state/nonstate concepts of, *see* Hypnotic state; Theories of hypnosis
scientific views of, 17
sleep and, *see under* Sleep
suggestibility as, *see* Suggestibility
therapeutic, *see* Hypnotherapy
trance logic in, 194–195
as trance state, *see* Trance state
Hypnosis Induction Profile (HIP), 129–141
personality structures and, 139–141
in psychopathology diagnosis, 134–138
as trance-capacity test, 129–137
Hypnotherapy
behavioral versus trance-state effects in, 258
in cancer pain alleviation, 232
as clinical, *see* Clinical context
depth of hypnosis and, 225–227
hypnotizability testing in, 139

as a methodological framework, 69, 82, 87, 119, 120, 143
patient's role in, 72, 73
patient-therapist relations in, *see* Subject-hypnotist relations
in psychosomatic disorders, 225–227
relaxation training and, 227
in skin disorders, 229
in surgery for hemophiliacs, 227
trance-state testing in, 129, 130
for unhypnotizable subjects, 51
warts treated by, 225, 229
Hypnotic analgesia, *see* Analgesia, hypnotic
Hypnotic behavior
experimental characteristics of, 259–260
explanatory account of, 279
somnambulism and, 253
specific distinctiveness lacking for, 15–16
Hypnotic induction, *see* Induction
Hypnotic interaction, *see* Subject-hypnotist relations
Hypnotic involvement, *see also* Absorption
antisocial acts and, 90
coercive power of, 90, 93–94
dissociated activity and, 58
experimental validity and, 88–89
experimental versus clinical contexts in, 86–87
extreme tasks in testing, 88
as involuntary response to suggestion, 208–220
quantification problem of, 86
rating of, in analgesia trials, 185
subject-hypnotist involvement and, 88, 90
suggestion-related imaginings and, 212
tolerance for incongruities and, 204
variable factors in, 90
Hypnotic state
characteristics of, 2–3, 14–18, 49, 251; *see also* Hypnosis; Trance state
non-state view versus, 40–44, 57–58, 194; *see also* Cognitive-behavioral theory; Suggestibility theory; Theory of hypnosis
waking state as distinct from, 50–51, 189
Hypnotic suggestibility, *see* Hypnotizability; Suggestibility
Hypnotic susceptibility, *see* Hypnotizability; Suggestibility

Hypnotic training, see Susceptibility training
Hypnotic trance, see Trance state
Hypnotist
    as actor-dramatist, 6–8
    as laboratory experimenter, see Experimenter-hypnotist
    as physician, see Clinical context
Hypnotizability, see also Suggestibility
    absorption and, 30, 109
    alpha rhythm activity and, 157, 158, 280
    analgesic affects and, 49–52, 175, 185–189
    189
    characteristics of, 48–49
    clinical context of, 143
    clinical measurement of, 129–141
    discontinuous distribution of, 56
    dream recall and, 166n
    evaluation of, 129–130; see also Hypnosis Induction Profile (HIP)
    in hallucinated incongruity response testing, 197
    hallucinatory experience and, 56–57
    high level(s) of, 139–140; see also Good hypnotic subjects
    hypnotherapy and, 56, 139, 225–227
    instruction and enhancement of, 83
    intact profile scores of, 131–134
    levels of, 56–57, 69, 83, 139–140
    modification of, 106, 121–124, 143–152; see also Susceptibility training
    optimal, 124
    overt-covert levels of, 52–57
    possible range of, 18, 123–124
    of subjects and simulators, compared, 54–55
    subject's capacity for, 50, 51
    testing progressive development of, 73
    therapist's versus experimenter's views on, 55
    verbal stimulation in, see Verbal preparation
Hypnotizability testing, see Testing for hypnotizability
Hypnotizable subject, see Subject
Hypothalamus, as factor in hypnotizability, 114

I chthyosis, hypnotherapeutic treatment of, 229
Ideomotor action, 208, 209
Imagining, see also Hallucination(s)
    control of, 126

    effecting overt responses, 109
    goal-directed fantasy (GDF) and, 211–212, 215
    hypnotic involvement and, 109, 212
    references on, 194
    in response to hallucination suggestions, 276
Incongruity (-ies), tolerance for
    adaptive regression and, 203
    characteristics of, 195, 199, 204; see also Trance logic
    cue structuring for, 195–199, 204
    hypnotized subject's capacity for, 194–195, 199, 202
    testing for, 199–203
Induction of hypnosis
    administration of, 39
    anxiety in, 78–79, 82
    basic components of, 250–251
    clinical testing of, 129
    clinical and experimental settings for, compared, 72
    counterfactual statements in, 12
    cue-response training and, 92, 100, 195–196
    densensitization and, 254
    as determinant of hypnosis phenomenon, 16, 18, 20–22, 34, 69, 72, 143, 251–252
    evaluation of, 130–137
    factors conditioning, 16, 51, 84
    in goal-directed fantasy study, 215
    hallucination and, 195–196, 256–257, 275
    involuntariness promoted by, 209
    neural integration process in, 80n
    speech patterning in, 8; see also Cue structuring; Verbal preparation
    relaxation and, 254; see also Relaxation training
    subject-hypnotist relations in, see Subject-hypnotist relations
    test-suggestion responses and, 34–44
    think-with instructions compared with, 40–44
    by videotape and live, compared, 268
Induction scores, of trance state realization, 132–134
Informational approach
    in hypnosis, 222–234
    in psychotherapy, 231
    in suggestibility differences, 232
Insomnia, hypnotizability and, 171–172
Intact profile scores, of hypnotizability, 131–134

Intelligence (IQ) testing, hypnosis and, 122–123
International Journal of Clinical and Experimental Hypnosis, 120
Introversion, hypnotizability and, 109
Involuntary motor responses
  characterization of, 208–209
  goal-direct fantasy (GDF) and, 211, 213
  induction of hypnosis and suggestion effects in, 209–210
  subject reporting of, 210–212, 217–219

Korsakoff's syndrome, 297
Kruskal-Wallis test, 39*n*

Linear type physique, suggestibility and the, 109–115

Medical hypnosis, *see* Clinical context
Meditation
  sleep traits and, 171
  suggestibility and, 171
Memory
  alteration of, in hypnosis, 19
  cognitive view of, 294–295
  conscious control of, 58
  continuity of, 48, 295, 296
  disorders of, 284
  failure of, 297
  loss and recovery of, 285, 287
  posthypnotic amnesia and, 287–288
  recognition versus recall in, 289; *see also* Recall
  searching of, 294–295
Mesmer, Franz Anton, mentioned, 17, 21, 222, 274
Mesmerists, Royal Commission investigation of, 21
Mesomorphy
  characteristics of, 107
  suggestibility and, 109, 113
Michigan State Suggestibility Profiles (MSSP), 74–76
Minnesota Multiphasic Personality Inventory (MMPI), 99–100, 106, 108
Missing watchhand test, 199*n*, 204
Modification training, *see* Susceptibility training
Morphine, analgesic effectiveness of, 176, 179, 182–185
Motivation
  in hypnotizability, 16, 105, 205, 260
  in posthypnotic amnesia, 292
  in susceptibility training, 125

Moving hand test, 75, 76
Muscular type physique, suggestibility and the, 108–113, 115
Music hallucination test, 35, 38

Nappers, *see also* Nonnappers
  hypnotizability of, 164, 166
  voluntary control of sleep by, 164–170
Negative hallucination tests, 199*n*, 200–201, 204
Neodissociation theory, 9, 56–59
Neurological factors
  in hypnosis, 17
  in hypnotic analgesia, 9, 10*n*
Nonnappers
  hypnotizability of, 167–168
  sleep control among, 168–170
Nonsense material recall, 286–287
Nonsuggestible subjects
  hypnotherapeutic effects in, 51
  inability to duplicate hypnotic behavior, 203
  motivation in, 16
  napping and nonnapping by, 166–171
  pain reduction in, 51
  psychopathology in, 134
  semantic-syntactic mode thinking in, 78
  as simulator comparison group, 23
  waking imagination in, 199–203

Occulomotor hypothesis, of alpha rhythm activity, 155–157
Olfactory-gustatory hallucination, 35, 38
Optokinetic nystagmus, in hypnotic hallucinations, 276

Pain perception, concepts of, 9
Pain reduction, *see also* Analgesia
  acupuncture in, 185, 188; *see also under* Acupuncture
  depth of hypnosis and, 225
  drugs in, *see* Aspirin; Diazepam; Morphine
  hypnosis in, 175
  hypnotic amnesia in, 52
  hypnotizability and, 49–53, 185–189
  in nonsuggestible subjects, 51
  two component theory of, 52–57
  by waking suggestion, 51
Paranoid Fantasy Scale, 106
Passive-dependent position
  anxiety counteraction to, 80, 82; *see also* Anxiety

in suggestibility potentials, 81; *see also* Dependency strivings
Patients, *see* Subjects
Perception(s)
auditory, 278–279
alteration of, as criterion of hypnosis, 19
falsified, in hypnosis, 274; *see also* Hallucination(s)
reality of, in hallucinatory suggestions, 274–279
visual, 275–278
Personality, hypnotizability and, 108, 109, 120–121, 139–141
Physician-hypnotist, relations with subject patient, 72; *see also* Subject-hypnotist relations
Physiological changes
psychic factors in, 230
suggestibility in, 227–228
Physique, suggestibility and, 107–115
Placebo effect
in analgesia, 176, 182, 184, 224
pain relief effected by, versus hypnosis, 178, 182–183, 191–192
in poor hypnotic subjects, 224
suggestibility and, 175, 224
Posthypnotic amnesia
characteristics of, 284–285
cognitive view of, 294–295
as compliance with expectations, 288
discontinuous distribution of, 94
disorganized recall and, 28
as forgetting, 225–258
heritability in twins, 106
memory processes effected by, 285–288
as neglect, 288–291
persistence of, 290–291
recall functions in, 285–288, 290–291, 293, 295–297
as repression, 291–294
as secret keeping process, 288–291
as suggestibility test, 75, 76
transference relationship in, 292
Posthypnotic suggestions(s)
amnesia as, *see* Posthypnotic amnesia
characteristics of, 265
as criterion of hypnosis, 19
conditioned response contrasted with, 58
dissociation and continuity of, 58
in hypnotic subjects versus simulators, 27–28
persistence of uncancelled, 264–272
suggestibility performance rating, 75
Pseudomemories, induction of, 29

Psychological health, hypnosis induction profile (HIP) distributions and, 135
Psychopathology
cerebral-hemisphere dominance correlations with, 138–139
Hypnosis Induction Profiles (HIP) in diagnosis of, 134–138
Psychosomatic disorders, hypnosis in treatment of, 225
Psychotherapy
hypnosis in, 238–248, 250
information processing approach to, 231
medical etiology and, 230–231
mind-body problem in explaining, 231
Pulse rate, hypnotic modification of, 228

Recall
cognitive view of, 295
in memory retrieval, 289, 293–295
posthypnotic amnesia and, 28, 293–295
recognition versus, 289
selectivity of, 293
Registration, without perception, 201, 203
Relaxation, 35, 38, 254; *see also* Relaxation training
Relaxation training
in behavior therapy, 251
electromyogram (EMG) feddback in, 146
hypnosis induction compared with, 254–256
in insomnia, 172
potentiation of, 150
suggestibility and, 146, 150–151, 251
therapeutic affects of, 227
Repression, posthypnotic amnesia as, 291–294
Response, simple, conditoned, and hypnotic, 58
Responsivity to hypnosis, *see* Suggestibility
Role enactment
concept of, 5, 7
as faking, in hypnosis, 4–6, 98; *see also* Simulation
hypnosis as, 4, 6, 20, 26
by hypnotic subjects, 8, 86, 98

Science, 189
Scientific method, in hypnosis inquiry, 4, 6, 11, 20–21, 36n
Second Conference on Psychophysiological Aspects of Cancer, 231

Segmental set, 134
Selective inattention, 194–206; *see also* Incongruity; Transparency response
Selective recall index, 293
Self-hypnosis, 51
Self-reporting
  absorption and, 220
  on acupuncture stimulation, 188
  of analgesic effects, 8–10, 186–187, 191
  of antisocial acts, 95
  of deafness, induced, 278
  on depth of hypnosis, 94
  on experimental procedures, 99
  fabrication in, 220
  on goal-directed fantasies, 211–215, 220
  "hidden observer" concept and, 8–9
  in hypnotic state characterization, 49
  on induction-cue response, 92, 94
  instructions on, 43–44
  involuntary hypnotic involvement and, 212–213
  of involuntary-motor responses, 210–212, 217–219
  neodissociation theory of, 9
  of overt and involuntary suggestion responses, 210–211, 215, 216
  of pain experienced, 52–53, 177
  of pain reduction, 186–188
  in posthypnotic amnesia, 8–9, 288, 290
  of posthypnotic suggestions, uncancelled, 270
  of relaxation feedback training, 151
  by simulator subjects, 53–55
  on subject–hypnotist relations, 93
  as trance-state theory contradiction, 253
  validity of, 8, 124
Semantic-somatic transduction, hypnosis as, 230–232
Semantic-syntactic mode
  in anxiety, 81, 82
  as cerebral-dominance factor, 70–72, 81–82
  disengagement of, in suggestibility, 77–78
  passive-receptive attitude and, 80
  subject suggestibility differences and, 78
Sensory restriction, suggestibility enhancement and, 144–146, 150
Sex distinctions, in suggestibility correlations, 110–114, 281
Shared neurosis, 238, 240, 241
Signal-detection theory, 189

Simulation
  applicability of, in suggestibility research, 29–30
  as conscious role playing, 26
  experimental hypnosis as reality, 86–87
  falsification of pain reduction in, 54–55
  in incongruity report testing, 195, 197
  as investigational control, 23–29, 92
  over-reaction in, 27–28, 54
  of posthypnotic amnesia, 288–290
  of posthypnotic suggestion responses, 27, 28, 265
  source amnesia in testing of, 27, 289
Sleep
  alpha-rhythm activity during, 154, 157
  control of, 164–172
  of good hypnotic subjects, 163, 168
  and hypnosis, 162–164, 171
  napping and, 164–170
  response to suggestions heard in, 222–223
  suggestibility and, 165–166, 168, 223
  trance state and, 251
Social stimuli, hypnotizability enhancement and, 144
Somatotonic temperment, 108
Somatotype(s), *see also* Physique
  classification of, 107
  hypnotizability and, 107
  temperment types and, 108
Somnambulism
  characterization of, 162, 163
  hypnotic behavior versus, 253
  training for, 123
Source amnesia
  characteristics of, 287–288
  simulators lacking in, 289
  validity of, 27
Spearman rank-order correlation, 296
Stanford Hypnotic Susceptibility Scales (SHSS)
  alpha rhythm correlations with, 158
  in antisocial act research design, 91–92
  in cue-structuring effects, 196
  in electromyogram (EMG) feedback training, 146, 147
  eye-roll (ER) test correlation with, 131
  in heritability study, 106, 107
  in hypnosis effects, 19, 35
  mentioned, 73, 105, 212
  in plateau susceptibility, 124
  in sensory-restriction enhancement testing, 144, 145
  in suggestibility testing, 91–92
  in temporal organization of recall, 296

in theta-feedback training, 149
think-with subject response to, 41
Stress-reduction hypnosis and relaxation in, 254–256
Subject(s), hypnotic
  accommodation of hypnotist by, 267; see also Subject-hypnotist relations
  anxiety of, 72
  behavior versus actual experience in, 25–26
  characterization of, with HGSHS, 185
  in clinical and experimental contexts, compared, 72
  coercion of, in antisocial acts, 90–103
  cue-structuring response by, 203–204
  deception of, in experimental context, 97–99
  enhancement training of, 119–123
  evaluation of potentials of, 10, 43–44, 129, 185
  informed consent of, 96–97, 99
  with low suggestibility, 143
  logical-incongruity tolerance by, 195; see also Incongruity, tolerance of
  nonhypnotizable, see Nonsuggestible subjects
  as own spectator, 11–12; see also Hidden observer; Self-reporting
  perception of experimental context by, 87–88
  perception of hypnotist's instructions by, 265
  personality traits of highly suggestible, 78; see also Good hypnotic subjects
  real and simulating, compared, 265
  relations with hypnotist(s), 92–93, 238–248; see also Subject-hypnotist relations
  screening of, 99–100, 185–186, 189
  sensory information processing by, 232
  sleep responsiveness of, 163
  submission to suggestion by, 69; see also Suggestibility
  training for suggestibility of, 123–124
  types and levels of responsiveness by, 16, 18, 49–51, 56–57, 123–125, 205, 222
Subject-hypnotist relations
  accommodations in, 267
  in anti-social act contexts, 88, 90, 92–93
  dependency strivings and, 81, 267
  ethical questions in, 96, 99
  in experimental context, 72
  in hypnotherapy, 72, 238–248

in induction, 16, 96, 99
self-reporting on, 93
shared neurosis in, 238, 240–241
of simulator subjects, 220, 238
as transference, in amnesia, 292
uncancelled posthypnotic suggestions and, 264–265
Subjectivity
  objective measurement of, 19
  as suggestibility factor, 143
Suggestibility, see also Hypnotizability; Induction of hypnosis; Susceptibility training
  as acquired ability, 120, 121
  acupuncture and, 175, 188–191
  analgesia and, 175, 187, 190
  in antisocial-act involvement, 90–92
  anxiety and, 78–82
  aptitude in, 122, 205
  assessment of, 69
  attention and, 78, 139–141, 144
  attitude as factor in, 34, 77, 105, 122, 126, 147–148, 205
  base-line level of, 124
  behavioral modification and, 151; see also Susceptibility training
  body morphology and, 105–115
  capacity for, 106, 130–134, 222
  cerebral-hemisphere laterality in, 69, 72, 78, 80, 114, 138, 279–282
  cognitive effort and, 150, 203
  concept of, 19–20, 120
  concentration and, 134, 139–141, 144 171
  constitutional traits and, 107–110
  cue structuring and, 203–204
  degrees of, in subjects, 51
  dependency strivings and, 72–73, 80–81
  discontinuity of, 56–57
  enhancement of, 69–80, 144–146, 150, 257; se also Susceptibility training
  endurance of, 224
  environmental conditioning and, 107
  experimental manipulation of, 77–78, 105–106
  extroversion and, 109
  eye-roll (ER) sign test of, 130–131
  of females, 114
  genetic factor in, 106, 107, 281
  growth phases in, 115
  hand-clasp test of, 139
  handedness and, 282
  hypnotherapeutic response to, 225
  hypnotic performance and, 144
  imagining and, 109, 212

insomnia and, 171–172
introversion and, 109
of males, 103–104
meditation and, 171
modification of, 119–126; *see also*
    Susceptibility training
motivation in, 16, 105, 205, 260
of nappers, 164, 166, 170
neuropsychological processes and, 83
nonhypnotic-type subject responses to,
    58, 203
nonintact profile scores of, 132–136
of nonnappers, 167–168, 170
passivity and, 69, 72, 77–81
personality and, 108–109, 120–121,
    139–141, 224
placebo affect and, 175, 224
plateau of optimal, 124
posthynotic amnesia and, 284
posthypnotic persistency and, 267–268
psychodynamics of, 69–72
psychpathology and, 134–138
relaxation instructions and, 146
"scare" instructions and, 145–146
sexual arousal and, 79
sleep and, 163–166, 223
subjectivity and, 143, 150
of subjects, as investigational factor,
    21–22, 91–92
testing for, *see* Testing for suggestibil-
    ity
theatricality and, 7–8
theories of, *see* Theories of hypnosis
trait-skill issue in, 120–121
trance logic and, 194–195
"twilight-state" instructions and, 149–
    150
in twins, 106–107
two-level theory of, 69–72, 80–82
Susceptibility training
attention in, 125
attitude in, 119, 126
behavior-modification training and,
    119, 151–152
clinical utility of, 122
cognitive strategy in, 126
conceptual issues in, 120–123
core components of, 125–126
criteria for for degrees of, 121–122
dependency strivings in, 72–73
effectiveness of, 123, 125
feedback in, 119, 125, 146–149
individual differences and, 123–124
information-control based, 119
methodological isues in, 124–125
methods of, 105, 119, 123

motivation in, 125
operant based, 119
optimal learning factors in, 119
relativity of, 122
relaxation training and, 146, 150–151,
    251
sensory restriction in, 144–146, 150
training effects in, 143–144

Taffel task, in posthypnotic amnesia
    testing, 289
Task-motivation instructions, *see* Verbal
    preparation
Temperature hallucination, 35, 38
Temperament, body build and, 108
Testing for suggestibility
    arm-levitation test, 35, 37, 131
    arm-rigidity test, 75–76, 215–217
    eye-roll (ER) test, 130–131, 189
    hand-clasp test, 139
    hand-levitation test, 35, 37
    hand-lowering test, 35, 37
    see Harvard Group Scales (HGSHS)
    head-fall test, 75, 76
    hypnotic induction and, 73–74
    instructions for control groups in, 83,
        124–125
    Michigan State Suggestibility Profiles
        (MSSP), 74–76
    missing-watchhand test, 199n, 204n
    moving-hand test, 75, 76
    music-hallucination test, 35, 38
    see Stanford Hypnotic Susceptibility
        Scales (SHSS)
    trait-item evaluation in, 74–77, 82–83
Theory(ies) of hypnosis
    as altered state of consciousness, 251
    as behavioral interaction, 258–260
    as behavioral therapy, 250–260
    cerebral hemisphere laterality in, 80,
        114, 138, 279–282
    cognitive-behavioral, 34–44, 194, 281
    cognitive-perceptive falsifications in,
        274, 279
    as conditional state, 18
    in experimental psychology, 9
    formist approach, 3–4, 18
    see "Hidden observer"
    of hypnosis as distinctive state, *see*
        Trance state theory
    individual responsiveness and, 9
    as motivational, 281
    needs and role of, 21
    neobehaviorist, 18
    neodissociationist, 9, 56–59

neural integrational, two-level, 69–72, 80–82
nonstate-state approach to, 57–58
in perceptual terms, 279
procedures as definitive of, 16, 18, 20–22, 34, 69, 72, 143, 251–252
of suggestibility, 80, 83
see Trance-state theory
two-step development in, 69–72, 80–82
Theta feedback, in susceptibility training, 148–151
Think-with instructions
administration of, 36, 41–42
evaluation of response to, 40–41
responsiveness scores in, 39
test-suggestion compliance with, 34
text of, 46–47
trance induction compared with, 40–44
Third signalling system, preconscious messages as, 151
Tolerance of incongruity, see Incongruity, tolerance of
Trance depth, see Depth of hypnosis
Trance induction, see Induction of hypnosis
Trance logic, 26, 194–195, 201, 281; see also Trance state; Trance-state theory
Trance state, see also Hypnosis
alertness as characteristic of, 129
borderline levels of, 131–132
behavioral concept versus, 258–259
characteristics of, 251
clinical measurement of, 129–130
cue-structured contexts of, 195
Hypnosis Induction Profile (HIP) rating of, 129–134
incongruity acceptance and, 194–195, 201
potentialities for, testing for, 129–134
registration without perception in, 241
theory of, see Trance-state theory
Trance-state theory
behavior therapy and, 251–254
cognitive-behavioral theory compared with, 40–44, 194
critiques of, 66, 251–253, 258–259
experimental-test evaluation of, 34–44
hallucination in, 256, 274, 279
historical developments in, 42
hypnotic phenomena in, 34–44, 143, 194, 258; see also Hypnosis

logical difficulties of, 252
postulates of, 34
self-reporting and, 253
Transcendence, of normal volitional capacities in hypnosis, 20, 22, 25, 29
Transference, in subject-hypnotist relations, 292
Transparency response, as test of tolerance for incongruity, 195–204
Twilight state
learning and, 148
suggestibility alteration in, 149–150
Twins, relative hypnotizability of, 106–107

Verbal preparation
in acupuncture trials, 189
behavioral compliance and, 151
in behavioral modification, 143–151
see also Cue structuring
in goal-directed fantasy studies, 213–214
in-hallucination, 256–257, 275–276
in hypnotic induction, 8, 22, 42, 92, 100, 195–196, 250–251, 268
in hypnotist-subject interaction, 267
for real and simulator subject differences, 265
in suggestibility, 143–144, 147–150, 230–232
in susceptibility training, 143–144
task-motivational instructions and, 42
in tolerance for incongruities, 195–199, 204–205
in uncancelled posthypnotic-suggestion persistence, 271
Viscerotonic temperment
characteristics of, 108
sugesstibility and, 109–110, 114
Visual hallucination, 75–76, 275–278

Waking suggestion
characteristics of, 50–51
hypnotic-state suggestion compared with, 22–23, 57, 189, 194; see also Cognitive-behavioral theory
in self-induced pain reduction, 51–52
Warts, hypnotherapeutic treatment of, 225, 229
Water hallucination, 35, 38